SECURITY FOR DEBT IN ANCIENT NEAR EASTERN LAW

CULTURE AND HISTORY OF THE ANCIENT NEAR EAST

EDITED BY

B. HALPERN, M. H. E. WEIPPERT

TH. P.J. VAN DEN HOUT, I. WINTER

VOLUME 9

TUTA SUB AEGIDE PALLAS · 1683 ·

SECURITY FOR DEBT IN ANCIENT NEAR EASTERN LAW

EDITED BY

RAYMOND WESTBROOK

AND

RICHARD JASNOW

BRILL
LEIDEN · BOSTON · KÖLN
2001

This book is printed on acid-free paper.

Library of Congress Cataloging-in-Publication Data

Library of Congress Cataloging-in-Publication Data is also available

Die Deutsche Bibliothek – CIP-Einheitsaufnahme

Security for Debt in Ancient Near Eastern Law / ed. by Raymond Westbrook and Richard Jasnow. – Leiden ; Boston ; Köln : Brill, 2001
(Culture and history of the ancient Near East ; Vol. 9)
ISBN 90-04-12124-2

ISSN 1566-2055
ISBN 90 04 12124 2

PRINTED IN THE NETHERLANDS

CONTENTS

Preface vii

Raymond Westbrook, Introduction 1

Edward Tomlinson, Comparative Historical Perspectives 5
I. Development of Creditors' Remedies in Medieval England 6
II. Bankruptcy as a Creditor's Remedy 9
III. Contemporary Security Devices 14
IV. Conclusion 30

Richard Jasnow, Pre-Demotic Pharaonic Sources 35

Piotr Steinkeller, The Ur III Period 47
Appendix 56

Raymond Westbrook, The Old Babylonian Period 63
I. Pledge 63
II. Suretyship 79
III. Joint Liability 83
IV. Distraint 84

Klaas Veenhof, The Old Assyrian Period 93
I. Introduction 93
II. Guarantee 104
III. Pledge 125
IV. Other Forms of Security 148

Kathleen Abraham, The Middle Assyrian Period 161
I. Introduction 161
II. The Sources 162
III. Typology 166
IV. Guarantor and Joint Liability 171
V. Instruments of Security 174
VI. Maturity and Default 184

VII. Other Measures to Satisfy the Creditor 189
VII. A Socio-Economic Analysis of Middle Assyrian Security 190
Appendices 199

Carlo Zaccagnini, Nuzi 223

Aaron Skaist, Emar 237

Tikva Frymer-Kensky, Israel 251
I. Introduction 251
II. Secured Loans 252
III. Results of Delinquency 256
IV. Remediation 258
V. Conclusion 261

Karen Radner, The Neo-Assyrian Period 265
I. Prolegomena 265
II. Prior Arrangement 266
III. Delinquency 272
IV. Insolvency 276

Joachim Oelsner, The Neo-Babylonian Period 289
I. Introduction 289
II. Case Studies 292
III. Types of Security 299
Appendix 303

Joseph Manning, Demotic Papyri 307

Raymond Westbrook, Conclusions 327

Indices 341
I. Sources 343
II. Terms 357

PREFACE

On March 19 and 20, 1999, the Society for the Study of Ancient Near Eastern Law held its second occasional colloquium at the Johns Hopkins University in Baltimore. Twelve papers on a single topic were presented by invited speakers and intensively discussed by some twenty-five participants. The speakers were drawn from different disciplines of the ancient Near East—Assyriology, Biblical Studies and Egyptology—and beyond, to include early Rabbinic and modern comparative law. The present volume comprises the edited conference papers, revised by their authors in the light of the conference discussions, together with an introduction and conclusions. We are grateful to the Israel Ministry of Justice for allowing one of their senior officials, Dr. Peretz Segal, to participate in the conference. Regrettably, Dr. Segal's onerous duties as a parliamentary draftsman prevented him from producing a written version of his lecture on early Rabbinic law.

The conference and resulting volume were made possible by the generosity of the Lucius N. Littauer Foundation of New York, Mr. Melvin Sykes of Baltimore, the University of Maryland School of Law, and the office of the Dean of Arts and Sciences of the Johns Hopkins University. The publication of this volume gives us a welcome opportunity to express our gratitude in public to them all.

We would like to thank Mr. Bruce Wells for his help in the preparation of the manuscript.

Raymond Westbrook and Richard Jasnow
Department of Near Eastern Studies, Johns Hopkins University

INTRODUCTION

Raymond Westbrook – Johns Hopkins University

There are certain problems which have existed since the very earliest legal systems and which continue to defy the best efforts of the law. An especially challenging set of such problems arises from the repayment of debts, or rather, the failure to repay. No legal system on earth can guarantee that payment will be made when it is due: that depends ultimately on economics, not law. The task of the law is to provide a framework within which legitimate expectations can be fulfilled, in this case the creditor's that he will be paid whatever can be paid. Even this modest goal, however, impinges upon a wide circle of conflicting interests, which may paradoxically include those of the creditor himself. All the wit and sophistication of modern legal science, with all the support that modern technology has to offer, still cannot reconcile them, nor provide a compromise that will set them at rest. On the contrary, legal opinion sways hither and thither like a clumsy gyroscope, as each new reform is perceived to have tilted the balance too far in one direction. It is therefore a particularly appropriate area in which to investigate the efforts of the earliest known legal systems. The solutions that they developed are but part of a continuum, a contribution to the ongoing debate that has characterized legal policy up to the present day.

Four main interests may be identified to which any legal system must have regard. The first, obviously, is that of the creditor. The law is expected to provide the creditor not only with access to the debtor's resources but also with protection from moral hazard—an expectation in the debtor that repayment will not be enforced, leading to the temptation to borrow beyond his ability to repay. It would seem at first sight that the greater the access and the greater the deterrent from moral hazard, the more secure the creditor will be. Too much security in law may, however, work against the creditor's longer-term interests, if overly harsh measures rob the debtor of the economic capacity to continue to generate resources from which the debt can be paid, or if financially sound persons are deterred from borrowing and the creditor is thus deprived of a profitable investment for his capital.

The second interest is that of the debtor. The honest debtor will seek protection from measures so harsh as to deprive him of livelihood, liberty, or his very life. As Deuteronomy 24:6 puts it: "One shall not take the upper millstone as pledge, for it is life itself that he takes as pledge." On the other hand, weakening the rules of security too far may have the same effect, if they make creditors unwilling to risk lending, and so deprive the debtor of access to credit.

The third interest to be considered is that of other creditors. Allowing a particular creditor to dedicate particular assets to securing his own debt alone may work unfairly against others who have lent money in good faith to the same debtor.

Finally, there is the interest of the economy as a whole, which requires the maintenance of productive capacity. The law has the unenviable task of providing a framework within which creditors retain an interest in investing and debtors an incentive to produce. The phenomenon of desperate debtors abandoning their farms and absconding is well known from the ancient Near East, and is not without equivalents in the modern world.

To ensure realization of the above interests, the law must provide mechanisms to resolve certain situations that arise in the context of default. First is the enforcement of prior arrangements between creditor and debtor for the contingency of default. Second is delinquency: measures to compel payment by a reluctant debtor and to deter/punish potential defaulters. Third is access to resources of the debtor which could be, but are not willingly, applied to payment. Fourth is insolvency: measures to distribute available resources equitably among the creditors and to provide (where feasible) for eventual payment of the balance. Fifth is hardship: the law must be prepared to provide means of escape from its own rules where the results will be inimical to justice and social stability. Individual legal systems will differ in the extent to which they enforce the parties' interests in each situation, but any judicial system with an ordered machinery for the creation and enforcement of debt (and the ancient Near Eastern systems all fall into that category) will have some arrangements for each of the above cases.

This volume represents an attempt to tackle the above questions in relation to the legal systems of the ancient Near East. The editors and contributors have no illusions as to their ability to answer these questions in the present state of our knowledge and source material. Nonetheless, it is hoped that we have made a useful beginning in organizing the amorphous mass of sources available and in bringing together evidence from many different periods and parts of the region in a comparable form. The volume begins with a comparative study of the historical development of modern law. Against this background, the remaining contributions are organized in accordance with the conventional political divisions of time and space in ancient Near Eastern history. Each contribution presents a report on salient features of the security arrangements and of their legal regulation in the period in question.

Note on Legal Terminology

A glossary of the modern terminology used by the contributors may be helpful to the reader, since English offers a confusing variety of terms for the instruments of security. There can also be difficulty in aligning the terms taken from modern Common Law systems with the German terms frequently used in scholarship on this topic. The following are definitions of how the terms are generally understood in modern law, without reference to specific legal systems.

Pledge (German *Pfand*) is property that the debtor gives or assigns to the creditor by way of security. It may also be referred to as a **lien** or **charge** on the debtor's property, terms which focus more on the imposing of a legal incumbrance on the property in the creditor's favor. If actually handed over, a pledge is **possessory** (*Besitzpfand*); if only assigned, it is **hypothecary** (*Hypothek*). (A mortgage is a special type of hypothecary encumbrance on land found in Common Law jurisdictions; the term has not been used in this volume for ancient instruments of security.) A pledge may be characterized as automatically **forfeitable** on a due date (*Verfallspfand*) or **redeemable** (*Lösungspfand*).

Suretyship (*Bürgschaft*), also called **guarantee**, is an obligation undertaken by a third party with regard to payment of the debt by the debtor. The person under obligation is called a **surety** or **guarantor** (*Bürge*).

Distraint refers to the seizing and holding of the debtor's property without his consent. A synonymous term is **distress**, which may also refer to the object taken by way of distraint. In the ancient Near East, as opposed to modern law, persons may be the object of distraint, in which case the term **distrainee** is used.

COMPARATIVE HISTORICAL PERSPECTIVES

Edward Tomlinson – University of Maryland School of Law

Historians disagree about when the commercial and intellectual life of Western Europe reached the nadir known as The Dark Ages. Did that point arrive with the collapse of the Roman Empire triggered by the Barbarian Invasions of the fifth century, or did it occur later when Arab expansion in the late seventh and early eighth centuries turned the Mediterranean into a Muslim lake?[1] On the other hand, most historians agree that by the twelfth century Europe was experiencing a revival whose effects continued at least until the arrival of the Black Death in the mid-fourteenth century.[2] That revival featured the appearance, first in the Italian city-states and then throughout northern Europe, of a substantial merchant class that developed trade networks extending from England in the north to the Crusader States in the east. That economic revival was accompanied by an intellectual revival whose hallmark was the study of Roman Law, primarily the *Corpus Juris Civilis* of the sixth century Eastern Roman Emperor Justinian.

The feudal system in which these developments occurred was not particularly responsive to the legal needs of merchant creditors. From a modern perspective, the creditor's security derives primarily from the availability of an effective legal system providing remedies for enforcing the debtor's duty to pay. In most cases, the availability of effective legal remedies provides the debtor with sufficient encouragement to pay when due without any need for the creditor actually to sue. Remedies available in feudal courts did not perform that function for merchant creditors. Rather, those courts focused on resolving disputes over land, including the services which tenants holding land owed to their lords. The procedures utilized by the courts were slow and often involved primitive methods of proof (trial

---

[1] The latter theory, espoused by the noted Belgian historian Henri Pirenne, has received considerable criticism. Lyon 1972.

[2] Haskins 1933. On the staying power of Haskins' work, see Cantor 1991.

by battle or ordeal) that assumed God would intervene to assist the righteous. Such a forum was not a propitious one for a nonresident merchant contemplating a lawsuit to collect a debt. Moreover, feudal law viewed a man's body, as well as his lands, as belonging to the lord. Therefore, it normally precluded the creditor from proceeding against the debtor's person by imprisoning him and from seizing the debtor's land to satisfy a judgment.[3]

I. Development of Creditors' Remedies in Medieval England

Creditors encountered similar problems in England despite that country's lead in developing effective legal institutions. By the twelfth century, the strong, centralized Anglo-Norman monarchy had created a system of royal courts applying a new body of law common to the entire kingdom.[4] One of the most significant remedies afforded by this new body of common law was the action for debt, "a procedure for compelling debtors to pay their obvious dues."[5] However, the procedures in an action for debt were cumbersome and allowed the debtor to escape liability by waging his law, i.e. by recruiting from among his friends a certain number of compurgators (in effect, character witnesses) who supplied their oaths in support of the debtor's oath that he did not owe the money.[6] In addition, the common law courts gave the creditor no remedy against the debtor's person. As explained by the leading historians of medieval English law, the common law knew at the time "no process whereby a man could pledge his body or liberty for payment of a debt."[7] The creditor could there-

---

[3] Cohen 1982. On imprisonment for debt, see text at notes 13 and 67 *infra*.

[4] The medieval common law was indigenous to England; it remained largely unaffected by Roman law. This situation contrasts sharply with the reception of a revived Roman law by most continental legal systems. The standard explanation for this English exceptionalism is chronological, that is, the Anglo-Norman kings in the generations after the Norman Conquest of 1066 developed their own legal system before the revival of Roman law had occurred. On the Continent, on the other hand, effective legal institutions arrived later at a time when Roman law was available as a model. See Van Caenegem 1992.

[5] Plucknett 1956: 363.

[6] *Id.* at 115–16.

[7] Pollock and Maitland 1895: II, 596. The situation on the Continent was less clear. Pollock and Maitland suggest that imprisonment for debt was permissible throughout the High Middle Ages in royal courts on the Continent. *Id.* The lead-

fore proceed only against the debtor's property, which in effect meant the debtor's personal property but not his land. This limitation appeared in the common law writs of execution which allowed the sheriff to seize the debtor's personal property to satisfy a judgment, but did not allow the debtor's dispossession from land, the chief source of wealth. The law treated the land as belonging to the debtor's lord; at most, the sheriff could levy on the crops or other proceeds from the land.[8]

The last three decades of the thirteenth century (the reign of King Edward I) brought significant changes to English law on "the fundamental business of debt-collecting."[9] Change came in the form of statutes, enacted by the newly inaugurated Parliament, which dealt harshly with defaulting debtors. Parliament excused this severity in the preamble to the first of these statutes (the Statute of Acton Burnett of 1283) on the ground that foreign merchants would not do business in England unless they were given a ready means for securing payment of their debts.[10] Plainly, the statute's drafters believed that a creditor's best security was the availability of effective legal remedies against a debtor who did not pay. Accordingly, the Statute of Acton Burnett, soon superseded in 1285 by the more comprehensive Statute of Merchants, gave the creditor three significant procedural weapons.

The creditor's first procedural weapon was a system of debtor recognizances. The Statute of Merchants required mayors to enroll debtors' bonds under the royal seal in local borough courts; in these bonds, debtors acknowledged their indebtedness. Creditors actively sought these recognizances because they eliminated any need to bring an action for debt; execution against the debtor, without any need for a trial or other procedures, followed immediately upon the presentation to a court of a bond in default.[11] For at least a century,

ing historian of French private law seems to agree. Brissaud 1912: 564–68. However, a French Ordinance of 1254, promulgated by Louis IX, echoed feudal concerns by expressly forbidding royal seneschals and bailiffs from seizing or holding the body of the debtor for a private debt. *Id.* at 568 note 2.

[8] Plucknett 1956: 390.

[9] Plucknett 1947: 137. Professor Plucknett mocks English conservatives who view Edward I's reign as the golden age of the common law. In fact, it was a time of radical legal change. Plucknett 1956: 396–97.

[10] Plucknett 1947: 139. The Statute of Acton Burnett proved to be an interim one; in 1285, Parliament superseded its provisions by enacting the Statute of Merchants.

[11] *Id.* at 144.

the borough and fair or market courts where these enrollments occurred had resolved commercial disputes informally by applying merchant custom, but their territorial jurisdiction was limited, and they lacked power to enforce a judgment outside the borough. This situation changed with the Statute of Merchants, which authorized the royal courts to enforce summarily debtors' recognizances enrolled in the borough and fair courts.[12]

To assure execution of these recognizances against the debtor, the Statute of Merchants gave creditors, as a second procedural weapon, the power to obtain from both the local and royal courts the immediate imprisonment of a debtor in default. The debtor's imprisonment had a coercive impact; it was intended to encourage the debtor to gather his assets together and to sell them to satisfy the debt. If the debtor did not satisfy the debt within three months, creditors received, as a third procedural weapon, the right to seize all the debtor's property, including both borough and feudal lands. Thus, the Statute of Merchants gave merchant creditors a remedy that the common law had long refused, i.e. the ability to control the debtor's land. Creditors became tenants or holders of the land by "statute merchant" and no longer needed to rely on the often uncooperative sheriff to collect the land's proceeds. In sum, these procedural weapons made the creditor more secure by creating a legal system which gave him "more chance of getting his money."[13]

The borough, fair, and later staple courts did not outlast the Middle Ages, but the royal or common law courts, which by the late fifteenth century had acquired most of the kingdom's mercantile litigation, implemented similar creditor-friendly procedures. First, the Statute of Westminster II, enacted the same year as the Statute of Merchants (1285), allowed a judgment creditor in the royal courts to hold one-half of the debtor's land until the debt was satisfied.[14] Second, the royal courts, starting in the thirteenth century, allowed creditors, before the creditor actually parted with his money, to pursue to judgment an action for debt. The Statute of Westminster II regularized this procedure by providing that such a debt of record

[12] In the fourteenth century Parliament established a similar machinery of debtor recognizances in staple courts for the convenience of foreign merchants dealing in wood, leather, and other staples. Plucknett 1956: 393.

[13] Plucknett 1947: 142. For the debtor's imprisonment, see *id.*, at 142–43. For the creditor's tenancy by statute merchant, see Plucknett 1956: 393.

[14] Plucknett 1956: 390–92.

(also called a recognizance) was not subject to further challenge.[15] Third, and most importantly, Parliament authorized the royal courts to imprison nonmerchant as well as merchant debtors. The first such law, called by a leading historian of the common law "one of the most drastic enactments in our history," authorized the royal courts to imprison servants and bailiffs whose accounts were in arrears.[16] A 1352 law extended this power to all actions for debt but required the creditor to choose between proceeding against the debtor's person (imprisoning the debtor to coerce him or his friends to satisfy the debt) or against the debtor's property (seizing the debtor's property to satisfy the debt). For centuries English law forced the creditor to make that choice.[17] It appears that the latter route was generally the more popular one.

II. Bankruptcy as a Creditor's Remedy

On the Continent, the legal changes which afforded the merchant creditor greater security took a quite different form. Starting in the twelfth century, the Italian city-states developed their own legal systems, applying a mixture of merchant custom and revived Roman Law.[18] Subsequently, similar systems appeared in fair towns and free cities throughout Europe. These new courts proceeded more informally and rapidly than did the preexisting feudal courts. More importantly, they afforded merchant creditors the potent remedy of "bankrupting" a defaulting debtor.[19] This initiative came from the Italian cities, which by the late thirteenth century had adopted statutes regulating bankruptcy proceedings. Bankruptcy itself derived from Roman law, which had recognized a creditor's right to initiate a

[15] *Id.* at 393–94. Summary judicial proceedings based on written instruments are often unfair; the instrument may be a forgery. To give the debtor some protection, the common law during the fourteenth century developed the writ *audita querela* allowing the debtor to present certain defenses. *Id.* The medieval recognizance nevertheless survives today in those states of the United States which recognize the cognitive note in which the debtor confesses judgment at the time he receives the loan. See *D.H. Overmeyer Co., Inc. v. Frick Co.*, 405 U.S. 174 (1972) (holding cognitive note enforceable between merchants).

[16] Plucknett 1956: 389.

[17] *Id.*

[18] Berman 1983: 356–403.

[19] The word "bankrupt" itself derives from the Italian *banco rotto*, meaning "counter" or "business broken." See Percerou 1935: 14 note 1.

proceeding against a defaulting debtor for the collective execution and distribution of the debtor's assets.[20]

The bankruptcy process, as it appeared in the medieval Italian city-states, was purely a creditor's remedy. Its purpose was to make creditors more secure and not to give the debtor a fresh start nor to allow a failing business to survive by reorganizing. These concerns, which often motivate modern bankruptcy legislation, were absent from bankruptcy's early history. Rather, the bankruptcy statutes of the Italian city-states afforded creditors an effective remedy against defaulting debtors. The mere stoppage of payment by a merchant allowed creditors to secure the debtor's arrest by the court. The creditors then elected a magistrate (later called a referee or judge) who designated a *curator* (now generally called a trustee) to collect and manage the debtor's assets. The liquidation which followed was largely creditor-controlled, and the debtor received a discharge only to the extent that creditors actually received payment. The debtor thus remained liable for any unsatisfied debts. Finally, the court could impose on a bankrupt person criminal penalties for any fraud or lesser fault. Even if the court found that the debtor committed no crime, a determination of bankruptcy was considered infamous, disqualifying the bankrupt person from many occupations and offices.

Creditors no doubt hoped that the repressive nature of bankruptcy proceedings would deter debtors from defaulting. For those debtors who did default, imprisonment was available as a means to coerce payment, as was the power of the referee to question the bankrupt under oath about the location of his assets. The only aspect of the procedure favorable to the debtor was the survival, alongside creditor-initiated bankruptcy proceedings, of the Roman law institution of *bonorum cessio*. That institution allowed the honest debtor to avoid bankruptcy by acknowledging his own insolvency rather than fleeing or being forced into bankruptcy by his creditors. The honest debtor could thus avoid the ignominy and imprisonment of bankruptcy if he turned over all his assets to his creditors. The threat of punitive bankruptcy proceedings provided the debtor with a strong incentive to cooperate with his creditors in this fashion.[21]

[20] On the history of bankruptcy, see *id.* at 3–67; Kohler 1891; Levinthal 1919a: 223–50.

[21] On the bankruptcy statutes of the Italian city-states, see Percerou 1935: 9–14 and Levinthal 1919: 241–44.

Bankruptcy did not officially arrive in England until 1542, when Parliament enacted the first English bankruptcy statute.[22] Earlier the borough and fair courts had developed, as part of the law merchant, procedures for the collective distribution of a defaulting debtor's assets,[23] but these courts had faded by the sixteenth century. Creditors found the common law remedies inadequate and obtained from Parliament in 1542 a statute directed "against such persons as do make Bankrupts." The statute's Preamble complained that debtors had avoided payment by concealing their assets, fleeing the country, or avoiding arrest by "keeping house" (i.e. by claiming their dwelling as a sanctuary). Parliament's initial response to this problem was penal; it enacted a criminal statute that did little more than punish debtors "who indulged in very prodigal expenses and then made off."[24]

One might wonder how creditors could use the 1542 statute against debtors whose dishonesty was less flagrant. To remedy that defect, Parliament developed more comprehensive bankruptcy procedures in subsequent statutes, principally ones enacted in 1570 and 1603. Under those statutes, as on the Continent, only merchant debtors were subject to bankruptcy. Commissioners, acting on behalf of the creditors, could imprison the debtor, seize his property, and examine persons (including the bankrupt) believed to be concealing the debtor's property from creditors. Finally, the creditors, acting under the commissioner's supervision, could administer and ultimately distribute the debtor's assets on a rateable basis. As on the Continent, the debtor did not receive a discharge from unsatisfied debts. That innovation did not come until a 1705 statute, and then only applied to debtors whose bankruptcy was attributable to misfortune. The earlier bankruptcy statutes had been strictly punitive; they sought to deter default by intimidating the debtor. For example, a 1623 statute provided that a debtor who failed to show that his bankruptcy was due solely to misfortune was subject to the pillory and the loss of an ear.[25]

---

[22] 34 and 35 Henry VIII, ch. 4 (1542).

[23] Holdsworth 1933: v, 97–98.

[24] Levinthal 1919b: 1. With Gallic aplomb, Professor Percerou castigates the 1542 English statute as "very inferior." Pecerou 1935: 15 note 7.

[25] On the English bankruptcy statutes, see Levinthal, 1919b. The general discharge provided by the 1705 statute was evidently intended as an interim measure occasioned by the hardship generated by the War of the Spanish Succession. See Holdsworth 1933: xi, 445. Jay Cohen argues that the 1705 statute survived, even though it gave merchant bankrupts a fresh start while nonmerchant debtors

Bankruptcy entered French law by the Ordinance of 1673 (France's initial commercial codification) and by the *Code de Commerce* enacted in 1807 under the First Empire. The latter statute, as proudly noted by the leading French scholar on bankruptcy, has had a grand influence in Europe, "both by the strength of our armies and by its own merits."[26] Its merits most assuredly appealed to creditors, given the exceptional severity of its treatment of merchant debtors, the only debtors covered by the Code. This hostility to debtors followed a number of spectacular business failures which evidently displeased Napoleon. The Emperor did not find severe enough the draft Code submitted to him for his approval upon his return to France after meeting with Emperor Alexander of Russia at Tilsit; Napoleon insisted (successfully, of course) that it be amended to require the automatic imprisonment of the bankrupt.[27] In addition, the 1807 Code eliminated the Roman Law *bonorum cessio*, which had been codified in the 1673 Ordinance promulgated by Louis XIV. Under the 1807 Code, therefore, all bankruptcies were either criminal or at least infamous, thus disqualifying the bankrupt from most trades and professions. In addition, the creditors took charge of administering and distributing the debtor's estate, and the bankrupt, unlike in England, did not receive a discharge for unpaid debts.

The French experience under the 1807 Code demonstrates that severe treatment of the bankrupt may not be the creditor's best security. The problem seems to be that not all bankrupts are crooks, and that those who are crooks are likely to dissipate most of their assets before their arrest by the bankruptcy court. The limited statistics available suggest that creditors rarely received anything close to full payment from the bankrupt's estate and that, at least until the French Parliament amended the *Code de Commerce* in 1838 and again in 1889 to revive the Roman Law *bonorum cessio* (now called

languished in prison, because it responded to a felt need to provide honest business owners with some form of limited liability. Owners can now limit their personal liability by doing business in corporate form, but that alternative was not available in the eighteenth century. See Cohen 1982.

[26] Percerou 1935: 36. Percerou is of course referring to Napoleon's armies, which in 1807 occupied most of Europe. Many of the occupied countries adopted one or more of the Napoleonic Codes. The leading German authority on bankruptcy acknowledges that it is indeed the French *Code de Commerce* which has served as the source of modern German bankruptcy law. Kohler 1891: 521.

[27] Percerou 1935: 36. Napoleon also believed that the law should provide only a modest allowance for the bankrupt's wife, but Cambacérès and other wiser heads prevailed on that point.

judicial liquidation), there were more liquidations through informal agreements between the debtor and his creditors than there were bankruptcy proceedings.[28] As confirmed in Balzac's novel *César Birotteau* (first published in 1837): "There are as many liquidations as bankruptcies in Paris. One thereby avoids the dishonor, the judicial delays, the attorneys' fees, and the depreciation of goods. Everyone believes that bankruptcy will produce less return than liquidation."[29] The Parliament responded, in 1838 and then definitively in 1889, by enacting new laws allowing insolvent debtors who surrender their assets to the courts to obtain the judicial liquidation of their assets without being stigmatized as a bankrupt.

Modern bankruptcy laws further demonstrate the limitation of bankruptcy as a security device for creditors. Take, for example, the federal Bankruptcy Act, enacted in 1898, which provides a uniform law of bankruptcy throughout the United States. Under that Act, the debtor may initiate bankruptcy proceedings, may obtain a discharge for unpaid debts, may escape imprisonment or any serious stigma, and may keep, subsequent to discharge, a considerable amount of exempt property, often including a dwelling. Modern bankruptcy law plainly serves other interests, which often conflict with the creditor's interest in security. It seeks to give debtors, today viewed more as unfortunates than as crooks, a fresh start, to protect employees and the tax collector, and, most importantly, to allow failing businesses to survive through reorganization. Accomplishing those goals sometimes requires the sacrifice of creditor interests. Often a failing business can survive only if the creditors agree to a suspension or even a partial discharge of claims so that the business can raise new funds and eventually pay off at least some of its prior debts. Such reorganizations in bankruptcy are commonplace in the United States.[30] The situation is now similar in France where the objectives of bankruptcy, as specified in the 1985 amendments to the French Bankruptcy Code, include "the survival of the enterprise, the maintaining of production and jobs, and the satisfaction of debts." Under their formulation, creditors' interests take third (and last) place.[31]

---

[28] Percerou 1935: 43–48; Jauffret 1997: 579–83.

[29] Balzac 1972: 301 (translated by myself and sentence order slightly changed). In the novel, Balzac placed the event described in 1819.

[30] For an overview of contemporary federal bankruptcy law, see Epstein 1995.

[31] Jauffret 1995: 609–10. The present French Bankruptcy Code, more properly

III. Contemporary Security Devices

The problems described above encouraged nineteenth- and twentieth-century creditors to seek more effective security for the payment of debts. Three principal techniques have emerged in Western Europe and the United States. First, the creditor's use of the debtor's real or personal property as collateral for a loan. If the debtor defaults on the loan, the creditor looks to the property for security. Second, the creditor's acquisition of more accurate information on the risk that his debtor will not repay a loan. Acquisition of this information allows the creditor to secure himself by choosing more intelligently to whom he loans money. Third, the creditor's arranging with other creditors to share the risk of the debtor's default so that each creditor assumes that portion of the risk he is best able to evaluate and handle. This risk-sharing approach, widely employed today in international trade through letter of credit transactions, provides merchant sellers with a degree of security which their medieval forbearers could never have imagined.

1. *The Debtor's Property as Security*

The use of a debtor's property as "collateral" or security for a loan derives from the ancient legal transaction known as pledge. However, the pledge, when it first appeared in early Germanic law, did not function as a security device.[32] Rather, it served as a provisional sale or, in the alternative, as a provisional method of payment. In the first case, the pledgor pledged his property (usually goods) to obtain from the pledgee property which he wished to purchase, while in the second case the pledgor pledged his property to satisfy the pledgee's claim for some wrong committed by the pledgor. These transactions were in effect cash transactions; not surprisingly, they occurred frequently in primitive societies that did not have a fixed medium of exchange (what we call money).

---

called the *Loi relative au redressement et liquidation judiciaires des enterprises*, appears as an Appendix to the *Code de Commerce*. As its title indicates, it applies only to businesses.

[32] On the history of pledge, see Wigmore 1896 and 1897. Professor Wigmore was one of the first great American comparativists. His magisterial study on the pledge idea remains unsurpassed.

In both cases, the pledgor gave the pledgee whatever property he had available at the time of the transaction, with the understanding that he could substitute more appropriate (or equivalent) property at a future date. However, the pledged property did not serve as security for an underlying debt. The pledgor had no obligation to reclaim it; if the pledgor chose not do so, the pledgee simply became its new owner. More importantly, the pledgee had no obligation to account for any surplus nor any right to obtain any deficiency, as he would have had if the pledged property had served as security for an underlying debt. Those features, essential aspects of a security transaction, were absent from the original pledge idea as found both on the Continent and in England. It was not until the late Middle Ages (fourteenth century and later) that the Germanic legal systems recognized that pledged property could serve as security for an underlying debt. In that case, the creditor (the pledgee) was liable for any surplus (the value of the property in excess of the debt) and could sue the pledgee for any deficiency if the value of the property did not cover the debt. In addition, if the debtor defaulted, the new law of pledge normally required the creditor to initiate a judicial or at least a public sale of the pledged property; the creditor could not simply keep the property by declaring a forfeiture.[33]

The use of the debtor's property as a security device was of limited utility until the nineteenth century. The principal difficulty was the requirement, applicable to pledges of personal property, that the creditor or a neutral third person actually take possession of the pledged property. No doubt a creditor is quite secure if he has possession of a debtor's goods equal in value to the debt, but most debtors are not in a position to offer that type of security. Would-be debtors normally seek credit to purchase goods or operate a business; the credit is of no utility to the debtor unless the debtor retains possession of the goods or business because the debtor expects to use them to generate profit. Despite the debtor's need for possession, the civil law systems on the European Continent have generally followed Roman law in requiring the creditor to take possession of pledged

[33] Thus, on the Continent, the newly revived Roman law treated as unenforceable forfeiture clauses (*pacta commissoria*) in security agreements. Huebner 1918. Article 2078 of the French Civil Code (enacted 1804) and article 1229 of the German Civil Code (enacted in 1896) codify this Roman law prohibition.

goods. This solution was codified in article 2076 of the Napoleonic Civil Code of 1804, which explicitly provided that a creditor retained a security interest in the pledged property only as long as the property remained in the possession of the creditor or of a third person agreed to by the parties. That text remains in effect today.[34] By mandating the debtor's dispossession, article 2076 assures that other creditors or potential creditors of the debtor receive notice that the pledged property is not available to satisfy any judgment they may obtain against the debtor.[35]

English law took a similar approach in treating the debtor's possession of pledged property as a fraud on the debtor's other creditors. In a well-known 1601 decision (*Twyne's Case*), the Star Chamber allowed the debtor's other creditors to avoid or set aside such a pledge on the grounds that the secured creditor's allowing the debtor to remain in possession of the pledged property was a fraudulent conveyance.[36] As a result, the secured creditor lost his security interest in the property, an interest which would have given him priority over other creditors in enforcing his claim. *Twyne's Case* later became a lead precedent, cited on both sides of the Atlantic as demonstrating the common law's abhorrence of nonpossessory security interests.[37]

This condemnation of "secret" liens did not apply, of course, if a carrier or warehouse rather than the debtor possessed the goods. In such cases, the common law readily recognized that documents of title (bills of lading or warehouse receipts) could be used, not only to control movement of the goods, but also to give the creditor a security interest in the goods. In addition, the condemnation of secret liens also did not apply to pledges of land (i.e. mortgages) because, even though the debtor remained in possession, the debtor's other creditors could receive notice of the pledge through public land records. However, land often proved to be an inadequate security device because the courts, particularly equity courts, intervened to

[34] The German Civil Code of 1896 contained a similar provision in article 1265 which likewise remains in effect today. See also article 2876 of the Italian Civil Code.

[35] Weill 1979: 82.

[36] *Twyne's Case*, 3 Coke 806, 76 Eng. Rep. 809 (Star Chamber 1601). Sir Edward Coke was the Attorney General who prosecuted and reported that case. He later became one of England's greatest judges and legal scholars.

[37] Gilmore 1965: 2, 39–47.

protect the debtor's interest in preserving the family homestead or business. Thus, the creditor had to follow cumbersome procedures and wait many years before foreclosing a defaulting debtor's right to redeem his ownership of the land by paying the debt.[38] Creditors, impatient to collect their money, needed a more timely and effective remedy.

In nineteenth century America, the need for credit made intolerable these common law restrictions on the use of the debtor's property as security. Manufacturers needed credit to buy goods (usually raw materials), to operate factories which turned raw materials into finished products, and to maintain an adequate inventory of goods for sale to their customers. Sellers and lenders responded by extending credit; those creditors took what the debtor had to offer, i.e. a security interest in the actual goods, machinery, or inventory. To protect the creditor's interest, creative lawyers drafted documents called chattel mortgages, conditional sales agreements, or trust receipts that purported to allow the creditor to seize and sell the property if the debtor defaulted. Sometimes courts enforced these contracts to give the secured creditor priority (at least with respect to the pledged property) over the debtor's other creditors and sometimes the courts did not. To achieve greater certainty, as creditors have no interest in gambling on enforceability, their lawyers then turned to the legislatures for relief in the form of statutes validating these new contracts. Legislatures responded affirmatively by enacting laws recognizing chattel mortgages, conditional sales, and other instruments creating nonpossessory security interests in personal property. Under these laws, a centralized recording system gave both the debtor's other creditors, as well as potential buyers from the debtor, legal notice of the creditor's security interest in the debtor's property. That notice dissipated the suspicion of fraud generated by the debtor's retention of possession. As a result, the secured creditor's interest in the property received priority over the interests of other creditors and of buyers.[39]

---

[38] Plucknett 1956: 603–08 and 690. French law also does not require the debtor's dispossession for real estate mortgages (*hypothèques*), but in France real estate rarely serves as security for debts other than those incurred by buyers in purchasing the land.

[39] On the history of security interests in personal property, see Gilmore and Axelrod 1948 and Gilmore 1948.

The most widespread of these new security devices was the personal property or chattel mortgage. By the early twentieth century, all forty-eight states had enacted statutes validating the chattel mortgage. These statutes favored the creditor by providing him with the remedy of self-help. Upon the debtor's default, the creditor could seize and sell the property without court intervention if he could obtain possession without a breach of the peace and if he followed statutory procedures (mainly giving notice) for a private or nonjudicial sale. While the creditor could not simply declare the property forfeit, he could purchase it at the sale, paying for it by forgiving all or part of the debt.[40] While protective of creditors, these statutes were popular because they served the interest of both creditors and debtors. Creditors wanted security and debtors (at least honest ones) wanted to be able to offer them security so that they could more readily obtain a loan.

The chattel mortgage statutes also addressed, but did not fully resolve, the more difficult problem of enforcing a shifting or floating lien. Goods in the debtor's possession do not remain static. Rather, the debtor uses tools, machinery, and other equipment (all of which wear out and eventually need replacing) to transform raw materials into finished products—goods which the debtor then maintains in inventory until sold to customers and replaced by new finished products hot off the assembly line. This constant processing and replacement of goods by the debtor posed a real problem for the common law, which had always viewed a creditor's lien as attaching to a specific piece of property. Upon that property's transformation, the creditor's security interest disappeared. Many merchant debtors therefore could not offer adequate security; the goods they possessed changed daily. The lawyers' response to this problem was to create a floating lien which followed the debtor's property through all these transformations. Specifically, this lien applied to property acquired by the debtor after the creation of the creditor's security interest and to proceeds from the sale of secured property. These innovations received confirmation in the Uniform Trust Receipts Act drafted by Professor Karl Llewellyn in the early 1930s. That model statute recognized a new generic instrument, called a trust receipt, creating a

[40] Gilmore 1965: 2, 1184–90 and 1211–16.

security interest in personal property which the creditor entrusted to his debtor.[41]

The culmination of this historical development was the Uniform Commercial Code, a statute drafted during the 1940s and enacted by forty-nine of the fifty states by the late 1960s.[42] Like the Uniform Trust Receipts Act, the new Code was the product of a movement to make more uniform the commercial law of the various states. The Code's drafters, spearheaded by Professor Llewellyn, were an elite group of judges, professors, and practicing lawyers joined together in the American Law Institute and the National Conference of Commissioners on Uniform State Laws; they presented their Code as a model for adoption by state legislatures. State legislatures responded enthusiastically by adopting it largely unchanged.

The Code itself covers the sale of goods (Article 2), negotiable instruments (Articles 3 and 4), and security interests in personal property (Article 9).[43] Those latter provisions codify all the advances made during the prior century. In particular, they present a simplified and unified structure for the creation of a security interest in personal property. Under the Code, a single instrument (called a security agreement) replaces the chattel mortgage and other instruments previously recognized by the law. The creditor obtains a security interest in the debtor's personal property by means of the security agreement. Upon perfection of that interest (usually obtained by recording of the agreement), the creditor obtains priority, at least with respect to the secured property, over the debtor's other creditors and over most buyers from the debtor. Furthermore, the Code ratifies the creditor's self-help and private sale remedies and preserves the floating lien by recognizing the creditor's secured interest in proceeds and other after-acquired property of the debtor. Finally, while the Code does not address what happens if the debtor goes bankrupt, federal bankruptcy law recognizes that secured creditors may enforce their interests in secured property in bankruptcy. Even if the bankruptcy court orders the reorganization of the bankrupt,

---

[41] Gilmore 1948: 761–65.

[42] Louisiana remains a partial holdout. Much of its law derives from the French Civil Code of 1804.

[43] The American Law Institute and the National Conference of Commissioners on Uniform State Laws publish the Official Text of the Code. The fourteenth edition appeared in 1995. Professor Grant Gilmore was the principal drafter of Article 9. For his magisterial summary of its provisions, see Gilmore 1965: 1, 287–400.

thus allowing the bankrupt to keep his property, the creditor must receive a note promising payment in full from the reorganized business.[44] In sum, the creditor's security is considerable. No doubt the secured property may deteriorate in value and there may be competing secured creditors, but secured creditors who adequately monitor their debtors are likely to receive payment in full.

Security interests in personal property have played a lesser role in modern civil law systems. Civil Codes normally retain the traditional rule that the creditor must acquire possession of the property to obtain an enforceable security interest.[45] In many civil law countries, nonpossessory security interests in personal property play a minimal role.[46] Other countries, such as France and Norway, have enacted special legislation recognizing nonpossessory security interests in specific types of property used for business purposes.[47] In France, a 1909 statute allows a creditor to obtain a security interest in a debtor's *fonds de commerce* (trade name, good will, leases, equipment) and a 1951 statute, intended to promote post-war recovery, recognizes security interests more generally in a business's tools and equipment.[48] Both statutes give the secured creditor a priority over the debtor's other creditors. However, no civil law system appears to have adopted anything comparable to the unitary security interest recognized by article 9 of the Uniform Commercial Code.[49]

On the other hand, civil law systems tend to provide the unpaid seller with more generous protection than does the common law. For example, an unpaid seller may, within generous limits, reclaim from a defaulting or even bankrupt buyer the goods sold.[50] In addition, in many civil law countries, the seller may include in the sales agreement a clause retaining the seller's title in the goods sold until

---

[44] 11 U.S.C. 1129(b)(2)(A) (1994). This "full priority" afforded secured creditors in bankruptcy is the subject of a lively debate among academics in the United States. See Bebchuk and Fried 1996, arguing that full priority is economically inefficient.

[45] See text at note 34 *supra*.

[46] Rajak 1995: 183–84 (Germany), 378–79 (Italy), and 574–75 (Spain).

[47] *Id.* at 120–22 (France) and 487–88 (Norway).

[48] Jauffret 1951: 202. The 1909 statute presents the disadvantage that the debtor can only offer security to one creditor.

[49] See Wood 1995. The closest analogy is the fiduciary trust recognized by case law in Germany and by the 1992 Civil Code in the Netherlands. *Id.* at 16–20. England and most other common law countries recognize a unitary or universal floating lien. *Id.* at 11–12.

[50] For example, the new Dutch Civil Code allows the unpaid seller to demand

the buyer pays for them in full. This retention of title clause creates a property and not just a security interest. This difference is significant because it allows the creditor to withdraw the property from the debtor's estate not only before any creditor claims are recognized but also before any reorganization of the debtor. Thus, under the 1985 French Bankruptcy Law, unpaid sellers of goods who retained title enjoy full priority, while the interests of secured creditors are often sacrificed, given the priority accorded by the new law to reorganizing (and saving) the enterprise.[51]

2. *Information as a Security Device*

Today in the United States, over 1,100 credit reporting companies supply creditors with information on the credit-worthiness of American consumers.[52] Creditors believe it worthwhile to purchase this information because it allows them to reduce their risks by declining to loan money to persons with poor credit ratings. In addition, the credit rating system gives creditors increased leverage in collecting existing debts. Many a debtor scrambles to pay when told by the creditor that a bad credit rating provoked by default will foreclose the debtor's access to future credit. The focus of the contemporary credit reporting industry is the consumer debtor, but when the industry first appeared in the 1840s, its purpose was to provide creditors with information on potential merchant debtors.

Business in early nineteenth-century America operated on a sea or web of credit.[53] Indeed, one could say that America had been founded on credit, as the majority of the early white settlers obtained their transatlantic passage on credit by agreeing to work as indentured servants for four to seven years after their arrival.[54] Even after

---

the return of the goods within six weeks after the debt has become due or sixty days after delivery. Rajak 1995: 456–57.

[51] See text at note 31 *infra*. One leading international practitioner goes as far as to say that in insolvency proceedings in France "security must be regarded as virtually worthless or at least highly unpredictable." Wood 1995: 159.

[52] Warren and Westbrook 1996: 8–14.

[53] Friedman 1985: 267 ("sea of credit"); Konesfky and King 1982: 89 ("web of credit").

[54] Friedman 1985: 82–85. At least in theory, these settlers were "free-willers" who had voluntarily agreed to work in return for their passage. In the seventeenth

American independence the chronic shortage of currency made the granting of credit inevitable. Foreign merchants sold goods on credit to American importers; importers or wholesalers in the large Eastern seaboard cities sold goods on credit to "country merchants" or retailers in the interior; and retailers then sold goods on credit to their consumer customers.[55] Both the foreign merchant and the Eastern city wholesale merchant or "jobber" primarily relied for security on the development of long-standing relationships with particular importers or retailers. In other words, they extended credit to persons whose prior record of trustworthiness made it likely that they would repay the loan. A few of the larger firms hired investigators to obtain information on strangers seeking credit, but most merchants found that option too expensive. In addition, some creditors solicited letters of recommendation from prospective debtors, but often those letters proved to be untrustworthy.[56]

Starting in the 1830s at least two factors seriously undermined the security of the wholesale merchant. First, the construction of canals and railroads greatly expanded the market area in the interior of the United States. More and more country or retail merchants who were unknown to the wholesale merchants presented themselves at the latters' showrooms. Thus, America's rapid expansion made the creditor's personal knowledge an inadequate basis for deciding whether to grant credit.[57] Second, an accentuated cycle of booms followed by busts made it likely that, in the hard times following a bust, some debtors who had always paid on time in the past would be forced to default. A debtor's past record on payment therefore no longer provided adequate security for a new loan. The Panic of 1837 proved to be a particularly severe bust, forcing many honest merchants to default on their debts.[58]

The credit reporting industry originated in the 1840s as a response to the growing need of wholesale merchants for more up-to-date information on the credit-worthiness of retail merchants seeking credit.

---

and early eighteenth century most of the northern colonies also enforced indentures for labor; a debtor in default could escape prison by agreeing to work under an indenture for a set number of years. Coleman 1974: 251.

55 Norris 1978: 3–4.

56 Wyatt-Brown 1966: 436–37.

57 Madison 1974: 166.

58 Wyatt-Brown 1969: 174–75 (suspension of payments by Arthur Tappan & Co.).

Its founder—Lewis Tappan—was a true American original. Tappan's career exemplifies de Tocqueville's contemporaneous observation that America was a nation of joiners.[59] A militant opponent of slavery and an outspoken evangelical Christian, Tappan was, in the words of his biographer, a member of "any and every league that had been founded for almost any purpose whatsoever, as long as it was benevolent, pious, and teetotaling."[60] Tappan also pursued several business careers and was a partner in his brother's silk goods wholesale business in New York when the Panic of 1837 struck, forcing that business to suspend payments for a time after its own debtors defaulted.[61]

Tappan's business experience led him to found in 1841 the Mercantile Agency, the world's first credit reporting firm.[62] To obtain up-to-date information on the credit-worthiness of the country merchants now arriving in droves in New York and other Eastern cities, Tappan retained as "correspondents" hundreds of lawyers and bankers living in the interior. Abraham Lincoln, then an aspiring young lawyer in Illinois, served as one of Tappan's early correspondents. These correspondents were charged with the responsibility of making inquiries on the retail merchants in their community and of presenting written reports to the Mercantile Agency in New York. As demonstrated by the following credit report, Tappan encouraged his correspondents to include information on the merchant's personal life and morality:[63]

> James Samson is a peddler, aged 30; he comes to Albany to buy his goods, and then peddles them out along the canal from Albany to Buffalo. He is worth $2,000; owns a wooden house at Lockport . . . has a wife and three children . . . drinks two glasses cider brandy, plain, morning and evening—never more; drinks water after each; chews fine cut; never smokes; good teeth generally; has lost a large double tooth on lower jaw, back, second from throat on left side . . . purchases principally jewelry and fancy articles.

---

[59] Alexis de Tocqueville, 1 *Democracy in America*.

[60] Wyatt-Brown 1969: vii. Wyatt-Brown is paraphrasing Henry James' classic portrayal of the antislavery lady, Miss Birdseye, in *The Bostonians*.

[61] See note 58 *supra*.

[62] On the history of the Mercantile Agency, see Wyatt-Brown 1969: 229–47 and Wyatt-Brown 1966: 432–50.

[63] Wyatt-Brown 1966: 235.

At least initially, Tappan did not pay his correspondents for their reports but promised them that, in return for their services, he would assure the referral to them of debt collection work. Tappan compiled the correspondents' reports in ledger books which were accessible to merchants who had subscribed to his service by paying an annual fee. By the later 1840s, the Mercantile Agency had over seven hundred correspondents and nearly eight thousand merchant subscribers. This remarkable growth occurred even though Tappan's well-known Abolitionist views made it difficult for him to recruit correspondents in slave states and even though Tappan himself refused any dealings with distilleries or other businesses he considered to be immoral.

By the end of the nineteenth century, commercial credit reporting agencies had evolved from a novel enterprise to an established business institution.[64] Tappan's original Mercantile Agency eventually became the well-known firm of Dun & Bradstreet. Over time, paid employees replaced the network of unpaid correspondents, and printed reference books and weekly updates replaced the ledger books inspected at the credit agency's office. The arrival of the telegraph made practicable the more rapid dissemination of up-to-date information. These innovations allowed Dun & Bradstreet and other credit reporting agencies to give subscribing merchants speedy access to the up-to-date credit information they needed about their customers.

Credit reporting services thrived in nineteenth-century America because, once a merchant extended unsecured credit, the means to assure payment were often woefully inadequate. In the absence of a federal Bankruptcy Act,[65] the law of debtor and creditor remained a state concern. Not surprisingly, given the continuing cycle of booms followed by busts, the matter of debtor relief often became a hot political issue. Since debtors outnumbered creditors, many state legislatures found debtor relief politically irresistible.[66] Most state legislation therefore favored debtors. By the Civil War, most states legislatures had abolished imprisonment for debt, thus depriving the creditor of a means for coercing his debtor to pay. In addition,

[64] Madison 1966: 186.

[65] Congress enacted Bankruptcy Acts in 1800, 1841, and 1867, but each of those laws was quickly repealed. An 1898 Bankruptcy Act proved to be more permanent; although much amended, it remains in effect today. See Warren 1935.

[66] Friedman 1985: 246.

Homestead Acts, enacted in most western and southern states, exempted the debtor's real property from execution. As in the feudal system of the Middle Ages, it was not possible for the creditor to satisfy a judgment by attaching the debtor's land, often the principal asset available. Finally, numerous state insolvency acts gave debtors a delay in payment or even a discharge from their debts. These statutes afforded debtors relief without providing creditors the advantages traditionally associated with bankruptcy proceedings. Creditors could not, as they could in bankruptcy, initiate a collective, inquisitorial-type proceeding designed to assemble and then distribute all the debtor's assets.[67]

Creditors fought back against this wave of debtor relief legislation. Usually, they found the courts more responsive to their concerns than state legislatures. Federal courts, for example, held unconstitutional state insolvency statutes that purported to discharge debts incurred before the date of their enactment.[68] Courts also tended to enforce the new security interests in personal property created by creditors' lawyers—the chattel mortgage and conditional sales agreements discussed in the prior section. Finally, state legislatures themselves often proved responsive to creditor interests if those interests corresponded with broader public interests. For example, legislatures enacted statutes giving mechanics and other artisans a lien on real property for improvements for which they had not been paid. In addition, state legislatures made debt recovery easier by enacting statutes which gave all persons better access to the courts and which simplified the often archaic common law procedures for debt collection. In particular, new statutes allowed judgment creditors to "garnish" money, wages, or goods owed the debtor by third persons.[69] These reforms presaged the enactment in the twentieth century of legislation such as the Uniform Commercial Code, which sought to balance more equitably debtor and creditor interests.

[67] For these debtor relief measures, see *id.* at 245–48 and 269–75 and Coleman 1974: 249–60.

[68] *Sturges v. Crowninshield,* 4 Wheat. 122 (U.S. 1819). Such laws violated the federal constitutional prohibition on impairing the obligation of contract.

[69] Friedman 1985: 243–45 and Coleman 1974: 262–68.

3. *Spreading Risk as a Security Device: Sureties and Letters of Credit*

A creditor can reduce the risk of a debtor's nonpayment by securing promises from third parties to pay the debt if the debtor does not. Those third party promisors, known as guarantors or sureties, are familiar figures on the contemporary legal scene. As in Roman law, their liability is normally secondary or accessorial in that the creditor can demand that they pay the debt only if the principal debtor has refused to pay.[70] Sureties nevertheless provide a creditor with considerable security, particularly if chosen for that role on account of their financial solvency. The creditor knows that he has recourse against a party of unquestioned solvency if the debtor defaults. However, commercial sureties expect a fee for their services and will not guarantee a debt unless they feel secure that they will be able to enforce against the debtor their own claim for reimbursement of any payments made to the creditor. Commercial sureties are therefore not likely to be available if the debtor is unable to provide them with security. Sureties remain useful in spreading the risk for the creditor, but they do not create security where none exists.

In early Germanic law, the surety played a more independent role. Custom often expected that relatives, friends, patrons, and even lords would fulfill the role of surety. That role was an onerous one because the creditor could hold the surety hostage until the debt was satisfied. Indeed, custom required obligors to provide hostages (pledges)[71] on all sorts of occasions, to guarantee the payment of a debt, an appearance in court, the execution of a judgment, or the preservation of the peace. Unlike Roman and modern law, early Germanic law normally treated the surety's or pledgor's obligation as primary, if not exclusive. The creditor thus looked to the surety for payment and often had no further remedy against the debtor once he took a surety hostage. Holding the surety hostage was a means of putting pressure on the debtor, as it was assumed that the surety would do everything possible to convince the debtor to pay.

---

[70] Loyd 1917 (history of surety at common law) and Weill 1979: 32 (accessorial liability of surety or *caution* under present French Civil Code). See also articles 765–778 of present German Civil Code, especially article 771 on the guarantor's secondary liability.

[71] In early medieval times a "pledge" (*plegius*) was almost always a person, not a thing. Plucknett 1956: 603 note 2.

By the twelfth century, the practice of the creditor's taking a surety hostage seemed to have disappeared, perhaps because creditors balked at the cost of feeding hostages. As the old adage goes, "The banquet of a hostage is a costly banquet." Suretyship, at least in England, became a contract, one of the few consensual contracts the common law enforced. However, until the end of the Middle Ages, the surety's liability remained primary and sureties were not usually commercial entities but rather individuals with personal ties to the debtor.[72]

In the modern commercial world, the documentary sale under a letter of credit is the paradigmatic device utilized to provide security by spreading the creditor's risk.[73] Take the case of a merchant seller in country A desiring to sell goods to a merchant buyer in country B. Modern communications permit the parties to agree on a sale without leaving their respective countries and before the seller ships the goods. However, the buyer is unlikely to want to pay for the goods until he obtains control over them in country B, and the seller is unlikely to agree to ship the goods until assured of payment. Shipping on credit is simply too risky for the seller even if the buyer has agreed to pay on delivery. The buyer may be unable to pay on account of insolvency or may reject delivery of the goods because the buyer no longer wants them or believes them to be nonconforming. Given the distance between the two countries, the seller may have no means of obtaining adequate information about the buyer to ascertain whether these problems are likely to occur. In addition, the seller may feel quite uncomfortable about pursuing legal remedies against the buyer in the unfamiliar legal system of country B, the forum where any dispute between the buyer and an unpaid seller is likely to be resolved.

The irrevocable letter of credit responds to the seller's insecurity about shipping on credit. It does so by expanding the transaction between the seller and buyer to include the buyer's bank, the seller's bank, the carrier, and the insurer of the goods. Each of these parties

[72] On the surety in early Germanic law, see Brissaud 1912: 571–74 and Pollock & Maitland 1895: II, 191. For the banquet quotation see Brissaud at 572–73. For the primary liability of the medieval surety, see Loyd 1917: 50–51.

[73] On the letter of credit, see Dolan 1996 (American law); Stoufflet 1957 (French law and international practice); Kozolchyk 1979 (comparative study). Professor Kozolchyk's book is part of the *International Encyclopedia of Comparative Law*. For a marvelously clear, albeit simplified, presentation on letters of credit, see Folsom, Gordon, and Spanogle 1996: 140–50.

assumes, for a fee, some of the risk that the seller would otherwise bear. To simplify a good deal, the buyer obtains from his bank in country B an irrevocable letter of credit payable to the seller for the purchase price of the goods. While irrevocable, the credit is only payable when the issuing bank receives from the seller a bill of lading—a document issued by the carrier confirming the seller's shipment of the goods. That bank, located in country B, naturally has better access to information about the buyer than does the seller; it also has greater familiarity with the legal system of country B. The buyer's bank therefore makes its own contractual arrangements with the buyer (usually called the applicant) for payment of the sum designated in the letter of credit. The bank is usually willing to extend credit to the buyer as long as the bank retains the bill of lading because that document of title gives the bank a security interest which the bank may enforce against the goods if the buyer does not pay the bank.

The buyer, of course, needs the bill of lading to obtain delivery of the goods. Prior to releasing the bill of lading to the buyer, the buyer's bank normally expects either payment or the execution of another instrument giving the bank a security interest in the goods. In the United States, that instrument used to be the trust receipt, which has now been subsumed under the unitary security agreement recognized by the Uniform Commercial Code. The trust receipt allowed the buyer to process or even sell the goods without the entrusting party (the bank) losing its security interest. The buyer could therefore use the goods to make the money which he needed to pay the bank.[74]

The international letter of credit, however, primarily benefits the seller. Remember that the seller does not ship (i.e. deliver the goods to a carrier in return for a bill of lading) until the seller obtains an irrevocable letter of credit. That letter makes the buyer's bank the primary debtor, thus providing the seller with additional security before he ships. Banks do occasionally fail, but they are more likely than merchant buyers to be solvent and to pay their debts on time. In addition, most sellers obtain a confirmation of the letter of credit by

[74] Kozolchyk 1979: 61–66. Professor Kozolchyk describes the more limited security devices available to the buyer's bank in other countries. His comprehensive analysis confirms the superiority of the Uniform Commercial Code in recognizing security interests in personal property.

a bank in their own country (country A). By confirming the letter of credit, the seller's bank becomes the primary debtor. The seller's bank is better able than the seller to inform itself about the banking system in country B and about the risk of default by the buyer's bank. The seller's primary security when he parts with the goods is therefore the confirmation by his bank of the letter of credit issued by the buyer's bank. While it is conceivable that the seller's bank could become insolvent and not pay (letters of credit are not insured by the government, as are savings deposits in the United States), that risk is one that most sellers feel comfortable about appraising and handling.

The letter of credit also assures that the seller receives prompt payment for the goods. There is a time gap between the seller's shipment and payment. The seller must ship first, but once he ships he can submit the bill of lading, proof of insurance, export license, and other required documents to his bank to obtain payment under the letter of credit. In other words, the seller receives payment before the buyer receives the goods because both the seller's bank and then the buyer's bank honor the letter of credit upon presentation of the documents submitted by the seller. Of course, the banks and other intermediaries all receive a fee for their services and any early payment received by the seller is always discounted to take into account the time value of money. For this reason, sellers and buyers who know and trust each other often do not go to the trouble of including a letter of credit as the payment term for a sale. Thus, most sales within one country and many sales within the European Union do not involve letters of credit. Under those circumstances, a seller desirous of obtaining security before shipping may feel sufficiently comfortable if he simply retains a security interest in the goods.[75] That technique is less likely to prove effective when the buyer is in a distant country with a different legal system.

The letters of credit transaction described above originated in mid-nineteenth-century England. Largely the creation of the London banks, it depends for its operation on the existence of functioning banking systems in both country A and country B. It also requires currency convertibility and cooperation between banks at the international level. Mercantile interests have insured that that cooperation

[75] *Id.* at 1–2.

has occurred. In most countries, however, the law on letters of credit remains largely customary.[76] Commencing in 1929, the International Chamber of Commerce headquartered in Paris has acted to standardize practices by issuing Uniform Customs and Practice (UCP) for Documentary Credits. The most recent revision dates from 1993.[77] The UCP rules are not mandatory, but most sales agreements providing for payment by letter of credit incorporate them by reference. In the United States, on the other hand, legislatures have intervened, and article 5 of the Uniform Commercial Code, adopted in all fifty states, provides rules on letters of credit. Once again, most of these rules are not mandatory but apply only if the parties do not provide otherwise by agreement. Both the UCP and the Code rules seek to insure that the seller receives payment upon presentation of facially adequate documents. Any dispute between the buyer and the seller over the quality of the goods or other matters must be resolved later, most likely in a lawsuit brought by the buyer in the seller's home forum.

IV. Conclusion

There is one security device—potentially a very effective one—which the Anglo-American common law has, fortunately, almost never adopted: debt slavery. The common law did at one time authorize courts, at a creditor's behest, to imprison debtors, but the purpose of the imprisonment was coercive, i.e. to pressure the debtor to disclose his assets or the debtor's family and friends to come to his aid. The debtor could not be forced to work, and, in most jurisdictions, the creditor was responsible for paying for the debtor's upkeep. Debtors' prison was therefore not debt slavery. Even if a debtor agreed to work for his creditor to pay off a debt, the courts normally refused to enforce the agreement. No doubt colonial courts did enforce some indentures for service,[78] but the Supreme Court decisively condemned debt slavery in *The Peonage Cases* in the early twentieth century. In those cases, the Court found unconstitutional,

---

[76] Dolan 1995: 3–22.
[77] *Id.* at 12–19.
[78] See note 54 *supra*.

under the 1866 constitutional amendment abolishing slavery, efforts by Southern states to require poor Blacks to work for landowners to whom they were indebted.[79]

The lesson of *The Peonage Cases* is that there are limits on the security which a creditor can expect from the law. A debtor is a human being, and the common law has traditionally imposed limits on an individual's power to renounce the autonomy which is a hallmark of that humanity. As recognized by John Stuart Mill, voluntary slavery is an oxymoron. One cannot be free not to be free. Therefore, an agreement by which a person would sell himself as a slave is null and void.[80] This bedrock proposition receives little confirmation from statutes or reported cases, perhaps because it is so basic that no one challenges it. Mill's value judgment nevertheless pervades our legal system and makes it unlikely that *The Peonage Cases* will arise again. Creditors may be a bit less secure as a result, but we are a better society for it.

[79] The lead case is *United States v. Reynolds*, 235 U.S. 233 (1914). For a fascinating discussion of the cases, see Schmidt 1982.

[80] Mill 1912: 125.

Bibliography

Balzac, Honoré de. 1837. *Histoire de la grandeur et de la décadence de César Birotteau.*

Bebchuk, L. and J. Fried. 1996. The Uneasy Case for the Priority of Secured Claims in Bankruptcy. *Yale Law Review* 105: 857–934.

Berman, H. 1983. *Law and Revolution: The Formation of the Western Legal Tradition.* Cambridge, MA: Harvard University Press.

Brissaud, J. 1912. *A History of French Private Law.* Translated from the second French edition by R. Howell. Boston: Little, Brown.

Cantor, N. 1991. *The Inventing of the Middle Ages.* New York: Morrow.

Cohen, J. 1982. The History of Imprisonment for Debt and its Relation to the Development of Discharge in Bankruptcy. *Journal of Legal History* 3: 153–171.

Coleman, P. 1974. *Debtors and Creditors in America: Insolvency, Imprisonment for Debt, and Bankruptcy 1607–1900.* Madison: State Historical Society of Wisconsin.

Dolan, J. 1996. *The Law of Letters of Credit. Commercial and Standby Credits* (rev. ed.). Boston: Warren, Gorham & Lamont.

Epstein, D. 1995. *Debtor Creditor Law in a Nutshell* (5th ed.). St. Paul, MN: West Publishing Company.

Folsom, R., M. Gordon, and J. Spanogle. 1996. *International Business Transactions in a Nutshell* (5th ed.). St. Paul, MN: West Publishing Company.

Friedman, L. 1985. *A History of American Law* (2nd ed.). New York: Simon and Schuster.

Gilmore, G., and A. Axelrod. 1948. Chattel Security I. *Yale Law Journal* 57: 517–548.

——. 1948. Chattel Security II. *Yale Law Journal* 57: 761–787.

——. 1965. *Security Interests in Personal Property.* 2 vols. Boston: Little, Brown.

Haskins, C. 1933. *Renaissance of the Twelfth Century.* Cambridge: Harvard University Press.

Holdsworth, W. 1933–. *A History of English Law.* London: Methuen.

Huebner, R. 1918. *A History of Germanic Private Law.* Translated by F. Philbrick. Continental legal history series, 4. Boston: Little, Brown.

Jauffret, A. 1951. La loi du 18 janvier 1951 sur le nantissement de l'outillage et du matériel d'équipement. *Revue Trimestrielle de Droit Commercial* 4: 202–219.

——. 1997. *Droit Commercial* (20th ed.). Paris: Librairie Générale de Droit et de Jurisprudence.

Kohler, J. 1891. *Lehrbuch des Konkursrechts.* Stuttgart: Ferdinand Enke.

Konefsky, A., and A. King, eds. 1982. *Legal Papers of Daniel Webster.* Hanover, NH: University Press of New England.

Kozolchyk, B. 1979. *Letters of Credit.* In International Encyclopedia of Comparative Law, v. 9; Commercial transactions and institutions, ch. 5. Tübingen: J.C.B. Mohr.

Levinthal, L. 1919a. The Early History of Bankruptcy Law. *University of Pennsylvania Law Review* 66: 223–250.

——. 1919b. The Early History of English Bankruptcy. *University of Pennsylvania Law Review* 67: 1–20.

Loyd, W. 1917. The Surety. *University of Pennsylvania Law Review* 66: 40–68.

Lyon, B. 1972. *The Origins of the Middle Ages.* New York: Nelson.

Madison, J. 1966. The Evolution of Commercial Credit Reporting Agencies in Nineteenth Century America. *Business History Review* 48: 164–186.

Mill, John Stuart. 1912. "On Liberty." In *Three Essays.* Oxford: Oxford University Press.

Norris, J. 1978. *R.C. Dun & Co., 1841–1900: The Development of Credit Reporting in the*

Nineteenth Century. Contributions in economics and economic history, 2. Westport, CT: Greenwood Press.
Percerou, J. 1935. *Des faillites, banqueroutes et liquidations judiciares* (2nd ed.). Paris: Rousseau.
Plucknett, T. 1949. *Legislation of Edward I*. Oxford: Oxford University Press.
——. 1956. *A Concise History of the Common Law* (5th ed.). Boston, MA: Little Brown.
Pollock, F., and W. Maitland. 1895. *A History of English Law before the Time of Edward I*. Cambridge: The University Press.
Rajak, H., ed. 1995. *European Corporate Insolvency* (2nd ed.). Chichester, NY: J. Wiley.
Schmidt, B. 1982. Principle and Prejudice: The Supreme Court and Race in the Progressive Era. Part 2: The Peonage Cases. *Columbia Law Review* 82: 646–718.
Stoufflet, J. 1957. *Le Crédit documentaire—Etude juridique d'un instrument financier du commerce internationale*. Paris: Librairies techniques.
Van Caenegem, R. 1992. *An Historical Introduction to Private Law*. Translated by D. Johnston. Cambridge: Cambridge University Press.
Warren, C. 1935. *Bankruptcy in United States History*. Cambridge, MA: Harvard University Press.
Warren, E., and J. Westbrook. 1996. *The Law of Debtors and Creditors* (3rd ed.). Boston: Little Brown.
Weill, A. 1979. *Droit civil. Les sûretés. La publicité foncière*. Paris: Dalloz.
Wigmore, J. 1896 and 1897. The Pledge Idea: A Study in Comparative Legal Ideas. *Harvard Law Review* 10: 321–350; *Harvard Law Review* 10: 389–417; *Harvard Law Review* 11: 18–39.
Wood, P. 1995. *Comparative Law of Security and Guarantees*. London: Sweet and Maxwell.
Wyatt-Brown, B. 1969. *Lewis Tappan and the Evangelical War against Slavery*. Cleveland: Press of Case Western Reserve University.
——. 1966. God and Dun & Bradstreet, 1841–1851. *Business History Review* 40: 432–450.

PRE-DEMOTIC PHARAONIC SOURCES

Richard Jasnow – Johns Hopkins University

The legal historian Pestman has emphasized that Egyptian law, for all its imperfections, did strive to maintain "equilibrium between parties and tries to look after their interests equally."[1] This ideal was certainly present in religious writings,[2] literary narratives,[3] wisdom texts,[4] and administrative didactic compositions.[5] The intrinsic sense of fairness found expression in practical legal procedure as well. In Demotic, for example, the interests of the two parties were protected through the institution of the trustee, the *ʿrbṯ*, who held the relevant documents in trust.[6]

The loan relationship and the web of mutual social and legal obligations bound up with it comprise a not unimportant part of that equilibrium mentioned by Pestman. However, the evidence for security and pledges in earlier Pharaonic Egypt is extraordinarily scarce, and that for loans not much more extensive. This is unfortunate, for the superficially dry topic of loans, pledges, and security raises intriguing, if often unanswerable, questions about conditions of life in the Ancient Near East.[7]

In a later chapter Manning discusses the substantial Late Period Demotic evidence for pledges and security; here I would like to comment on the lack of written evidence on loans before the seventh

---

[1] Pestman 1961: 182.

[2] "I made every man like his fellow; and I did not command that they do wrong," declares the creator-deity in the Coffin Texts, translated in Lichtheim 1975: 132.

[3] See for example, *The Eloquent Peasant*, translated in Lichtheim 1975: 169–84.

[4] The advice to the judge considering the pleas of petitioners in the wisdom text of Ptahhotep. Lichtheim 1975: 68.

[5] An excellent illustration is the passages emphasizing the the objectivity of judges in the "Installation of the Vizier Rekhmire." Lichtheim 1976: 23.

[6] The third-party trustee holds the deed of sale (*sẖ ḏbꜣ ḥḏ*) and the deed of cession (*sẖ n wy*); see Manning in this volume.

[7] These questions, raised by contributors to this volume, concern the need of the debtor (compare Manning and Radner); the legal or relative social status of the persons involved (Abraham); their legal or economic options; the choice between surety and pledge (Oelsner).

century BCE.[8] Anyone researching the subjects of borrowing, lending and security quickly observes that they are not prominent in the Egyptological literature on law and economy.[9] One reason for this state of affairs is the generally meagre sources for law and economy in Pharaonic Egypt. Perhaps in part due to chance of preservation, but perhaps in fact also partly because the Egyptians felt little need as a rule to document such transactions, the quantity of relevant texts from Pharaonic Egypt is inconsiderable in comparison with the vast numbers of tablets from Mesopotamia. Similarly, the lack of surviving systematic law codes in Egypt until the Hermopolis Legal Code,[10] written in Demotic, removes another potentially rich source of information regarding debt and loans. Consequently, it is hardly surprising, for example, that Janssen's pioneering article "Prolegomena to the Study of Egypt's Economic History During the New Kingdom" does not once mention loans or security.[11] The same author's massive volume on *Commodity Prices during the Ramessid Period*, which because of its subject matter covers a great range of text types, similarly scarcely brings up loan or security.[12]

While they seldom find expression in formal legal documents, the basic notions associated with the pledge and security naturally do exist in Pharaonic Egypt. The family of a fugitive may be imprisoned to compel an absconder to return to corvée-labor in the Middle Kingdom, an example of distraint.[13] In the school text of P. Lansing, the farmer's family is seized as security because that unfortunate cannot pay his taxes.[14] Some scholars have interpreted the confiscation of the poor peasant's donkey by an unscrupulous official as an exam-

---

[8] According to Malinine (1947: 123), the institution of "guaranty" ("caution") is only attested in the Ptolemaic demotic texts. In O. Chicago 12073, it has been suggested that a third party stands bail or surety for the debtor, but this is by no means clear; see Manning et al. 1989: 120. McDowell (1990: 32) states in her discussion of O. Chicago 12073 that "the concept of standing surety is otherwise unknown in the village." On that interesting text, see also Janssen 1975a: col. 292; Pirenne 1974b: 169–72.

[9] See Menu 1973, 1998; Pirenne 1974a, 1974b; Boochs 1984.

[10] See Allam 1993.

[11] Janssen 1975c.

[12] Janssen 1975b. A possible example is mentioned in 1975b: 532. See also footnote 17 *infra*.

[13] For this example of distraint in the Middle Kingdom, see Hayes 1955: 44; Quirke 1990: 136.

[14] A translation is in Lichtheim 1976: 170–71. The relevant passage is uncertain, however; see Erman and Lange 1925: 65–70. See also Pirenne 1974b: 167–68; Allam 1977: 89–90.

ple of security or pledge in the Middle Kingdom Tale of the Eloquent Peasant, a debatable point.[15] In the New Kingdom Tale of Wenamun, the long-suffering hero, robbed of his goods in Tjeker territory (on the Phoenician coast), takes 30 deben of silver from a Tjeker ship, apparently with the intention of holding it until he is compensated for his loss.[16] These are, to be sure, all rather vague and unsatisfactory examples of the ideas of pledge and security.

Given the present state of the evidence, little can be done to remedy the situation. Especially from the Old and Middle Kingdoms, we simply have no clearly formulated loan documents, but merely references to loan transactions.[17] One of the earliest attestations of the only word for "loan" (*ṯ3b.t*, "Darlehn [an Korn]") given in our standard Egyptian dictionary,[18] occurs in a literary description of a chaotic, reversed universe dating to about 2000 BCE. The author declares:

> See, the one who earlier had not seed is (now) possessor of a granary.
> The one who earlier had to take a loan of seed, gives it now.[19]

Local authorities or rulers in the troubled First Intermediate Period (ca. 2135–2040 BCE) may speak of making such "seed-loans" to distressed communities, but they provide few details as to the conditions under which the loans were made.[20]

---

[15] See Shupak 1992: 8.

[16] Again, a damaged passage; see Lichtheim 1976: 225.

[17] Ray 1973, for example, suggests that P. Kahun 13 deals with debts and the cancelling of debts. He also discusses there the possibility of debt imprisonment, which occurred in Roman Egypt. In discussing the important Middle Kingdom Hekanakht documents, Goedicke (1984: 77) has proposed that the debtor's property served as security. Janssen (1975b: 532), in analyzing a possible instance of joint ownership, remarks: "It does not seem likely that one party borrowed a sum of 'money' and that the other acquired a share in the object by way of security." I quote also his footnote 62 of that page: "Prof. Pestman informs me that he knows of no clear instance of such a pledge from Egypt, except in the case where the lender was given right to dwell in a house of the borrower's." For a discussion of terms for instruments of security, see also Goedicke 1986: 94.

[18] *Wb.* 5, 354/10 ("Darlehn an Getreide"). See Goedicke 1986: 79.

[19] Admonitions 9/5:
mtn ỉwty pr.t = f m nb šnw.t
ỉn n = f ṯ3b.t m dd pr = st
"Seht, wer kein Saatkorn hatte ist Besitzer einer Scheuner, und wer sich en Saatgut darlehn holen musste, ist einer, der es ausgibt." Helck 1995: 43.

[20] More specific than usual is Cairo 43371, quoted by Goedicke 1986: 79: "As for any man whom I found in this district with a seed loan for another against him—I paid it to its holder (owner) from my estate."

The New Kingdom evidence for debts and non-payment of debts is greater, but still not very informative about pledges and security. In the corpus of Deir el-Medina texts, one of the chief sources for our knowledge of New Kingdom legal practice, we do find debts recorded. In O. Gardiner 204, for example, there is a list of the objects of A which B has received (measured according to standard units of value: "x worth so-and-so-much"). The text then states that A has been given a partial repayment, but that there is still a remaining debt to be satisfied.[21] Nothing in this document suggests that the lender received or demanded any sort of security or pledge before making the "loan." It is just possible that in O. Cairo 25572, a garment described as "with" the lender, and equal in value to the debt, may be a form of security, but this is not certain.[22] Although the pledge and security do not seem to be much used as legal tools, there was naturally a concern that debtors make good their debts. Thus, in O. Cairo 25553 from Deir el-Medina the court apparently appoints an official to see that the debtor pays his debt:

> Then the man of the work-gang PN was found to be in the wrong. One had him swear an oath by the lord. He said: "If I do not repay the food-stuffs, then they will be against me doubled." One placed the chief PN behind (*m-sꜣ*) him.[23]

So, in the Deir el-Medina material there are "debts" recorded in documents, but hardly very explicit or elaborate loan agreements, and scarcely any mention of security in connection with these debts.[24]

The authors of Egyptian wisdom texts, which occasionally deal with legal topics, do in fact imply that one could become indebted with dire consequences, perhaps due in part to the loss of the pledge or security. One New Kingdom composition advises (Any 6/6):

> Do not rely on another's goods
> Guard what you acquire yourself;
> Do not depend on another's wealth,
> Lest he become master of your house.[25]

---

[21] Janssen 1994: 130–31. See also Allam 1973a: 189–90; 1973b: 18.
[22] Janssen 1994: 132.
[23] Following Allam 1973a: 58.
[24] Compare the remarks of Janssen 1975b: 508.
[25] Lichtheim 1976: 139; Quack 1994: 102–03:
m-ỉr mḥ ib = k (m) ỉḫ.t ky

The Egyptians become somewhat more informative regarding loans in this later (post-New Kingdom) biographical text from about 900 BCE (Statue Inscription of Djedkhonsefankh):[26]

> (The deceased boasts of his generosity)
> I was constant in lending grain to the Thebans, in nourishing the poor[27] of my town. I did not rage at him who could not pay. I did not press him so as to seize his belongings. I did not make him sell his goods to another, so as to repay the debt he had made. I sated (him) by buying his goods and paying two or three times their worth.

Clearly formulated loan documents first appear in Egypt during the First Millennium. An excellent example, written in hieratic, is P. Berlin 3048 (Twenty-second Dynasty):[28]

> Year 13, first month of summer, day 11.
> There has said PN, son of PN, to the prophet of Amun, overseer of the treasury PN, son of PN:
> (I) have received from you 5 *deben* of the treasury of (the god) Heryshef.
> It is I who will give it to you, they being 10 (*deben* in) year 14, first month of summer, day 11, without there being anything in the world to say with you.[29]
> Through the hand of the document scribe PN, son of PN, so he spoke.
> (There follow six witnesses)
> In the presence of the prophet of Khonsu PN, so he spoke.
> In the presence of the prophet of Amun, overseer of the treasury PN, so he spoke.
> In the presence of the god's-father PN, so he spoke.
> In the presence of the prophet of Amun-Re, lord of the gods PN, so he spoke.
> In the presence of the god's father of Amun, PN, so he spoke.
> In the presence of the prophet of Amun-Re, king of the gods, overseer of the treasury of Pharaoh, PN, so he spoke.

---

s³w ṯ ỉry = k n = k
m-ỉr hn = k (ḥr) nk.t ky
bw-ỉr = f ṯ³s m pr = k

[26] Twenty-second Dynasty; Lichtheim 1980: 17 = Jansen-Winkeln 1985: 13. The transliteration is: *rwd.kw m dỉ.t ṯ³b.w n W³s.ty sʿnḫ nmḥ.w nw nỉw.t = ỉ n fnd = ỉ r šw m ḏb³ n sḥs sw r ỉṯ wnn.t = f n rdỉ = ỉ dỉ = f ḫ.t = f n ky r mḥ ḥr.t-ʾ n ššp n = f ss³.n = ỉ swn.n = ỉ m nw = f dỉ = ỉ pr = w ḥr = f m wḥm ḫm.t* (= p. 437).

[27] Literally, *nmḥ.w*, "poor, orphans," *Wb.* 2, 268/4–8. The word comes to mean "private person, freeman."

[28] Möller 1921: 298–304.

[29] The interest on this "money-loan" is a rather high 100 percent.

Another loan (of grain) is P. Louvre E 3228b (704 BCE—reign of Shabaka).[30] This text also mentions interest, which only begins if the loan is not paid back on time. The possibility of a court dispute is envisioned, so that one party declares that he will pay back the debt "without any contesting the matter with you." The transaction is witnessed by eight persons. An interesting feature of this document is that it has been annulled, if that is the correct interpretation of the 12 vertical lines drawn through the text.[31]

The mechanism of security appears in other legal contexts in the first millennium BCE. It has been suggested that in the few preserved early marriage documents, beginning from the Ninth Century BCE, the groom addresses the bride's father directly. He gives to the father the "gift of a woman," and "pledged his property to his (future) father-in-law as a security."[32]

Nevertheless, the Pharaonic Period evidence for pledges, security, and loans in general, scarcely rivals the Mesopotamian tradition. This problem is naturally one aspect of the larger issue of the pharaonic Egyptian economy, currently the object of vigorous study.[33] While much remains obscure, it is perhaps safe to state that the economic conditions prevailing in Pharaonic Egypt were not overly conducive to the development of a sophisticated system of pledges, sureties, and security. Egypt has nothing to compare, for example, with the intricate economic and legal world of the Assyrian trading colonies in Anatolia.[34] In Pharaonic Egypt when we hear of the acquisition of luxury items, ivory and other goods from Nubia, they seem generally to come about through royal missions, e.g. Harkhuf in the Old Kingdom.[35] So too there does not seem to have been a significant class of totally "free" labor in Egypt, although there may indeed have been some latitude within narrow parameters. It is possible, for example, that even in the Old Kingdom artisans may have had at least some say in their labor-obligations and compensation, while the Deir el-Medina artisans may have done some work "on

[30] Malinine 1953: 5.
[31] Malinine 1953: 5.
[32] Johnson 1994: 156.
[33] See, most recently, Warburton 1997.
[34] On the need for large sums of money, and on the complexity of their loan and security arrangements, see Veenhof in this volume.
[35] His autobiography describing his journeys to Nubia, where he procured valuable goods is translated in Lichtheim 1975: 23–27. But see the remarks on trading of Janssen 1975c: 162–63.

the side."[36] Nevertheless, the role of the free market in Egypt, that is, unsupervised by the state, is much debated.[37] Such historians as Janssen have doubted that "profit" was an especially "driving" force in the economy.[38]

The figure of the independent or semi-dependent merchant appears repeatedly in the following chapters of this volume. It is precisely the dependent or independent status of the merchant class, the group which might have had most use of security and pledges, merchants, which is much disputed in the Pharaonic Period. As Tomlinson implies, the rise of an important merchant class necessitated or encouraged the development of rules of credit and loans.[39] The merchant class is rather hard to document in Egypt.[40] There is certainly some evidence for itinerant merchants, but they are a murky lot.[41] Janssen points out that in our most important text corpus for New Kingdom law and economy, from Deir el-Medina, the word *šwty*, "merchant," never appears to occur.[42]

I should like to conclude with a few remarks on other aspects of debt and security in ancient Egypt.

Several contributors to this volume discuss how various Near Eastern peoples took steps to ease the situation of debtors, or at least showed awareness of their dilemma. Naturally, the Biblical material stands out, as in Deut. 24:18: "You cannot take the garment of a widow in pledge,"[43] but other peoples also display such an awareness or sensitivity.[44]

---

[36] "Kemp has pointed out that in el-ʿAmarna the houses of the officials were surrounded by those of the lower classes, in which he sees an indication of the existence of free labourers." Janssen 1975c: 159.

[37] See, for example, Eyre 1998.

[38] 1975c: 138–39. One finds relatively little evidence in Pharaonic Egypt for buying objects in order to resell them at a profit.

[39] Tomlinson, in this volume, points out that the feudal system was not especially responsive to the legal needs of merchants.

[40] Very interesting in this respect is the statue of a merchant from Naukratis, from the Late Period, to be sure: Jansen-Winkeln 1997.

[41] Janssen 1975b: 542. Such persons are described in the New Kingdom literary text Papyrus Lansing "The merchants travel downstream and upstream. They are as busy as can be, carrying goods from one town to another. They supply him who has wants. But the tax collectors carry off the gold, that most precious of metals." Lichtheim 1976: 170.

[42] 1975b: 561. The village may be atypical, however.

[43] Discussed by Frymer-Kensky.

[44] Compare Veenhof on the city in the Assyrian trading colonies sometimes acting to make it easier for a defaulting debtor to redeem an important pledge like

Among the actual Egyptian legal documents, forgiving of loans is not prominent. Nevertheless, evidence for a social conscience is certainly not lacking. One may quote, for example, the New Kingdom Wisdom text of Amenemope (xvi, 1), which has, to be sure, to do with a loan, not a pledge:

> If you find a large debt against a poor man,
> Make it into three parts
> Forgive two, let one stand
> You will find in it a path of life.[45]

Several contributors to this volume have emphasized the social problems caused by debt bondage.[46] The resulting situation could demand periodic intervention by kings, although the regularity of the *Dror*, mass remissions every seven or 50 years, presumably heavily impacting on the economy, seems unusual. Once more Egypt is a contrast. Debt-slavery to my knowedge is hardly attested for Pharaonic Egypt until, perhaps, the Abnormal Hieratic or Demotic period.[47] I do not know of debt-annulment decrees isssued by any Pharaoh.

As is true generally in Egyptian lexicography, detailed studies of individual words and phrases with legal meanings pertaining to loan, debt, and security remain a desideratum. For example, the usual Late Period Demotic term for "surety" is *šp tr.t*, "to receive the hand (of someone)."[48] Quack has discussed the phrase *šsp ḏr.t* in the New Kingdom Wisdom text of Any, which may be then a possible early example of that idiom.[49] As Manning points out in this volume, the common Demotic word for "pledge, security, surety," *ỉwy.t* is found

---

the family house. Oelsner remarks in connection with the Neo-Babylonian material, that a court case could develop since a pledge had been improperly alienated. Especially interesting is the detailed mechanism in the Middle Assyrian period, discussed by Abraham, by which ownership over pledged property was transferred to the creditor, who may have been required to compensate the debtor for the market difference.

[45] Lichtheim 1976: 155–56.
ỉr gm = k wḏꜣ ꜥꜣ n nmḥ
ỉ-ỉr sw m 3 tny.t
ḫꜣꜥ 2.t ỉm mn wꜥ
gm = k sw mỉ wꜣ.t n ꜥnḫ (Lange 1925: 79).

[46] See especially Radner (on debt slavery), Steinkeller, and Westbrook (Old Babylonian period).

[47] See, for example, Bakir 1952: 74, 119–20.

[48] Erichsen 1954: 500.

[49] Quack 1994: 101–02, 167.

in the sense of "human substitute" in the New Kingdom.[50] A ninth century BCE example of *ỉwy.t* in its later Demotic sense of "pledge, security," possibly appears in the still unpublished P. Berlin 3048 verso b.[51]

It may well be that future analysis of the scattered corpus of legal or economic texts and terms, or the discovery of new material, always a possibility in Egypt, will reveal a more substantial use of such legal mechanisms as pledge and security in Pharaonic Egypt. At present, however, only the Late Period Demotic documents provide significant information concerning pledge and security.

[50] See also Gardiner 1951.
[51] Menu 1982: 194.

Bibliography

Allam, S. 1973a. *Hieratische Ostraka und Papyri aus der Ramessidenzeit.* Tübingen: Im Selbstverlag des Herausgebers,

——. 1973b. *Das Verfahrensrecht in der altägyptischen Arbeitersiedlung von Deir el-Medineh.* Tübingen: Im Selbstverlag des Herausgebers.

——. 1977. Les Obligations et la familie dans la société égyptienne ancienne. *Oriens Antiquus* 16: 89–97.

——. 1993. Traces de "codification" en Égypte ancienne (à la basse époque). *RIDA* 40: 11–26.

Bakir, Abd el-Mohsen. 1952. *Slavery in Pharaonic Egypt.* Supplément aux Annales du Service des Antiquités de l'Égypte Cahier 18. Cairo: Institut français d'archéologie orientale.

Boochs, W. 1984. Zur Problematik von Schuld und Haftung im altägyptischen Recht. *GM* 78: 27–31.

Erichsen, W. 1954. *Demotisches Glossar.* Copenhagen: Ejnar Munksgaard.

Erman, A. and H. Grapow, eds. 1926–31. *Wörterbuch der ägyptischen Sprache.* 5 volumes. Leipzig and Berlin: J.C. Hinrichs Verlag.

Erman, A. and H.O. Lange. 1925. *Papyrus Lansing. Eine ägyptische Schulhandschrift der 20. Dynastie.* Det Kgl. Danske Videnskabernes Selskab. Historisk-filologiske Meddelelser X. 3. Copenhagen: Bianco Lunos Bogtrykkeri.

Eyre, C. 1998. The Market Women of Pharaonic Egypt. In *Le Commerce en Égypte ancienne,* eds. N. Grimal and B. Menu. Pp. 173–91. BdE 121. Cairo: Institut français d'archéologie orientale.

Gardiner, A. 1951. A word for "representative", "substitute", or the like. *JEA* 37: 111.

Goedicke, H. 1984. *Studies in the Hekanakhte Papers.* Baltimore, Md.: Halgo Inc.

——. 1986. Bilateral Business in the Old Kingdom. *DE* 5: 73–101.

Hayes, W. 1955. *A Papyrus of the Late Middle Kingdom in the Brooklyn Museum.* Wilbour Monographs 5. Brooklyn: The Brooklyn Museum.

Helck, W. 1995. *Die "Admonitions" Pap. Leiden I 344 recto.* Kleine Ägyptische Texte 11. Wiesbaden: Harrassowitz Verlag.

Jansen-Winkeln, K. 1985. *Ägyptische Biographien der 22. und 23. Dynastie.* ÄAT 8. Two Volumes. Wiesbaden: Otto Harrassowitz.

——. 1997. Ein Kaufmann aus Naukratis. *ZÄS* 124: 108–15.

Janssen, J. 1975a. The Rules of Legal Proceeding in the Community of Necropolis Workmen at Deir el-Medina. *Bibliotheca Orientalis* 32: 291–96.

——. 1975b. *Commodity Prices from the Ramessid Period.* Leiden: E.J. Brill.

——. 1975c. Prolegomena to the Study of Egypt's Economic History during the New Kingdom. *SAK* 3: 127–85.

——. 1994. Debts and Credit in the New Kingdom. *JEA* 80: 129–36.

Johnson, J. 1994. The Persians and the Continuity of Egyptian Culture. In *Achaemenid History VIII. Continuity and Change,* eds. H. Sancisi-Weedenburg, A. Kuhrt, and M. Cool Root. Pp. 149–59. Leiden: Nederlands Instituut voor het Nabije Oosten.

Lange, H.O. 1925. *Das Weisheitsbuch des Amenemope.* Det. Kgl. Danske Videnskabernes Selskab. Historisk-filologiske Meddelelser xi, 2. Copenhagen: Bianco Lunos Bogtrykkeri.

Lichtheim, M. 1975. *Ancient Egyptian Literature: A Book of Readings. Volume 1: The Old and Middle Kingdoms.* Berkeley, Los Angeles, London: University of California Press.

——. 1976. *Ancient Egyptian Literature: A Book of Readings. Volume 2: The New Kingdom.* Berkeley, Los Angeles, London: University of California Press.
——. 1980. *Ancient Egyptian Literature: A Book of Readings. Volume 3: The Late Period.* Berkeley, Los Angeles, London: University of California Press.
McDowell, A.G. 1990. Jurisdiction in the Workmen's Community of Deir el-Medina. Leiden: Nederlands Instituut voor het Nabije Oosten.
Malinine, M. 1947. Notes juridiques (à propos d'l'ouvrage de E. Seidl). *BIFAO* 46: 93–123.
——. 1953. *Choix de Textes juridiques en hiératique "anormal" et en démotique (xxve–xxviie Dynasties).* Première Partie. Paris: Librarie ancienne Honoré Champion.
Manning, J., G. Greig, and S. Uchida. 1989. Chicago Oriental Institute Ostracon 12073 Once Again. *JNES* 48: 117–24.
Menu, B. 1973. Le pret en droit Égyptien. Nouvel Empire et Basse Époque. *CRIPEL* 1: 59–141.
——. 1976. Note sur la vente à terme et la notion de crédit en droit égyptien ancien. *CRIPEL* 4: 131–37.
——. 1982. Les rapports de dépendance en Égypte à la Basee Époque. In *Recherches sur l'histoire juridique, économique et sociale de l'ancienne Egypte.* Pp. 184–99. Brassac-Les-Mines: L'Imprimerie la Margeride.
——. 1998. Modalités et réglementation du prêt en Égypte à l'époque de la première domination perse. In *Recherches sur l'histoire juridique, économique et sociale de l'ancienne Égypte II.* Pp. 385–99. BdE 122. Cairo: Institut français d'archéologie orientale.
Möller, G. 1921. Ein ägyptischer Schuldschein der zweiundzwanstigsten Dynastie. *SPAW.* Pp. 298–304.
Pestman, P. 1961. *Marriage and Matrimonial Property in Ancient Egypt.* Leiden: E.J. Brill.
Pirenne, J. 1974a. La caution dans l'antiquité orientale. Rapport de synthèse. *Recueils de la Société Jean Bodin pour l'histoire comparative des institutions* 28: 155–65.
——. 1974b. Les suretés personnelles dans le droit égyptien. *Recueils de la Société Jean Bodin*, 28: 167–68.
Quack, J.F. 1994. *Die Lehren des Ani.* Orbis Biblicus et Orientalis 141. Freiburg Schweiz and Göttingen: Universitätsverlag and Vandenhoeck and Ruprecht.
Quirke, S. 1990. *The Administration of Egypt in the Late Middle Kingdom.* New Malden Surrey: Sia Publishing.
Ray, J. 1973. A Consideration of Papyrus Kahun 13. *JEA* 59: 222–23.
Römer, M. 1992. Der Handel und die Kaufleute im Alten Ägypten. *SAK* 19: 257–84.
Schenkel, W. 1965. *Memphis. Herakleopolis. Theben. Die epigraphischen Zeugnisse der 7–11. Dynastie Ägyptens.* Ägyptologische Abhandlungen 12. Wiesbaden: Otto Harrassowitz.
Shupak, N. 1992. A New Source for the Study of the Judiciary and Law of Ancient Egypt: "The Tale of the Eloquent Peasant." *JNES* 51: 1–18.
van den Boorn, G. 1988. *The Duties of the Vizier. Civil Administration in the Early New Kingdom.* London and New York: KPI International.
Warburton, D. 1997. *State and Economy in Ancient Egypt.* OBO 151. Fribourg and Göttingen: University Press and Vandenhoeck and Ruprecht.

THE UR III PERIOD

Piotr Steinkeller – Harvard University

The security arrangements for loans during the time of the Ur III dynasty (2100–2000 BCE)[1] cannot be evaluated properly without first considering the nature of Ur III loaning practices themselves, since, in the final analysis, it is the legal and economic parameters of a loan transaction that determine (and explain) the character of any security arrangements that a given transaction may involve.

The question of Ur III loaning practices has been treated at considerable length in my paper "Money Lending Practices in Ur III Babylonia: The Issue of Economic Motivation," which I presented at the conference International Conference on Ancient Near Eastern Economies, Fourth Colloquium (New York, Nov. 12–13, 1998).[2] Although meant for a slightly different audience, and concerned more with economic than legal issues, that contribution was written with the objective of the present volume in mind as well, to provide a theoretical and factual foundation from which the issue of Ur III security arrangements may be studied in specific detail. Since the ensuing argument rests on the conclusions presented there, the reader is asked to read the two papers together, treating the New York paper (henceforth referred to as "Money Lending Practices") as Part 1 of a larger, logically connected whole.

The main points I argued in "Money Lending Practices" are as follows:

As an introductory general observation, it may be said that what the loan is depends on the economic and social environment in which it operates. In other words, the presence of the mechanism of loaning, meaning essentially the advancement of capital in the expectation of an economic gain, does not necessarily mean that the same economic gain is always obtained through it. To put it differently,

[1] As far as I know, Ur III sources offer the earliest evidence on the security for loans that is available from ancient Mesopotamia.

[2] To appear, under the same title, in Steinkeller 2001.

"interest" is a variable, whose value and function is determined by outside factors.

In ancient Babylonia, as in other ancient societies, most loans were made with objectives other than interest-generated profit in mind. As the extant data demonstrate clearly, the lender's primary objective in advancing loans was to get possession of either the borrower's labor or his land or often both. In such instances, interest was a tool and not an economic end in itself, being therefore devoid of real economic value. Its rate was largely irrelevant vis-à-vis the amount of the loan, except that it had to be sufficiently high to make it impossible for the borrower to repay the capital.

Naturally, this does not mean that *all* Babylonian loans were purely fictitious arrangements. A great variety undoubtedly existed in this matter, depending on the place and period, and even more so, on the economic context. In fact, the expectation of profit through the accruing of interest is detectable behind a whole range of transactions, such as partnership loans and various credit arrangements among merchants.

Let me also make the following point of broader significance, which emphasizes the economic dimension of the phenomenon of loans: loaning practices—and with them, the issue of security—cannot be treated in abstraction separate from the underlying socio-economic situation. If I am permitted to invoke a crass Marxist dictum, the economic structure determines the nature of the superstructure. As formulated long ago by Marx, the economic structure is the "foundation on which arises a legal and political superstructure and to which correspond definite forms of social consciousness."[3]

What this dictum—and it does not take a Marxist to recognize its inherent truth—means for the topic under discussion is this: although ancient loaning practices may appear to share *formal* similarities among themselves, and may seem to be *formally* identical with or at least analogous with modern loaning practices, one must assume that in each case we are dealing with a different phenomenon, whose precise nature is determined by the economic and social context in which it occurs.

Yet another important point to keep in mind in this connection is the difference between commercial and agrarian loans. And that difference is quite dramatic.

---

[3] Marx 1971: 21.

These general observations about the nature of early Babylonian loaning practices have important ramifications for the interpretation of security-like provisions, such as those stipulated in at least some of the surviving loan documents. The fundamental question one needs to consider here is the following: is it at all possible to speak of Ur III "security" instruments, at least in the sense of this term in modern legal praxis? In my opinion, this depends entirely *on the economic motivation behind the issuing of a given loan*. If the lender's economic goal was primarily to profit from the accrued interest, and if he expected to recover his loan eventually, then a pledged property—if, indeed, one was supplied by the borrower—would fall very closely under the modern definition of security. However, if it was the pledge that the lender was really after (as in the case of Shylock's infamous bond), then the word "security" seems to be singularly inappropriate to describe the phenomenon at hand. It is hardly the lender who requires legal protection in such an instance! To my knowledge, there is no modern legal label that applies to this particular type of arrangement. The term "bondage instrument" perhaps comes closest, but this would be speaking from a primarily economic perspective.

In view of the above distinction, it is essential that the Ur III evidence on security instruments be studied on a case-by-case basis, with the goal of determining in each instance the true nature of the lender's motivation. Most of the Ur III loan documents involving possible occurrences of "security" have been reviewed in "Money Lending Practices"; the remaining examples are presented and discussed in full in this presentation (see Appendix). Unfortunately, the phraseology used by these sources tends to be vague and economical in the extreme, which makes it exceedingly difficult to comprehend the background of the transactions with which they are concerned. In most instances, only a block of documentation illustrating the activities of a particular lender provides a real understanding of the legal and economic particulars of transactions.

However, before we undertake a review of the extant sources, a few words need to be said about the Ur III loan documents and in general about the security instruments which were available to the early Babylonian law.

With regard to its form,[4] the Ur III loan document consists of a statement (the so-called "operative section") to the effect that the

[4] See Lutzmann 1976: 17.

borrower received from the lender x capital (usually grain or silver) as an interest-bearing (or interest-free) loan. This is followed by the borrower's sworn promise to return the loan at a specific date (usually after the harvest), an optional penalty clause, a list of witnesses, and the date. The document is usually sealed by the borrower and, in some instances, also by the guarantor.

As for the security instruments, the following types are documented:

a) Guarantor or surety, who functioned as a co-obligor.[5] In loan transactions, his role was that of a co-borrower. If the borrower failed to repay the loan, the creditor had the right to approach the guarantor, who would then be liable to meet the obligation. The use of guarantors as part of loan transactions appears to have been rather rare in the Ur III period; only some ten Ur III loans mention a guarantor specifically.[6] As noted earlier, the guarantor, in at least some instances, sealed the loan tablet.

b) Babylonian law of the Third Millennium also knew the institution of personal pledge, called šu-du$_8$/dù-a, "hostage, captive," in Sumerian.[7] Documented cases of this are found already in the Pre-Sargonic and the Sargonic periods.[8] In this type of security arrangement, which resembled the early medieval bail or hostageship,[9] the obligor put at the obligee's disposal another individual, who pledged his own person—becoming thereby a virtual hostage—to guarantee the performance of a promise or obligation. The most common purpose of such personal pledges appears to have been to ensure the appearance of the obligor.[10] Some of the cases involving šu-du$_8$-a's may have arisen from unpaid debts, or perhaps even loans, but there are no instances of such pledges being stipulated at the time of a loan agreement itself.

---

[5] See Steinkeller 1989: 80–92.

[6] Owen NATN 163, 346, 472, 539; Çiğ-Kizilyay NRVN 1 104, 197; RA 8, 197 no. 21; UET 3 11; YOS 4 7, 55. See Steinkeller 1989: 87–88.

[7] See Falkenstein 1956: 116–18; Sauren 1970. The usual formulation used in such documents is PN$_1$-ra PN$_2$-e šu-du$_8$-a-ni in-gub, "PN$_2$ pledged with his own person for PN$_1$," lit.: "PN$_2$ placed his bound hands (as a substitute) for (those of) PN$_1$." For šu-du$_8$/dù-a, Akk. *kamû*, "captive, prisoner," see CAD K, 129; Kienast 1994: 160.

[8] CT 50 31 ii' 1–5 (Pre-Sargonic); TuM 5 48, 216 (both Sargonic); ITT 4 7449 (Sargonic); ITT 5 6710 (Sargonic); MAD 4 36 (Sargonic).

[9] See Holmes 1963: 196–97.

[10] As in the following examples:

^{I}Pu-ka árad Á-la-la-kam Á-la-la igi-ni ì-ši-gar mu lugal ud ba-zàh-dè-na-gá šer$_7$-da

c) Still other means of protection were the witnesses and the loan document itself.[11]

d) And finally, one finds instances of land or individuals being transferred, seemingly as security, by the borrower to the lender as part of the loan transaction. These are the cases which preoccupy us specifically in this study. At least some of these transactions appear to have been antichretic arrangements, in which the usufruct of pledged property was meant to repay interest.

Among the sources falling under this category we can list the following ones:

(1) TIM 3 149, belonging to the SI.A-a dossier, which is edited and discussed in "Money Lending Practices."
(2) YOS 4 21, Fish Catalogue 60, MVN 3 336, FAOS 16 1244, 1282, belonging to the Ur-Bau dossier, which is discussed in "Money Lending Practices."
(3) YOS 4 5, from the Ur-Ninsiana dossier, which is discussed in "Money Lending Practices."
(4) Various loan transactions involving the pledging of fields (see Appendix nos. 1–5).
(5) Various loan transactions involving the pledging of individuals (see Appendix nos. 6–11).

---

hé-a bí-in-dug$_4$ Za-an-me-ni ama-ni ù Géme-^{d}Suen nin$_9$-na-ni šu-tu nu-zàh-da ba-an-gub-éš; 7 witnesses; date.

Puka, slave of Alala, approached Alala and declared: "By the name of the king! If I run away, it would be a crime indeed!" Zanmeni, his mother, and Geme-Suen, his sister, became pledges (for him) that he will not run away. 7 witnesses. Date (BE 3/1 1; Šu-Sin 5/xiii; Nippur).

A-e-lí dumu Ba-zi ù Da-gu-ma-⸢at⸣ dam Šu-a-bi Šu-ku-bu-um nu-bànda šu-du$_8$-bi ⸢šu⸣ ba-ti Nu-úr-^{d}Šu-^{d}Suen Nibru^{ki} gin-ni ka abul gub-da mu lugal-bi al-pàd; before 13 witnesses.

Šu-kubum, the colonel, took hold of A'ili, son of Bazi, and Takun-ma[t], wife of Šu-abi, as pledges (for Nur-Šu-Suen). That Nur-Šu-Suen will go to Nippur (and) present himself at the entrance of the city gate, it was sworn by the name of the king (by Nur-Šu-Suen). Before 13 witnesses (Çiğ-Kizilyay NRVN 1 60; undated; Nippur).

^{I}Ur-^{d}Šul-pa-è udul Ur-^{d}Nanše-ke$_4$ šu-du$_8$-a-ni in-gub ^{I}Níg-^{d}Ba-ú dam-gàr-ra [Dug$_4$]-ga-zi-da sanga šu-du$_8$-a-ni in-gub lú gud Lú-dingir-ra-ka ba-zuh-a-me.

For Ur-Šulpae, the cow-herd, Ur-Nanše became his pledge; for Nig-Bau, the merchant, [Du]gazida, the temple administrator, became his pledge. These men (Ur-Šulpae and Nig-Bau) are the ones who had stolen the cattle of Lu-dingira (ITT 2 6225; undated; Girsu/Lagaš).

[11] See Steinkeller 1989: 104–10, 146–49.

(6) the Ur-Meme texts, edited in Appendix as nos. 12–21, and discussed here and in "Money Lending Practices."

Of all of these documents, the easiest to interpret are the sources grouped under (5), which appear to involve an antichretic arrangement in which the interest on a loan is to be repaid by the labor of a pledged person.

The documents grouped under (1), (2), (3), and (4), all of which involve the pledging of fields, also appear, at least on the surface, to be *bona fide* antichretic arrangements, with the interest on a loan to be repaid by the produce of a pledged field. An obvious difficulty in assessing the nature of these transactions is presented by our incomplete knowledge of their background. One particular problem is that the texts never say explicitly who is to cultivate the pledged field, the creditor or the debtor, nor whether the debtor is entitled to participate in the harvest proceeds.[12] We also do not know whether the debtor would eventually recover his pledge, even if he had failed to repay the loan. Would it happen automatically, after a lapse of, let's say, seven years?

---

[12] As is suggested by comparative ethnographic data, there probably was no strict rule regarding these matters. For example, in similar types of loan arrangements practiced in Malaya, a pledged field could be cultivated by either its owner or his creditor. In the first case, the owner kept half of the produce for himself as compensation for his labor; but, if the lender cultivated the pledged field, the owner received nothing. Significantly, the amount of the produce was not related to the amount of interest on the loan: "If a man has rice lands, then these can be *pereto* or *pegang* by the lender of the money, i.e. 'governed' or 'grasped' . . . From the lands thus taken as security the lender gets half the crop; the owner of the land works it and gets the other half of the crop for his labour . . . [But] if the lender is a rice planter he will probably work the land himself and take the whole of the produce. If he is not a rice planter, then he will get someone else to work the land in accordance with the customary system called *pawoh*, under which the worker gets half of the produce, and the owner—or in this case the person to whom the land has been pledged—gets the other half. But according to the ethics of the system, if the man who has pawned the land is a rice farmer, it is the right thing to allow him to *pawoh* the land himself, so that he gets half the produce in return for his labour on it. The system differs from the simple and direct taking of interest in that the half-share of the produce goes annually to the lender of the money, *irrespective of the proportion which the size of the loan bears to the value of the land* [italics added]. Moreover, considered as return on capital, this half-share of the produce varies according to the particular season . . . The system of pledging land differs from the system of mortgage as we know it in two main respects. Firstly, the interest obtained is at a variable, not a fixed rate; secondly, the productivity of the goods on which the loan is secured passes over to the lender, and the borrower can be deprived of it altogether" (Firth 1946: 169–71). On the other hand, in the *balal* system known to the

These uncertainties notwithstanding, it may be surmised that in many (if not in all) of these transactions the lender's real expectation was to get possession of the pledged field, on account of the borrower's failure to repay the loan. This is indicated, in my view, by comparing the amount of interest on attested loans with the amount of produce that creditors could realistically have expected from the cultivation of pledged fields. For example, in text no. 1, 9 iku of land were given in exchange for a loan of 9 shekels of silver. At an average yield of 30 gur of barley per 1 bùr (= 18 iku) of land, which is well documented in Ur III times,[13] 9 iku of land would have been expected to yield 15 gur of barley (= 15 shekels of silver). In contrast, the interest on the loan in question was only 2.2 shekels.

One finds similarly disproportionate ratios in other texts as well: the equivalent of 30 shekels of silver expected from the produce versus 2 shekels yielded by the interest (no. 2); 6.66 shekels worth of produce (assuming that the field in question was 4 iku in size) against 5/6 shekel of interest (no. 3); 120 shekels worth of produce against 6 shekels of interest (TIM 3 149); 120 shekels worth of produce against 1.8 shekel of interest (FAOS 16 1282).

Even if one subtracts the expenses that the creditor would have incurred in connection with cultivating a pledged field, namely, the cost of seed-grain and labor (human and animal), and the irrigation tax (máš a-šag$_4$-ga), the disparity between a harvest income and interest income is so great as to deny any possibility of the two being equivalent. One can, therefore, only wonder, why, given the economic advantage of cultivating the field himself, would the owner

---

Ifugao of the Philippines, a pledged field was cultivated by a creditor, with the produce being considered, in the manner of a true antichretic loan, the exact equivalent of the interest on the loan: "In case a man finds himself under the necessity of raising a considerable sum of money—usually in order to provide funds for a funeral feast or a sacrifice—he frequently borrows the sum, giving a rice field into the hands of his creditor as a security and as a means of paying the interest on debt. The creditor holds, plants, and harvests the field until the debt be repaid. The field is to all purposes his, except that he cannot sell it. He can, however, transfer it as a *balal* into the hands of another. But he must transfer it for the same or a less amount of money; that is, if he has loaned fifty pesos on the field, he must not borrow more than that sum, unless, of course, he be able to secure the owner's consent. This is a very wise provision of Ifugao law that insures the prompt return of the field to the owner as soon as he be able to get together the amount needed to redeem the field" (Barton 1969: 37).

[13] See Maekawa 1974: 40.

of the field borrow money under such unfavorable conditions? The obvious answer to this question is that, in many of the transactions discussed here, the borrowers simply had no choice: almost certainly, because of their prior indebtedness to creditors,[14] the latter were able to impose those particular conditions on them.[15]

If that was the case, then transactions of this type do not fall under the category of antichresis. Nor can the fields pledged in such arrangements be properly described as security, since creditors procured them with objectives other than simply protecting the capital advanced (i.e. holding a "security" in the legal sense of the term).

The Ur-Meme texts (nos. 12–21) represent a special case. Although formulated as field rentals, and not as loans, these sources (excluding nos. 20 and 21, which appear to be genuine rental agreements, and are cited for the sake of comparison only) may plausibly be explained as pledges of land resulting from unpaid loans.[16] What apparently happens in these transactions is that the creditor "leases" the debtor's allotment field (šuku) when the latter fails to repay a loan. The creditor pays no rental fee, although he recompenses the debtor for taxes (máš a-šag$_4$-ga) the latter owes to the state on account of his field. It is less clear who is to cultivate the field; in three instances (nos. 16, 18 and 19), the cultivator is apparently the debtor. As to how the produce is to be divided, we are in complete darkness. Is the creditor to keep the entire produce for himself? Or is he to share it with the debtor? And what happens to the pledged field after the stipulated "rental" period is over and the debtor, in all likelihood, fails to repay his debt again? Does the creditor at that point take outright possession?

I would suggest that pledged fields classify as "security" only if their primary purpose was to protect the lender. Such was the case, for example, in Roman law, where the primary function of real security was to insure the repayment of a debt, rather than to provide a lender, as in the modern mortgage, with a source of investment.[17]

[14] This can be demonstrated for the debtors appearing in the sources from the Ur-Bau and Ur-Meme dossiers. See "Money Lending Practices."

[15] In this connection, note that, in no. 1, it is additionally stipulated that failure to repay the loan on time will result in a 40% penalty, i.e. double the standard interest on silver loans. Clearly, the creditor sought to make sure that the borrower would not be able to repay the loan!

[16] See in detail "Money Lending Practices."

[17] Early Roman law knew two forms of real security, *fiducia* and *pignus*. The for-

In contrast, the Ur III transactions treated here—however one wants to define them from a legal perspective—unquestionably functioned as investments first. Although pledged property provided a lender with the additional benefit of protection, his primary expectation was to profit from it economically. This was true even if he never assumed outright ownership of pledged property. As long as he was able to keep debtor's land in his possession, the income he gained from it was much higher than what he would otherwise have obtained as the accrued interest on loans.

In summary, the evidence for security on loans in the Ur III period is meager, if not completely negative. Apart from the basic means of protection that were available to Ur III law—such as the guarantor, witnesses, and the option of providing the creditor with a written record of the loan transaction—one fails to find any certain instances of "security" in the modern legal sense of this term. What we find instead are various types of quasi-antichretic arrangements, in which a loan and its interest are secured with land or labor. Although land and labor pledged in this way superficially resemble modern security, the fact that their primary objective was other than protecting lenders, argues, in my view, against lending them this classification. In fact, this phenomenon escapes all modern legal definition, which underscores once again the conceptual autonomy of ancient and "primitive" legal systems, and the difficulty of conforming their facts to our own understanding of normative legal and economic behavior.

mer, which involved a transfer of ownership, was a conveyance subject to a covenant for reconveyance on the payment of the debt. The latter, which involved a transfer of possession only, was the form of security in which physical custody of the thing pledged could be, though was not necessarily, given to the creditor, but in which the ownership was not transferred to him. See Nicholas 1962: 149–53; Diósdi 1970: 116–20; Watson 1971: 84–90.

According to Nicholas 1962: 149–53, the primary purpose of real security in Roman law was to ensure the payment of the debt. He contrasts this situation with the modern mortgage, which is usually an investment. In the latter "the mortgagor (the borrower) is concerned to obtain the use of capital for some considerable time and the mortgagee (the lender) is concerned to get an adequate and steady return on his money" (ibid. 150). On the other hand, in ancient Rome "the use of real security as an investment seems to have been but little developed; if a man wished to invest in land he seems to have preferred the direct investment provided by an out-and-out purchase to the indirect investment offered by a mortgage" (ibid. 150).

Appendix: Documentation

(A) Various loan transactions involving the pledging of fields

No. 1 (ZA 53, 87 no. 24; Šu-Sin 1; Nippur?)
10 lá 1 gín kug-babbar maš-bi 2 gín igi-6-gál 6 še ki Gá-a-kam-ta Ur-[d]En-líl-lá engar šu ba-ti 9(iku) gána nam-apin-lá-šè in-na-an-sum kug-bi ki-sur_{12}-ta sum-mu-da bí-in-dug_4 tukumbi ku[g-bi l]a-ba-an-sum 1 g[ín kug-babbar]-a 1.2. še gur-ta ì-á[g]-gá mu lugal-bi in-pàd; before 4 witnesses; date.

Ur-Enlila, the farmer, received from Gakam 9 shekels of silver (as an interest-bearing loan), the interest being 2.2 shekels (= 25%). (In lieu of the interest) he (i.e. Ur-Enlila) gave (to Gakam) 9 iku of land for tenancy. He promised to return this capital at the threshing-floor (following the harvest). He swore by the name of the king that, if he does not return this capital, for each shekel of silver he will measure out 420 liters of barley (= capital + 40%). Before 4 witnesses. Date.

The field is to repay the interest on the loan. If the capital is not returned on time, a 40% penalty will be added to it.

No. 2 (Owen NATN 305; Šu-Sin 3/i; Nippur)
10 gín kug-babbar ki [giš]Eren-d[a-ni-ta] [I]Ni-in-š[i-...] [Id]En-líl-[...] [I]Ka-tar 3 a-[n]e-ne máš 10 gín kug-babbar-šè gi-ne 1(bùr) gána a-$šag_4$ ba-ši-ni-gub-éš tukumbi inim bí-gi_4 10 gín-šè 1/3 ma-na-àm lá-dè—7 witnesses—mu lugal-bi al-pàd; date.

Ninš[i-...], Enlil-[...], (and) Katar, three of them, (received) 10 shekels of silver from Erend[ani] (as an interest-bearing loan). For the interest on 10 shekels of silver they deposited 18 iku of land as a "security." In the presence of 7 witnesses they swore (lit.: it was sworn by them) by the name of the king to weigh out 20 shekels of silver, in place of the (original) 10 shekels, should the agreement be revoked (i.e. they take the field back). Date.

The field is to repay the interest. If the field is taken back, the borrowers are to pay double the amount of the original loan.

No. 3 (Owen NATN 17 tablet and case; Ibbi-Suen 2/iii; Nippur)
2 1/2 gín kug-babbar 1.1.4 še gur-ta ab-ši-gá-ar KI.UD ág-e-dè ki Ur-LI DINGIR-ra-bí šu ba-ti a-$šag_4$ nam-10 Ku-da-núm DINGIR-ra-bí uru_4-e-dè Ur-LI in-na-sum mu lugal-bi in-na-pàd; 3 witnesses; date. Seal: DINGIR-ra-bí/dumu Lí-e-dan.

2 1/2 shekels of silver (is the loan). For each (300 liters) of barley 400 liters were assessed (i.e. the interest is 33%). It is to be measured out at the threshing-floor. Ili-rabi received (this loan) from Ur-LI. (In lieu of the interest) Ili-rabi gave to Ur-LI for cultivation the nam-10 field (probably 4 iku in size) of Kudanum. He (i.e. Ili-rabi) swore by the name of the king for him (i.e. Ur-LI). 3 witnesses. Date. Seal of Ili-rabi, son of Li'e-dan.

Note: nam-10 denotes a unit of ten soldiers (éren), under the command of an ugula ("lieutenant"). Each member of such an unit held a šuku field of 4 iku. Cf. the Ur-Meme texts nos. 12–19.

No. 4 (Çiğ-Kizilyay NRVN 1 239; IS 2; Nippur)
nam-10 Ku-ru-ub-É-a apin-lá-šè Ì-lí-ra-bí Ur-LI ì-na-sum mu lugal-bi im-pàd tukumbi šuku-ra-ni al-⸢ág(?)⸣; 2 witnesses; date. Seal: DINGIR-ra-bí/ dumu Lí-e-⸢dan⸣.

Ili-rabi gave to Ur-LI for tenancy the nam-10 (field) of Kurub-Ea. He (i.e. Ili-rabi) swore that, if his šuku field (is taken back?), (the grain loan in question plus x) will be ⸢measured out?⸣. 2 witnesses. Date. Seal of Ili-rabi, son of Li'e-⸢dan⸣.

No. 5 (Owen NATN 836 tablet and case; Šu-Sin 5/v; Nippur)
2 gín kug-babbar ki Ìr-ib-ta Tu-ra-am-ì-lí šu ba-ti 6(iku) gána nam-apin-ne-lá-šè ki Tu-ra-am-ì-lí-ta Ìr-ib ì-dab$_5$ kug-bi máš (ì-)tuku-tuku a-šag$_4$-bi máš (ì-)tuku-tuku; before 3 witnesses; date.

Turam-ili received from Ir'ib 2 shekels of silver (as a loan). (At the same time) Ir'ib took from Turam-ili 6 iku of land for tenancy. This capital has an interest (and) the field has a máš payment (i.e. the interest will pay off the máš payment; in other words, the lender will not recompense the borrower for the máš payment on the field, and the borrower will not pay the interest on the loan). Before 3 witnesses. Date.

For this transaction, see Steinkeller 1981: 115–16 n. 13.

(B) Various loan transactions involving the pledging of individuals

No. 6 (TuM n.F. 1/2 32 tablet and case; Ibbi-Sin 1/vi; Nippur)
7 gín kug-babbar máš-bi-šè Ù-ba-a-a gé[me-ni] ab-da-gub ki Šeš-da-da-ta Šu-na šu ba(-an)-ti tukumbi gá-la ba-an-DAG á ud-da 5 sìla ág-e-dam mu lugal-bi ì-pàd; 3 witnesses; date. Seal: Š[u(?)-na] / dumu ⸢X-x⸣.

Šuna received from Šeš-dada 7 shekels of silver (as a loan). In lieu of the interest, he placed Uba'a, his slave [woman] (with Šeš-dada). He (i.e. Šuna) swore by the name of the king to pay a daily wage of 5 liters (of barley), should she abstain from work. 3 witnesses. Date. Seal of Š[una?], son of ⸢X-x⸣.

A reconstruction d[am-ni], "his w[ife]" (in place of gé[me-ni]), is also possible.

No. 7 (Owen NATN 307; Šu-Sin 9/vii; Nippur)
[x.] še gur máš-bi-šè ˡŠe-li-bu-um dumu Ì-lí-mi-šar Ì-lí-mi-šar-e mu 5-àm in-gub nu-da-kar-ri-a mu lugal-bi in-pàd; before 5 witnesses; date.

[x bushels] of barley (Ili-mišar received from X as an interest-bearing loan). In lieu of the interest, Ili-mišar placed Šelibum, son of Ili-mišar, for 5 years (with X). He (i.e. Ili-mišar) swore by the name of the king not to take him away (during that period). Before 5 witnesses. Date.

No. 8 (BE 3/1 19; date unreadable; Nippur)
[x gí]n kug-babbar [ki Ur]-^{d}Nuska-ta ⸢A⸣-a-na-tum-e šu ba-ti; Ma-ad-ì-lí mu 4-àm gub-dè á-ni-šè su-su-dè mu lu[gal-bi ì-pà]d-[dè]-éš; 2+[x] witnesses; date.

A'anatum received from [Ur]-Nuska [x] shekels of silver (as a loan). They (i.e. A'anatum and Mad-ili) swore by the name of the king to place Mad-ili (with Ur-Nuska) for 4 years, and to repay (the interest?) with his wages. 2+[x] witnesses. Date.

No. 9 (Çiğ-Kizilyay NRVN 1 192; Šu-Sin 4; Nippur)
1 gín kug-babbar maš-bi-šè ud ⸢6⸣-kam nam-nagar ki Á-da-a-ta Bí-ša-ḫi-lum šu-ba-ti; before 3 witnesses; date.

Pišaḫ-ilum received from Ada'a 1 shekel of silver (as a loan). As its interest, (he will provide) 6 days of carpenter's labor. Before 3 witnesses. Date.

No. 10 (AUCT 2 121; AS 8/x-Reichskalender; provenience uncertain)
5. še gur še ur$_5$-ra máš-bi-šè 5 munus ur$_4$ sum-mu-dè ki Lú-dùg-ga-ta Lú-^{d}Inanna ⸢. . .⸣ Lú-^{d}Geštin-an-ka-⸢ke$_4$ (?)⸣ šu ba-an-ti; date.

Lu-Inana, the ⸢. . .⸣ of Lu-Geštinana, received from Lu-duga 1,500 liters of barley, a barley loan. As its interest, (he promised) to supply 5 female shearers. Date.

No. 11 (MVN 8 168; Ibbi-Sin 2; SI.A-a dossier)
1 ma-na ⸢kug⸣-[babbar] máš-bi-šè A-⸢da⸣ -làl nagar ì-gub ki SI.A-a-ta Nam-[z]i-tar-ra ⸢šu ba⸣-ti A-da-làl nagar níg-⸢x⸣-šè igi [. . .] ⸢sám(?) til(?)⸣ [. . .] ì-l[á(?)-e] I-lu-ba-na si[mug(?)] kug-lá; 7+[x] witnesses; date.

Namzitara received from SI.A-a 1 mina of silver (as a loan). As its interest, he (i.e. Namzitara) placed Adalal, a carpenter, (with SI.A-a). Adalal, the carpenter, ⸢. . .⸣ [. . .] ⸢the full? price?⸣ [. . .] he will ⸢weigh out?⸣; Ilubana, the s[mith?], was the weigher of silver (in this transaction); 7+[x] witnesses. Date.

(C) The Ur-Meme texts

No. 12 (TuM n.F. 1/2 249; Šu-Sin 5/v; Dusabara)
4(iku) gána a-šag$_4$-^{d}Šul-pa-è apin-lá-šè šuku ^{d}Nin-MAR.KI-ka Ur-Me-me ì-dab$_5$ máš-bi .2.3 še <gur> lugal ki Ur-Me-me-ta ^{d}Nin-MAR.KI-ka šu ba-ti mu ^{d}Nin-MAR<.KI>-ka-šè kišib Lú-bala-šag$_4$-ga; date.

4 iku of land, in the field Ašag-Šulpae, the šuku plot of Nin-MAR.KI-ka, Ur-Meme took for tenancy. Its (i.e. of the field) máš payment, 150 liters of barley, Nin-MAR.KI-ka received from Ur-Meme. In place of (the seal of) Nin-MAR.KI-ka, the seal of Lu-balašaga (was rolled). Date.

For Nin-MAR.KI-ka, cf. nos. 17, 18, and 19. Lu-balašaga seals also in no. 14.

No. 13 (Owen NATN 748; ŠS 5/v; Dusabara)
⸢4(iku)⸣ gána a-⸢šag$_4$⸣-^{d}Šul-pa-⸢è⸣ [apin]-⸢lá⸣-šè ⸢šuku⸣ Lú-^{d}Utu Ur-Me-me-ke$_4$ ì-dab$_5$ 1/2 gín kug máš-bi SI.A šu ba-ti a-šag$_4$-bi KA.NE íb-gi-né igi ^{I}Ur-^{d}Nin-gír-su igi ^{Id}Nanna-dalla-šè igi ^{I}Di-NE-šè lú-inim-ma-bi-me šag$_4$ Gír-su^{ki}; date.

4 iku of land, in the field Ašag-Šulpae, the šuku plot of Lu-Utu, Ur-

Meme took for tenancy. Its máš payment, 1/2 shekel of silver, SI.A received (from Ur-Meme). KA.NE guarantees for this field. Before Ur-Ningirsu, Nanna-dalla, (and) Di-NE, the witnesses. (The transaction took place) in Girsu. Date.

For SI.A, cf. nos. 16, 17, and 18.

No. 14 (FAOS 16 932; ŠS 5/v; Dusabara)
4(iku) gána a-šag$_4$-^{d}Šul-pa-è apin-lá-šè šuku Ur-^{d}Ig-alim Ur-Me-me ì-dab$_5$ máš-bi 1/2 gín kug-babbar ⸢še⸣ ŠU.IGI.DU ur$_5$-šè .1. še <gur> lugal-kam ki Ur-Me-me-ta mu Ur-^{d}Ig-alim kišib Lú-bala-šag$_5$-ga íb(!)-ra; date.

4 iku of land, in the field Ašag-Šulpae, the šuku plot of Ur-Igalim, Ur-Meme took for tenancy. Its máš payment, 1/2 shekel of silver, on account of the barley of a previous(?) loan, (amounting to) 60 liters of barley (Ur-Igalim received from Ur-Meme). In place of (the seal of) Ur-Igalim, the seal of Lu-balašaga was rolled. Date.

Note that Ur-Igalim appears also in no. 15, where he pays the máš payment on behalf of Ur-Meme. Lu-Balašaga also seals in no. 12.

No. 15 (FAOS 16 933 tablet and case; Šu-Sin 5/vi; Dusabara)
4(iku) a-šag$_4$-^{d}Šul-pa-è apin-lá-šè šuku Úr-AN má-laḫ$_4$ Ur-Me-me ì-dab$_5$ máš-bi .2.3 še <gur> mu Ur-Me-me-šè ki Ur-^{d}Ig-alim-ta Úr-AN šu ba-ti; date. Seal: Úr-[AN] / má-laḫ$_4$ PA.⸢AL(?)⸣.

4 iku of land, in the field Ašag-Šulpae, the šuku plot of Ur-AN, the sailor, Ur-Meme took for tenancy. Its máš payment, 150 liters of barley, Ur-AN received from Ur-Igalim, (who was acting) on behalf of Ur-Meme. Date. Seal of Ur-AN, the sailor of the ⸢majordomo?⸣.

Note that Ur-Igalim also appears in no. 14, where he is one of the contracting parties.

No. 16 (TuM n.F. 1/2 250; Šu-Sin 5/x; Dusabara)
4(iku) gána a-šag$_4$-^{d}Šul-pa-è šuku {AN} Igi-An-na-ke$_4$-zu Ur-Me-me ì-dab$_5$ máš-bi .2. še <gur> Igi-An-na-ke$_4$-zu šu ba-ti iti ezen-maḫ-ta mu Šu-Sin 5-ta uru$_4$-dè mu lugal-bi in-pàd igi Ka$_5^{a}$-šè igi Gú-ni-na-kal igi Lugal-an-ki kišib SI.A íb-ra.

4 iku of land, in the field Ašag-Šulpae, the šuku plot of Igianakezu, Ur-Meme took (for tenancy). Its máš payment, 120 liters of barley, Igianakezu received (from Ur-Meme). He (i.e. Igianakezu) swore by the name of the king to cultivate (this field for Ur-Meme) from the 10th month of the year Šu-Sin 5 on. Before Ka, Guninakal, and Lugal-anki (the witnesses). The seal of SI.A was rolled.

For SI.A, see nos. 13, 17, and 18.

No. 17 (TuM n.F. 1/2 253; Šu-Sin 5/x; Dusabara)
4(iku) gána šuku ^{d}Nin-MAR.KI-ga-ka 4(iku) šuku Ama-tu-da šag$_4$ a-šag$_4$-^{d}Šul-pa-è iti ezen-maḫ mu Šu-Sin 5-ta uru$_4$-dè ⸢^{d}⸣Nin-MAR.KI-ga ù Ḫu-ud-da dam Ama-tu-da-ke$_4$ Lú-^{d}Inana-ra in-na-ab-sum máš a-šag$_4$-ga-bi-šè 1. še gur

šu ba-an-ti-éš igi ^{I}SI.A engar-éren-na-šè igi ^{I}Šag$_4$-kug-ge àga-ús igi ^{I}Ur-^{d}Šu-maḫ-šè lú-inim-ma-bi-me šag$_4$ Du$_6$-sa-bar-ra^{ki}.

4 iku of land, the šuku plot of Nin-MAR.KI-ka, (and) 4 iku of land, the šuku plot of Amatuda, in the field Ašag-Šulpae, to be cultivated from the 10th month of the year ŠS 5 on, Nin-MAR.KI-ka and Ḫudda, wife of Amatuda, gave to Lu-Inana (for tenancy). As the máš payment of these fields, they received 300 liters of barley (from Lu-Inana). Before SI.A, the chief farmer of the soldiers, Šakuge, the gendarme, (and) Ur-Šumaḫ, the witnesses. (The transaction took place) in Dusabara.

For Nin-MAR.KI-ka, cf. nos. 12, 18, and 19. For SI.A, cf. nos. 13, 16, and 18.

No. 18 (TuM 1/2 n.F. 247 tablet and case; Šu-Sin 5/xi; Dusabara)
4(iku) gána a-šag$_4$-^{d}Šul-pa-è šuku Lú-^{d}Utu Ur-Me-me ì-dab$_5$ ŠU.IGI.DU-bi-šè .1.2 še <gur> Lú-^{d}Utu-ke$_4$ šu ba-ti iti ezen-an-na mu Šu-Sin 5 uru$_4$-dè mu lugal-bi in-pàd igi SI.A(-šè) igi Dùg-úr-šè mu Lú-^{d}Utu-šè kišib ^{d}Nin-MAR.KI-ga íb-ra. Seal: ^{d}Nin-MAR.KI-[ga/ka]/dumu Lú-Urub$_x$ (URUxKÁR)$^{[ki]}$ / ⌈àga-ús⌉ PA.[AL(?)].

4 iku of land, in the field Ašag-Šulpae, the šuku plot of Lu-Utu, Ur-Meme took (for tenancy). On account of the previous(?) (loan), Lu-Utu received 80 liters of barley. He (i.e. Lu-Utu) swore by the name of the king to cultivate (this field for Ur-Meme) from the 11th month of the year Šu-Sin 5 on. Before SI.A (and) Dugur, the witnesses. In place of (the seal of) Lu-Utu, the seal of Nin-MAR.KI-ka was rolled. Seal of Nin-MAR.KI-[ka], son of Lu-Urub, the ⌈gendarme⌉ of the major[domo?].

For SI.A, cf. nos. 13, 16, and 17. For Nin-MAR.KI-ka, cf. nos. 12, 17, and 19.

No. 19 (TuM n.F. 1/2 254; Šu-Sin 5/xi; Dusabara)
4(iku) gána a-šag$_4$-^{d}Šul-pa-è šuku Ur-mes dumu A-a-kal-la ^{d}Nin-MAR.KI-ga Ur-Me-me-ra ì-na-sum .2.3 še <gur> ur$_5$-šè ^{d}Nin-MAR.KI-ga šu ba-ti iti ezen-an-na mu Šu-Sin 5-ta uru$_4$^{ru}-dè mu lugal-bi in-pàd.

4 iku of land, in the field Ašag-Šulpae, the šuku plot Ur-mes, son of A'a-kala, Nin-MAR.KI-ka gave to Ur-Meme (for tenancy). On account of a (previous?) loan (or: as a loan), Nin-MAR.KI-ka received 150 liters of barley (from Ur-Meme). He (i.e. Nin-MAR.KI-ka) swore by the name of the king to cultivate (this field for Ur-Meme) from the 11th month of the year Šu-Sin 5 on.

For Nin-MAR.KI-ka, cf. nos. 12, 17, and 18. Note that in no. 12, dated 6 months earlier, he gives his own plot to Ur-Meme.

No. 20 (TuM n.F. 1/2 246; Šu-Sin 4/ii; Dusabara)
1(bùr) gána A-gàr-TUR.TUR 2-a-bi ús-sa-du Ur-É-an-na-ka a-šag$_4$ Lú-^{d}En-ki-ka Ur-Me-me-ke$_4$ apin-lá-šè ì-dab$_5$ a-šag$_4$-a-^{giš}geštin-na-a a<-šag$_4$>-^{giš}ma-nu-ka gú íd-^{giš}sug-e-dar-ra; date.

18 iku of land, in the *Flur* Agar-TUR.TUR, in two (separate plots), bordering on (the field of) Ur-Eana, the (šuku) field of Ur-Enki, Ur-Meme

took in tenancy. (This land) is located in the field Ašag-ageština (and) in (the field) Ašag-manu, on the bank of the canal Sugedara. Date.

No. 21 (TuM n.F. 1/2 248 tablet and case; Šu-Sin 4; Dusabara)
1(bùr) gána a-šag$_4$ Ur-É-an-na(-ka) Ur-Me-me-ke$_4$ apin-lá-šè ì-dab$_5$ máš-bi 1 gín lá igi-4-gál kug-babbar kin šuku(-ra)-šè engar-ra sum-mu-dam 1 gín lá igi-4-gál kug-babbar a-šag$_4$ ég zi-zi-dam a-šag$_4$-sag-dù gú Íd-sug-e-dar-ra; date. Seal: Ur-É-an-na/dub-sar/dumu Pirig-dalla.

18 iku of land, the (šuku) field of Ur-Eana, Ur-Meme took in tenacy. Its máš payment, 3/4 shekel of silver, for the (irrigation) work on the šuku (field), is to be given to the cultivator (i.e. Ur-Meme) (by Ur-Eana). (Another?) 3/4 shekel of silver (Ur-Eana will give to Ur-Meme) to raise dikes in the field. (This land is located) in the field Ašag-sagdu, on the bank of the canal Sugedara. Date. Seal of Ur-Eana, scribe, son of Pirig-dalla.

Bibliography

Barton, R.F. 1969. *Ifugao Law*. With a New Foreword by F. Eggan. Berkeley: University of California Press.

Diósdi, G. 1970. *Ownership in Ancient and Preclassical Roman Law*. Budapest: Akadémiai Kiadó.

Falkenstein, A. 1956. *Die neusumerischen Gerichtsurkunden, Erster Teil*. Bayerische Akademie der Wissenschaften, Philosophisch-historische Klasse, Abhandlungen, Neue Folge Heft 39. Munich: Bayerische Akademie der Wissenschaften.

Firth, R. 1946. *Malay Fishermen: Their Peasant Economy*. London: Kegan Paul, Trench, Trubner & Co.

Holmes, O.W. 1963. *The Common Law*, ed. by M. DeW. Howe. Cambridge, MA: Little, Brown & Co.

Kienast, B. 1994. *Glossar zu den altakkadischen Königsinschriften*. Freiburger Altorientalische Studien 8. Stuttgart: Franz Steiner.

Lutzmann, H. 1976. *Die neusumerischen Schuldurkunden*. Heidelberg: Published by the author.

Maekawa, K. 1974. Agricultural Production in Ancient Sumer. *Zinbun: Memoire of the Research Institute for Humanistic Studies, Kyoto University* 13: 1–60.

Marx, K. 1971. *A Contribution to the Critique of Political Economy*. London: Lawrence & Wishart.

Nicholas, B. 1962. *An Introduction to Roman Law*. Oxford: Oxford University Press.

Sauren, H. 1970. Zum Bürgschaftsrecht in neusumerischer Zeit. *ZA* 60: 70–87.

Steinkeller, P. 1981. The Renting of Fields in Early Mesopotamia and the Development of the Concept of "Interest" in Sumerian, *JESHO* 24: 113–45.

_____. 1989. *Sale Documents of the Ur III Period*. Freiburger Altorientalische Studien 17. Stuttgart: Franz Steiner.

_____. Money Lending Practices in Ur III Babylonia: The Issue of Economic Motivation. In *Debt and Economic Renewal in the Ancient Near East*, ed. by M. Hudson and M. Van De Mieroop, Peabody Museum Bulletin 8 (Cambridge, MA, 2000) (in press).

Watson, A. 1971. *Roman Private Law around 200 BC*. Edinburgh: Edinburgh University Press.

THE OLD BABYLONIAN PERIOD

Raymond Westbrook – Johns Hopkins University

The sources on security in this period are limited in quantity but varied in type. Evidence may be culled from contractual documents, law codes, royal edicts and private letters.

The contractual means of security available to the creditor were pledge, suretyship, and joint liability of co-debtors. If consensual means failed, distraint of persons was an option. On the other hand, a striking feature of the period that emerges from its official (i.e. palace-originated) sources is the intervention of the authorities to restrain self-help and to reduce or even nullify any assurance that the creditor might have of being repaid.

I. Pledge

Kienast and Skaist have made detailed studies of the Old Babylonian pledge documents.[1] Skaist has collected 55 pledge documents in total, very unevenly distributed over the region of southern and central Mesopotamia, with more than a third coming from a single site: Kisurra. The latter is the focus of Kienast's study, which also surveys the material from other Old Babylonian sites.

There is evidence for both possessory and hypothecary pledges, although the former are preponderant. The object of the pledge could be land or persons, among whom are found wives, sons, daughters, male or female slaves, and even the debtor himself.[2] Pledge of valuable movables is mentioned in letters, but not in legal documents. Apparently it was not thought necessary to draft a legal instrument for movable property; mere deposit with the creditor was sufficient proof of the transaction.

---

[1] Kienast 1978; Skaist 1994. See also Eichler 1973: 48–83.

[2] VAS 13 96; also ARM 8 52, following the interpretation of Eichler 1973: 60–61.

1. *Possessory Pledges*

1.1. *Terminology*

1.1.1. The standard Sumerian formula in its fullest form is kù.ta.gub.ba.šè . . . íb.ta.gub, although frequently shortened by ellipsis.[3] Usually, but not invariably, a further formula is added to show that the pledge is antichretic. For land the standard phrase is "for its (the loan's) interest" (máš.bi.šè).[4] A clause in Manana 29:8 provides that the creditor will have the usufruct of the field ("will eat" al.kú.en) for two years. For persons, the following formula is found: "the slave does not have her hire; the silver has no interest" (gemé á.ni [nu.]ub.tuku kù máš nu.ub.tuku: ARN 105:11), a clause that becomes widespread in later periods. In UET 5 323, the debtor further promises to pay the maintenance of the slave he has pledged for a loan expressly stated to bear no interest.

1.1.2. The standard Akkadian term, and the equivalent of the Sumerian expression above, is *mazzazānum* or the abstract *mazzazānūtum*, with a variety of verbs, or the verb *šuzzūzum* alone.[5] No supplementary clause is given to indicate the antichretic nature of the pledge, which seems to be assumed. Note especially ARM 8 31+72, where the loan is referred to as interest-bearing (ur_5.ra = *ḫubullum*) but, atypically, no interest rate is specified. Instead, a slave is given *ana mazzazānūtim* and is redeemable on repayment of the principal (Eichler 1973: 59–60). An express statement of the pledge's function is found in an Alalakh *mazzazānūtum* text from the Old Babylonian level: the sons of a fowler given as pledges must perform the work of a fowler

---

[3] Cf. *ana ittišu* 2 IV 21'–23', 27'–29'.

[4] Kienast (1978: 75) assumes that any pledge in the Kisurra corpus not containing this formula is not antichretic. We would hesitate to make this assumption. It should be remembered that a cuneiform legal document is always only a record of an oral transaction and frequently an incomplete one. In the particular circumstances of the case the parties may have deemed it unnecessary to make express mention of this aspect of the pledge. Silence does not in any case resolve all ambiguity when an income-bearing object is pledged, since the income could either be applied to repayment of the principal or not be applied to the debt at all, becoming a bonus for the creditor. Appeal to oral transactions and customary practice is indispensable. Kienast avoids this problem by assuming that all such pledges are hypothecary (1978: 83–87), but see the criticisms of Skaist (1994: 204–8).

[5] Cf. *ana ittišu* 2 IV 21'–23', 27'–29', discussed by Eichler 1973: 49–51.

for the creditor.[6] In one document only is the arrangement so short-term that a pledge designated by this term might be deemed non-antichretic, but the circumstances are somewhat unusual.[7] Even in that case, antichretic exploitation of the pledge for the short period of its duration is not excluded, although it was undoubtedly not the main purpose of the transaction.

1.1.3. *šiprūtum* was apparently the standard term for pledge of movable objects, mentioned occasionally in letters. AbB 8 81 refers to a gold sun-disk and CT 4 26a to a bronze axe and ingot.[8] A slave is referred to as a *šiprūtum* in one legal document (Edzard Tell ed-Der 21).

1.2. *Formation*

The documents do not indicate when the pledge transaction takes place. Since in the majority of documents it is interleaved with the granting of the loan, it may be assumed that it is co-terminous with the original loan. For example:

> 22 shekels of silver—for its interest he has pledged a house, the inheritance share of X—D son of X has received the silver from C . . . (Kienast Kisurra 4:1–8)

In some documents, however, the principal transaction appears to be the pledge itself, which may indicate that it was given subsequent to the loan:

> A slave, X by name, is given as a pledge (*ana mazzazānūtim izzaz*) from Y for 6 shekels of silver . . . (Harris 1955: no. 3:1–6)

VAS 13 96 definitely involves a pledge given upon default, but to a third party who pays off the original loan:

> X has pledged himself voluntarily to Y for 5 shekels of silver. Y has paid 5 shekels of silver for his debt (*iḫiltišu*). When X brings the silver, he may take (himself) away.[9]

---

[6] Wiseman Alalakh 18: 5–11. For restoration, see Eichler 1973: 66–67.

[7] ARM 8 71, discussed by Skaist 1994: 210, 220; Eichler 1973: 62–3, and see below.

[8] Cf. *ana ittišu* 2 IV 35'–38', 49'–53', and Assyrian *šapartu*.

[9] Cf. ARM 8 71, discussed below.

1.3. *Interest*

By its nature, the interest on an antichretic pledge is uncertain, being the income from the asset pledged. In a few contracts, however (all formulated in Sumerian), a fixed rate of interest in barley is stipulated on a silver loan, notwithstanding the pledge. Kienast Kisurra 9 is a loan secured by pledge of land in the usual manner, but with a fixed interest clause instead of the standard "for its interest" clause. The same is true of Manana 35, although a redemption clause for the slave pledged leaves the possessory nature of the pledge in no doubt. These fixed interest clauses could indicate that the loan is not antichretic, i.e. that the property handed over may be exploited by the creditor while the debtor is still liable for interest. On the other hand, it could be that these contracts merely set a limit on the amount of income from the pledge that may be claimed by the creditor, the balance (of the field's yield or the slave's hire) being returned to the debtor. In Kienast Kisurra 5, the interest clause is actually in addition to the standard clause stating that the land is pledged "for its interest."

By contrast, the *šiprūtum* pledge of a slave (Edzard Tell ed-Der 21) imposes both fixed interest (probably 20 percent) and a rate of hire for the slave (payable by the creditor). Edzard (1970: 51–4) considers that the stipulation of hire was merely *pro forma*, no actual payment being made. Instead, the hire would have been deducted from the interest, and if necessary the principal, on repayment of the loan. Thus the pledge was purely to secure the capital of the loan and not in any way antichretic, which accords with the more typical function of *šiprūtum* in this period as a pledge of unproductive assets.

1.4. *Non-performing Antichretic Pledges*

Some contracts contain provisions for the contingency that the pledge may cease to perform its role as a source of income for the creditor. In the case of persons as pledges the circumstances contemplated are that the pledge dies, is ill, runs away or disappears (ARM 8 31; Harris 1955: no. 3; 5; Manana 63). The circumstances under which land is lost are less clear: the verbs used are "is lost" (ú.gu . . . dé: Kienast Kisurra 6), "goes out" (*uṣû*: Kienast Kisurra 193), or "he dispossesses (him) of it" (*īkimšu*: Kienast Kisurra 8). The references may be to removal by the debtor himself or to dispossession by other creditors.

The sanctions imposed were of two types. If the creditor chose to maintain the contract, the debtor would be charged directly with a sum equivalent to the interest lost (Kienast Kisurra 8) or to the daily hire of a substitute worker.[10] Doubtless this remedy occurred where the creditor was fairly confident of the debtor's ability to repay, and may have been intended to encourage the debtor to provide another pledge as soon as possible. Alternatively, the creditor could call in the loan, demanding that the debtor pay the principal (ARM 8 31; Kienast Kisurra 193; Harris 1955: no. 5:15–18), or principal and interest (Harris 1955: no. 5:8–14; Kienast Kisurra 6). In the latter case, the extra penalty was possibly due to deliberate removal of the pledge by the debtor (Kienast 1978: 93). Manana 63 gives no specific penalty for death or flight of the pledge, but concludes with the statement "oath of the king." This may be an oath by the creditor calling down on himself unstated penalties if the pledge ceased to be available.[11]

1.5. *Antichretic Interest without Pledge?*

Certain special types of arrangement seem to be intended not to secure the lender's capital but solely to provide interest.

1.5.1. X leases a field from Y on a sharecropping basis, and gives Y an advance payment in the form of a loan. The clearest example is Manana 47:

> X has leased from Y 6 iku of field, next to the field of Z, for cultivation of barley, peas and sesame, (on the basis of) half shares. Y has received from X 1 shekel of silver and 15 seah of barley (as a loan) not bearing interest. He shall pay it in the seventh month.

[10] SHLF viii 3–10; PBS 13 39 (two model contracts); Harris 1955: no. 3. See Skaist 1994: 212–213. In Kienast Kisurra 203, a field is secondarily pledged to cover the loss of income if the primary pledge, a slave, is lost. See the restoration and interpretation of this fragmentary text ad loc. pp. 178–79.

[11] Cf. the neo-Sumerian pledge contract NATN 307: x kor of barley, for its interest A has pledged B son of A for 5 years. He (A) swore the oath of the king that he (B) would not run away (nu.da.kar.re.a mu lugal.bi in.pà).

The creditor thus has an interest in the field that is limited in time—until the harvest, when the principal will also be repaid. In Dalley Edinburgh 35, where the creditor's share is one-third, the debtor is also surety for repayment of the principal, which suggests that the field itself was not security for the principal and would not be forfeited on default.[12] Nonetheless, the creditor's control of the field in the interim would appear to give him a ready means of ensuring repayment, by taking it directly from the debtor's share of the crop. That situation is expressly at issue in the second type of arrangement.

1.5.2. A common form of lease at Susa has the following pattern:

> X has leased a field (of x location) from Y for "gather and take away!" (*esip tabal*). He has paid 1 shekel of silver and leased the field. (MDP 23 250)

Koschaker (1934: 90–4) already noted that the Susa documents were not a real lease, but an antichretic pledge arrangement, by reason of the advance payment of the whole "rent." The true nature of the transaction is confirmed by LH 49:

> If a man borrows silver from a merchant and gives the merchant a field prepared for barley or sesame and says to him "Cultivate the field and gather and take away the barley or sesame that is grown!" (and) if a farmer grows barley or sesame in the field, at the harvest the owner of the field will take the barley or sesame grown in the field and will give the merchant barley for the silver that he borrowed from the merchant, plus its interest and the expenses of cultivation.[13]

The *esip tabal* contract in LH envisages the creditor being paid both principal and interest from the harvest, but not being able to take the whole harvest in lieu of principal and interest. Koschaker (1934: 95–8) considered that LH went too far in protecting the rights of the debtor, effectively destroying the security afforded by the lease granted in the Susa contracts. His view, however, makes two assumptions, both of which may be questioned.

The first is that the Susa contracts allowed the creditor to take the whole harvest. They certainly give that impression, but it is by

[12] Previously published as PSBA 33, no. 29 = HG 1465.

[13] LH 50 provides the same ruling for an already cultivated field, where the farmer's services are dispensed with, and LH 66 (= Roth ¶a) likewise for a date-palm orchard.

silence, whereas contracts do not have to spell out rules imposed upon them by the law. Rules of fairness imposed by the courts often act as hidden parameters for a contract, contributing no less than express clauses to the contours of the agreement. We would suggest that reimbursement of the balance to the debtor (after deduction of principal and interest) may well have been an equitable rule imposed by the courts. On this understanding, the provisions of LH were not so much a radical restructuring of the contractual arrangement as an attempt to prevent its abuse, namely the creditor helping himself first and giving the debtor whatever he chose to regard as the balance.

The second assumption is that if the debtor defaulted, the creditor had no security. Koschaker cited in support LH 52, which rules that if the farmer hired to cultivate the land failed to produce a crop, he (presumably the creditor who hired him) "shall not alter his contract." But risk of the security being unproductive—which the creditor would bear even under the most favorable lease arrangement—is not the same as lack of security for default. As Driver and Miles pointed out (1952: 147), the *esip tabal* contract as restricted by LH would still entitle the creditor to seize the grain if not paid at all with it. In other words, it was the pledge of a future crop, rather than a pledge of the land itself. Like any hypothecary pledge, it protected the creditor against the claims of third parties upon the debtor's assets, and it could become possessory in the event of default, whether by non-payment or by alienation to a third party.[14]

1.5.3. Manana 29 differs from the above leasehold arrangements in that the debtor's field is expressly pledged to secure the loan. However, it also contains a clause allowing the creditor to enjoy the usufruct of the land pledged for two years (8: mu.2.kam a.šà al.kú.en), followed by a clause obliging the debtor to repay the loan in the second month (9: iti gu_4.si.sá ì.lá.e). As Skaist (1994: 214) points out, since the loan was made in the tenth month, it was only of four months' duration. The curious situation thus arises where the creditor had use of the pledge far beyond the duration of the loan. It is possible that if the debtor failed to repay at the due date, the field

[14] The lessee in the sharecropping arrangements discussed above may have been similarly constrained with regard to possession of the land and use of the crop for repayment of the principal.

would be immediately forfeit, thus providing an incentive for him to pay on time even though he did not regain the use of his pledge. The land would at that point cease to be security; it would merely be a source of income, in the nature of a gratuitous lease. Another possibility is that the repayment date was intended to specify when in the second year the loan and its security matured, i.e. after 14 months.

1.6. *Termination*

The natural end to a pledge contract is that the debtor either repays the loan and redeems his pledge or defaults and forfeits it to the creditor. This simple schema may have many variations, however, with restrictions both on the redeemability and forfeitability of the pledge. The picture presented by the sources is indeed far more complex and fragmented, due to a variety of factors.

With one exception (ARM 8 71, discussed below), the pledge documents do not explicitly refer to the powers of the creditor over the pledge upon default. Most of them do not even specify a date for maturity of the loan. YOS 14 35 is exceptional in that it contains three provisions that relate to the question of termination of the pledge:

> X and Y have received from Z 6 iku of field in (x location) as pledge (*ma-za-za-nu*) for 3 shekels of silver. The silver and the field "look at each other" (*i-ta-ṭà-la*). In the month of Girritum he shall pay the silver and redeem the field . . .

The Sumerian Laws Handbook of Forms contains a parallel formula in a model clause:

> The slave woman and the silver look at each other: when he brings the silver, he may take away his slave woman.[15]

In other Old Babylonian contracts the "look" clause is found alone, without mention of payment or redemption (Harris 1955: no. 4:5–7; Kienast Kisurra 4:9–10; 63:2–4), as is a variant form from Kisurra: "the silver is like the field" (Kienast Kisurra 1:9: kubabbar a.šà.gi.me.en; 5:3 (Case); 22:5 (Case): kù ù a.šà).

[15] Col. viii 11–15: géme ù kubabbar igi.ne.ne.du$_8$ u$_4$ kù mu.un.tùm.da géme.ni ba.an.tùm.mu. (Ed. Roth 1995: 46–54.) Cf. *ana ittišu* 2 IV 30'–34'.

As Kienast (1978: 100–101) has pointed out, the clause establishes the equivalency of value of pledge and debt, and can only relate to the acquisition of the pledge by the creditor on default. That is not to say that absence of the clause means that the pledge is not forfeitable. The clause assumes forfeiture of the pledge, and seeks to regulate its execution. It is in the interest of the creditor, who would want to keep all the proceeds from sale of the pledge. Without it, it is reasonable to suppose that at the least the creditor would have been accountable to the debtor for the difference between the value of the debt and that realized by the pledge.[16] In the absence of indications to the contrary, therefore, we should assume that the possessory pledges in these very tersely worded documents were forfeit to the creditor on default.

The lack of a due date in the document might be such an indication, but the presence of a due date is so rare that it cannot be a reliable criterion. Many agricultural loans will have had a customary date of maturity, usually in the harvest season.[17] On the other hand, ARN 105: 12–14, which contains a due date and a provision for penal damages on default, certainly did not intend forfeiture of the pledge at that juncture.

Kienast (1978: 101–102) suggests that automatic forfeiture did not obtain in cases where a supplementary form of security was present. Of the examples that he gives it is certainly true of one, Dalley Edinburgh 35, but that contract, as we have seen, was a special arrangement in which the land itself was not in fact pledged. The other examples are beside the point, since in all of them the pledge is a person, and persons are capable of disappearing—hence the need for extra security. Providing they were still available on default, it would not be a bar to their forfeiture to the creditor.

More difficult of interpretation are documents where a seemingly open-ended redemption clause is found, without due date or "look/like" clause.[18] Delay by the debtor in repaying the debt was often to the

---

[16] The principle involved is articulated in a fragmentary section of the Middle Assyrian Laws (C+G7): [If . . .] or anything is held in the house of an Assyrian as a pledge [. . .] and the due date pas[ses . . .], if the silver (i.e. the principal of the debt) amounts to as much as its value, [it is acquired and] taken; if the silver does not amount to as much as its value [. . .] he may acquire and take [but(?)—] he shall cause (him) to abandon [. . .], the principal of the silver [. . .] . . . there is no . . .

[17] See Skaist 1994: 148–166 and cf. Manana 63.

[18] ARM 8 31+72; Manana 35; UET 5 300; UET 5 323; VAS 13 96; YOS 8. 78. The clause is also found in a model contract: PBS 13 39 ii 8'–9'.

advantage of a creditor secured by an antichretic pledge: he would simply continue to exploit its income. In economic if not in legal terms, the accumulated income would ultimately amortize the whole debt; indeed, the longer the creditor held the pledge, the more profitable the arrangement would be for him. Consequently, it is not absolutely necessary to assume a fixed term to the pledge arrangement; the same open-ended arrangement (*Lösungspfand*) is found in later periods. Furthermore, such contracts may have been colored by principles of social justice imposed by the courts during the Old Babylonian period, which allowed redemption to be exercised long after the right would normally have expired.

1.7. *Social Justice*

1.7.1. *Redemption*

The sources attest to rules allowing redemption even after sale by a debtor, under limited circumstances and for limited categories of property. *A fortiori* their provisions must have applied to property pledged. Slightly different rules are found in relation to land and persons.

1.7.1.1. Land. According to LE 39:

> If a man becomes weak and sells his house, whenever the buyer will sell, the owner of the house may redeem.

The law establishes the principle of open-ended, if contingent, redemption, even beyond the point of sale. The condition of becoming weak is a reference to impoverishment, which would almost invariably involve indebtedness. In any case, the holder or buyer of a forfeited pledge logically should not be in a better position than a buyer direct from the debtor. Indeed, what the law does is to assimilate sale to pledge, in giving the property sold the redeemable character of a pledge.

The law does not explain what is meant by "his house," but there are a number of house purchases in which it is noted that the buyer "redeemed his father's house."[19] This suggests that it was the ancestral family home that the law was seeking to protect.

A direct association with pledge is attested by a common clause in land sale documents from Susa: "not redemption, not pledge (*maz-*

[19] See Westbrook 1991: 93 n. 2.

zazānum); full price. As a father buys for his son, X has purchased . . . in perpetuity."[20] The clause is designed to resist the possibility that the transaction will be deemed a pledge, and therefore redeemable. The character of the purchase that assures the distinction is "full price," which must in this context refer to the value of the property. It suggests that in order to establish clear title, a buyer at Susa had to circumvent a law similar to that of LE 39, protecting impoverished sellers whom necessity had forced to sell at a discount.

The question of full value brings us back to the "look/like" clause in the pledge documents. It is possible that where the land pledged fell within a category protected by social laws, the clause served to protect the creditor and subsequent owners from redemption claims after forfeiture and sale.

1.7.1.2. Persons. LH 119 reads:

If a debt seizes a man and he sells his slave woman who has borne him children, the owner of the slave may pay the silver that the merchant paid and redeem his slave woman.

A fortiori we may conclude that members of the debtor's family were subject to redemption even after sale. The slave concubine is deemed a family member by reason of her having borne children to the head of household. The provision that the redemption price is to be the original sale price shows that it is regarded as analogous to the redemption of a pledge.

A good proportion of the pledge documents have as their object not a slave but a wife, son or daughter, or even the debtor himself (ARM 8 52; 71; Grant 1938: no. 6; Harris 1955: no. 5; VAS 13 96; YOS 8 78; YOS 14 85). At Alalakh they represent the standard type of *mazzazānum*-pledge.[21] Most of these documents contain no other clauses, so that the rules of redemption and forfeiture must be presumed to have followed customary practice and principles of law such as those illustrated by the above provisions of the law codes.[22] It is in the light of those principles and practices that the only document to contain an express right to sell, ARM 8 71, should be understood. The contract reads:

[20] Discussed by Eichler 1973: 78–80 and Westbrook 1991: 102–07.

[21] Collected and edited by Eichler 1973: 63–75.

[22] Two have open-ended redemption clauses (YOS 8 78, VAS 13 96) and one has a due date, but the rest of the clause is unfortunately broken.

> X went surety for Y for 6 1/2 shekels of silver. W the wife of Y was assigned to X. If he does not pay the silver within 2 months, W wife of Y will be sold.

The situation is unusual and extreme: the debtor had evidently defaulted on his loan and was saved by the intervention of a surety, who gave him a breathing space of two months. The surety, however, demanded security in his turn, and on terms most probably harsher than those of the original debt. Since they involved the debtor's wife, there was the possibility that the courts would restrict the creditor's powers. On the other hand, since the creditor was a third party who had stepped in to rescue an already insolvent debtor, the terms were arguably justified. Against this background, the sale clause was neither restating a right that was self-evident nor creating a right that would otherwise not have existed, but was asserting its unfettered exercise under the special circumstances.

1.7.2. *Release*

It was the practice of Old Babylonian kings to issue edicts cancelling existing debts, on a limited or nationwide basis.[23] Devastating as this might sound for creditor confidence, they had several features which tempered their long-term effect. Firstly, they applied essentially to "consumer" debt (in ancient economic terms these would have been mostly agricultural loans), commercial debt being expressly excluded. Secondly, each edict was a one-time, retrospective measure. Thirdly, they were singular events and difficult to predict. The timing of the edict was entirely within the discretion of the king: it would usually occur on the accession of a new ruler to the throne, but further debt cancellations could also be decreed at irregular intervals in the course of a reign, triggered by political or religious considerations.

These edicts not only attacked debt directly, but might also release persons who had been pledged or sold by reason of a debt. Paragraph 20 of the Edict of king Ammi-ṣaduqa reads:[24]

> If a debt is incurred by a son (= citizen) of Numhia, Emutbal, Idamaraz, Uruk, Isin, Kisurra, or Murgu and he [gives] hims[elf], his wife or

[23] The fundamental work of reference is Kraus 1984, where the texts are edited and all other Old Babylonian references to debt release edicts are collected and analyzed.

[24] Edited by Kraus 1984: 181.

> [his children] in sale, in penal servitude[25] [or as ple]dge (*ana mazzazānim*)—[because the king] has decreed equity [for the land, he is rele]ased, his restoration (*andurār-šu*) is established.

The relationship between debt, pledge, and sale is made explicit in this provision. Sale is the direct result of an unpaid debt.[26] Here the law intervenes to break the creditor's security *ex post facto*, for the benefit of certain privileged classes of persons, namely citizens of the cities named. In the context of a debt release decree, extinction of the security can only mean that the debt is annulled also.

The beneficiaries are not identified by their family connection, as was the case with the redemption law, but being free citizens it may be presumed that they had been reduced to servitude by the head of their family or by themselves. The term *andurārum* does not mean release in the abstract, but restoration to one's previous status, which in this case would mean return to one's family and one's position within it. They would revert to being free citizens, as the term "released" (*wuššur*) emphasizes (Charpin 1987).

LH 117 is a close, but not exact, parallel:

> If a debt seizes a man and he sells or gives into penal servitude his wife, son or daughter, they shall work in the house of their purchaser or holder in penal servitude for three years; in the fourth year their restoration shall be established.

The relationship between this cyclical release and the release of the edict is problematic.[27] For our purposes, it is sufficient to note the significant omission of *mazzazānum*. It is not, in our view, accidental. A pre-ordained time limit to the security and thus to the debt

[25] *ana kiššātim*. See Westbrook 1996.

[26] Eichler (1973: 82) was concerned that this provision seems to contemplate that the pledge was given only on default, like sale, whereas he considered that a pledge could only be given at the time of the loan. While we would not restrict the time of pledging so narrowly, a *mazzazānum*-pledge was certainly not designed to be given on default. On the other hand, there is no need to interpret pledge and sale as strictly parallel in this context. Three different causes of servitude are envisaged, each of which had its own procedure.

[27] See Hallo 1995: 90–91. It should be noted that the precise situation contemplated may be different in the two sources. The edict talks of an obligation binding a man (*e'iltum i'ilšu*), whereas the law code talks of it "seizing" him (*iṣbassu*). The latter may imply a more extreme situation, unsuited to antichretic pledge. Perhaps it indicates default on the original debt and the intervention of a third party, as in ARM 8 71 above.

is a very different concept from the occasional retrospective forgiveness of debts. The theoretical basis is evidently that three years' work of the family member is regarded as amortizing the debt. Amortization of this sort would not have been compatible with an antichretic pledge.[28]

Paragraph 21 of the Edict presents a case where the creditor's security is shielded from the effects of the royal decree:[29]

> If the male or female house-born slave [of][30] a son (= citizen) of Numhia, Emutbal, Idamaraz, etc. or (of) a son of the land for the [full] price is sold or bound in penal servitude or left in pledge, his restoration shall not be established.

Here the restoration of the slave would be to his previous status as slave of the debtor. Where the pledge is equal in value to the debt, however, as we have seen with redemption, the bargain was not considered oppressive, and would be allowed to stand. A house-born slave was apparently not enough of a member of the family for this principle to be overriden.

2. *Hypothecary Pledges*

Hypothecary pledges are less well attested. They tend to be associated with more complex transactions. CT 33 29 in our translation reads:

> X has given Y 6 shekels of silver to take possession of land (*ana qaqqarim ṣabātim*). If Y does not pay X the silver, X will stand on the land (*eli qaqqarim izzaz*).

The transaction is in our interpretation a loan for the acquisition of land.[31] It is unlikely that the first clause refers to the creditor taking the land as pledge, as it would make the second clause superfluous.[32]

---

[28] Cf. LL 14: If a man has returned his slavery to his master and it is confirmed (that he has done so) twofold, that slave shall be released.

[29] The text has almost exact parallel versions in Edict X (§ H), the Edict of Samsu-iluna (§ 3') and in a fragment, NBC 8618, which may be from the latter Edict. See Kraus 1984: 154–62; Hallo 1995. The present translation is based on NBC 8618, with restorations from the other two texts.

[30] or: see Hallo 1995: 84.

[31] *Contra* Kienast 1978: 74 n. 317: "gegen 'Packen' eines Grundstückes . . .", and Skaist 1994: 215–17.

[32] Cf. CAD *ṣabātu* vol. 16, p. 14 mng. 3d.

Failure to describe the location of the land suggests that it has not yet been acquired. A loan for purchase (or for some other payment necessary to acquisition) is an obvious occasion for a hypothecary pledge.

Kienast (1978: 101) suggests that the effect of the phrase "will stand on the land" was merely to turn the hypothecary pledge into a possessory one, not to transfer ownership. Kienast's interpretation is supported by a similar phrase used to describe a possessory pledge in RA 8, 70: "until he pays the silver, X (creditor) will stand upon the land." Default on a hypothecary pledge could, however, lead directly to ownership. The outcome depended on the individual contract, as is shown by two contrasting documents from Kisurra, both demonstrating the role of the hypothecary pledge as a secondary security.

In Kienast Kisurra 203, a fragmentary text, it appears that the debtor has given a person in antichretic pledge. Should that person die or run away, the debtor must compensate the creditor for the loss of income with a fixed rent supplied from a field given in hypothecary pledge. At most then, the creditor could take physical possession of the pledge, pending default on the principal. In Kienast Kisurra 92, on the other hand, flight of the debtor, who has apparently pledged himself, allows the creditor to succeed (*iredde*) to his "house and orchard." This non-specific description of the debtor's estate is, as also attested in later periods, an indicator of hypothecary pledge.

A further clause states that if two named persons claim the land, they must pay the debt. Kienast (1978: 91) assumes that these are other creditors, which would raise interesting questions concerning the priority of competing creditors. It is more likely, however, that these are potential heirs of the debtor, who would naturally seek to contest the succession to his estate with his creditor. What the clause does indicate is that the pledge was not intended as a substitute payment for the debt. As successor in title to the land, the creditor may have been able to resist any claim to reimbursement of the difference in value between the debt and the pledge as long as he held the land (indeed, this may have been the purpose of the "succession" clause). Ultimately, however, he could not disregard the rights of the debtor's successors in title, which once exercised would reduce his rights to his true interest: the value of the original debt.

YOS 8 35 also concerns the securing of a creditor against flight of the pledge, but is more remotely connected to the original debt.

The parents of a slave receive him into their custody from his master, the financier Balmunamhe of Larsa. If the slave runs away, the parents' house and orchard, i.e. their whole estate, is forfeit to Balmunamhe.

Van de Mierop (1987: 6–12) has explained the background to this and similar texts concerning Balmunamhe. The financier released slaves during periods of low agricultural activity—on leave so to speak—with guarantees that they would return to work when needed.[33] Presumably the slave in this case was originally sold to Balmunamhe by his parents by reason of debt, but that debt was not at issue in the present transaction. Probably the same arrangement lies behind VAS 13 73, in which another known Larsa financier, Ubar-Shamash, released a slave to his parents, who pledged their house and orchard as security against his absconding.[34]

Finally, Waterman 37 shows how practicalities might determine whether a pledge of land was hypothecary or possessory:

> X received 33 shekels of silver from Y. Y received a field of 2 1/2 iku in (x location) from X. The field and the silver look at each other. At the harvest X shall measure out to Y 100 seah of barley, produce of the field, at the threshing-floor. If he does not measure it out, Y will dispossess him of the field and will cultivate (it himself). Apart from the terms of his tablet of the field of the entirety.

As Kienast points out (1978: 91–2), the amount of barley to be supplied equals 10% of the value of the silver. The specific injunction that the interest be paid from the pledged field shows the antichretic nature of the transaction: the amount stipulated is thus a limit on the antichretic interest, as we have seen above. The further requirement that the debtor himself hand it over to the creditor gives the transaction its hypothecary character.[35] Should the debtor fail to pay even the limited interest, the creditor would be obliged to take over the field, and by way of compensation award himself at the least a

[33] In the other texts adduced by Van de Mierop no security is involved; the parties responsible for the loss of the slave must pay compensation or make substitution.

[34] The situation is somewhat complicated by the unexpected appearance of a second person, Sin-damiq, in lines 3–4, from whom the parents actually received their son. He may have been an agent or partner of Ubar-Shamash, who is named as the slave's master in line 2.

[35] Cf. Koschaker, commentary to HG 1467. Kienast's view (1978: 84) that the creditor could not take possession because the contract was prior to sowing is criticized by Skaist (1994: 217 n. 61).

more generously interpreted share (as in the *esip tabal* contracts) or even the whole of the crop—his exact entitlement is not clear.

The enigmatic final clause has generally been interpreted as referring to another parcel of land. In our view, it is intended to establish that taking possession of the crop on default of interest is without prejudice to the right of the creditor to acquire ownership in the field on default of payment of the "entirety," i.e. the principal, as adumbrated in the "look" clause.

II. Suretyship

1. *Typology*

Sureties were widely used in the Old Babylonian period, and for a variety of purposes. There were two main types of suretyship:

1) to secure the appearance of a person at a given date or venue (*Gestellungsbürgschaft*), e.g. the accused at a trial (AbB 1 101; 9 269), an abducted wife (VAS 8 26), or the return of a slave from furlough (BIN 7 210); or else to insure against the flight of a person, an antichretic pledge (Kienast Kisurra 109), or a hired worker (Meissner BAP 61). This type of suretyship only incidentally involved security for a debt.

2) to secure payment of a debt should the principal debtor default. As with *Gestellungsbürgschaft*, the surety's liability was secondary—only if the debtor defaulted could the creditor claim from him. In AbB 7 75, the writer asks in astonishment: "Why are they suing me for the silver (just) because I stood surety for X?"

2. *Terminology*

Various expressions are used for the assumption of liability as a surety.

2.1. The surety was said to "take the hands" of the debtor (Sum. šu.du$_8$.a.ni . . . šu ba.an.ti/Akk. *qātāti leqûm*).[36] For example, YOS 14

[36] Cf. *ana ittišu* 3 II 51–53.

158:1–6 records that X and Y borrowed 10 shekels of silver from Z. G "took the hands" of X and Y from Z.[37]

2.2. The surety was said to "hold the head" of the debtor (*qaqqadam kullum*).[38]
Both these expressions apply to suretyship assumed together with the granting of the loan. Malul has interpreted them as referring to the surety's assumption of control over the debtor (as in later periods), the basic role of the surety being to assure the availability of the debtor for payment or for personal execution.[39]

2.3. The impersonal expression "the hand of X is removed" (*qāti* X *nasḫat*) is applied to many different situations, among which is suretyship.[40] Landsberger (1937: 119) explained the word *qātum* in this context as involvement (*Beteiligtsein*) in the widest sense with a matter, claim, etc. The full phrase thus means to sever such involvement. It can be used for the rejection of a plaintiff's claim by the court, or for the termination of a creditor's claim, whether by settlement or by the intercession of a third party (Kümmel 1974–7: 75–9). It is in this latter function that it is used for suretyship. The situation arises where the debt has matured and the debtor is unable to pay. The surety intercedes on his behalf and either pays the debt or agrees to pay it within a short time. PBS 8/2 207 states:

> Regarding 15 shekels of silver that X borrowed from [Y]. Z acted as surety (šu.du$_8$.a <*ilqi*>) and paid the 15 shekels of silver to Y. The hand of Y is removed from X and Z.

Since the debt has been settled in its entirety, the document quite logically records that the involvement of both the debtor and the surety with the debt has been severed. Where the surety has taken over the debt but not yet paid it, it is only the debtor's hand that is removed (e.g. YOS 13 273). The same phrase can equally well refer to the situation from the creditor's perspective, as in PBS 8/2 245:

---

[37] Cf. YOS 5 114; UET 5 425. A surety was referred to as "he of the hands" (*ša qātātim*), e.g. Wiseman Alalakh 22.

[38] BIN 7 210; Gautier Dilbat 51; cf. Meissner BAP 61, where the surety is called the "holder of his (debtor's) head" (*mukil qaqqadišu*).

[39] Malul 1988: 219–31, reviewing the earlier literature.

[40] Cf. *ana ittišu* 3 II 54–55.

> 20 shekels 150 grains of silver, the balance of the price of a slave, which X and his brother Y were owed by Z: the hands of X and Y are removed. Z will pay the silver to G in 10 days.

Here it is the involvement of the creditors with the debt that was severed, leaving the debtor obligated to pay a third party, who must have been the surety.

2.4. The phrase "to give (X) for hands (to Y)" (*ana qātātim nadānum*) appears in a few sources, but in contexts so obscure that its import cannot be discerned. The most detailed is a letter (AbB 6 73) in which the addressee is enjoined to hold (*kullum*) a person given to him by two others *ana qātātim* until the writer should arrive. Possibly the primary debtors had defaulted and execution against the surety was contemplated.[41]

3. *Conditions*

As might be expected, the surety would normally be liable not only for the principal of a loan but also for its interest. In YOS 14 158 the surety paid 15 shekels to satisfy a two-year-old debt of 10 shekels. In a letter, the addressee is said to have stood surety "for silver and interest" (AbB 9 27).[42] On the other hand, it seems that the surety could limit his liability. In AbB 2 113 the addressee is requested to stand surety for a third party "up to one mina of silver" (*a-di* 1 ma.na kubabbar).

4. *Regress*

If the debtor defaulted and the surety settled the debt in his place, he stepped into the shoes of the creditor and had full right of regress against the debtor.[43] In ARM 8 71, discussed above under pledge, the surety took the debtor's wife as pledge to ensure repayment. In PBS 8/2 245, also discussed above, the debtor, having been relieved

---

[41] Cf. AbB 3 55 (the writer complains that "they have written to me and have given me *ana qātātim*"). Also *ana ittišu* 3 II 41–45. See CAD Q 169, mng. 1b.

[42] See Ries 1981: 81–4; cf. Gautier Dilbat 51.

[43] For a full discussion of the sources, see Ries 1981.

of liability to pay his creditor by a surety, was given 10 days in which to pay the surety. YOS 14 158 renders a graphic account of the problems surrounding regress:

> X and Y borrowed 10 shekels of silver from Z. G acted as surety for them. They absconded and Z seized G, and G after their (departure) paid Z 15 shekels of silver for 2 years (*ša* mu.2.a). His heart is satisfied. If Z sees X and Y he shall not sue them; G in the town where he sees them may take the silver from whichever of them is solvent.

The term "seize" is a reference to a formal act initiating a lawsuit (Dombradi 1996: 295–302). The creditor took the surety to court, but the absence of the usual account of judicial procedure shows that the document records an out-of-court settlement.[44]

A letter (AbB 9 27) suggests that once the debtor had defaulted, the surety could act in anticipation of fulfilling his secondary obligation. The writer urges the surety not to sleep on his rights, but to sue the debtors pre-emptively:

> . . . Concerning the sons of X, for whom you acted as surety for silver and interest, Y . . . is on his way to you with a soldier of the king. Seize the men, cause them to pay the silver and interest and give it to the gentleman. Don't abandon the suit on your own (or) you will pay the silver and interest from your own hand!

The underlying nature of Old Babylonian suretyship as *Gestellungsbürgschaft* is evident here. The surety's essential duty was to make sure the debtor paid. If it was a practical possibility, he could extract payment from a defaulting debtor directly, rather than pay first and seek reimbursement afterwards. The only condition was that the creditor be paid promptly.

5. *Purpose*

We have seen that suretyship covered a wider range of obligations than pledge. Even within the sphere of debt, suretyship seems to have been the preferred method for securing commercial loans. In

[44] See Dombradi 1996: 183–84. Ries (1981: 85–6) wondered how a private agreement could impose obligations on absent third parties—the debtors—but it should be understood as a regulation as between the creditor and surety of the exercise of rights that they both had against the debtors by virtue of the original contract to which the debtors were parties.

CT 8 33a advance payment was made for the purchase of wool, which was not delivered. The surety took over the debt and agreed to deliver the wool at wool-plucking time at the price then prevailing. A similar purchase may lie behind the assumption by a surety of the obligation to deliver a cow (YOS 13 42) within two days. Suretyship offered a quick and flexible means of ensuring that a credit transaction could proceed, and may account for the very short payment times—usually not more than one month—imposed on the surety taking over a debt that had fallen due.[45] Given the surety's right of regress, the debtor's obligation would in theory only be deferred by the same amount of time.

Larger commercial transactions also made use of sureties. In AbB 2 113, the writer urges the addressee to act as surety for a third party ("my brother") for up to one mina (a considerable sum!) for a few days until the writer arrives, adding: "He has no father beside you." The familial terms are clearly not to be taken literally here; they seem rather to apply to business relations.[46] CT 48 108 records a complicated commercial arrangement involving Princess Iltani: she delivered 2 talents of wool at a price of 12 shekels to X, Y and Z. G had a tablet drafted concerning the wool received. On the due date in that tablet, X, Y and Z will "remove the Princess's hand" from G.[47]

III. Joint Liability

Where a loan was made to more than one debtor, a joint liability clause was frequently added to the repayment clauses of the contract. Although frequently abbreviated, the fullest version can be reconstructed as follows: "he (creditor) will take the silver from the sound and solid one" (Sum. ki lú.silim.ma ù lú.gi.na.ta kubabbar šu

---

[45] See the table in Kümmel 1974–7: 80–83. Not all such transactions were commercial. Some involved payment of taxes. One tax in particular, *kezērum*, seems to have been payable by a woman upon marriage, and liability fell equally upon her husband. Perhaps the use of a surety facilitated the couple's marriage. See, YOS 13 312, 315, 327 and CAD K 315–16.

[46] *aḫu* is well attested in OB as colleague or business associate (CAD A/1 201, mng. 2a2'b'); *abu* rather as a term of respect (CAD A/1 71, mng. 2a2').

[47] The possible scenarios behind this contract are discussed by Kümmel 1974–77: 78.

ba.ab.te.gá/Akk. *itti šalmim u kīnim kaspam ileqqe*).[48] The purpose was clearly to make each debtor liable for the whole of the loan, leaving the risk that any single debtor would be unable to contribute his share to fall upon his fellow debtors, not upon the creditor.

IV. Distraint

The only measure of self-help allowed to the Old Babylonian creditor was to detain a member of the debtor's household pending payment of the debt. The person detained was referred as a *nipûtum* of the debtor and the act of distraint by the verb *nepûm*, often with *nipûtum* as its object. It applied not only to loans outstanding, but to debts arising from any cause—taxes (AbB 11 79), dues on crown land (AbB 10 5) and for the return of a borrowed pig (AbB 13 131). It was also used to enforce corvée duties (AbB 9 253; 10 1), especially at Mari.[49] In the case of loans, it could be justified by arrears of interest alone (AbB 3 20).

The consent of the debtor was not required (Jackson and Watkins: 1984). The creditor could even act in the debtor's absence (AbB 7 68). Nor was any court order necessary, although distraint frequently accompanied the initiation of litigation (AbB 1 93). For this reason, there are almost no contractual documents dealing with distraint; our evidence comes from a few paragraphs in the law codes and from letters, where it was a frequent subject of correspondence—so frequent that there were even model letters on distraint that were copied by scribes as a school exercise (Kraus 1959–62: 26–9).

Any subordinate member of the household could be taken for this purpose: wife (AbB 9 41), children (LH 116) and slaves (AbB 10 5), but also a daughter-in-law (AbB 9 270) and a sister-in-law (AbB 6 41), perhaps because they were living in the debtor's household. Occasionally an animal is mentioned (TCL 1 2). There are no references to male slaves, and in practice (and perhaps for practical reasons) the efforts of creditors centred on females. The distrainee, never identified by name, is often marked with a female determi-

---

[48] Cf. *ana ittišu* 2 II 68–69. The Old Babylonian references are collected and discussed by Skaist 1994: 231–32.

[49] See CAD N/2 250 mng. d).

native (SAL *nipûtum*). More than one person might be distrained at the same time.

The place of detention must normally have been the creditor's house, although it is seldom specified. In AbB 7 125, an embittered brother claims that he was brought into his father's house not by way of adoption but as a distrainee (cf. AbB 6 172 *ina maḫrīa*). Other buildings include a mill (AbB 1 137) and a barn (AbB 9 270). The school texts speak of the debtor's family being put in prison (*ṣibittum*: Genouillac Kich 2 D 39; TCL 17 74; UET 5 9). Where a type of prison called *nupārum* is named, there seems to be some connection with the king: the debtor has been denounced by the king (AbB 2 114; 5 228; cf. AbB 5 234: *ṣibittum*) or must plead with the king (AbB 7 68).[50]

The purpose of distraint was not to satisfy the debt. On the contrary, LH 113 penalizes a creditor who helps himself to grain from the debtor's granary or threshing-floor: he must return the grain taken and forfeit the amount of the original loan (Jackson and Watkins 1984: 411–14). The terminology of distraint is in fact never used with inanimate objects or commodities.[51] It is used of female slaves, who were regarded as a commodity, but their different role is neatly illustrated by AbB 11 158, where a court ordered the creditors to release two *female* slaves whom they had distrained from the debtor's business partner on the grounds that they had been reimbursed by the sale of a *male* slave of the debtor. As far as the economic value of the distrainees was concerned, Jackson and Watkins (1984: 417) assert that the *nipûtum* was normally put to work, but there is no direct evidence. Since the term *nupārum* could also mean a workhouse, perhaps those distrained by government authorities (at least in connection with corvée duties?) were expected to work.[52] At all events, the distrainee's work was not applied to the loan, whether by way of amortizing the capital or as antichretic interest (Jackson and Watkins 1984: 417–18).

The essential function of distraint was to put pressure on the debtor to pay the debt. The distrainee was a kind of hostage: at the

[50] The two terms may be synonymous in a royal context: see Scouflaire 1989.

[51] As pointed out by Jackson and Watkins 1984: 417. We disagree with Yaron's assessment of the creditor's powers (1988: 247): "A fortiori he would also be entitled to seize other property belonging to the debtor, subject, probably, to specific rules exempting from seizure certain kinds of property."

[52] See CAD N/2 341–42 and Scouflaire 1989: 158.

very least it forced the debtor to make the next move. As the creditor in AbB 6 200 put it: "Until he comes to me, I will not release his distrainee." It was intended to be an interim measure, but in a war of nerves between debtor and creditor it could drag on, not necessarily to the creditor's advantage. In AbB 11 106 a *nadītum* complains of her dilemma:

> . . . I hold his distrainee (SAL *ni-pu-us-su ú-pa-sú-um*) but he has not sent me the barley. If I send his distrainee to him, he will be negligent in sending me the barley. Write to the judges . . . let them tell him to send me the barley so that I may send him his distrainee. I have been feeding the distrainee for 5 months; if he does not send me the barley, shall I release the distrainee? . . .

Nonetheless, distraint could be very effective. The model letters emphasize the debtor's need for haste and the danger of delay (UET 5 9):

> Since you went on a journey, after your departure X came and said: "He owes me 20 shekels of silver." He distrained your wife and daughter. Come here and redeem your wife and daughter before they die from detention in prison!

In AbB 1 89 the debtor was so desperate to redeem his distrainee that he attempted to raise a loan from a third party for that purpose.

A measure that did not require the creditor to use the courts might justify their intervention if abused. This time, however, it would be the debtor who sought the court's help. The writer in AbB 9 238 justified his order in those terms:

> . . . distrainees of X shall not be distrained; let them distrain distrainees of Y. If he is wronged, since Z (presumably the creditor) is present here, let him (Y) come and we will do him justice.

The law codes anticipate unjustified distraint and impose punishments for it. According to LH 114:

> If a man is not owed grain or silver by a man and distrains his distrainee, he shall pay 20 shekels of silver per distrainee.

For the wrongful distraint of a slave woman in the same circumstances LE 22 imposes a payment of "as much as [the value(?)] of the slave-woman."[53] To resolve the factual dispute, it imposes an

[53] Restore š[ám]. See Yaron 1988: 276–7.

oath by a god on the debtor, a burden that would not have been regarded as easy to discharge.

The assumption that these laws concern the claim of a fictitious debt has been questioned by some scholars, who propose that what is contemplated is rather the wrongful retention of a distrainee after the debt had been paid (Szlechter 1954: 127–32). Jackson and Watkins find it hard to imagine circumstances in which a creditor could, knowingly or not, create a false debt; disputing the settlement of an existing one is a more credible scenario (1984: 415–16).

In our view, the law covered both possibilities. On the one hand, failure to return the distrainee after a debt had been settled was a common complaint (AbB 3 67; 6 208; 11 158). On the other, distraint was used for indebtedness arising from many causes, not only loan, and there were many opportunities for abuse. Consider the writer's argument in AbB 10 1:

> . . . regarding X the *kalûm*-priest . . . he deposed to me as follows: "No one has ever tried to conscript me as a bearer. Now the official (*šāpir mātim*) has sent a message and has distrained my distrainees (*ni-pa-ti-ia it-te-pú-ú*)." The man is under my authority . . . he is no foreigner . . . If you love me, let no one claim against his house (*ana bītišu mamman la išassi*).

Imposition of corvée duties or of taxes (which would be collectible in silver or grain) on a person supposed to be exempt from them was a known bureaucratic hazard (AbB 6 41; 9 216), and one not entirely unfamiliar to modern societies. Furthermore, complications could arise if the purpose of the transfer of silver or grain were disputed, as between sale, gift, deposit or loan.[54] The assertion that X owed Y a debt could therefore infer a multitude of possible transactions.

The formation of the laws is ambiguous as to whether they punished errors in good faith or whether more deliberate misconduct was necessary. Distraint was a drastic act of self-help, but to penalize its use by a creditor acting on a genuine belief would have severely reduced the security for debt afforded by the law. Old Babylonian courts had the power to impose a penalty on an unsuccessful plaintiff if he acted "not knowingly" (*ina lā idîm*), which from

[54] Cf. Edict of Ammiṣaduqa 7, where various different purposes for the presence of silver or grain in a person's possession are given. See Kraus 1984: 172–3.

the contexts seems to mean without reasonable cause.[55] In AbB 6 6 the writer, reporting to his superior on a dispute over a field, hastens to assure him that as a result of his intervention certain parties

> . . . have not distrained a distrainee and not one shekel of silver has been collected. I will send the men to Babylon to my lord. If they have claimed without cause (*lā idâm idbubū*), let my lord punish them.

The letter suggests that distraint would have been an aggravating factor had the claim turned out to be baseless. A more objective standard than the fraudulent state of the claimant's mind, it would have been particularly apt for dealing with high-handed bureaucrats or with financiers who relied on their economic strength to act intemperately against debtors.

The law codes also consider the liability of a creditor for the death of the distrainee while in his custody. LH 115 rules that there is no liability where death has occurred through natural causes, but LH 116 provides:

> If the distrainee in the house of his/her distrainer dies from beating or maltreatment, the owner of the distrainee shall prove it against his creditor (lit., "merchant"): if a son, they shall kill his son; if a slave, he shall pay 20 shekels of silver and forfeit as much as he gave (as a loan).

Jackson and Watkins (1984: 417) assume that death was not deliberately inflicted, since there was no benefit to the creditor thereby, but resulted from a work regime. It is true that the creditor would not profit by the distrainee's death, but he would profit from the threat of death. The creditor could not unilaterally sell the distrainee to realize the sum owed. Even if the distrainee was expected to work, only a limited amount could be extracted from wives, children and female slaves (without the added insurance against absence or death provided by antichretic pledge contracts). There would have been a temptation to add to the pressure on the debtor by maltreating members of his household, or at the least to save money by starving them. As the model letter above (UET 5 9) assumes, there is a distinct possibility that the distrainees could die from imprisonment. By that pressure the creditor could hope, if not for payment, then at least to extract an agreement from the debtor to sell himself or the

[55] CT 47 63:49 where a penalty is imposed on relatives of the *de cuius* who claimed the estate from an adoptee.

members of his family into slavery in lieu of the debt, or to allow them to be sold to a third party, as we have seen in ARM 8 71 and LH 117. For such an alternative to be tolerable to the debtor, the physical conditions of distraint had to be worse than those of debt slavery.

LE 23–4 takes the situation a step further, considering the case where death has been caused by one who distrained without justification. For a slave the penalty is twofold restitution.[56] For a son, ". . . it is life, the distrainor who distrained shall die." In other words, in the aggravated circumstances of the offence, the penalty of vicarious liability in LH 116 (a son for a son) is increased to the death of the head of household himself.[57]

In view of the fact that distrainees were typically female, the possibility of sexual abuse would seem an obvious problem. In fact, only one text alludes to its existence. YOS 8 51 reads:

> Concerning X daughter of Y whom Z had distrained and concerning (whom, namely) X daughter of Y, Z had sworn the oath of the god at the Gate of D not to approach or take sexually:
> Y swore the oath of king Rim-Sin: "Henceforth, be it for 5 years or for 10, I shall keep my daughter for Z and I shall indeed give her to him in marriage."

The contract records an agreement whereby a girl is released from distraint into the custody of her mother in return for a promise of marriage. The distrainor's solemn oath not to take sexual advantage of her suggests that it was considered a natural privilege of the creditor. All the more reason for the debtor to make haste in paying his debt.

Finally, LH 241 seeks to place a limitation on the type of property subject to distraint. It fines a creditor 20 shekels for distraining an ox. The rationale is obvious: without the ox a poor family would be unable to cultivate their land and would thus be deprived of the means to repay their debt. As with other rules of social justice in the law codes, it is open to question how systematic their application was. In a letter to one of his senior officials, Hammurabi orders him to investigate and judge the case of a petitioner who, inter alia,

---

[56] Yaron (1988: 278) notes that in LE 22–3 the wrongdoer pays double, which in his view makes the offence equivalent to theft, on the basis of the penalty for theft in LE 49.

[57] For this interpretation, see Westbrook 1988: 55–7.

has complained that three oxen of his have been distrained on account of his nephew (TCL 1 2). The circumstances leading to the distraint and the outcome of the hearing are not preserved. It would not appear, however, that the distraint was regarded as being in itself illegal.[58]

[58] Another provision that might be considered relevant to distraint is LH 151, according to which spouses may make a nuptial agreement to bar creditors from seizing (*ṣabātum*) one of them for the other's pre-marital debts. It is more likely, however, that it means simply being the defendant in litigation. The continuation in 152, which concerns post-marital debts, speaks of both of them *paying* the creditor (i.e. satisfying the claim).

Abbreviations

Harris 1955 = Harris, R. "The Archive of the Sin Temple in Khafajah (Tutub) *JCS* 9 (1955) 31–119.

LE Laws of Eshnunna

LH Laws of Hammurabi

LL Laws of Lipit-Ishtar

Manana	1–24	= Rutten, M. "Un lot de tablettes de Mananâ," *RA* 52 (1958) 208–224.
	25–41	= idem, *RA* 54 (1960) 19–40, 147–152.
	42–46	= Charpin, D. "Nouveaux textes de la Dynastie de Mananâ," *RA* 72 (1978) 139–150.
	47–59	= idem, *RA* 73 (1979) 121–133.
	60–68,45	= idem, *RA* 74 (1980) 11–128.

SLHF *Sumerian Laws Handbook of Forms*. Edited by Roth 1995: 46–54. Law Collections from Mesopotamia and Asia Minor. Writings from the Ancient World, 6. Atlanta: Scholars Press.

Bibliography

Charpin, D. 1987. Les décrets royaux à l'époque Paléo-Babylonienne, à propos d'un ouvrage récent. *AfO* 34: 36–41.

Dombradi, E. 1996. *Die Darstellung des Rechtsaustrags in den altbabylonischen Prozessurkunden.* Stuttgart: Franz Steiner.

Driver, G.R., and J. Miles. 1952. *The Babylonian Laws.* Vol. 1. Oxford: Clarendon Press.

Edzard, D. 1970. *Altbabylonische Rechts- und Wirtschaftsurkunden aus Tell ed-Der im Iraq Museum, Baghdad.* Bayerische Akademie der Wissenschaften, philosophisch-historische Klasse. Abhandlungen, N.F. 72. Munich: Verlag der Bayerischen Akademie der Wissenschaften.

Eichler, B. 1973. *Indenture at Nuzi.* Yale Near Eastern Researches, 5. New Haven: Yale University Press.

Grant, E. 1938. Ten Old Babylonian Contracts. In *The Haverford Symposium on Archaeology and the Bible*, ed. E. Grant. Pp. 225–45. New Haven: American Schools of Oriental Research.

Hallo, W. 1995. Slave Release in the Biblical World in Light of a New Text. In *Solving Riddles and Untying Knots*, ed. Z. Zevit. Pp. 79–93. Winona Lake: Eisenbrauns.

Harris, R. 1955. The Archive of the Sin Temple in Khafajah (Tutub). *JCS* 9: 31–119.

Jackson, B. and T. Watkins. 1984. Distraint in the Laws of Eshnunna and Hammurabi. In *Studi in Onore di Cesare Sanfilippo* Vol. V. Milan: giuffrè.

Kienast, B. 1978. *Die altbabylonischen Briefe und Urkunden aus Kisurra.* Vol. I. Wiesbaden: Franz Steiner.

Koschaker, P. 1934. *Über einige Griechische Rechtsurkunden aus den östlichen Randgebieten des Hellenismus.* Sächsische Akademie der Wissenschaften, philologisch-historische Klasse. Abhandlungen 42. Pp. 1–122. Leipzig: Hirzel.

Kraus, F. 1959–62. Briefschreibübungen im altbabylonischen Schulunterricht. *Jaarbericht Ex Oriente Lux* 16: 16–39.

——. 1984. *Königliche Verfügungen in altbabylonischer Zeit.* Studia et Documenta ad Iura Orientis Antiqui Pertinentia XI. Leiden: Brill.

Kümmel, H. 1974–7. Ein Fall von Sklavenhehlerei. *AfO* 25: 72–83.

Landsberger, B. 1937. *ana ittišu.* Materialien zum Sumerischen Lexikon (MSL) I. Rome: Pontifical Biblical Institute.

Malul, M. 1988. *Studies in Mesopotamian Legal Symbolism.* AOAT 221. Kevelaer: Butzon & Bercker.

Ries, G. 1981. Zu Haftung und Rückgriff des Bürgen in altbabylonischer Zeit. *ZA* 71: 73–86.

Roth, M. 1995. *Law Collections from Mesopotamia and Asia Minor.* Writings from the Ancient World, 6. Atlanta: Scholars Press.

Scouflaire, M.-F. 1989. Premières réflexions sur l'organisation des "prisons" dans le royaume de Mari. In *Reflet des Deux Fleuves (Mélanges Finet)*, ed. M. Lebeau. Pp. 157–60. Leuven: Peeters.

Skaist, A. 1994. *The Old Babylonian Loan Contract.* Ramat Gan: Bar-Ilan University Press.

Szlechter, E. 1954. *Les Lois d'Ešnunna.* Paris: Sirey.

Van de Mierop, M. 1987. The Archive of Balmunamhe. *AfO* 34: 1–29.

Westbrook, R. 1988. *Studies in Biblical and Cuneiform Law.* Cahiers de la Revue Biblique 26. Paris: Gabalda.

——. 1991. Property and the Family in Biblical Law. JSOT Supplement Series 113. Sheffield: JSOT Press.

——. 1996. zíz.da/*kiššātum. WZKM* 86: 449–59.

Wiseman, D. 1953. The Alalakh Tablets. Occasional Publications of the British Institute of Archaeology at Ankara, 2. London: British Institute of Archaeology at Ankara.

Yaron, R. 1988. *The Laws of Eshnunna.* 2nd ed., Jerusalem: Magnes Press.

THE OLD ASSYRIAN PERIOD

Klaas R. Veenhof – Leiden University

I. Introduction

1. *Text Corpus and Historical Context*

Nearly all Old Assyrian texts known today, most of which date to the nineteenth century BCE, were discovered in the commercial district in the lower town of the ancient Anatolian city of Kanish, in Central Anatolia. This lower town harboured a large Assyrian trading colony, whose administration also served as the centre of a network of more than thirty Assyrian commercial settlements all over central Anatolia. Local diggers and since 1948 official Turkish excavations thus far have brought to light approximately twenty thousand cuneiform tablets from perhaps close to one hundred different archives, which may comprise between a few dozen and more than thousand records each.[1] Of these, about four thousand have been published in some form and I am familiar with the contents of another 2500 unpublished tablets, not all of which, however, I can quote or use here.

Though all texts are in Old Assyrian script and language, we have to distinguish two groups. In the first place those written by and for Assyrians, which document their business practices and legal customs. In the second place those written for and in part also by native Anatolians, in which only persons with Anatolian names figure, which must reflect local Anatolian social and legal customs. Even though the influence of the Assyrians, through the use of their language and the impact of their commercial practices was important, we cannot simply consider legal forms and substance embodied in Anatolian documents as reflecting Assyrian legal custom. There is sufficient evidence, in the area of family law, of distinctive native Anatolian customary law to make us careful. Moreover, loan and credit operations,

---

[1] See for general information on Kanish and the Old Assyrian trading colony there, Veenhof 1995a.

which concern us here in particular, are in some respects different among Anatolians from those among the Assyrian traders.

The tablets from the archives of traders reflect a highly developed and versatile overland trade, in which commercial loans and credit played an important role and where security must have been an important issue. Since written Old Assyrian laws, which did exist,[2] have not thus far been found, our reconstruction of the legal customs has to be based entirely on practice documents, such as contracts, judicial records of various kinds, and commercial letters. Though it is not always easy to distill generally prevailing rules and devices from a large variety of individual cases, the sources usually are numerous enough to reveal what was customary and what were less common, ideosyncratic or perhaps new solutions to obtaining security. Since the trade must have developed over the period of more than a century during which it is attested, we may expect developments also in the rules and legal devices meant to provide security. The growth of the trade, both in size, complexity, and range of action (a growing network of commercial settlements), required more capital supplied by more investors and moneylenders, and more participants, especially employees and traveling agents who were given lots of merchandise in consignment for the purpose of credit sale. All these features must have increased the need for legal instruments to protect investments, loans and credit granted. However, since most dated texts, which actually means most contracts bearing on loans and credit, are from the later years, when the trade was in full swing, while there is little evidence from the earlier, presumably formative period, it is difficult to trace developments in the commercial procedures and legal devices.

While most records found in the Assyrian archives of *kārum* Kanish were written in Anatolia, they also include a substantial number of texts—mostly letters, but also judicial documents and some contracts—written in Assur and sent to Kanish, which thus reflect legal customs of the mother-city. Though there was no difference between the legal rules prevailing in Assur and in its colonies in Anatolia, we have to bear in mind that the nature of the transactions in Assur and in the colonies was rather different and required different devices for providing security. In Assur firms were founded, which meant long- or short-term investments in a trader's capital (called "money-

[2] See Veenhof 1995b.

bag" *naruqqum*), commercial trusts (*qīptum*), and long term loans (*ebuṭṭū*). Merchandise for export to Anatolia was purchased in Assur by paying cash silver which had arrived from Anatolia as the proceeds of a previous business trip or was borrowed at interest (*ana ṣibtim laqā'um*) from business relations or "at a merchant's house." Occasionally merchandise could be bought on credit from wholesale dealers and probably also from the "city-office" (*bēt ālim*).

On the Anatolian scene the most important feature was the sale of the imported merchandise; again, when possible, for cash, but usually on credit, either directly to customers, such as the local palaces, dignitaries and traders, or by consignment (*qīptum*) to middlemen, especially travelling agents called *tamkārum*. Both usually received credit, which resulted in debt claims (*ḫubullum*, "debt"). Credit granted to customers who were to pay later was called "to leave behind" (*ezābum*) and resulted in "outstanding claims" (*bābtum*), a term, however, also used for what was due from consignment. Travelling agents to whom lots of merchandise were "given" (*tadānum* with personal dative; also "to lay upon" *nadā'um ina ṣēr*) or "entrusted" (*qiāpum*) as consigment, had to sign promissory notes payable in silver after a fixed number of months. The claims on them were protected primarily by default interest, among Assyrians usually of thirty percent per year. Granting commercial credit, notwithstanding regular insistence on using only reliable agents, always entailed the risk of delayed payment and (temporarily) insolvent or unwilling debtors, which is the subject of many commercial letters and legal confrontations.[3] Nevertheless, instruments of security other than default interest are not frequent in the relevant contracts. The local palaces and their high officials, important and powerful customers but regularly late in paying and even in issuing acknowledgments of their debts,[4] had to be handled with care. But Anatolian individuals, who were usually also charged a higher default interest, frequently had to supply various forms of security, a custom even more developed in loans granted by Anatolian traders and moneylenders to fellow Anatolians.[5]

[3] See for Old Assyrian credit operations, Veenhof 1999a.

[4] Called *iṣurtum*. See for the behaviour of the palaces Veenhof 1995c: 324f.; lists of claims in silver and copper on the palace and local officials in CCT 1, 21d and CCT 6, 34a. But note EL 273, a verdict of the *kārum*, ordering a commercial boycott of a high palace official who did not pay his debts to an Assyrian trader.

[5] See for the analysis of the business of one particular Anatolian moneylender, Veenhof 1978 and also Donbaz 1988.

2. *Evidence on Security*

Information on instruments of security derives in the first place from a variety of debt-notes and related records,[6] but the relevant data are not very frequent and usually short and laconic, mentioning only that an item or person serves as pledge or guarantor. Such debt-notes must have been written in big numbers, as shown by the large memoranda which were drawn up periodically by traders to have an overview of their outstanding claims, and which basically consist of excerpts of such debt-notes. Most are lost, however, because the debtor upon payment received "his tablet" (recording his liability and sealed by him) back, which was regularly was destroyed ("killed"; the sealed envelope was broken and the tablet thrown away). Thus the number of surviving debt-notes, which includes duplicates and copies of original contracts, is comparatively small.[7] It must have included unpaid, bad debts, for which security is more likely to be required.

Our second source are business letters and judicial records, which usually provide more detailed information on security. They contain reports on problems with bad debtors, on the designation and actions of guarantors, and on acquiring and using pledges. Such reports frequently are in the form of testimonies (depositions) on what was said or agreed during private summonses or official lawsuits started by creditors against overdue or fraudulent debtors or by guarantors who had been obliged to pay for debtors and were seeking regress by various legal means.

In our sources we meet various kinds of security. In the first place and most clearly security provided by persons or objects, such as guarantors and personal and impersonal pledges. In the second place

---

[6] A representative collection was edited in a typological classification with comments as EL. After more than sixty years, although in need of certain corrections, it can still be relied upon. Unfortunately, the systematic "Juristische Erläuterungen," mentioned and even referred to by paragraph in the commentary, have never been published. About hundred additional debt-notes were edited by Rosen 1977, and later additions are in KKP, KKS and TPK.

[7] In all about 250 original debt-notes are known to me. The number of surviving debt-notes in two regularly excavated archives (those of 1990, published in TPK and of 1991/2, which I am preparing for publication) amounts to about one every two years. Almost none of the debt-claims listed in memoranda is represented by its original debt-note, which implies that they were paid and subsequently discarded. See for the problem, Veenhof 2000: § 4.

security in the form of various legal devices, which allow a creditor to recover his claim or to indemnify himself at the expense of his defaulting debtor. The latter, known from specific clauses inserted in loan contracts and debt-notes, are the liability of each member of a plurality of debtors for the whole debt and the authorization of the creditor to borrow the unpaid debt from a moneylender at the expense of the debtor. A non-consensual type of security, hence not stipulated in debt-notes but usually reported in letters, is distraint.

The important question why a particular kind of security was preferred and why so often no security at all was demanded is not easy to answer, since the ancient texts do not present them, let alone discuss them, as alternatives. Choices must have been determined by the nature of the relationship between creditor and debtor, the record and current financial status of the latter, and the nature of the transaction. The security demanded usually correlates with the risk calculated. Though the trade in general was profitable and relatively risk-free, certain persons apparently were considered more risky than others. In particular, credit or loans granted to Anatolians are more often protected by security and their default interest usually is higher than that demanded of Assyrians. We also have examples of Assyrian traders in financial difficulties who could only borrow money if the loan was secured by a guarantor or a substantial pledge. For understanding transactions between Assyrians, knowledge of the background of the parties is vital and it appears that demanding security from relatives and close partners was unusual. But when there were problems help from relatives who granted "favours" (*gimillum*), advanced money, gave soft loans or acted as guarantors was not rare. Something similar is attested for employees or trusted agents of an Assyrian firm, for whom financial help in the form of a secured loan, under strict control of the boss/creditor, was an option which might prevent bankruptcy and allow "recovery" (*balāṭum*, lit. "revival"). Information on such matters usually can only be derived from letters and judicial records in the context of archives, because loan contracts and debt-notes seldom reveal their background.

In Old Babylonian it is, to some extent, possible to conclude from the wording of a contract whether one has to do with a "new" debt, resulting from a loan ("the debtor received/acquired . . . from the creditor"; *itti* C D šu ba.an.ti/*ilqe*) or a liability with a history, recorded in a debt-note (Germ. *Verpflichtungsschein*), "the creditor has a claim. . . . on the debtor"; C ugu D in.tuku/*eli . . . išû*). The latter may refer to a novation, the balance of a debt, a liability due to arrears, etc.[8] In Old Assyrian practically all debt-notes use the second formulation,[9] "creditor has a claim of x silver (etc.) on debtor" (*iṣṣēr* debtor *išû*), which makes it virtually impossible to distinguish true loans from financial liabilities resulting from credit sale, consignment, settling accounts, or arrears in paying fees or taxes. For this reason I use "debt" in a rather broad sense to include several financial liabilities, in particular those resulting from credit sale, loan and consignment. In the case of consignment, the contract has the form of a normal debt-note, which, unfortunately, does not specify the merchandise received, but only mentions the resulting debt, which is the price, the amount of silver the debtor/agent in due time will pay for the merchandise received. Knowledge about the persons involved (which includes the distinction between Assyrians and Anatolians), the size of the debt (large amounts usually involve consignment),[10] and the terms (those of credit sale and commercial consignment almost never exceed one year) help us to reconstruct the nature of the liability and hence, at times, the nature of and reason for the security.

3. *Cumulation of Security*

Some commercial letters and a number of contracts, especially those between Anatolians, contain evidence of a cumulation of instruments of security. An example is the letter BIN 4, 4, in which Ilwedaku reports to Buzazu on a consignment of merchandise entrusted to two agents:

> 8 Akkadian textiles, 1 *kamsu*-textile, and 10 Abarnian textiles, at 45 shekels of silver apiece, 20 *kutānu*-textiles at 30 shekels apiece, plus 4

[8] Stol 1983: 6f. discussed this aspect in connection with the question when a guarantor was provided.

[9] There are very few contracts which state that the debtor "has received" (*ilqe*) the amount due; see for them and a possible reason for this formulation, Veenhof 1995/6: 20, with note 53. TPK 1, 85 is a rare contract using *C ina libbi D išû*, "C has an claim on D," which refers to an existing debt; the expression *ina libbi PN* is very common in lists and letters to record that a debt "is (still) owed by PN."

[10] But there are also many smaller debts originating from credit-sale, e.g. of a few textiles, such as the one edited as Kienast 1984: no. 33. We have to realize that by Mesopotamian standards 30 shekels (approx. 250 grams) of silver, the sale price of one expensive woollen textile, was a substantial sum, equal to two to three times the annual wage of a labourer.

> normal textiles we "gave" (in consignment) to B. and Š. for 25 minas (pounds) of silver and we drew up their sealed debt-note for payment within four weeks. A pledge (*šapartum*) has been made available (*nadā'um*), the debt is "bound" to whichever of them is (financially) sound (solvent), and B. is guarantor. If they do not pay (in time), they will add interest. For a lot of 200 normal textiles I have agreed with them for a price of 10 shekels of silver apiece. When they deliver the gold and the copper as pledge I will release the textiles to him (Š., the principal debtor).

Hence a pledge (and from the related letters CCT 4, 29b and AnOr 6, 19 we know that it was a packet of 10 minas of gold), liability of both debtors for the whole of the debt, a guarantor, and default interest. Such a cumulation of security, including a valuable pledge (equal to approx. 80 minas of silver, more than the total value of the goods!) is exceptional and there must have been special reasons for requiring it. In BIN 4, 4 the cumulation of consigments may have been a factor, since the second (200 textiles) will only be "released" when the agents actually deliver the pledge. Another example is in the debt-note TC 3, 232, which combines pledge, guarantee and default interest.

> 3 minas of refined silver $Š_1$. and A. owe to "the creditor" (*tamkārum*), $Š_2$. is guarantor; A. and S. and their houses are pledges (*erubbātum*). (Reckoning) from the week of (the eponyms) L. and B. they shall pay within six weeks. If they do not pay they will add 1 1/2 shekel of silver per mina per month (= 30% per year). Witnessed by A. and E.

In the Assyrian debt-note I 475, for a debt of two minas of silver, to be paid within three months, not only the debtor's wife, slave-girl and house serve as pledge, but it is also stipulated that, if the debtor fails to pay when his term is over, the creditor is entitled "to enter a merchant's house to borrow silver at interest, which interest the debtor will compensate" (lines 10ff.).[11]

Thus cumulation of security in this way was not impossible,[12] but it raises questions. Were the various forms of security alternatives or could they be used simultaneously? Was there an order of priority, either customary or at the choice of creditor or debtor? Was the

---

[11] See for this type of security, below IV.2.

[12] See for this issue Kienast 1975/6, esp. 225f. He maintains that pledges which occur alongside or in competiton with other security, such as "Solidarhaftung," "Bürgschaftsleistung" or "Verzinsung," are not "Ersatzpfand" but only "Sicherungs-

cumulation a reflection of growing financial problems of the defaulting debtor, who may have been forced to offer the creditor in due time more and better security? Without background information of an archival nature we cannot answer such questions.

4. *Conditioning Factors*

Old Assyrian stipulations on security should be understood against the commercial, social and legal background which determines the practice of the trade. A few such factors should be mentioned in this introduction.

The first is the frequently enormous value of the commercial loans and credit transactions. Debts of up to 30 minas (15 kilograms) of silver are frequent and even higher amounts are not rare, as the letter just quoted shows. The record AKT 3 no. 27 itemizes the contents of five debt-notes of one trader, a total of nearly 40 kilograms of silver, "all this the debt of the scribe Adada." The same man, in AKT 3 no. 28, engages in a contract whereby he obtains (borrows) in Anatolia 46 kilograms of silver for a trip to Assur to buy merchandise. Upon his return to Kanish his creditor, if he wishes, can take this merchandise or Adada can keep it, if he is ready to pay back after [x] weeks its double, 92 kilograms of silver. Even for successful and rich Assyrian merchants it must have been difficult to provide security for debts and claims of such magnitude. The instruments current in Babylonia (antichretic pledging of fields, houses, slaves, family members, with the possibility of eventually acquiring them for good) in most cases would have provided only a very limited security, far less than the value of debt. Hence, it is not surprising that the evidence for security in connection with commercial debts between Assyrians resulting from investment, credit sale and loans is limited; there is not a single example of a field pledged. Few of the relevant debt-notes mention a pledge and the number of occurrences of a guarantor is small (in less than ten percent of the preserved debt-notes). This no doubt also had to do which the fact that in general such commercial transactions went fairly smoothly and

---

pfand," even though the contract he quotes clearly states that the creditor will leave (*waṣā'um*) the house he holds as pledge, a "dogmatic" interpretation which goes back to considerations of P. Koschaker.

profits were big, which usually allowed debtors to pay back what they owed. Delayed payments due to the nature of the caravan system (during the winter no caravan travelled in Anatolia), the behaviour of customers or middlemen, or too heavy investments, causing temporary shortages of money, occurred regularly. But guarantors and pledges apparently were not the normal devices or deemed necessary to secure the resulting claims. The problems frequently could be solved by advances[13] from friends or by taking out short-term interest-bearing loans, while creditors in the meantime were satisfied by the high default interest stipulated for exceeding terms. Real problems arose when this interest "became too much"[14] or the capital itself could not be repaid. In such cases we meet guarantors securing loans taken out by people in trouble or the handing over of valuable pledges, such as expensive houses in Assur or tablets recording high debt-claims.

The second feature is that in a trading society bankruptcy usually benefits neither debtor nor creditor. I know of no texts which describe how an indebted trader or agent, who had lost all his assets, was seized as personal pledge or sold into (debt) slavery, although the fear of getting into debt-servitude is occasionally expressed.[15] Of course, we cannot exclude the possibility that some of the Assyrian slaves or slave-girls we meet owe their fate to financial problems, perhaps rather in Assur than in the colonial society. But what we observe is that creditors use their (virtually bankrupt) debtors' capacity for work and commercial experience by extending them new, well-secured loans for a caravan trip to Assur. There they have to buy tin and textiles to be sold in Anatolia with profit which by contract will serve as (partial) payment of the old and the new debt.[16] Such a situation can be compared with that of working for a creditor in debt-servitude, but the relevant texts, essentially loan contracts with specific clauses, do not use the terminology current for antichretic pledging. This terminology states that the object or debtor handed over "is held by the silver" (*išti kaspim uktâl*) owed to the

[13] A typical request to advance silver for a purchase in Assur uses the words "allow your silver to get out of your control for a few months" (*kasapka warḫam ištên u šina libbe'elka*, see Veenhof 1972: 409ff.).

[14] There are numerous letters which warn against "interest becoming (too) much" and ask to immediately send silver to prevent worse.

[15] In BIN 6, 27:5–11: "Why do I hear that over there you register as guarantor? Must I enter into somebody's debt-bondage?" (*ana mamman ana wardūtim errab*).

[16] See for details, Veenhof 1999a: § 3, 'Special arrangements'.

creditor. In TPK 1 no. 156, an Assyrian, redeemed(!) by a woman from his Anatolian creditor for 26 1/3 shekels of silver, "is held by the silver for five years," during which period he has to pay off his debt by working for her, probably as a donkey driver.[17] The same terminology ("he is held by the silver" he received) and stipulations about breaking the contract and leaving the employer are standard in dozens of Old Assyrian service contracts. For that reason Kienast[18] seems to consider all such employees as defaulting debtors working in antichretic debt-servitude. But this interpretation is refuted by the fact that such debts in most cases are of standard size, usually 25 or 30 shekels of silver. These amounts are not unpaid, old debts for which debt-service is now performed, but new and interest-free silver loans, called *be'ūlātum*,[19] put at their disposal in order to allow them to earn their own wages.[20] The conceptual link between debt-servitude and this type of employment is a service obligation which arises from the acceptance of the creditor's silver and also the fact that in such contracts no interest is stipulated for the debt/loan, since the service could be considered to be antichretic for it ("no interest and no wage," as some Old Babylonian texts write). In the case of real debt-bondage the service is the exploitation of a security for an *existing debt* at the expense of a defaulting debtor; but for Old Assyrian caravan personnel the service obligation is *created* in exchange for a new interest-free loan, made available when the term of service starts. Since most Old Assyrian hired employees were therefore not working in debt-servitude, we shall disregard these so-called *be'ūlātum* loans in what follows.

A third feature to be noted is that by customary law a creditor had various means to enforce his claims, even when no security had been contractually agreed upon. There are many examples of creditors putting pressure on debtors, seizing (*ṣabātum*) or distraining

---

[17] If he leaves his employer she will hire a substitute and he has to pay the latter's wages at a rate of 1 shekel per double hour. Read in line 6: *ta-áp-ṭur$_4$-šu*; the expression for "to serve" is *qassa iṣabbat*, "he will grasp her hand," "support her."

[18] Kienast 1989.

[19] The noun designating this loan, *be'ūlātum*, is a substantivized passive participle of the verb *be'ālum*, "to have authority over," whose logical subject is the debtor hired to work. Some contracts state that the loan is given to them *ana be'ālim* and in a few cases the debtor/hireling is the subject of the verb itself (*ibe'el*). See the observations in Veenhof 1994.

[20] Part of it is normally used to buy a few woollen textiles in Assur, which they could sell in Anatolia with great profit; they are mentioned separately in caravan reports as "textiles belonging to the caravaner."

(*katā'um*) their assets or family members; in Assur, also by sealing their houses.[21] The letter TC 3, 60, written by a trader to an employee of his who travels around to catch a fugitive debtor, puts it eloquently:

> You are lying when you tell me "I have to catch Š.!" When you were in Kanish, Š. was staying there too, in your presence, but you did not seize him and did not force him to pay the silver! You are running around over many miles (lit., "ten double hours distance"). Does he not have a slave-girl and a slave in Kanish? When you read this letter, take his slave-girl and slave as distress/security (*katā'um*) and (so) take your silver!

Below we will discuss the verb *kat'āum*, but here it suffices to show that there were other means than contractual security for protecting claims. In the contract kt 91/k 200, in which a man accepts responsibility for a debt of his father-in-law, he has to promise that he will not allow the creditors to "seize" (*ṣabātum*) his newly wedded wife.[22] The debt-note originally passed between the father-in-law and his creditors may have stipulated that his daughter served as pledge, but it is equally possible that the father feared that his daughter would be distrained by his creditors.[23] The meaning of the verb "to seize" unfortunately is too general to decide whether a pledge or a distraint is involved.

Finally, there is the fact that Assyrian creditors not only dealt with fellow Assyrians but also with Anatolians. We know that security could be demanded and given when a loan was taken out, but it could also be contractually agreed upon only at a later stage, when the debtor defaulted and the creditor forced him to provide a pledge, a guarantor (comparable to the Roman *vindex*), or could be authorized (in a verdict) to "seize" his assets, his house or members of his household. The relative rarity of contractual stipulations on security in debt-notes and the more numerous references to them in letters and judicial records suggest that such "second-stage" security agreements or actions were more frequent with commercial debts among Assyrians. But in loan contracts concluded with Anatolians, which may have been considered more risky (the rate of interest was usually

[21] In the letter AKT 2, 31:16f., where a silver loan, secured by a guarantor, is contracted in order to acquire a house, the creditor (a woman) "comes regularly (with the intention) to seal the house."

[22] Published in Veenhof 1997c: 360f.

[23] Apparently even after her marriage, but this may be due to the fact that she still belonged to her father's household, since her husband seems to have moved in with her father.

higher also), more pledges occur and claims are regularly stated "to rest on" (*iṣṣēr . . . išû*) not only the person of the (male) debtor, but also on his wife, children, house, slaves, fields, etc. (see below IV.1). Perhaps actually seizing or distraining defaulting Anatolian debtors may have been more difficult for Assyrians, because it involved the local Anatolian authorities.[24] For that reason, contractually agreed security may have been preferred here as providing a safe legal basis for such actions.

II. Guarantee

1. *Terminology*

1.1. *qātātum and ša qātātim*

In Old Assyrian, where guarantee has to date not been studied in detail,[25] the guarantor, as in Babylonian, is called *qātātum* or *ša qātātim*. The latter is no special designation of the "Gestellungsbürge," as was assumed in EL 123ff., but the distinction is basically a grammatical one. *Qātātum* is used when the guarantor is named and determined—"PN is guarantor," so always in debt-notes;[26] "you are my guarantor"; "the guarantor of PN"[27]—*ša qātātim* when not. The latter occurs in "to ask for *ša qātātim*" (CCT 3, 8b:14), in EL 238:4f., where the duty of "a guarantor" is stated,[28] and especially in the expression *ana ša qātātim tadānum*, "to give to/for *ša qātātim*," which

[24] In the interesting contract EL no. 184, a local Anatolian ruler and his wife hand over an indebted Anatolian with his family to an Assyrian creditor, whereupon a high Anatolian official acquires them by guaranteeing the creditor half the amount of their debt to be paid in two annual instalments.

[25] But see EL I, 175–182, "3. Bürgschaft und Schuldübernahme," with texts nos. 183–188 and EL II, 122–126, on texts nos. 332–334; Matouš 1976: 206–210; Kienast 1984: § 99–103.

[26] Usually at the very end, before the witnesses, occasionally in the absolute state, used for the predicate of a nominal sentence, *P.N qātāt*, e.g. BIN 4, 4:15 and EL 227:33. Seemingly undetermined *qá-ta-tum* is the personal name Qātātum.

[27] In statements such as "a debt for which I am the/your guarantor" (Kennedy-Garelli 1960: no. 1; TPK 1, 166:7; ATHE 64:15), "for which PN, his brother, is guarantor" (EL. 227:33), "for which A. is my guarantor" (CCT 2, 49a:11f.), "a trust of K. for which he (S.) is guarantor" (BIN 6, 35:10).

[28] Correct EL's reading to *ša* [5] *[qá]-ta-tim [ša t]a-ú-ra-am* [6] *ú-ta-ra-kà!-ni ša-zi-/iz-ma* [7] *lū nušširka*, "appoint a guarantor who will not fail to bring you back; then we will let you go."

we may render by "to give to a guarantor/for guarantee." A few times, occasionally in the mouth of the creditor,[29] we meet the combination *bēl(ū) qātātim*, with and without possessive suffix, with the same meaning.

In many letters and judicial records where we read that persons "are/have registered as guarantor," the verb *lapātum*, "to book, inscribe" is used, both in the passive/reflexive N- and Gt-stems, which seem to be synonymous. Since the active G-stem is not used and being registered as guarantor implies the guarantor's consent, we may translate both "to be registered" and "to have oneself registered."[30] Occurrences may mention the guarantor (G) only, or relate him to the debtor (D), the creditor (C), and the debt. The debt is usually mentioned in the main clause ("the debt for which (*ša*). . . .").[31] Examples of the various constructions are:

- without reference to D or C: a debt for which "the three of us are registered as G" (*litaptāni*, stative Gt, *JCS* 14, 10 no. 5); "you are registered as G" (*nalputāti*, stative N, CCT 5, 8a:26);[32]
- with reference to G and to D by means of his name, a pronominal suffix or a genitive: "the silver for which PN registered as your G" (*ša PN qātātika iltaptu*, Gt, AKT 3, 59:17; with stative N, *nalputu*, AKT 2, 31:6); "at a merchant's house I was registered as D's G" (*qātāt D allipit*, past tense N, TC 3, 67:12); "for which PN has been registered as D's G" (*ša PN qātātim ša D iltaptu*, with stative Gt, kt m/k 126:8).
- with reference to G, D, and C, the relation to C being expressed by the dative (preposition *ana*, "for") and that between G and D

[29] ICK 1, 86 + 1, 141:4. In TPK 1, 157:5 the buyers of a house refer to him as the one who has to protect them against vindication. See also kt 89/k 231:25 and TPK 1, 171:11f.

[30] *CAD* L 89 2,b, takes Gt also as "to write down" (somebody as a guarantor), but the fientic forms of this stem have to be translated, with *CAD* Q 170, 3,a, as "to register as guarantor," where "to register" is intransitive with the guarantor as subject. In the last text quoted in *CAD* L, CCT 5, 24b:7 (see C. Michel, *Innāya II*, no. 202), *altaptu* must be a mistake for *iltaptu*. Note that the unique occurrence of **qātātim naṣbutum*, in EL 325:45f., can be deleted, since the tablet has *nalputāku*, "I have been inscribed" (see my copy in VAS 26 no. 112:46).

[31] Once introduced by the preposition *ana*: "Who is there, who will register as guarantor for all that silver?" (*ša ana kulišu kaspim qātātim iltapputu*, CCT 3, 8b:21).

[32] In both cases *ša* might serve a double duty, as relative pronoun introducing a dependent clause and as *ša* preceding undetermined *qātātim* (hence for **ša ša qātātim nalputātini*), but note BIN 6, 27:7 *ammakan qātātim taltapputu*, "that you getting registered there as guarantor" (and not *ša qātātim*).

by a genitive: silver for which "I had (been) registered as D's G on behalf of C" (*qātāt D ana C altapat, RA* 60, 123:2; cf. *ana C qātātim ša D nalputāku*, KTH 15:6; *G qātāt D*, his brother, *ana C iltaptuni*, kt v/k 156:12, courtesy Donbaz; *ana C qātātišu nalputāku*, EL 326:26). G himself writes: "x silver *ša C qātāt D altapat*" (BIN 6, 123:7f.), but may also omit the verb, saying to his debtor: "You (D) owe x silver to C and I am G" (*anāku qātātum*, BIN 6, 109:5f.), while D himself, referring to the same contract, can state: "I owe x silver to C, PN is G" (PN *qatātum*, BIN 4, 218:17f.).

1.2. *izēzum and šazzuztum*

Guarantee can also be expressed by means of the verb "to stand for" (*izēzum ana*), with the guarantor as subject and the creditor on whose behalf and the debt for which one guarantees in the dative (preposition *ana*). A man who in kt 91/k 200:8ff. "stands for the debt" (*ana ḫubullim izzaz*) of his father-in-law, in the related record kt 91/k 127:4f. is said to be his guarantor" (*ša qātātuni*). In O 3684 (see note 42) a creditor asks the guarantor: "Do you accept responsibility towards me for the debt?" (*ana* x silver. . . . *tazzazzam*). CCT-MMA 1, 84 12ff. mentions a debt-note for 10 pounds of silver due to *tamkārum* together with one stating "that A. will stand for me: for this debt," apparently a separate record recording that A. accepts liability for the debt, perhaps a guarantor. The verb is also used in the causative stem, with the debtor as subject and the guarantor as object, e.g. in EL 238:4ff. (see note 28), where the debtor is asked "to provide/appoint (*šazziz*, imp. Š-stem) a guarantor[33] who will not fail to bring the debtor back" (to the creditor). The same verb, without mention of a guarantor, occurs in EL 254:1–10, where the son of C seizes D, when the latter is about to leave for Assur, saying: "Appoint for me/provide me (*šazzizam*) somebody who, when your term expires, will pay me cash the 5 pounds of silver belonging to E."[34] The verb has a somewhat different meaning when used with the preposition *warki*, "behind," as attested in KKS 5. Here D, whose term has nearly expired, asks C: "Why have you made the boy

[33] EL's original reading is corrected in EL II 184; D does not supply a slave as pledge, but a guarantor "who will bring him back."

[34] See also KKS 3, where a trader liable for clearing a colleague, "if he travels to the countryside shall provide to him" (*ušazzassum*) somebody to take over his reponsibility.

"stand" behind me?" (*ṣuḫāram warkia tušazziz*). When C answers: "You are about to leave, pay me 1/3 pound of silver, since you have only a few days (left) to keep it," D assures him: "Should I leave, I will pay your silver." Making a boy (servant) "stand behind the debtor"[35] clearly is a security measure, taken by the creditor, in order to prevent the debtor from leaving without paying. In this use of the verb *izēzum* "to stand for" and its derivatives the notions of pledging and guaranteeing meet, as is clear from the Old Babylonian *mazzazānum*, "pledge."[36]

The noun derived from this causative stem, *šazzuztum*, well known with the meaning "representative," is also used for the guarantor, in AKT 3, 8:8ff.: "The silver which A. owes to the *kārum* and for which I am the *šazzuztum*—I have indeed paid that silver out of my own funds." This is hardly surprising since being a guarantor is a specific way of representing, acting for another person.

1.3. *apālum*

Finally we mention the verb *apālum*, usually translated by "to answer," but in the Old Assyrian commercial contexts frequently "to answer for" in the sense of "to accept responsibility for." In EL 186 (according to the editor a case of "Schuldübernahme") two persons "answered for"[37] a debt of 13 pounds of silver of the debtor and "shall pay the silver when his term is over." In EL 254:11 the persons which the debtor had "to provide to the creditor" (*šazzizam*, line 5), in order to pay him the silver due when his term had expired, declare "we guaranteed for him" (*nēpulšu*). In EL 186 and 254 the term "guarantor" is not used and hence it is not clear whether the persons "answering for" the debtors had indeed been registered as guarantors in the debt-notes. One gets the impression that they only got involved when the due date approached and the creditors had doubts about the availability or solvency of their debtor. This may also have been the case in EL 238, where the the duty of the person designated as "guarantor" is also expressed by the verb *apālum*; here the

---

[35] Exactly the same expression, *ṣuḫāram warki D šazzuzum*, also in the unpublished text kt n/k 1139:22 (courtesy S. Çeçen).

[36] See *CAD* M/I, 232f., which quotes a lexical text which has *ana manzazānim ušziz*.

[37] EL's "werden begleichen" assumes a present-future tense, *eppulū*, where I prefer a past tense, *ēpulū*. See for the verb also EL II p. 85 note c.

representatives of the creditor tell the debtor that the "Gestellungsbürge" shall be "answerable to us" (*lēpulniāti*) for bringing him back.

The verb *katā'um*, notwithstanding the meaning of some derivatives in other periods of Akkadian, does not refer to guarantee but to distraint (see below IV.3 with note 148).

The verb *ka'unum*, contrary to the translation ("feststehend/ortsbeständig machen") and comments in EL on text 184, does not refer to "Gestellungsbürgschaft,"[38] but to "proving" or "confirming" a liability.

2. *Guarantor and Creditor*

The frequent expression "to register as guarantor" (see II.1.1 above) shows that it was customary to record in writing that a particular person was guarantor, and this is reflected in debt-notes (and excerpts from them in memoranda), which mention the name of the guarantor ("PN is guarantor"). The guarantor accordingly had to seal the contract as proof of the acceptance of his liability, as is shown by the presence of his seal impression on a few debt-notes still encased in envelopes.[39] That only a relatively small number of debt-notes (thus far about twenty) mention a guarantor, shows that only a limited number of loans were secured by guarantors right from the beginning. We can only guess why, since the short debt-notes normally tell us nothing about their background. See for a possible explanation the observations made in I.4 above.

Debt-notes also do not tell us what the liabilities of a guarantor were. This must have been familiar from customary law and they are illustrated by references in judicial records and letters which show that a guarantor had basically two obligations. In the first place, he had to see to it that the debtor was available to the creditor when the debt matured for collecting payment or taking measures against him if he defaulted. This obligation, called "Gestellungsbürgschaft" by German scholars, is attested in a group of records in which the

---

[38] This idea has influenced Lutzmann 1976: 26, § 44, where, with an indirect reference to Old Assyrian, its Sumerian equivalent g i n is also, in my opinion incorrectly, claimed for "Gestellungsbürgschaft."

[39] Seal impressions of guarantors on ATHE 55:63–65; 75; KKS 8; 13; kt 89/k 307.

creditor "gives the debtor for guarantee" (*ana ša qātātim tadānum*) and makes the guarantor accept his liability. The second obligation, which according to a number of records applied if he failed in the first, but also more generally if the debtor did not pay, was to pay in his stead. This liability for subsidiary payment for the debtor is attested in records and letters which deal with the guarantor's payment, his attempts to acquire security for doing so or to get his money back (the guarantor's regress on the debtor), and the fate of the original debt-note, which changed hands during these procedures. That contracts about "Gestellungsbürgschaft" mention subsidiary payment as a conditional, second duty could be taken as an indication that delivering the debtor is the older and primary one,[40] but it is difficult to prove this. Where both liabilities obtain, their sequence and the conditional nature of subsidiary payment is only logical. Moreover, there are many cases where guarantors (are forced to) pay for debtors without any hint of a failed "Gestellungsbürgschaft" (in a statement of the type "Because you did not supply the debtor . . ."). Gestellungsbürgschaft" must have been useful in a society of travelling traders, where debtors might be absent at due dates and deadlines for payment were important because caravans to Assur would leave with regular intervals. Specific contracts stipulating it and making subsidiary payment dependent on it may therefore have been an Old Assyrian innovation.

2.1. *"Gestellungsbürgschaft"*

A particular type of document, mostly judicial records of various kinds, sheds more light on this obligation of the guarantor. A clear example is EL 306 (= TC 1, 103):

> Puzur-Aššur!(C) "gave" Zaha (D) to Ennanum (G) "for guarantee." Puzur-Aššur said: "Tomorrow you shall bring the man (= D) back. Should you not bring my man back, you shall pay me, in accordance with the valid record of my witnesses, half a mina of silver!" Ennanum answered: "I will pay you." Zaha said: "Retain what (I state) with an oath by the City and the Ruler, that, although I do not owe him

[40] As already assumed by Koschaker 1911: 57, 70; elsewhere he considers this obligation typical for "archaic law," where "Zahlungsgarantie" and "subsidiäre Zahlungsverpflichtung" had not yet developed.

> anything, he keeps holding me [by the hem of my garment and tries to 'give me for] guarantee'."[41]

Similar records are 0 3684;[42] ICK 1, 86 + 2, 141; EL 238 (see note 33); TPK 1, 171;[43] kt a/k 300 (unpubl.); kt 89/k 352 and 419 (both courtesy Y. Kawasaki). The last one reads:

> Ilabrat-bani "gave" Šu-Išhara "for guarantee." Ilabrat-bani said: "Tomorrow you shall bring back the man. If you do not bring (him) back, you shall pay to me ten pounds of silver with its interest, which he owes to my father in the City according to his valid debt-note (*ṭuppum ḫarmum*), a tablet which belongs to me, my mother and my sister on the basis of my father's testamentary disposition. I went to him (the debtor) for the ten pounds of silver and the interest on it, but he (said): "You, although I do not owe you anything, either in the City or in Anatolia, you hold me by the hem of my garment and try to 'give me for guarantee.' Bring me proof in the presence of these persons here, whether my father or I myself are indebted to you. What else can I say?'[44]

These records are of two types. The first and basic type is a *contract*, before witnesses, between C and G, starting with the statement that C "gave" D "for guarantee" to G, followed by C's address to G and the latter's acceptance of his liability. It is attested in EL 306, I 478, kt a/k 300, and kt 89/k 352, all of which mention C,[45] D and G by name. EL 306 includes the protest of D, who denies his debt and may appeal to the court (end broken), whereas in the other texts D only figures as object. Kt 89/k 419, which does not mention G by name, nor his reaction to C's request,[46] probably was a draft, drawn up by C when he intended to approach G, and might have served as the basis for a record comparable to EL 306.

The second type, represented by EL 238, ICK 1, 86+, TPK 1, 171 and O 3684, is a *deposition*. The report on the agreement between C and G occurs in the framework of a testimony given by people who had been "seized" as witnesses by C when he tried to reach

---

[41] Read in lines 20ff.: [*lá ḫa-b*]*u-lá-ak-šu*!*-ni-/ma* [21] [*sí-ki*] *uk-ta-/*[*n*]*a-lu-ni* [23] [*ú a-na*] *ša qá-ta-/tim* [*i-ta-na-dí-ni*] . . . (cf. TC 3, 28:24ff.; ICK 2, 141:29ff.).

[42] Garelli 1987: 110f.

[43] Misunderstood by the editors, see Dercksen 1997/8: 338, but problems remain for lines 15ff. and note that D is absent and that in line 13 G starts to speak.

[44] Lines 24ff. *maḫar annên ru'amma mīnam aqabbe.*

[45] In I 478 C is the scribe/secretary, who represents the Assyrian authorities, because the debt is a fine imposed by the City.

[46] It adds a report on C's earlier summons of D with the latter's protest.

an agreement as recorded in the contracts of type one. This testimony was given when the agreement had been frustrated or D had objected and the case had ended up before a *kārum*-court. Such a court usually started its proceedings by hearing (recorded) testimonies from those who had witnessed the earlier confrontation. Its final lines state that this testimony was given under oath, because "the *kārum* (court) had given us for this affair."

According to these records the obligation of the guarantor is "to bring back"[47] the debtor, who is occasionally designated as "my man."[48] It can be taken literally, if we assume that the debtor stayed or intended to go elsewhere, but we can also translate "to turn/hand over." The verb also occurs in EL 188, where an Anatolian guarantor, who had obtained the release of a debtor, since he could only promise payment of half the debt (in two annual instalments), "turned over" (*uta'er*) the debtor to the son of his (by now dead?) creditor.[49] The meaning of *ta'urum* in our texts cannot have been different from that of *abākum*, "to bring along" (frequently followed by *nadānum*, "to hand over, deliver"), current in neo-Babylonian guarantee contracts. Most texts state that "handing over" has to be done "tomorrow" (*urram*), but O 3684 has "within one month." If we take "tomorrow" literally, the action would have taken place only one day before the due date, which is rather late; hence rather "presently," "in the near future."

Securing the availability of D to C at the due date was important because debtors in difficulties might try to flee or, more likely in a society of overland traders, might (have to) leave on a business journey. In the letter CCT 3, 8b:13–15 a D, who has received goods on consignment (*qīptum*) from his C, is afraid that the latter "will require a guarantor (*ša qātātim*) from me when I am to leave on a journey, which would put me to shame." EL 238, ICK 1, 86+, and kt 89/k 419 show that debtors whom a creditor wanted "to give for

[47] EL 238 stresses the duty of the guarantor by writing "You shall not fail to bring my man back!" in Assyrian by adding a paranomastic infinitive to the finite verbal form.

[48] Cf. the designation *amēlūtī* for the debtor in texts from Emar.

[49] See for the verb also the damaged record EL 297, where an Anatolian debtor asks his guarantor, who wants to exercise his right of regress by "turning him over" (to the creditor?), not to do so, but to take along "his boys" (children, slaves?) and to sell them. EL define the verb as "die Verbringung einer Person oder Sache an den eigentlich Berechtigten, namentlich nach Wegfall eines anderen Rechts" (I:273).

guarantee," were actually prevented from leaving. They complain of being "held by their hem" (*sikki D ka'ulum*) by a creditor who, according to EL 238:5f., will only "release" (*waššurum*) them if a guarantor has been provided (*ša qātātim šazzuzum*).

While in nearly all cases G's obligation is to make D available for payment (and if he fails, to pay for him), EL 238 is an exception. Two representatives of C, after D has provided a guarantor, address D as follows (lines 10–20):

> He (the guarantor to be appointed) shall not be answerable to us for the silver (*ana kaspim lā eppalniāti*), he shall be answerable to us (only) for bringing you back, so that we can have you transferred here in accordance with the verdict of *kārum* Kanish. Even if you wish to pay us silver or gold, we will not take it, we will bring you to court (*niraddeka*).

As stated above, I see no reason to consider *ša qātātim* a specific term for "Gestellungsbürgschaft," but this role may be fulfilled by the verb *tadānum*, "to give, to hand over," with the creditor as subject. "To hand over a debtor to a guarantor" is more comprehensive and concrete than "to make a guarantor pay for the debtor"; it indicates that the guarantor acquires a grip on the debtor, hence the use in O 3684 of "entrusting (*paqādum*) the debtor to a guarantor." This makes the expression as a whole suitable for "Gestellungsbürgschaft," which implies that the guarantor has power over the debtor and acts in the interest of the creditor, who accordingly is the subject of the action.

2.2. *Paying for the debtor*

Most texts mentioned thus far state that the guarantor, if he fails to meet his obligation as "Gestellungsbürge" has to pay D's debt. Some do it by quoting the short dialogue between creditor and guarantor, in which the latter accepts his liability: "I will pay" (EL 306:13; kt a/k 300; kt 89/k 352), "I will be responsible to you (for the debt)" (O 3684:26).

Describing the liability of the debtor taken over by the guarantor in some detail—its exact amount, background and written evidence—was useful in order to prevent later problems. In EL 306 the debt is specified as a sum of silver as recorded in a "valid deed (deposition) of my witnesses," in kt a/k 300 a large amount of copper, qualified as "a balancing payment owed at 60% interest," in TPK

1, 171 also "copper plus interest on it, according to a valid deed," and in ICK 1, 86+ a large amount of silver "which D's father E. owed to my grandfather L." Kt 89/k 419 registers "ten pounds of silver with its interest, on the basis of a valid deed, which he (D) owed in the City to my father and which now belongs to me, my mother and my sister on the basis of my father's last will." In kt 89/k 352 the guarantor has to pay "in accordance with the later verdict of the *kārum* and separately a fine of 4 pounds of silver," and in O 3684 "45 shekels of silver or what has been purchased for it, owed for five years, both earlier and later items."

While we do not know whether every guarantor, when not bound by a contract as discussed under a), had the duties of a "Gestellungsbürge," it is clear that paying for the defaulting debtor was a general liability. There is ample evidence for the fact that guarantors did pay for debtors, especially from letters and in records which deal with attempts to get their money back (the guarantor's regress on the debtor) and mention problems concerning the transfer of the debt-note and the payment of interest due; see below II.3. An interesting case is that of a son-in-law who agreed (in the framework of the marriage contract?) to act as guarantor for a debt of his father-in-law and actually paid for him. This is clear from the receipt issued by the latter, which states that the debt-note in which the name of the guarantor was registered was now invalid, apparently because it had not been returned and hence could not be cancelled.[50]

The obligation of subsidiary payment is also clear from occasional variations in the description of the same debt. In a number of cases it is stated—presumably from the point of view of the creditor—that debtor and guarantor are jointly liable for the debt (see below IV.1),[51] and when the clause of joint liability is absent, one of the two debtors may figure as guarantor.[52] In the file consisting of EL 331–333 (with BIN 6, 35) all three descriptions are used of the same liability: two debtors, joint liability, and debtor with guarantor. While this variation is understandable, because the guarantor had to pay for the defaulting debtor and was *de facto* an accessory debtor, it did not mean that the distinction between the two was completely blurred. Some contracts, with joint liability, explicitly state who is debtor and

[50] See for this case Veenhof 1997c.
[51] EL 226:34–44, BIN 4, 4:12ff., kt 87/k 293, kt 91/k 125, and BIN 6, 238.
[52] CCTMMA I, 84a:15f., 25ff.; EL 321 compared with the letter KTH 15:6f.

who guarantor, while others specify that the debtor and not the guarantor was the one who had acquired the sum borrowed.[53] But for the creditor this may have made little difference, since he could get his money back from both.

This variation also reflects the flexibility of the Assyrian traders for whom contracts and legal rules were instruments to promote their commercial interests, not only to protect their claims, but also to secure the best results. As an example, which calls our attention to the functionality of legal constructions, I refer to the letter TC 3, 110, which I have recently analysed in detail.[54] It shows how a trader, registered as guarantor for a colleague when they (*sic*) borrowed copper, and apparently having paid for him, subsequently decided that it would better to record that they were joint debtors ("the debt is our debt and not that of you alone"). Still later he changed his mind and wrote a tablet which stipulated that his former co-debtor "would enjoy half of the profit and would be responsible for half of the losses," thereby turning their relationship into one of a risk-sharing commercial partnership.

2.3. *Other duties*

There are a few occurrences of guarantors mentioned in connection with a sale. In ICK 1, 19,[55] a woman and her daughter as guarantors have to protect the lady who buys a slave-girl against vindication; they have to "clear" her and if they fail to do so they must pay more than twice the sale price and can "take the girl along."[56] A perhaps similar case is TPK 1, 157, where L, "our guarantor" (*bēl qātātini*) has to clear the buyer if the house sold is vindicated. In both cases the presence of a guarantor probably implies an earlier forced sale by a defaulting debtor and where normally the original

[53] Kt 87/k 293 (courtesy Kawasaki): Two debtors, jointly liable, but "the silver has been taken in the name of D_1, D_2 is guarantor"; similarly kt 91/k 135: debt of D., Š. is guarantor, jointly liable, but "Š. did not take anything, D. has to pay it (back)," and BIN 6, 238: Debt of D_1 and D_2, "D_1 took their silver, D_2 is guarantor."

[54] Veenhof 1999a: 79f.

[55] Edited as Kienast 1984: no. 28.

[56] This final clause suggests the possibility of redemption, at a higher price; normally one would expect those vindicating the slave to take her along if the claim was not refuted, not the failing guarantors!

owner has to protect the new one after a second sale, the guarantor now has this duty.

2.4. *The meaning of ana ša qātātim tadānum*

The meaning and implications of this expression, rendered by "to give a debtor for guarantee," is not clear and two questions can be raised. The first is as to procedure, since at times either D or G seems to be absent or passive, but D can also raise protest or appeal to a court. The second is whether C tries to obtain security from a guarantor already registered in the debt-note (hence when the debt was contracted, comparable to the Roman *fideiussor*), or one only found when the debtor threatened to default (comparable to the Roman *vindex*)? Or, to put it differently, was a "sleeping" guarantor/*fideiussor* activated by a formal, witnessed procedure, whereby the debtor was "given to him" and he had accepted his liability as stated by the creditor? Or was it problems with the debtor that motivated the creditor to find and enlist a guarantor/*vindex*, whose availability and obligations had accordingly to be agreed on and recorded in a contract?

Contracts of the first type (see II.2.1), which record that a debtor is "given for guarantee," always mention C, D and G by name and it seems likely that all three were present, although only EL 306 has D speaking. Records of the second type reveal more variation: witnesses may state that they had been seized by C against G (O 3684, TPK 1, 171) or against D (ICK 1, 86+, EL 238) and both may record what D said in reaction (TPK 1, 171, ICK 1, 86+) or ignore him (O 3684). In TPK 1, 171 G does not seem to answer C, but D addresses C, who answers him;[57] in EL 238 C's request of guarantee is answered by D himself, who supplies (*šazzuzum*) Š. as guarantor.

We can imagine two different situations. In the case of debt not secured by a guarantor, the alarmed C summons D to demand security, which is the scenario of EL 238, where D himself supplies a guarantor. If a guarantor was already available, either on the basis of the original debt-note or because he had been found recently, C would summon him, as recorded in the depositions O 3684 and TPK 1, 171, where the witnesses state that C had seized them against

[57] Due to damage these words of D and C are not clear.

G. C then made a contract with him, as recorded in the texts of type 1, where the acceptance of his liability by G is always recorded. ICK 1, 86+, where C summons D before witnesses, "hands him over for guarantee" and addresses the guarantor in direct speech, after which D raises protest, presents a problem, because G remains anonymous and, more important, his acceptance of his liability is missing. Either the formulation is for the account of the witnesses, who present the confrontation as essentially one between C and D, since its main focus is D's protest against C's action and the claim on which it is based.[58] Or the deposition reports on a later confrontation between G and C, where C's earlier seizure of D and his attempt to "hand him over for guarantee" are mentioned as facts in the past ("C had given D for guarantee and said to his guarantor . . ."); the new fact is D's protest and appeal to the *kārum*, which may have made G's name and answer irrelevant. The first solution seems more likely to me.

Another problem is that according to the records of contracts between C and G, D occasionally speaks up to fight C's claim. One would expect C's action of "giving D for guarantee" to take place only in cases where C's claim was clear and provable, as suggested by the strictures of a creditor who admits "having been afraid to hand over D for guarantee, since I did not have my witnesses at hand" (CCT 2, 14:8–13). But in EL 306, as in ICK 1, 86+, D fights the claim and this is also reported in kt 89/k 419. According to this draft, quoted under II.2.1, C had earlier on summoned D, who had denied the claim and requested proof. C, however, pressed on and must have decided to try "to hand him over for guarantee" and the long description of the nature of the debt, given in the words (to be) spoken to the guarantor, may be understood as explanation and proof of his claim. C's action here should thus have resulted in a contract of type one, where he tried to kill two birds with one stone: silencing D's protests[59] and obtaining security.

The question whether the guarantor to whom D was given was

[58] The claim is mentioned only indirectly, by quoting the words addressed by C to G. D objects to what C tries to do, because the *kārum* had granted him a respite of six months to check C's claim against written evidence, and C's action makes him lose precious time ("my term is running out," *ūmū'a imallû*, line 26).

[59] Perhaps by bringing proof, since the testamentary dispositions of his father to which he refers normally would have been recorded in writing, before witnesses and testamentary executors.

one already registered in the debt-note or one who only became it through a contract of type one, is not easy to answer. In the absence of clear indications to the contrary I favour the interpretation suggested by EL 238 and assume that the contracts we have (and those reported on in depositions) record a new initiative of the creditor to obtain security, because he foresaw problems with a debtor about to leave and/or default. Merely activating a "sleeping" guarantor, already registered in the debt-note, would not have needed such a formal contract. People "registered as guarantor" according to letters and judicial records never mention that they subsequently were (had to be) summoned by the creditor in order to make them meet their liability. The rarety of guarantors registered in debt-notes correlates well with the necessity of contracting them later, when problems arose.

This also fits the picture of the letters which mention the "giving of a debtor for guarantee." They reflect a variety of situations, which are more complicated than that of involving a guarantor on the basis of an existing debt-note. In TC 3, 28 a trader who asks his agent(?) A. for silver entrusted to him, is told to go to Kanish where it is and to talk (negotiate) with P.; refusing to do so he now "holds A. by his hem and tries to hand him over for guarantee." The writer of KTS 38a gives instructions to do the same, if a certain debtor refuses to pay, but it clearly is an *ad hoc* and presumably temporary measure, because he adds "until I myself arrive." This must also be the case in the letter VAS 26, 37, where a trader, about to arrive in order to clear accounts with the writer, should be detained and not allowed to leave on a business trip without guarantee, before the writer arrives. In kt n/k 101 (courtesy Çeçen) the creditor who tries to do the same is told that the debtors are only ready to pay him if he presents written evidence of his claim.[60] All these cases report on new, at times unexpected developments, which made creditors try to[61] secure their interests by "handing over the debtors for

[60] The situation is complicated because it is an indirect claim; the person acting does so for two others who owe him silver and who in turn seem to have a claim on the persons held.

[61] This nuance I derive from the frequent use of the iterative or Gtn-stem of the verb "to give" (occasionally also of the verb "to hold," in the parallel expression "to hold by the hem"), which does not refer simply to a repeated action, but to continual attempts to do so; VAS 26, 37:10f. even uses the imperative of the Gtn-stem (*ana ša <qá>-ta-tim itaddinaššu*).

guarantee." They were not prepared to let them go unless security was provided.[62]

The contracts and records of guarantee quoted above support this interpretation in showing that the act of "giving a debtor for guarantee" represents a stage in a running conflict. Some refer to an earlier verdict of the *kārum*, which in EL 238 had authorized the creditor to have his debtor transferred to Kanish for a lawsuit,[63] in kt 89/k 352 had resulted in a fine, while in ICK 1, 86+ the creditor is accused of violating a verdict of the *kārum* which had granted the son of a debtor six months' respite. In EL 238 too, the debtor may have been granted a term for appearing in court and it seems likely that the creditor/plaintiff demands of him security for his timely appearance now that he is about to leave. Kt 89/k 419, where the action of the creditor is linked to the liquidation of a dead trader's assets, reports upon an earlier, apparently unsuccesful attempt of the creditor to force the debtor to pay. ICK 1, 86+, where the original creditor and debtor are dead, the debtor's son, summoned by the creditor's grandson, refers to an earlier lawsuit. In O 3684 the debt is five years old, which makes it unlikely that this is the first attempt to collect it. In EL 306 the creditor does not refer to "my valid tablet" (the original debt-note, where the guarantor might have been registered) as proof of his claim, but to "the valid record of my witnesses" (*ṭuppum ḫarmum ša šībē'a*), hence a (later) deposition, which implies earlier legal action, perhaps resulting in a confirmation of the claim.[64] A special case, finally, is I 478,[65] where a scribe, acting for some local Assyrian authorities, "gave S. to L. for guarantee" with the words: "Herewith I entrust (*paqādum*) the man to you." The guarantor promises to turn S. (who only figures as object and may not have been present) over to the authorities, when a certain I. leaves for Kanish, and is told: "If you fail to do so, you shall pay 53 1/2 pounds of silver, his (I.'s) fine (*arnum*), which the City of Assur had imposed on him." The measure has to make sure that

[62] The debtor in TC 3, 28 asks for help against a creditor who detains him, because "he does not want to be tied down during his journey" and the one in VAS 26, 37 complains that his creditor "refuses to let him go on his journey."

[63] For such actions a plaintiff could make use of the executive power of the *kārum*, even when he undertook them on his own responsibility; see Larsen 1975: 255ff.

[64] Note also that kt 89/k 419 speaks of the debt as "the silver and its interest," which was therefore already overdue—not surprising, since the original debtor had died.

[65] See also Matouš 1976.

the departure of the fined debtor I. is matched by new, local security, in the form of a certain S, whose presence and availability to the local authorities are made the responsibility of the guarantor L, to whom S "is entrusted."[66]

CAD Q 172[67] translates *D ana ša qātātim tadānum* "to make a debtor provide a guarantor," which assigns a rather active role to the debtor. This would fit EL 238, where the dialogue is between C and D, and D himself provides (*šazzuzum*) a guarantor, but here the expression "to hand over for guarantee" is not used! Where it is used, D is never the subject of the verb and even his presence at the transaction is not always certain. Above I have preferred the translation "to hand over D for guarantee" and not "to a guarantor" because there are several examples of the full expression *D ana G ana ša qātātim tadānum*, where the name of the guarantor is known. The undetermined *ša qātātim*, also because of the repetition of the preposition *ana*, is better not taken as apposition, but as prepositional adjunct, "for guarantee."

We may define what happens as a legal action by the creditor in order to secure his debtor's availability on the day of maturity of the debt—in most cases because he fears default by absence—by "entrusting" (I 478) him to a guarantor, who will "hand him over" when payment is due. If, as seems very likely, no guarantor had previously been available, the question is how he was secured. While in EL 238 the creditor's summons makes the debtor himself supply a guarantor, the other texts only show that one is somehow available, not how and by whom he was found, and I have been unable to discover evidence on the relations between C or D and G. The function of a guarantor basically was a double one: he comes to the aid of the debtor (especially by paying for him),[68] but also serves the creditor by making the debtor available and paying for him if he defaults. This second function dominates in our contracts and actually earns him the name "guarantor," since he guarantees C the payment of the debt; to quote Koschaker, he serves as "Exekutionsorgan

[66] We need more information on the relation between the the debtor, his "stand-in," and the guarantor to understand what happens, but from I 445 it is clear that I. and S. worked together.

[67] Possibly at my instigation!

[68] Old Babylonian contracts may state that he "pulls the hand (of the creditor) away" from the debtor.

des Gläubigers" whom he supplies a "Zahlungsgarantie."[69] Could we then consider him a person found (and rewarded?) by the creditor, whom the debtor had to accept as his trustee? That would imply the availability of guarantors of a different kind, ready to assume liability on the basis of an agreement with a creditor, in the knowledge that they enjoyed the right of regress against the debtor, which might offer them certain advantages (exploiting the debtor, repayment of the debt with a surcharge?). They would be comparable to some Old Babylonian capitalists, who exploited debt-slaves taken over from their original creditors. Though perhaps not too far-fetched for the inventive and money-minded Assyrian traders, there is no evidence to support it. More insight into the identity and relations between C, D and G might help.

The guarantor, in order to be able to live up to his obligation of "handing over" an (unwilling?) debtor, had to enjoy certain coercive powers. They are nowhere stated, but implied in EL 238, where the debtor himself agrees to supply a guarantor "who will not fail to hand you over." We may assume that the debtor in the other cases too had to accept the legal power granted to the guarantor, but since none of these contracts was found in its envelope, we have no seal-impressions of the debtors to prove it. There was also another justification for the power of the guarantor: his liability for subsidiary payment must have been the basis for granting him powers similar to those any creditor had over a defaulting debtor, such as distraint or taking a pledge.

3. *Guarantor and Debtor*

Most debtors were members or employees of family firms and mutual guarantee must have been rather common among brothers, sons and business partners. It must have been less common for a defaulting, bad debtor than for somebody well known, who had a temporary cash shortage or had to leave for business reasons some time before his due date and needed to be helped. Further prosopographic studies in archives will probably shed more light on the relations between D and G. In CCT 5, 8a:17ff., a daughter of the deceased Pushuken

[69] Koschaker 1911: 67f.

reminds her brothers in Anatolia that they had registered as guarantors for a debt of thirty pounds of silver of their father.[70] In EL 227:30ff. and kt v/k 156 the debtor's brother is his guarantor, in EL 75 the debtor's wife, in EL 215 a sister and son of the debtor, in EL 226:46f. a member of the same firm, and in kt 91/k 127 and 200[71] a man for his father-in-law. The fact, noted above, that guarantors may appear as co-debtors or be included in the clause of joint liability, also implies a relationship between the two.

3.1. *Risks and protection*

Acting as guarantor for outsiders and strangers was unusual, and even inside the Assyrian community it could entail risks. The addressee of BIN 6, 27 voices concern when he heard that the writer was registering as guarantor: "Must I enter into debt-slavery with somebody?"[72] His fear may have been somewhat exaggerated, but there are several examples of guarantors who could not escape their obligation to pay for an absent or defaulting debtor, even when this created problems for themselves. A well-documented case is that of a guarantor called Dadaja, who had to pay eight pounds of silver for the debtor M. and, having no silver at hand, was forced to take out a loan with a banker (*tamkārum*). The documentation reveals how he obtained a verdict of the City Assembly of Assur, which allowed him "to take M.'s silver wherever it is available" (also that invested in merchandise or assets). Moreover, according to a legal ruling on a stele with Old Assyrian laws (referred to in a letter), he is authorized to charge his debtor interest and compound interest ("interest on interest"), apparently both the interest he was entitled to for the sum he had paid for him and that which he himself had to pay to the money-lender. The case, which I have analysed elsewhere in more detail,[73] is important in showing that verdicts of the City of

[70] An unpublished letter in Ankara, dealing with the financial situation of same family after the death of the father, states: "One mina of silver, for which our father had registered as guarantor of D, has been added to our debt." Refusing to consider a potential liability an actual debt, I take "our debt" as "debt owed to us." Because the father had paid as guarantor, he had the right of regress and his claim was thus an asset inherited by his sons.

[71] Veenhof 1997c.

[72] *miššu ša aštanammeʾu qātātim taltapputu, ana mamman ana wardūtim errab?*

[73] Veenhof 1995a: 1722ff.

Assur were passed and even regulations drafted in order to help unlucky guarantors to get back what they had lost. While the regulation may have applied to all such cases of forced borrowing for the benefit of somebody else, the authorization granted by the verdict, which was therefore the result of a separate decision, may have taken into account specific factors which are not mentioned (we do not have the text of the verdict itself).

Guarantors in turn could protect themselves against risks. From CCT 5, 8a:15ff., mentioned above, we learn that the house in Assur with its furniture served as security for a debt of P., for which his son has registered as guarantor,[74] and the same protection is recorded in the contract kt 91/k 173, where two Assyrians are guarantors for a debt of 11 pounds of silver. Lines 9ff. state: "If the silver is collected to the debit of (*iṣṣēr*) the guarantors, the debtor's house in Assur serves as pledge (*erubbātum*) for the silver."[75] Something similar may be the case in TPK 1, 170, where the question is asked whether a packet of meteoric iron, called "one pledge with my seals," has been given to any guarantors (*mamman bēlū qātātim*). An interesting but not unique case is reported in the letter TC 3, 67,[76] where the trader E. writes that he has registered as guarantor of his agent K. at a banker ("merchant's house"), where the latter had taken out a loan of thirty pounds of silver. Apparently K. was in financial difficulties, perhaps in fact because of debts to E., and to overcome them he had (been allowed to) borrow money for a business trip, if E. served as guarantor. E., aware of his risk and at the same time knowing that a profit realized by K. would enable the latter to pay off (part of) his debts, took measures to check and control K's commercial activities. He established a claim ("laid his hand") on the silver shipped to Assur and asked his representatives in Assur to do the same, once the merchandise bought for it was shipped back to Anatolia. And there are other, similar cases.

---

[74] Read lines 15ff. *bēt Aššur ú ú-/* [16] *tù-up-tù-šu* [17] [erasure] *ana 30 mana* [18] [*š*]*a qātātišu* [19] [*n*]*alputātini*. A verb is missing, since the next line has to be read: [*a-w*]*a-tum i-za-ku-wa*?. "When the affair is cleared up. . . ."

[75] This device is already attested during the Ur III period. According to Falkenstein 1956–7: no. 195 a slave-girl had been pledged to a guarantor, who had problems in actually acquiring her after he had paid on behalf of the debtor.

[76] Edited Larsen 1967: 10, type 2:1.

3.2. *Regress*

Guarantors who paid for a debtor enjoyed the right of regress, and several records deal with this issue. Efforts to indemnify oneself and get the money back, referred to as "suing" (*še'āum*) the debtor, could be based on the law and supported by verdicts of the City (see the previous paragraph on Dadaja). If G paid C, the latter had to give him the original debt-note, to serve as a kind of receipt and as proof of his claim on D. The records documenting this, as usual, deal with problems and complications.

Uncertainty about the payment by D is reflected in Kennedy-Garelli 1960: no. 5, an arrangement between the three guarantors (G_{1-3}) concerning a debt of 5 2/3 pounds of silver, initiated by G_2, who has so far received nothing back:

> Of this silver G_2 did not receive anything. If G_1 and G_3 still have to sue him (D), G_2 will sue him together with them for his share. If G_1 and G_3 already have been satisfied (by D) with this silver for which the three of us have registered as G's, G_2 also is (counts as) satisfied.

Guarantors probably could be paid back in various ways, usually in silver, but in the context of the trade also by balancing assets and debts or by giving merchandise. An interesting case is recorded in EL 215, where an Assyrian D owes 15 shekels of silver to an Anatolian C, whereby C's sister figures as G. Unable to pay silver, D gives a plot of land "instead of the 15 shekels of silver" to C and G together. Perhaps the Assyrian D had been married to C's sister, both of whom are now paid in kind.

Guarantors apparently were also liable for the normal or default interest if D could not pay. In an unpublished letter we read: "As for the 40 pounds of silver for which D has become indebted to C, the interest on which, 21 5/6 pounds of silver, we as D's guarantors promised (verb *apālum*)—C has been satisfied with that silver." A related letter mentions that payment had taken place and was recorded in the presence of two witnesses in two copies, perhaps because there were more G's or because both the G's and D were entitled to a copy. In the letter CCT 5, 8a:24ff., mentioned before, a sister tells her brother that "7 1/2 pounds of silver have been paid from your silver as interest on 30 pounds of silver for which you are registered as guarantor."

Payment of interest is also mentioned in some of the contracts whereby a debtor "was given for guarantee" (see above II.3.1) and it is an issue in TPK 1, 166, which reports a discussion between P. and his guarantor S., but is difficult to understand. When S advises P. to take (borrow?) a sum of silver, the latter has serious doubts: "Which silver then should I take? One might charge me interest where you are registered as my guarantor and should I then take (borrow?) silver?" S. answers: "Where you have received it in trust, you will add 20% interest, (but) where I have entrusted it (merchandise belonging to P., handled by S, line 9) they will add for you 30% interest." The meaning of these words perhaps is that interest charged for money received in trust (*qīptum*) from a money-lender and secured by a guarantor is less than a trader can charge himself when he sells goods on credit via an agent.

The receipt kt 91/k 127,[77] which records that D paid back to G, concerns "the silver and the interest on it": either interest due to G because D was late in paying him back, or rather interest due to C, since the involvment of a guarantor implies payment problems of D (hence delay and default interest, which is a common feature in Old Assyrian debt-notes).[78] In AKT 3, 59 a creditor urges his debtor to pay the remainder of his debt, secured by a guarantor; if not, he will charge interest[79] and collect it "in accordance with the tablet where I. is registered as your guarantor." This probably means that he will collect it from the guarantor, who of course will indemnify himself at the expense of the debtor.

The law authorized a G who had to borrow in order to meet his obligation the right to charge D "interest and interest on interest" to cover the extra costs of the loan he had contracted with a money-lender (see above under II.3.1).

3.3. *The debt-note*

The rule was that when a debt was paid, C would return the debt-note to D; if G paid he would obtain it to return it to D when he was paid back. The unpublished letter kt 89/k 231 (courtesy Kawasaki) connects payment to G with the release of the debt-note: "Sell here the full amount (as much as is needed to pay the debt?) of mete-

[77] Veenhof 1997c: 362f.

[78] See for problems concerning interest to be paid for a debt secured by a guarantor also AKT 2, 31.

[79] Lines 13ff. perhaps: "I will certainly not [waive]? the interest."

oric iron for silver and give the silver to A., so that we can give it to our guarantors (*bēlū qātātini*) and they may give up (*waššurum*) the debt-note which I. and his partners (the D's) have validated." But debt-notes could get lost, which is the issue of Kennedy-Garelli 1960: no. 1, a deposition by G:

> As for the five pounds of silver which D owes to C and for which I am guarantor, when I asked him (C) for the debt-note he said: "It is lost!" I (G) am the one who has paid (with emphasis, *anāku šaqqulāku*). Should the tablet of the five pounds of silver, D's debt, turn up, it is invalid.

G needs the tablet as proof of payment and as evidence of his claim on D, who in turn would ask him for it if he repaid. In the absence of the tablet he has this statement of the facts recorded before witnesses, and the clause on the invalidity of the tablet has to protect G and in due time D.

The whereabouts of a debt-note for 15 pounds of silver, owed by D to C and secured by a G, are at stake in CCT 1, 13a. It must have been drawn up in connection with the liquidation of D's assets after his death (which is also the subject of other documents) and records that various persons have seen this tablet "with the seals of D and G in the house of I., among his memoranda and notes which are (now) in the possession of I.'s son P . . ." The fact that this tablet was missing, without having been cancelled, must have been a worry, in particular to the guarantor, the well-known trader Pushuken. The absence of a debt-note is also the reason why kt 91/k 127 (see note 77) records that the guarantor had been paid back by the debtor (his father-in-law) adding, as is usual for Old Assyrian receipts, that it is invalid if it turns up.

III. Pledge

Pledging has been analysed in Kienast 1976 and data on closely related features such as conditional sale, redemption, and acquisition of pledges of defaulting debtors in Kienast 1984: §§ 95–103. A substantial increase of data, thanks to new text editions,[80] allows additions

[80] Occasionally also by improved readings of old texts, e.g. EL 190:6ff. (see note 90) and 179 (note 90).

and corrections. I will more or less follow the line of Kienast's analysis, referring to it by paragraph number.

1. *Terminology*

1.1. *šapartum*

The main terms are *šapartum* (also attested in Babylonia and Assyria) and *erubbātum*. *šapartum* (henceforth *š*., Kienast 1976: §§ 3–5), according to Kienast "reines Fahrnispfand," hence movable objects, especially utensils, household goods, slaves, and (among Assyrians) also gold and copper. It is preferred in Anatolian contracts, where it is even used for houses (BIN 6, 236) and persons (EL 15) and hence figures as a term for "Pfand schlechthin." Derivation from the verb *šapārum* is of course correct,[81] but this verb is never used for sending goods, only for sending persons and (via them) messages. Starting from its basic meaning, "to manage (by order, letter), administer, direct" (*šāpirum* 'manager, boss'), we can define a pledge as something over which the creditor has power of disposition. There is hence no *a priori* reason to limit its use to movable objects (Germ. *Fahrnispfand, Sendepfand*) and the word is indeed also used of real estate in the Middle and neo-Assyrian periods. But Kienast is correct in observing that in Assyrian documents it is never used of real estate and persons and hence does not occur in Assyrian debt-notes. When a man seized for a debt of 20 shekels of silver protests because he had given a silver cup weighing 22 1/2 shekels of silver as *šapartu*-pledge, the writer of TPK 1, 21 blames his addressee for not having registered the cup as pledge in his document.

1.2. *erubbātum and erābum*

This term (Kienast 1976: § 6) is used in Assyrian and Anatolian contracts for persons and real estate and seems to refer to a contractually agreed pledge. It is registered in a number of debt-notes and we have written contracts with clauses on the return and the release of such pledges. In one instance a tablet recording a debt-claim of

---

[81] Once we meet the masc. plural *šaprāni* (AKT 2, 18:8) which, if not a scribal error, has one parallel in neo-Assyrian.

20 pounds of wool(!) is called *erubbātum*.[82] The noun seems to be typically Old Assyrian, but there is one occurrence in a text from Northern Babylonia (Tell Harmal), where it is used of a house.[83] Derivation from the verb *erābum*, "to enter" (into the house/power of the creditor), widely used for pledges,[84] suggests that its use for pledged real estate (houses) may be secondary, which makes it understandable that Anatolian documents occasionally use *šapartum* for them. The etymology suggests that C acquired possession of the pledge until the debt was paid, but according to Kienast (§ 11ff.) it was rather a "Sicherheitspfand." We will address this issue in III.3.

The verb *erābum*, "to enter (as pledge)," is attested in EL 86 (the defaulting D and his wife will "enter C's house"), kt c/k 1340[85] (an Anatolian family enters the house of a man who provided for them), BIN 6, 27:10f. (see above II.3.1), and kt a/k 447a, where D's sons make two slaves "enter" with the creditor for (*ana*) a large amount of copper, which probably implies (antichretic) service.[86] The D-stem[87] occurs in TPK 1, 106:2' and 194:13ff., where houses are pledges,[88] and in EL 2:13, where a person is the object.[89] In TPK 1, 194 the pledged house "is held with the silver" (*bētū išti kaspim uktallū*) until the Ds pay, whereupon "they take the house (back)."

The number of references for *erubbātum* in debt-notes has increased since Kienast § 6.[90] Alongside simple *erubbātum*, "x is pledge," and neutral *erubbātūšu*, "x is his (C's) pledge," we have also more occurrences of *erubbātū'a*, "x is my pledge," in debt-notes which otherwise

---

[82] "Neukirch Letter," quoted EL I p. 231 note d.

[83] IM 63153, for a debt of half a pound of silver (interest 30% per year, the typical Old Assyrian rate!). Cf also the Hebrew nouns *ʿērābōn* and *ʿ^arubbā*, Ugaritic *ʿrbn*, and Greek *arrabōn*, presumably (indirect) loans.

[84] Note its use in texts from Alalakh (82:11f., 83:5f., 84:4f.: *ana* ŠU.DU$_8$.A *ana C erēbum*).

[85] Balkan 1974: 30 note 12: a couple with their daughter *ana bēt U. ērubū uballissunu*.

[86] Texts mentioned in EL I p. 177 note b, under "Ausfallbürgschaft," are not relevant, since C and not D is the subject of "to enter with a trader/banker." See below IV.2.

[87] The use of the D-stem suggests a specific, technical meaning, otherwise one would have used the causative *šērubum*, "to bring into."

[88] TPK 1, 106: [D a house] *ana C ú-ri-bu*; 194: for a silver debt *bēt A. ú-ri-bu*.

[89] Emending *ú-ru-bu-šu*, "they shall (not) pledge him," into *ú-<šé>-ru-bu-šu*, "they shall bring him into," is unlikely since this last form cannot be used in an absolute sense.

[90] Note EL 190 6ff., where two houses and two slave-girls are designated as "his pledges" (*e*!*-ru-ba*!*-tù-šu*).

use the objective third person style.[91] This suggests that it is a literal quotation of the words by means of which C claimed the pledge, similar to the use of the first person of the verbs *ṣabātum* and *dagālum*, mentioned under c), and in "I will enter a banker's house," discussed under IV.2.

Contrary to Hirsch 1969, *mazzāzum* is not a pledge, but presumably a metal statuette, which could be pledged;[92] *mazzazānum* is not used in Old Assyrian. Equally uncertain is *maškanum*, which probably designates a deposit, which occasionally may have served as security; as such we find merchandise (CCT 5, 2a:21ff.; TC 3, 63:29ff.) and tablets (kt k/k 16, courtesy K. Hecker).

1.3. *Some verbs*

Several other verbs occur in texts which mention sureties for C.

1) *ṣabātum*, "to seize," in the sense of bringing under one's power. In EL 91, if a debt of 22 1/2 shekels of silver is not paid in time, C will seize Z. (one of the debtors) and the woman N. EL 292 (above under III.1.1) shows that *ṣabātum* does not necessarily mean high-handed action such as distraint; it can be used of a mother who wants to get back her daughter sold into debt-slavery (Kienast 1984: text no. 10:5). If the creditor's right to "seize" an object or person belonging to a defaulting debtor is stipulated in the debt-note (EL 91), pledging is meant, not distraint, which is never contractual. Without context we cannot decide which of the two is as stake, as is the case in AKT 2, 32, where "one seized 5 pounds of silver, the house of his father-in-law and his wife" for a substantial silver debt. Note that the tablet of EL 91 has C speaking in the first person (*aṣabbat*), while the envelope uses the third person (*iṣabbat*).

2) *qātam šakānum ina*, "to lay hands on," in the sense of "to establish/have a claim on," frequent in commercial contexts, where traders obtain security or establish a claim by "laying their hands on" merchandise. Attested in TPK 1, 100 (case of the tablet kt 91/k 107), where for a debt of two pounds of silver "C's hand rests on" (*qāti C šaknat*) a mule and 125 fleeces, in EL 226:1f., where for a silver debt C's hand "rests on" a lot of textiles, and in OIP 27, 59:30,

[91] AKT 1, 44, KKS 15, Larsen-Moller 1991: 230 no. 3 line 13; TC 3, 232; 222; kt 86/k 202.

[92] See Dercksen 1997: 84f.

where "C's hand rests on W.," the wife of D (damaged duplicate EL 24). In the last text, a debt-note, it clearly means that the person/object mentioned is a hypothecary pledge.

3) *dagālum*, "to look at," occurs in debt-notes usually (not in EL 92) in the first person singular with C as subject and the pledge as object; see below III.2, table 2, notes h-j, kt d/k 43:18 (object: the debtor's house), and three unpublished occurrences all in the first person singular. The verb is usually translated as "to own,"[93] but it is also used as "to have a claim on," especially in some unpublished debt-notes, where "for the silver (owed) the creditor looks at whichever (of the debtors) is solvent and available" (*ana kaspim šalmam u kīnam idaggal*). While both meanings are conceivable with pledges, the verb cannot be taken as evidence of a possessory pledge, as Kienast 1976: par. 18 does. As will be argued below (III.3 end) it states that the creditor has a claim on, a title to property of the debtor, without indicating how this claim has been or will be realized.

4) *izēzum ana*, "to stand for," used of guarantors who "stand in" for a debtor or creditor (see above II.1), but when the subject is impersonal it may denote a pledge as security. In EL 217:24ff. a debtor's house, slave-girl, slave, furniture and whatever he owns "stand for this silver" (*ana kaspim annîm izzaz*).

5) *ka'ulum* is frequent in connection with pledges, to express the idea that the creditor "holds" the pledge, or that "the pledge is held" (passive stem; *šapartum* etc. *uktâl*); note the imperative in EL 262:7, when silver and gold are offered as security. It is a common verb, generally used for "detaining," "keeping" persons and objects (merchandise, tablets, etc.), which focuses on the effects and not on the legal basis of the action.[94] Hence, in the absence of the words "as pledge" (*ana šapartim*), it may equally well imply pledging or distraint or simply "retaining, withholding" an object or person and the choice is not always easy.[95] Most people "held" (also "by the hem of their

---

[93] See *CAD* D, 22, c; also in kt 91/k 426: a woman lives in another person's house, but does not own it (*lā tadaggili*).

[94] Note its use in Larsen-Moller 1991: 227, in a debt-note which stipulates interest "if D keeps the silver."

[95] *CAD* K 509ff. complicates matters by listing under c), "to hold valuables as security or for other reasons," both references which add "as pledge" and others which certainly do not imply pledging. Moreover, it adds a separate meaning e), "to hold back, to detain a person or an animal as pledge, security, or for other reasons," which lists a dozen OA references, most of which do not refer to pledging, but also CCT 1, 11a:17, which adds "as pledge," and ICK 1, 61 ("hold the

garment") are no pledges, and letters may report that merchandise is seized and "held" in order to force its owner to meet his obligations. The iterative Dtn-stem[96] occurs in EL 180 and probably means antichretic use of a pledge: L. gives an amount of silver to S. "for holding the storeroom" which she will leave when, at her request, the silver is returned.

6) *šēṣu'um*, lit. "to make go out," "to obtain the release of," like *ka'ulum* has a wide use and is particularly frequent for the release of a debt-note after the debt has been paid, which is similar to the release of a pledge. It is used for the release of a pledge which had "entered" into the power/house of the creditor, with the one who pays (debtor or guarantor) as subject. It is attested in BIN 6, 68:28 of *š.*-pledges held by an Anatolian creditor, but in several cases what is released is not called a pledge, in OIP 27, 12:13 and kt 89/k 313 (a debtor out of the house of his Anatolian' creditor by paying his debt), EL 252:23 (a slave-girl), TC 3, 51:20 (a textile "held" for four shekels of silver"), and AKT 2, 53;18 (a bronze object). This makes it difficult to distinguish between pledging and distraint.

7) *waššurum* denotes the release of an object or person retained or detained by the person who "holds" it. It is frequent in the trade ("release of merchandise" upon payment or when a security is offered), but also occurs with pledges *and* deposits.[97]

8) *rakāsum*, "to bind," is very frequent in the expression that the debt "is bound on/on the person of" (*ina ṣēr/qaqqad . . . rakis*),[98] which turns what is mentioned before *rakis* into a co-debtor or security, a kind of hypothecary pledge (see also below IV.1). Items mentioned in this

slave-girl until I give you your silver," to be connected with EL 252), where pledging is very likely.

[96] *ana kuta'ulim*, also used of a pledged house in kt n/k 1528 (*pace* Kienast 1976: 220 note 10, who assumes a passive stem; not in *CAD* K). Note the use of the iterative stem of the verb "to cultivate" in Middle Assyrian texts (KAJ 13:35 and 21:22) for antichretic used of pledged fields.

[97] See for this verb EL II p. 53 and note the exceptional use of the basic stem in VAS 26, 1:11, with a tablet given in deposit as object.

[98] The preposition *iṣṣēr* can be used with persons and objects, but *qaqqudum*, also current in the expression for joint liability (*ina qaqqad šalmišunu kīnišunu rakis*), originally referred to a person (cf. *ina qaqqidišu u bētišu rakis*, EL 20). *ina qaqqad* subsequently developed into a compound preposition used when persons pledged are followed by inanimate objects, such as houses, and even when no persons at all are listed (kt 89/k 282:15: *i-qaqqad bētišunu u mimma išû rakis*). Note *i-qaqqad šalmišunu bētišunu*, TC 3, 218 alongside *i-qaqqad šalmišunu u kīnišunu i-bētišunu u bābišunu rakis*, AKT 3, 10.

formula are wives, sons, daughters, children (*šerrū*; also "youngsters" *ṣuḫrum*), slaves, slave-girls, houses, fields (kt f/k 171), a gate (*bābum*, AKT 3, 10), other property (*alānu*, EL 188), and "whatever there is" (TC 3, 238; kt 89/k 282). Such a listing at the end of the debt-note is similar and presumably equivalent to an initial statement, in the "debt formula" (*C iṣṣēr D išû*), where D is followed by his family, slaves, house, property, etc., such as in TC 3, 237 and 238 (includes "his oxen"). The same reality is expressed when KTK 95:5–7 writes: "slave-girl(s), slave(s), house, his children and fields are of C," and all these formulations seem to secure the creditor a kind of general lien.

2. *Occurrences and items pledged*

As observed in Kienast 1976 (§ 3), *šapartum* occurs in letters and judicial documents, but not in Assyrian debt-notes, which suggests that this type of pledging was normally effected by oral contract, before witnesses. This explains occasional problems about the identity and status of objects in somebody else's possession, presumably similar to those anticipated in LH 122ff. for deposits. In EL 179 (collated) a disagreement concerning the nature and number of objects handed over as pledges was solved:

> Before these men (seven arbitrators), the *š.*-pledges which I. had put at the disposal of Š. were enumerated: one hammerstone(?), and 6 *qablītu*-objects and 2 cups(?)—these he had put at the disposal of Š. son of A. as pledge for half a pound of silver as interest.[99]

Similar problems are recorded in EL 292.[100] When A. demands the return of household items (*unūtum*) which his wife Z. had given to another couple "for safekeeping" (*ana nabšêm*), i.e. as deposit, the other wife admits having obtained (*ṣabātum*) them, but as pledge,

[99] After cleaning the dirty tablet I could read in lines 9–16: [P]*Ip-qú-um* DUMU *A-bi a-e*[?] [10] [P]*Šu-Anum* DUMU *Ku-da-a* [11] *a-wi-lu-ú a-ni-ú-tum ga-me-er* [12] *a-wa-tim ša Iliš-tikal* [13] [*u*] *Šu-Anim* [14] *maḫar awīlē* [15] *anniūtim ša-áp-ra-tum* [15] *ša I-lí-iš-tí-kal a-na* [16] *Šu-A-nim i-dí-ú-ni i-zi-ik-ra*. That the silver is called *kaspum ša ṣibtim*, "silver as interest" (rather than "silver at interest"), may imply that the pledges had been given to secure the (default?) interest, not the principal.

[100] Now CCT 5, 17a, with its duplicate TC 3, 266.

because Z. had borrowed silver at interest from her. Moreover, she had loaned Z. another sum of silver in exchange for a *š*.-pledge. She is ready to yield the items (*unūtum*) if she is repaid. Z. confirms the latter transaction, secured by a pledge, but denies the existence of the former debt: "I did not put any *unūtum* at your disposal as pledge!." A similar problem[101] is related in VAS 26, 1, where D's representatives paid his debt, obtained his debt-note, and left it for safekeeping (*ana nabšêm ezābum*) with I. Later I. refuses to relinquish it to the debtor, asserting that it was deposited with him as pledge (*ana šapartim iddi'unissu*), which D emphatically denies and tries to prove by means of witnesses.

In Anatolian debt-notes *šapartum* is used for all possible pledges, including houses (BIN 6, 236 and TC 3, 240 + TC 2, 66) and slaves (ICK 2, 116). The variety of items attested as *š*.-pledge both in Anatolian and Assyrian texts has increased since Kienast 1976 and now includes meteoric iron (TPK 1, 160), jewels (a golden pectoral, ICK 1, 190: 28; a ring of *amūtu*-iron, KTK 68), gold (CCT 4, 29b:31f.; kt 89/k 119), golden (statuettes of) gods (kt 92/k 212:5),[102] silver (ICK 1, 171:6f.), tin (VAS 26, 60:14, KTS 13:28), a silver cup (TPK 1, 21a), a hammerstone (CCT 4, 35:13; EL 179:17), various copper and bronze objects (*supannum*, kt 91/k 179; *itqurum*, BIN 6, 90:18; *šugarria'um*, TC 2, 61:3), household objects (*unūtum*, EL 292, KTS 47c:20, CCT 3, 42b:16), wool and a saddle rug (ICK 1, 37b:17).

Not mentioned by Kienast, but important in the context of Old Assyrian trade, is the use as pledges of "valid tablets," usually debt-notes which embody a claim, which their indebted owner may offer to his creditor as pledge. Examples are AKT 3, 98:27f., CCT 3, 42b:6f., VAS 26, 1:11f. (pledge or deposit), kt 92/k 179:26f. (a tablet of 34 1/2 pounds of tin), BIN 4, 112 (= EL 320 + CCT 6, 17a; debt-notes called *iṣurtum*, which the *kārum* had made available as pledge),[103] kt 92/k 212:6f. (a debt-note of 100 shekels of silver), and the unpublished letter quoted in EL p. 231 footnote d, which reports on the

[101] Also for us, in less explicit contexts, because for both actions the same verbs, "to give," "to put at the disposal of" (*nadā'um*), and "to leave to" (*ezābum*) can be used.

[102] Written DINGIR-*li ša ḫurāṣim*, and in the parallel memorandum kt 92/k 206:12ff. *20 ilū munūtam ša ḫurāṣim*.

[103] See for this text and *iṣurtum*, Veenhof 1995c: 324f., and for tablets treated as assets ("Aktivwerte") already EL II p. 53.

transfer of "a valid tablet of 20 pounds of wool(!), being the debt of P., pledge of the creditor" (*erubbāt tamkārim*).

Even more interesting are indications that debt-notes could be drawn up for the sole purpose of serving as security or pledge for a creditor. This possibility was first suggested by EL in their comments on text 102[104] and I found new evidence of it in AKT 3, 104. Here the debtor S. hands over to his creditor a debt-note of his brother for exactly the same amount as his own debt, due to an anonymous creditor (*tamkārum*), which is deposited as security in a sealed packet, in the house of a third person. The letter was written because S. had paid and is now entitled to receive the pledged tablet back.[105] The question how a creditor could use pledged debt-notes is treated in 3.4 below.

Pledges played a role in commercial traffic, but commercial debts secured by an *erubbatu*-pledge are not very numerous and the debt-notes in which they occur do not specify the reasons for requiring them. We can only go by the names of the debtors (Assyrians or Anatolians, men or women) and the size of the debt. In KTH 13 the instruction is given to sell imported textiles to the local palace only for cash, "do not give them (at credit), not even if they offer a *š.*-pledge," and when imported tin is deposited as *š.*-pledge, the writer of VAS 26, 60 is warned: "your tin should not be tied up!" (lines 14f.). There were other methods of securing commercial debts and the best attested one is that of "laying one's hand on" assets of the debtor, as is recorded in the memorandum EL 226:1f. for a commercial debt of 5 pounds of silver. This is a formal act, performed publicly, before witnesses ("in the city gate," according to TC 3, 69:27f.), and the claim thus established prevents others from seizing the assets in question.

---

[104] The contract mentions the possibility that the creditor "satisfies himself" for a debt of 14 pounds of good copper "by means of an outstanding claim" of his debtor. Since the possibility of that claim yielding more or less than his debt is not considered (as it is in EL 297, in connection with the sale of pledged slaves), the size of his debt may have equalled the value of the outstanding claim and EL 102 have been drawn up for the purpose. Note, however, that nothing is said about returning the ceded debt-note "if he has not received anything" and that the amount of the debt is rather small (ca. 10 shekels of silver), which may have suggested an "easy" solution.

[105] See Veenhof 1997a: 359.

Table 1. Debt-notes registering an *erubbātu*-pledge

text	*cred.*	*debtor*	*debt in silver*	*term in weeks*	*interest d(efault)*	*pledge*	*other data*
AKT 1,44	Ass.	Ass.	20 sh.	—	30 %	woman +daughter	extra security[a]
EL 190	Ass.	Ass.	102?	—	—	2 houses, 2 slaves	guarantor?[b]
EL 227:27f.	Ass.[c]	Ass.	40	—	30 %	slave-girl	guarantor
I 475	Ass.	Ass.	120	13 w.	—	wife, slave, house	extra security[d]
KKS 15	Ass.	Ass.[e]	20	—	60 %	slave-girl	
FT 3[106]	Ass.	Ass.	60[f]	—	—	slave-girl, slave	
TC 3, 222	Ass.	Anat.[g]	20	—	120 %	house	
TC 3, 232	Ass.[h]	Ass.	180	6 w	30 % d.	2 women +house	guarantor
TC 3, 233	Ass.	Ass.	91 1/2	7 w.	30 % d.	slave	
kt n/k 1716	Ass.	Anat.	45	52 w.	30 % d.	slaves, sister, house	
kt 86/k 202	Ass.	Ass.	36	—	30 %	slave	joint liability
kt 89/k 312	Anat.	Anat.	30	—	—	person[i]	redemption
kt 91/k 1	Anat.	Anat.	11 2/3	?[j]	50 % d.	slave-girl	joint liability
kt 92/k 1038	Anat.	Anat.	30	—	120 %	woman + *ṣuḫrum*	

[a] "Until he satisfies me nobody shall approach them" (the pledged women; lines 9–11).
[b] Not very clear: "Silver which from C D took; D took the silver, P. (a guarantor?) is not involved" (*lā ṭaḫḫu*), but the pledges are "of (belonging to or supplied by?) P."
[c] C = *tamkārum*, guarantor is D's brother.
[d] If D defaults C can borrow the silver at D's expense with a merchant.
[e] D = two Assyrian women.
[f] 30 shekels *be'ūlātum* and 30 shekels cash.
[g] D = ZI-*a*, Anat. woman?
[h] C = *tamkārum*.
[i] Ḫamarši, man or woman?
[j] The festival of Ana.

Only fourteen debt-notes record such a pledge and the debts secured by it in general are not very big. There are only four of more than one pound of silver and none is a substantial commercial debt in the range of five to thirty pounds of silver, the result of credit sale and consignment to agents. For lack of background information we do not know why these debts were secured by pledging, but several clearly were considered risky, since they register additional security such as a guarantor, joint liability, or borrowing by the creditor (note

[106] Larsen-Moller 1991: 230 no. 3.

d). The five cases of a pledge for debts of Anatolians also fit this pattern and three of them also stipulate a much higher (default) interest, which is also the case in KKS 15, with two Assyrian women as debtors. I also note that nine of these debts have no payment term, that four stipulate no interest at all, six interest right from the beginning, and four default interest, which is therefore not incompatible with security by pledging. When neither a term of payment nor interest is stipulated, the pledge might well have been in the hands of the creditor, perhaps for antichretic use, but this is only certain for kt 89/k 312, where the debtor, when she pays the debt, "will take along" (*itarru*; hence, get back) the pledge. The extra security stipulated in AKT 1, 44, which "reserves" the pledge for the creditor, must have been useful whether the pledges were in the possession of the creditor or not (yet).

The few occurrences of *erubbātum* outside debt-notes offer the following picture: KTS 2, 9: two (expensive) houses in Assur pledged for a debt of 49 pounds of silver; kt 92/k 173: a house in Assur as hypothecary pledge for two guarantors "if the (11 pounds of) silver is collected" at their expense; Neukirch letter (EL I p. 231 note d): transfer of a debt-note for 20 pounds of wool(!), called *erubbāt tamkārim*, "pledge of (accorded to) the creditor." While the monetary value of the last debt is not high (perhaps between 5 and 10 shekels of silver), the first two are substantial commercial debts and they fit the pattern of using expensive houses in Assur as security.

Evidence for *šapartu*-pledges is more extensive and more varied than that for *erubbātu*-pledges, especially in letters and judicial records, but occurrences in debt-notes, as pointed out by Kienast 1976: § 3, are rare. In the following table I add to debt-notes mentioning *šapartu*-pledges others where pledging is stated in a different way.

Table 2. Debt-notes registering *šapartu*- and other pledges

text	*cred.*	*debtor f(amily)*	*debt in silver*	*term*	*interest*	*pledge š(apartum)*[a]	*other data*
EL 15	Anat.	Anat. f.	15 sh. +grain	summer	—	*š.* daughter	joint liability
TC 3, 240	Anat.	[f]Anat.	18 sh.	sowing	—	*š.* house[b]	
BIN 6, 236	Anat.	Anat	24 3/4 sh.	—	—	*š.* house	
kt 92/k 178	Ass.	Ass. f.	30 sh.	—	30%	*š.* tablet	joint liability[c]
kt 92/k 228	[...]	2 [f]Anat.	[ ]	1 month	x%	*š.* [ ]?	joint liability[d]

table cont.

text	*cred.*	*debtor f(amily)*	*debt in silver*	*term*	*interest*	*pledge š(apartum)*[a]	*other data*
kt m/k 118	Ass.	Ass.	15 sh.	—	40%	*š. supannum*	
kt v/k 171	Ass.	Anat.	75 sh.	—	10%	house[e]	
kt 87/k 96	Ass.	Anat.	72 sh.	—	grain	house, fields[f]	
TPK 1, 88	Ass.	3 Ass.	12 sh.	—	—	house[g]	
AKT 1, 45	fAnat.?	fAss.	9 sh.	harvest	—	1 person[h]	
EL 14	Ass.	Anat.	60 sh.	x months	—	house, wife, children[i]	
EL 92	Anat.	Anat.	90 sh.	—	—	house + 3 persons[j]	
EL 24	Ass.	Ass. f.	20 sh.	—	30%	wife of D[k]	
EL 91	3 Anat.	Anat.?	22 1/2 sh.	autumn	—	2 persons[l]	
kt 87/k 104	Ass.	2 Ass.	9 sh.	—	—	1 person[m]	
EL 86	Anat.	Anat. f.	27 sh.	summer	—	2 debtors[n]	

[a] Expressed by *ana šapartim ka'ulum*, active or passive stem.
[b] "When she pays the silver they (3 creditors) will leave the house."
[c] Memorandum, creditor *tamkārum*, debtors I., fA.$_1$ and 2 sons of A.$_2$; B. "assisted the debtors."
Pledge is a debt-note for approx. 34 1/2 pounds of tin (equivalent to approx. 5 pounds of silver).
[d] Interest 1/2 shekel of silver per month, hence a debt not greater than about 10 shekels; "if they do not pay, the *š.*-pledges will be taken away" (*ittabbalā*).
[e] "If D satisfies (the creditor), D will leave for (i.e. return to) his house (*ana bētišu ittallak*).
[f] Courtesy Hecker; pledges *išti kaspim annîm uktallū.*
[g] Pledge is "the house held by the silver" (*išti kaspim bētū uktallū*); "if they chase him (C) away (*ṭarādum*) they will give him back the 12 shekels of silver and he will leave (the house)."
[h] Creditor *Ku-ri-ba*; pledge: "for the silver I 'look at/own' (*adaggal*) I."
[i] "I (C) look at/own (*adaggal*) his house, his wife, his children."
[j] For this silver he (C) looks at/owns (*idaggal*) the house, K., the girl and the slave-girl; who pays the silver to C takes the house."
[k] Debtor is Ass. with Anat. wife fW.; pledge: "C's hand rests on fW." (see duplicate OIP 27,59:30).
[l] Creditor *Ta-ta-a*; "if they do not pay I will seize (*ṣabātum*) Z (third debtor) and fN."
[m] Courtesy Hecker; "if they do not pay they will take along (*tarā'um*) K. instead of their silver."
[n] "If they do not pay they will enter the house(hold) of the creditor."

The debts in most cases are small. Three of those for more than one pound of silver have Assyrian creditors and in the fourth, for 90 shekels, the well-known Anatolian moneylender Tamuria is creditor. Some of the smaller debts may have been commercial, but most probably were domestic and consumptive. Note that none of those with Anatolian creditors stipulates interest.

In letters and various records we find approx. thirty references to a variety of *šapartu*-pledges (mentioned above), which are made available, held or returned. These references, in combination with those listed in the two tables, can give us some idea about the value of the items pledged, especially in relation to the size of the debt. In many cases we cannot be sure, because the value of houses, slaves and various objects used as pledge is not stated and will have varied, but some conclusions are possible. Houses, children or slaves pledged for relatively small debts must have offered a good security, especially the houses pledged for 12 (TPK 1, 88), 18 (TC 3, 240), 20 (TC 3, 221), 24 3/4 (BIN 6, 236) and 30 (kt n/k 1830) shekels of silver, and slaves pledged for debts ranging from 9 to 40 shekels, listed in the tables above. A clear example of an attempt to strive for equivalency is TPK 1, 21, where a debt of 20 shekels of silver plus interest is secured by pledging a silver cup (*kāsum*) of (weighing) 22 1/2 shekels.[107] ICK 1, 37 surprises us by mentioning that even for a debt of only one shekel of silver a quantity of wool and a saddle rug had been given as *šapartu*-pledge (and had been given back after payment). On the other hand, even two (expensive) houses in Assur are not equivalent to a debt of 49 pounds of silver (KTS 2,9).

Traders of course were well aware of the value of pledges and in EL 297:x + 9ff. an Anatolian debtor, unable to pay, tells his Anatolian creditor "take my boys (slaves) along, sell them for silver, satisfy yourself with the silver you are entitled to and let the rest of that silver count as owed by you." In other cases, however,[108] a possible difference between the size of the debt and the yield of the sale of the pledges (slaves and a house) is not considered. With large commercial debts the yield of pledges, when sold, could be deducted (*ṣaḫḫurum*) from the original debt, when accounts were settled.

3. *Hypothecary or Possessory Pledge*

Kienast 1976: § 11f. correctly assumes that movable objects figuring as *šapartu*-pledge were usually handed over as security to the creditor (and are thus "Besitzpfand"),[109] but he rejects this for real property

[107] But silver cups served as "concrete money"; they occur together with silver and gold, at times with their weight/value specified, see *CAD* K 254,1,a,1'.

[108] Adana 237E (debt of 30 shekels of silver) stipulates: "If the debtor does not pay, the (female) creditor can sell the slave and the house and so get her silver."

[109] In EL 292 a woman "took" (*ṣabātum*) such a pledge from another woman when she borrowed only 1 1/2 shekels of silver! Note also, in a trader's last will, the bequest of "the *šapartu*-pledges he has in possession" (Garelli 1965: 153, Sch. 23:58f.), mentioned alongside slaves and donkeys. When kt 91/k 228 stipulates that, if a debt is not paid within one month, "their *šapartu*-pledges will be fetched"

and persons, both among Anatolians (as *šapartu*-pledge) and among Assyrians. An Assyrian *erubbātu*-pledge would have been no "Besitzpfand" or "Ersatzpfand," but merely a hypothecary "Sicherungspfand," much better suited to "commercial ideas." Arguments for this view are 1) absence of evidence for antichretic use of the pledge and (hence) also no special clauses to protect their possessor against risks; 2) competition with other liabilities which provide security to the creditor—such as a) (default) interest, b) joint liability by a plurality debtors, and c) availability of a guarantor—which would make possession of the pledge improbable and superfluous; and 3) occurrence of anonymous *tamkārū* as creditors, hence the possibility of ceding debt-claims, which would create problems with possessory pledges. Consideration 2) also makes him reject the idea that the pledge would automatically become the property of the creditor if the debtor defaulted (§ 17), but for what happened if other security failed he can only refer to one letter, where a debtor's house is sold.[110] The "Eigentumspfand," whereby the pledge becomes the property of the creditor, with the possibility of redemption and occasionally with certain restrictions, would have been alien to Old Assyrian law, but a feature of Anatolian law (§§ 17–20).[111] Kienast's words "Pfandbestellung in der Form der Eigentumsübertragung" (§ 18) imply that this was not the conveyance to the creditor of an existing (hypothecary or possessory) pledge, but pledging by formal transfer of property rights, which Kienast, consequently, does not present as a consequence of the debtor's default.

Existence of the hypothecary pledge is clear from some of the contracts listed in table 2 (see notes d, k, l, m, and n) which stipulate that the creditor will only acquire them if the debtors default. According to kt 87/k 104 the creditors in that case "will take along the person pledged instead of (*kīma*) their silver." Kienast's denial of the existence of the possessory pledge, however, is problematic in view of the data of our sources. And while his theoretical arguments, partly negative and circumstantial, partly based on what he calls

(*šaprātušina ittabbalā*), this probably means that the creditor obtains pledges on default of payment, not that he takes possession of hypothecary pledges, which in that case should have been registered.

[110] The unpublished letter quoted in EL p. 231 footnote d, already mentioned above; but the debtor's house which is sold is not identified as *erubbātu*-pledge!

[111] As proof he refers to contracts now edited in Kienast 1984 as nos. 10, 26, 27, and 32 (TC 3, 255 is not included there).

"Haftungskonkurrenz," have some force, they cannot decide the issue. In paragraph I.3, on the cumulation of security, also among Assyrians, we met a *šapartu*-pledge in the form of a packet of gold, no doubt in the possession of the creditor, alongside a guarantor, joint liability, and default interest. There is no reason why possessory *erubbātu*-pledges could not also occur in combination with joint liability or default interest. Moreover, default interest is a compensation or penalty for not paying in time, but does not secure the return of the principal, for which both a hypothecary and possessory pledge would be useful. When in kt 91/k 228 the debtors default "their pledges will be taken away and they will add interest." It is also doubtful whether we may apply the "logic" observed for Assyrian contracts to those between Anatolians, where cumulation of security (in particular joint liability in combination with pledging and occasionally guarantors) is frequent. It seems better to start from a detailed analysis of what the sources say.

Important is the interpretation of the debt-note TC 3, 240 (between Anatolians), which states that when the debt is paid the creditor "will leave (*waṣā'um*) the house held as *šapartu*-pledge," hence a clear example of a possessory pledge. Kienast (§ 16) takes this, "trotz des Wortlautes," as a guarantee clause which states the right of the creditor to claim ("beanspruchen") the pledge until he is paid. While it is not easy to determine in whose interest the guarantee clause is,[112] it is unacceptable to read into "leaving" (the house) only the right of "claiming it," thereby turning it into a hypothecary pledge. The same verb is used in other texts where a building is held as pledge: in EL 180 the creditor will leave the storehouse held as (presumably antichretic) pledge, when D returns the silver, and in TPK 1, 88 (above table 2, note g) the creditor does the same with a house held as pledge, if the debtors "chase him away" (*ṭarādum*). The last verb, as other occurrences show,[113] implies that the creditor possesses,

---

[112] Literally: "She (D) pays and then they (C's) leave," without conjunction. A clue could be the linking of the two verbs not by the simple connective *-ma*, but by *-ma ù*, which could mean "only when," but this requires proof, especially for an Anatolian contract. Note a similar construction in EL 180:13ff.: "Whenever (*immati*) C demands her silver back, D returns the silver and then C leaves the storehouse" (held as pledge; *kaspam tutārma ù tuṣṣi*), where C has the initiative, and in TPK 1, 88:8ff., where D has the initiative. We have debt-notes which show that the notion Kienast prefers, "until he is paid," are explicitly rendered by the conjunction *adi*, "until," e.g. in AKT 1, 44:9 and KTK 95:20.

[113] Note the unpublished contract H.K. 1005–5534, quoted in Veenhof 1997b: 143 footnote 58, where its object is a woman "living in the house."

occupies it, and this is confirmed by EL 92 (above, table 2, note j), where he who pays "takes (*laqā'um*) the house," *scil.* from the creditor, as is also the case in TPK 1, 194, where the debtors, if they pay back the guarantor, "take their house."

Possession of the pledge is also clear from kt v/k 171 (above, table 2 note e), where after payment the debtor "leaves for his house," which means that he could return home, leaving his creditor's household. This situation is also implied by kt v/k 157 (courtesy V. Donbaz), where the creditor after payment has to "release" (*waššurum*) a (pledged) girl to the debtor, on penalty of a heavy fine. Unambiguous is kt 89/k 312 (above, table 1, note i), where the debtor, if she pays, "takes along" (*tarā'um*), hence gets back, the person held as pledge.

Clauses protecting the creditor as possessor of a pledge are rare but not totally absent. The stipulation that "nobody shall approach" two women held as *erubbātu*-pledge until the debt is paid,[114] is more likely when the pledge is in the possession of the creditor. When in EL 297 the debtor S. offers his creditor N. his "boys/slaves to take them along to sell them," N. only accepts if S. promises that "whether they perish/die or live,"[115] it is for the account of the debtor. The rules concerning a possessory pledge may have been similar to those obtaining for a (pledged?) person sold into debt-slavery "instead of" the amount of the debt. In Kienast 1984: no. 32, the availability of a male substitute protects buyer-creditor in such a case against vindication or flight of the girl bought. Evidence for antichretic use in the form of obligatory service can be found in TPK 1, 156a, where an indebted Assyrian, redeemed (line 6: *tapṭur!*) by a woman, "is held by the silver" (she paid for him) "and will serve/assist her[116] for five years."[117] Antichretic used of a pledged house "held for silver" is probably contained in kt a/k 1044,[118] where it is occupied by the creditor's wife, who has to leave it when he is paid.

The conclusion must be that both hypothecary and possessory pledges occur among Assyrians and Anatolians. It is impossible to decide in each case which of the two is meant, because most pledges in debt-notes occur in nominal clauses, which say nothing about

---

[114] AKT 1, 44, see above table 1, note a.

[115] Lines x + 17: *iḫalliqū*[*ma*. . . .], line x + 22: *i-mu-tù i-ba-lu-ṭú-ma*, see *CAD* B 56,3,a,1'.

[116] *qassa iṣabbat.*

[117] Contrast Ka 1096 (Donbaz 1971/2), where the redeemer has a simple debt claim on the father of the redeemed person.

[118] Bayram-Veenhof 1993: 90, c).

their transfer and the verbs used ("to hold," "to look at") are ambiguous. Their hypothecary nature is clear when their transfer is linked to default of payment ("If D does not pay . . ."), when it is said that "the creditor's hand rests on it" (TPK 1, 100), or when the verb is clearly in the future tense ("the creditor will seize . . .," EL 91). Their possessory nature is obvious when upon payment the creditor has to "leave" the pledged house or the debtor/guarantor "takes along" the pledged person. I consider it rather likely that in many cases persons or houses "held as pledge" actually came into the hands of the creditor, as attested in some texts (see III.1.2). This is also suggested by the use of this same terminology ("to be held by/with the silver") in Old Assyrian service contracts. The great majority concern employees who in exchange for receiving an interest free loan "are held by the silver" and have to serve its owner.[119] Their situation is comparable to that of antichretic personal pledges, as formulated in Old Babylonian contracts, where "the capital has no interest, the antichretic pledge no wage,"[120] and this parallelism supports the idea of antichretic use of pledges.

We may introduce a further distinction by assuming that on default of payment pledged items could become the legal property of a creditor also by transfer of title only, without physical delivery of the pledge. Such a solution is suggested by occurrences of commercial debts secured by the creditor establishing a claim ("lay his hand upon") on merchandise of the debtor to make sure that the proceeds from their sale will be available to satisfy him; see TPK 1, 100, discussed below (III.4 with note 130). Legal ownership without physical possession is likely in case of a kind of general lien, when the contract states that "until the the creditor has been satisfied all he (the debtor) owns belongs to him" (KTK 95), or when some contracts use the verb *dagālum* with the creditor as subject, if that really means "to own" (see table 2, notes h, i and j, and III.1.3 on this verb). Kienast 1976: § 18, taking this meaning for granted, considers them as "das Eigentumspfand begründend." The purpose of these clauses may have been to secure their easy, automatic conveyance in case

[119] See Veenhof 1994, also for criticism of Kienast's view that most such contracts were concluded to provide security for existing, unpaid debts.

[120] See Eichler 1973: 50ff. The comparison may include the statement that the father who rented out his son in this way, "when he returns the silver takes his son along where he wants" (EL 161), with the verb *tarā'um* typical for freeing pledged persons.

of default of payment, as with a "Verfallspfand." This is clearly the case in kt n/k 71,[121] where indebted parents sell a son for 45 shekels of silver to the creditor and we read: "He (the father) will pay the silver within four years; if he does not pay he (the creditor) will take him along."

While the ambiguous and laconic formulation of many contracts makes us guess at what really happened, EL 92 suggests still another distinction. After stating that for a debt of 1 1/2 pounds of silver the creditor "looks at" the debtor's house, son(?), daughter and a slave-girl, there follows: "Who pays the silver to C takes the house." This suggest that the single verb *dagālum* covers the general notion of a security claim on possessions of the debtor, without by itself specifying whether this security is hypothecary or possessory. It may therefore cover different realities: the house as possessory pledge, which the creditor will hand over (give back) to whoever pays the debt (the debtor or a guarantor?), while the members of D's household seem to have served only as a hypothecary security, automatically annulled by payment. This suggests that in many more cases where (all) the possessions and members of the debtor's household are covered by a security clause ("general lien") such distinctions are possible. It supports the idea that where a debt was protected by various types of security, on default certain priorities or preferences, presumably of the creditor, came into play, as also suggested in Kienast 1976: § 15. What the clauses, perhaps at times deliberately vague and ambiguous to provide the creditor with a choice of security, actually meant or could imply only becomes clear when we can see what happened when the debtor really defaulted.

4. *Default, Seizure, Forfeiture, and Foreclosure*

Clauses in some contracts (above, III.2 table 2, notes d, l, m) show that on default of payment the creditor could take possession of a hypothecary pledge, by "taking along" personal pledges, "instead of his silver" (kt m/k 104, see III.2) and by occupying a pledged house. The letter KTS 2, 9:13 instructs its addressee to "seize both houses" which had been registered as *erubbātu*-pledge for a debt of 49 pounds

[121] Donbaz 1988: 48f.

of silver. To make sure such actions were possible C's claim on the pledge had to be protected (see AKT 1, 44, table 1, note a). The seizure of a consensual pledge, registered in a debt-note, in general should not have presented problems, but occasionally we see authorities play a role when debtors were handed over to their creditor. In kt a/k 477 an Assyrian *kārum*-court decides that four persons (two sons and two slaves) "will enter and be held by" a creditor for a large copper debt, and in EL 188 it is the local Anatolian ruler who "hands over" an Anatolian family to an Assyrian creditor. Unfortunately we do not know the background of these cases, nor whether the people involved had served as pledges, but it is anyhow clear that the Anatolian authorities could be involved in the sale of countrymen into debt-slavery.[122]

How the pledge was used to satisfy the creditor is rarely mentioned. While antichretic use is likely when houses had become the creditor's possession or persons had entered his household (TPK 1, 156a), their exploitation usually will not have yielded the creditor more than the (default) interest due. To get the principal back more drastic steps were necessary, usually the sale of the pledge. This is suggested by the text Adana E where, if a debt of half a pound of silver is not paid, the creditor "will sell the slave-girl and the house and so obtain her silver," but in kt f/k 82 the debtors themselves promise to sell a (pledged) girl in order "to satisfy the creditor" with what she yields. At times more creditors had to be satisfied and kt 88/k 1050[123] describes how all the creditors of the Anatolian Ḫ. convene and liquidate his family: the family members are given to his Assyrian creditors, three Anatolian ones receive the debtor's brother, and ten others (sell and) divide one pound of silver, the price of his house. Kt 89/k 371 records the redemption of a debt-slave sold by "all creditors and money-lenders" and kt v/k 28[124] the sale of a house by the debtor together with his eight creditors. All these

---

[122] This refers to the so-called "notarization" of deeds of sale, which mention at the end: "Through the hands of (*iqqāti*) the ruler and the head of the stairway," which must imply some form of authorization or ratification of the transaction. Note also the role of the Anatolian "overseer of the market" in Kienast 1984: no. 29, where he brings back a person sold into debt-slavery, who had "fled for his debts"; perhaps not simply because he had witnessed the sale according to Kienast no. 15, but as evidence of "staatliches Eingreifen in Zusammenhang mit der Rückführung des Sklaven" (Kienast 1984: 146).

[123] Bayram-Veenhof 1993: 89b.

[124] Günbattı 1989: 54f. no. 4.

examples show that many creditors/money-lenders were not really interested in acquiring and keeping the person or object pledged, but converted it into silver by selling it, which was of course almost inevitable if more creditors had to share a pledge.

The nature of such a sale is clear when instead of the usual "for (*ana*) x silver" we read "instead of (*kīma*) x silver," as is the case in Kienast 1984: no. 32 (sale of slave; see also above III.2) and EL 215, where a plot of land is "given instead of 15 shekels of silver."[125] Sale to cover a debt is clear in kt b/k 121,[126] where the price of a house is called "x silver plus the interest on it" and when sales stipulate the possibility of redemption or impose certain restrictions on the buyer, treated in Kienast 1984: 74ff., §§ 95–98 ("Schlussklauseln beim bedingten Verkauf"). But since it is usually not mentioned whether the items sold had been pledged before, they could also be examples of *datio in solutum*, as assumed for EL 215. Forced sale of houses of defaulting debtors by creditors (including the authorities of Assur)[127] is mentioned several times in Old Assyrian letters,[128] but again we usually do not know whether the houses had been pledged before.[129] In Assur, according to TPK 1, 46, an indebted Assyrian family had "three years ago entrusted for silver the paternal house with its stores" (*ana kaspim paqqudā*)[130] and when "this was not enough," another house was sold. But now, the writer of this letter is happy to report, "the god Assur has had mercy upon his City: a man whose house had been sold" (line 22f.) could get it back. Not by a remission of debts, but by a measure which facilitated redemption and whose formulation ("A man who . . .," *awīlum ša*. . . .) suggests a legal ruling of general validity. Its existence shows that such forced sales were not rare and that the society took measures to prevent the loss

[125] Sale is clear from the seller's obligation "to clear" (*šaḫḫutum*) the buyer, common in sales (Kienast 1984: §§ 74f.).

[126] Bayram-Veenhof 1993: 96 no. 2.

[127] Illustrative is TPK 1, 26 where, because of a silver debt due to the city-house in Assur, inspectors seize and hold (*ṣabātum, ka'ulum*) a house, deliver an ultimatum (an order to pay), and subsequently "offer the house for sale" (*ana šīmim kallumum*, where the verb, "to show," may refer to a public auction), actions basically identical to what a private creditor would do.

[128] See examples in Veenhof 1999a: 80.

[129] In the Neukirch letter (EL I p. 231, note d), contrary to Kienast 1976: 221 with note 14, the house is not identified as pledge.

[130] For details, see Veenhof 1999b, § I. The term "to entrust" does not belong to the terminology of pledging; perhaps a final sale had not yet taken place or the house had been charged as security for a loan.

of the family house, where the ancestors would be buried, due to debts.

What happened when various types of security had been stipulated is not clear and Kienast may be right in assuming that recourse to the possibilities offered by joint liability or the availability of a guarantor took priority over appropriating and selling pledges. While sale of a pledge required authorization and time, joint-debtors or guarantors could be forced to pay the creditor principal and interest in cash, which was also the advantage of allowing the creditor to borrow at the debtor's expense (I 475, above table 1, note d). But we must bear in mind that various pledges or other instruments of security could play different roles, as indicated by EL 92, quoted in the previous paragraph.

There are only a few indications that at forfeiture the pledge sold was valued at the level of the loan. The best example is EL 297, where D, summoned by C (perhaps originally his guarantor), says: "Take my boys (slaves?) along and sell them for silver and satisfy yourself and you will be indebted to me for the remainder of the silver" (lines 9ff.). D thus claims any surplus that their sale might yield. It seems likely that among Assyrian traders the value of a pledge or the proceeds from its sale was applied to the balance of the debt, as is also indicated by TPK 1, 46, where the yield from the first house "was not enough," but we have almost no information on such procedures. An indication of how this may have worked is contained in the debt-note kt 91/k 107 (tablet) + TPK 1, 100 (damaged case; between Assyrians). For a debt of two(!) pounds of silver the creditor has established a claim ("his hand rests on") on a mule (*perdum*) and 135 woollen fleeces of the debtor. Mule and fleeces will be converted into silver within three months and the creditor will satisfy himself; "if there is a deficit of silver the debtor will be responsible, if there is a surplus he will take it."[131] There is no reason to assume that this solution was restricted to purely commercial debts. In CCT 5, 8a:8ff., where a house together with its stores (*išittum*) serves as security for a debt to the City of Assur, the

[131] Lines 16ff. *šumma kaspum batiq D izzaz šumma watar D ilaqqe*. Note that satisfaction of the creditor is expressed by *uštabba*, "he will satisfy himself," and that the sale of the pledged merchandise is not described as an act of the debtor, but by the impersonal form "they will be converted," both of which suggest legal ownership of the pledges by the creditor.

writer promises the addressees "to write them how much of your debt remains when the price of the house has been deducted in the *līmum*-office."

An important question is whether and how tablets (with debt claims of D), pledged as security, could be used by C to recover his claim. Since I have recently discussed this question[132] and concluded that this was to some extent possible, I only mention here the main evidence. The writer of CCT 3, 42b:6ff. speaks of tablets left to a trader and handed over as *šapartu*-pledge and he wants to know "how much silver he took, where (from the man to whom) he has given the (pledged) tablet." This could refer to collecting the debt recorded in the tablet or perhaps even its sale. The writer of AKT 3, 98 accuses a man of having gained access to his tablets and of having used them "to deposit them as pledges" and he wants to know whether the man "has collected silver over there or anywhere else or has given tablets as pledges." Finally, EL 320 (joined with CCT 6, 17a) mentions that a trader had left to his representative "records"[133] which the organization of traders had put at his disposal as pledges. "Did you collect in my name any copper, yes or no?" This last text offers a clue, in showing that such use of pledged records was possible among close associates, partners and relatives, or when a debt-note avoided mentioning the creditor by name and added a clause stating that "the bearer of this tablet is the creditor." In III.2 I already mentioned that there are even a few cases were it is likely that such bonds were drawn up to serve as security to be deposited in a third party's house until a financial obligation had been met. Assyrian traders seem to have been the first ones to use and develop this type of security.

Contracts recording the sale of persons by defaulting debtors usually contain a stipulation about the possibility and conditions of redemption and may impose certain restrictions on the creditor/buyer; see Kienast 1984: 74ff. But most contracts say nothing about how long redemption was possible and which restrictions obtained, i.e. when the person sold became the creditor's full property which he could sell again to regain his money. An exception is TC 3, 252 (Kienast 1984: no. 32; between Anatolians), where a girl, sold "instead of" an amount of silver, can be redemeed within one month, after

[132] Veenhof 1997a: 351ff. on "Anonymous creditors and bearer cheques."
[133] *iṣurātum*, regularly used for debt-notes issued by the local Anatolian palaces.

which the buyer/creditor is free to sell her where he wishes, i.e. she becomes a chattel slave. In LB 1218[134] the person sold into debt-slavery can redeem himself and his daughter (only?) if he is treated badly by his creditor. Both cases concern redemption at the original sale price, which probably was the amount of the debt (note the use of "instead of" in TC 3, 252 and some odd prices) and this possibility must have been restricted in time. Most conditional sales do not impose a time limit on redemption, but fix the ransom at double the original price, which must have made redemption difficult if not illusory.[135] In ICK 2, 116 (Kienast 1984: no. 27) the buyer of the (debt-)slave shall not sell her nor get rid of her, but redemption is possible at twice the original sale price. The contract kt n/k 75,[136] where a whole family together with its house is sold to the Anatolian money-lender Ašēd for 40 shekels of silver, stipulates: "they will pay ten shekels of silver on each (of the next four) festivals of Nipas; they are held with the silver." The transaction is thus a sale, which turns family and house into the creditor's property, but for the time being they "are held" as (possesory) pledges or debt-slaves, with the possibility of redemption. The implication here and in similar conditional sales seems to be that, when they fail to pay in time, they automatically become the full property of the creditor, without the necessity of a further formal conveyance.

Redemption of houses sold for debts is implied by the letter TPK 1, 46, treated above, but the evidence from relevant sale contracts is meagre: EL 215, kt b/k 121, and kt v/k 28, mentioned above. It is usually even difficult to determine whether a house sold had been pledged before and was sold to cover debts (although an odd price as in Kienast 1984: no. 6 suggests it), because contracts of houses, clearly sold for debts, surprisingly do not contain a redemption clause.

A unique conditional sale of a field among Anatolians is recorded in kt 84/k 169,[137] where two Anatolians buy a field in cultivation (*eqlam mērаštam*) from an Anatolian father and his two sons for 15 shekels of silver. The buyers "will cultivate their field for five years. If they (D's) give them back the silver within five years, their 15

---

[134] Veenhof 1978: 292; not in Kienast 1984.
[135] See the table in Kienast 1984: 76.
[136] Donbaz 1988: 51.
[137] Veenhof 1993, 92ff. with comments.

shekels of silver, they will take their field back." The possibility of redemption shows that the field had been conditionally sold (it may have been pledged before) by defaulting debtors, with the (theoretical) possibility of redeeming it within five years. Lacking information on the field's size, speculations on the yield of the crop in relation to the size of the debt (plus interest), hence its antichretic value, are impossible. The long duration of the usufruct bought evokes comparison with similar Middle Assyrian contracts, which assured the creditor the factual ownership (and yield) of the field, for a long period, which must have diminished the chances of the original owner of redeeming it. By drawing up a sale contract (and not one of pledging a field for antichretic use) and stipulating a time limit for the possibility of redemption, the problem of the unclear legal status of non-redeemed pledges, mentioned above in connection with pledged persons, was prevented. The field would become the full property of the creditor after the term for redemption had elapsed. In the case of fields this may have been more urgent, in view of the creditor's investments in it.

IV. Other Forms of Security

Finally, three other forms of security will be briefly discussed: two consensual and registered in the debt-note, one not and a form of legal self-help. Default interest, stipulated in the contract, might also be considered an instrument of security, comparable to antichretic use of a pledge, but it is of a different nature and I will not discuss it.

1. *Joint Liability*

A special clause, usually called one of "joint liability," appears in debt-notes with a plurality of debtors. In Old Assyrian it appears at the end of the contract and reads: "the silver (etc.) is bound to the person ('head') of whichever of them is *šalmum* and *kīnum*" (*ina qaqqad šalmišunu u kīnišunu rakis*); I call it the "*rakis*-clause." While the full form is most frequent, a short version without *kīnum* appears regularly.[138] In addition we have formulations of the type *šalmam u kīnam*

[138] There are also two examples with *kīnum* alone (I 500 and kt v/k 160), a few

išaqqal,[139] where the adjectives are best taken as adverbial; it may be compared with the guarantee clause *šalmam u kīnam adaggal* (above, III.1.3 no. 3). "Joint liability" occurs not only in debt-notes, but also with other liabilities resting on two or more persons, such as an investment in the *naruqqu*-capital managed by two partners: "the *naruqqum* is bound on whichever of them is *šalmum*" (EL 328:17ff.).

Although there is a difference of opinion about the (original) meaning of the adjectives *šalmum*—presumably "sound, in good condition" and hence solvent—and *kīnum*—"reliable, firm" and hence available at the maturity[140]—the purpose of the formula is not in doubt. Each debtor is liable for the whole of the debt; if one of them does not or cannot pay his share the other has to pay it. The expression is frequent in Old Assyrian because there were many cases of business partners or relatives taking out commercial loans, and it is also regularly used with Anatolian married couples or families as debtors. But there are also quite a few cases where, for no obvious reason, the formula does not occur. In one instance it is missing on the tablet, while the envelope of the debt-note has it (EL 91).

The legal situation created by inserting the formula is described in EL 325a:5 by stating that "a tablet is written of both of us together" (*kilallīni*). In the letter TTC 14:27ff. we read: "Should A. say: "take my share (in the debt)," do not to accept it from him, (since) the silver is bound *ina qaqqad šalmišunu*. Take it only if he pays in accordance with (read *ma-lá*) their tablet!" The debt "remains the liability of them jointly until they satisfy (the creditor) with that amount of silver" (KTK 94:10ff.). In kt a/k 1411:14f. a trader is ready to give textiles "to one of you who are jointly liable" (*ana ištên šalmikunu*).[141]

---

where in the full formula *kīnum* comes first (EL 21, JCS 14, 17f. no. 12) and a single occurrence of "bound on the head of whichever of them is *šalmum* and *balṭum*" (ICK 2, 43, collated), where the formula is confused with the one used in soft loans, to be paid back when the creditor is (again) "sound and healthy."

[139] ATHE 75:19f. (between Anatolians; "(Betrifft) den Wohlbehaltenen und (Orts)beständigen: er wird zahlen"); Kennedy-Garelli 1960: 18 no. 12:12ff. (between Anatolians; "A l'endroit même et en entier il paiera"); TPK 1, 108:12f. (between Assyrians; "Il payera la totalité de ce qu'il convient"). *CAD* K 392a, 2', in my opinion wrongly, takes it as referring to the "quality of the payment," presumably on the basis of EL 94, where payment is stipulated "without (deduction of) transport costs *šalmam u kīnam* in Kanish." But similar stipulations use *šalmum*, "the complete amount," alone (ATHE 64:34, TC 3, 29:6, ICK 2, 262:2; KUG 48:25, etc.), and EL 94 hence presumably conflates two expressions.

[140] See for a discussion and earlier literature Skaist 1994: 231ff.

[141] Balkan 1967: 398 no. 8.

Since joint liability with more debtors is not a legal norm, doubt may exist when the original contract is not available. The arbitration in EL 328:17–30, concerning a *naruqqu*-capital managed by two cooperating traders, spells out the consequences of both possibilities so that the solution can always be effectuated. POAT 12 is a settlement between two creditors and one (E.) of two presumably jointly liable debtors concerning debt recorded in two (separate?) tablets. It may have been concluded because, according to the closely related record kt c/k 680,[142] the other debtor (K.) had already paid part of his debt. If E. pays part of his share the creditors will sue (*šeʾāum*) K. for his half, but if he fails to do so the agreement is cancelled and both will be liable for their half of the whole debt. kt c/k 680 is more explicit and states that K.'s respresentatives will inspect the tablet of the agreement between him and E. to establish "whether the shares of K. and E. are really separate shares (*qātum ša K. qātat*, etc.) or "bound to the person of whichever (of them) is solvent."[143] An example of a debt owed by a group of persons without joint liability, where each is responsible for a proportional share of the debt, is the receipt kt 89/k 341 (courtesy Y. Kawasaki). It records that of two Anatolian couples who together owed a sum of two pounds of silver (no clause of joint liability), one has satisfied the creditor with "their half," whereupon he promises not to come back on them, their children or property. This promise may have been added because with only half of the debt being paid the original debt-note could not be returned, but is equally possible that it was necessary to prevent recourse of the creditor who might treat them as jointly liable debtors.

The purpose of the "*rakis*-formula" can also be served by stating at the beginning of a debt-note that the creditor has a claim which rests on (*iṣṣēr . . . išû*) two or more debtors; I call it the "debt-formula." It regularly occurs with Anatolian couples, where the wife is included in the formula as co-debtor. The joint liability may be repeated by mentioning the couple again in a "*rakis*-formula" added at the end, e.g. in EL 15. At times, nearly always with Anatolian debtors, both formulae are expanded to include other items. The "debt-formula" of TC 3, 237 states that the debt rests on the couple, "his(!) children and his house" and the contract ends with the

[142] Balkan 1967: 401f. no. 14.

[143] Read in POAT 12:14–17 *ša mišlišu* [*u*]*šabbiuniātima ana ša K. K. nišeʾu.*

simple "*rakis*-formula" (similarly EL 67). In AKT 3, 10, on the other hand, a normal "debt-formula" (covering six Anatolian debtors) is followed by an extended "*rakis*-formula," which also mentions "their houses and gates" (*i-bētišunu u bābišunu*; similarly TC 3, 218 and TPK 1, 138). ICK 1, 41, with several Anatolian men in the "debt-formula," ends with a "*rakis*-formula" which now includes "their wives." And this is not all, because both the "debt-formula" and the "*rakis*-formula" can be combined with a stipulation about a personal pledge (EL 86, the Anatolian debtors, when defaulting, "will enter the creditor's house") or a guarantor (EL 55 and 226:42). Above (II.2.2) we observed that the difference between being a co-debtor and a guarantor with subsidiary liability is rather theoretical. In the same way, there must have been little difference between a debt-claim resting on a whole family and one resting on the couple only, but secured by including family members or slaves (AKT 3, 14) in the "*rakis*-formula." Similarly, a debt resting on a man, a couple, or a whole family together with its house, slaves and fields "and whatever there is" (kt f/k 71, TC 3, 238) is hardly different from one resting on a man or a couple, whereby the "*rakis*-formula" covers the person and the house of the debtor (EL 20, TC 3, 218, cf. AKT 3, 10).

If persons and possessions mentioned in the "debt-formula" and in the "*rakis*-formula" of Anatolian debt-notes were equally vulnerable to forcible measures taken by the creditor on default, their unequal distribution over both formulae becomes understandable, as does the fact that occasionally the enumeration on tablet and envelope are not identical.[144] This makes it likely that the variety (at times also confusion) in Anatolian contracts is mainly a matter of formulation and reflects the creditor's concern to obtain maximal security by using both formulae and so establishing a kind of general lien on the members and possessions of the indebted household. The use of the term hypothecary pledge seems justified, because none of these Anatolian debt-notes registers a formal pledge (*šapartum*). The only combination of joint liability with a formal *šapartu*-pledge (the debtor's daughter) occurs in EL 15, where, however, we have a simple "*rakis*-formula" which mentions only the indebted couple itself (*šalmu-kīnu*-formula); no children or possessions. This allows the conclusion that the extended "debt-formula" and/or "*rakis*-formula" serve the same

[144] In kt f/k 94 (courtesy L. Umur) the tablet includes in the "*rakis*-formuka" the debtor's house and wife; the envelope, his wife and children.

purpose as a formal pledge. Did the choice of a particular formulation affect the possibilities of the creditor to indemnify himself? One might argue that family members and possessions included in both formulae could be summoned, detained or seized in order to enforce payment, while only a formal pledge could be taken along by the creditor to become a possessory pledge. I doubt whether this distinction applies in the Anatolian sphere, even apart from the fact that there is hardly any practical difference between a distraint and a pledged person who has entered the creditor's household.

In purely Assyrian contracts this is different, and the distinction between the liability of the debtor(s) and the security provided by pledging persons or property is clear. What is pledged is mentioned separately and never included in the "debt-formula," and the "*rakis*-formula" mentions the joint liability of the debtors only. Here only the practical identification of the status of co-debtor and guarantor obtains, but both were still kept apart, as the references in note 53 show.

2. *Borrowing by the Creditor*

The second consensual type of security, of which I know a dozen occurences,[145] occurs in debt-notes where the creditor states: "if the debtor does not pay back (if his term has elapsed), I will enter a merchant's house and I will take silver at interest (at his expense)."[146] The creditor is thus entitled to indemnify himself by taking out a loan for the amount owed to him with a banker or money-lender, of course ultimately at the expense of the debtor. Since the creditor cannot make the banker draw up a debt-note in the name of the debtor, the creditor figures as debtor and is also liable for the interest due.[147] But he is authorized to claim both the capital and

---

[145] Published ones are AKT 1, 34; EL 87; 185; ICK 2, 95, 147; I 475; TPK 1, 169.

[146] See for details Veenhof 1999a: 66ff. The older interpretation, still found in EL 87 (with comments) and in the translation of I 475, is that the defaulting debtor would enter the house of the creditor. We now know from ICK 2, 147:19' ("we will enter and borrow silver," with one debtor and two creditors) that it is the creditor who is speaking in the first person, stipulating his right.

[147] Old Assyrian knows debt-notes where the creditor remains anonymous and is called *tamkārum*, "the creditor," but there is no proof that they are the loans taken

the interest from his debtor: I 475 writes that the creditor borrows at interest, but that his debtor "shall compensate (*mallu'um*) the interest," and TPK 1, 169 explicitly states, addressing the debtor: "And you will be responsible to me for the silver and the interest on it." This responsibility in some contracts is expressed by adding a dative suffix to the verb: "I will take for him," i.e. for and at the expense of the debtor. That the statement by the creditor is always in the first person means that the contract quotes *verbatim* the words by means of which he established the right to indemnify himself in this way, which the debtor granted by signing (sealing) the debt-note. The use of the first person by the creditor is similar to that attested when he calls pledges "my *erubbātu*-pledges" or states his right to them by saying "I will seize . . .," "I hold . . .," "I look at . . ." (see above III.1.2 and III.1.3).[148]

This device is rather rare in debt-notes, even rarer than the stipulation of a guarantor, and the debts which it has to secure in general are not very large. Hence, it seems likely that it was a legal instrument to secure for creditors in need of cash (rather traders than bankers and money-lenders) the possibility of collecting small debts quickly and easily, without resort to legal measures, when debtors were late in paying. Some occurrences which speak of "borrowing silver (to make up) for a deficit" (*ana bitiqtim*, sing. and plur.) and use the verb "to supply, compensate" (*mallu'um*), probably concern the balance of partially paid debts. In such cases the device offered an efficient way of settling affairs. Contracting a loan at the expense of a debtor is only sensible if the creditor urgently needs the money and feels sure his debtor will refund him in due time. This fits the picture of traders who liked to have their capital working all the time and hence from time to time (if payments by agents or the silver caravan from Anatolia were late) were confronted with temporary cash problems. For normal and consumptive debts this legal device would not have worked and the traditional means of

out by creditors with bankers at the expense of debtors. Debt-notes with *tamkārum* as creditor, moreover, are very numerous, while the stipulation on borrowing by the creditor is relatively rare. See for reasons for not identifying the creditor by name, Veenhof 1997a: 351ff.

[148] Occasionally also in the joint liability clause, e.g. kt v/k 161: "my silver is bound on whichever of them is solvent." Note also TPK 1, 91, where the creditor states: "I will obtain (lit. *a-kál*, 'I will enjoy') one shekel of silver for six shekels of silver" (a very favourable rate of exchange).

securing or enforcing payment (hostages, pledges, debt-servitude) must have been more effective.

3. *Distraint*

Non-consensual security could be obtained by distraint, in Assyrian the verb *katāʾum*,[149] used in the basic stem, in the doubled stem with plural object (CCT 3, 24:42, TC 1, 25:16, 43:8) and in the iterative Gtn-stem (refers to repeated attempts to take a distrainee; TC 2, 46:7, kt k/k 114:18), twice with the object *kutuʾātum*, "(female) distrainees" (CCT 3, 11:12 and kt n/k 519:45, courtesy C. Günbattı). The verb denotes the seizure and detention of items, usually persons, not as material compensation for the debt but as a forcible means to obtain satisfaction from a defaulting debtor. In kt n/k 519:38f. it happens because "the term has elapsed"; in CCT 3, 11:10ff. the action is preceeded by attempts "to hold the debtor by the hem of his garment," a measure which prevents him from leaving.

Distraint is based on the conviction that the loss of the distress will urge the debtor to pay as soon as possible. In KTS 29b:5f. the distraint of a slave-girl buttresses the creditor's request of silver. It is an act of intimidation and in TC 2, 46:7 and CCT 3, 24:41ff. is combined with the verb "to frighten" (*šaḫdurum*). Both texts show that the measure worked; in the second the creditor "has frightened the house and taken slave-girls as distrainees, whereupon your representatives have settled the affair and I paid 45 shekels of silver." Distraint followed by payment is also clear in TC 1, 25:14ff. and in the letter TC 3, 60. When its addressee is ordered not to chase a debtor over a great distance, but "to distrain his slave-girl and slave in Kanish and so get the silver," the writer does not mean silver from the sale of the distrainees, but payment by the debtor who wants to get them back.

In the Old Babylonian period, where this action is rendered by the verb *nepûm*, it could mean detaining persons in the creditor's house (see Codex Hammurapi §§ 114ff.), but also putting them in jail (*ṣibittum, nūparum*), which is a standard topic in Old Babylonian

[149] See *CAD* K 308b. Note that the verb and its derivates in Old Assyrian are not used for security, guarantee, as they are in contemporary and later Babylonia and in texts from Alalakh (see *CAD* K s.v. *kattû*).

school letters.[150] Old Assyrian sources do not tell us what happened to a distrainee and there is no evidence for putting them in jail. In the dozen occurrences known to me[151] its objects are once household items (*unūtum*, in the later text OIP 27, 35:9), once a slave (CCT 4, 3b:19), twice slaves and slave-girls (TC 1,25: 14f.; 3, 60:20), in all other cases slave-girls.[152]

Though not consensual, the action was not illegal, since even the *līmum*-official of the city of Assur practised it (TC 2, 46:7f.; kt n/k 519:45f., courtesy C. Günbattı), because of debts owed to the city. The right of a creditor to put pressure on a defaulting debtor apparently was granted by common law, but it is relatively rare in Old Assyrian. It may have been practised only when other ways of summoning a debtor did not work (as in TC 3, 60), in situations where no other security had been stipulated, or with debts not arising from borrowing but from arrears in paying, such as those due to the city-office in Assur. Unfortunately we have no information on the fate, rights and release of distrainees.

---

[150] See Kraus 1967: 26ff. nos. m-t; the fate of the distrainee is the reason for writing a letter to the absent debtor.

[151] Read in TPK 1, 192:8 *lu-ša̓!-dí-šu*, "I will make him pay"; unclear is BIN 6, 178:11 (Michel 1991: II, no. 3), "they have warned me by distraining . . ." (*ina* GA-*tí kà-tù-im*).

[152] In the difficult text TC 1, 43:8, *mammana lā ú-kà-tí-ku-nu* could mean "nobody has taken you as distrainees" or "has taken distrainees from you" (ablative accusative).

Abbreviations

AKT 1–3	*Ankara Kültepe Tabletleri (Ankaraner Kültepe-Tafeln/Texte),* I. Emin Bilgiç e.a. Türk Tarih Kurumu Yayınları VI. Dizi—Sa. 33. Ankara: Türk Tarih Kurumu Basımevi, 1990. II. Emin Bilgiç—Sabahattin Bayram. Türk Tarih Kurumu Yayınları VI. Dizi—Sa. 33a. Ankara: Türk Tarih Kurumu Basımevi, 1995. III. Emin Bilgiç—Cahit Günbattı. Freiburger Altorientalische Studien. Beihefte 3. Stuttgart: Franz Steiner Verlag, 1995.
ArAnat	*Archivum Anatolicum. Anadolu Arsivleri.* Ankara Universitesi Dil ve Tarih-Coğrafya Fakültesi, 1ff. Ankara: Üniversitesi Basımevi, 1995ff.
CTMMA	*Cuneiform Texts in the Metropolitan Museum of Art.* Vol. 1. *Tablets, Cones and Bricks of the Third and Second Millennia B.C.* Ed. I. Starr. New York: The Metropolitan Museum of Art, 1988. Pp. 92–142, Old Assyrian Texts, by M. Trolle Larsen.
EL	G. Eisser – J. Lewy. *Altassyrische Rechtsurkunden vom Kültepe,* I–II. MVAeG 30 und 35/3. Leipzig: J.C. Hinrichs, 1930–1935. Quoted by text number.
I+number	Old Assyrian cuneiform text in Prague as published (in the order of their I numbers) in Karl Hecker – Guido Kryszat – Lubor Matouš, *Kappadokische Keilschrifttafeln aus den Sammlungen der Karlsuniversität Prag.* Praha: Univerizita Karlova, 1998.
kt a/k (etc.)	Unpublished texts from Kültepe (kt), found in *kārum* Kanish (/k), since the first year of the excavations, 1948 (= a), until 1972 (= z).
kt 73/k (etc.)	Kültepe tablets excavated in *kārum* Kanish since 1973.
POAT	W.C. Gwaltney Jr., *The Pennsylvania Old Assyrian Texts.* Hebrew Union College Annual Supplement 3. Cincinnati: Hebrew Union College, 1983.
TPK 1	C. Michel – P. Garelli, *Tablettes paléo-assyriennes de Kültepe volume. 1 (Kt 90/k).* Institut francais d'études anatoliennes Georges Dumezil. Istanbul. Paris: De Boccard, 1997.

Bibliography

Balkan, K. 1967. Contributions to the Understanding of the Idiom of the Old Assyrian Merchants of Kanish. *Or.NS* 36:393–415.

——. 1974. Cancellation of Debts in Cappadocian Texts. In *Anatolian Studies Presented to H.G. Güterbock on the Occasion of his 65th Birthday*, ed. K. Bittel et al. Pp. 29–42. PIHANS 35. Istanbul: Nederlands Historisch-Archaeologisch Instituut.

Bayram, S., and K.R. Veenhof. 1993. Unpublished Kültepe Texts on Real Estate. *JEOL* 32:89–100.

Dercksen, J.G. 1997. The Silver of the Gods. *ArAnat* 3:75–100.

——. 1997/8. Review of C. Michel and P. Garelli, *Tablettes paléoassyriennes de Kültepe, volume 1 (Kt 90/k)*, in: *AfO* 44/45:333–339.

Donbaz, V. 1988. The Business of Ašēd, an Anatolian Merchant. *AfO* 35:48–63.

——. 1971/2. The Old Assyrian Month Name Kanwarta. *JCS* 24:24–28.

Eichler, B.L. 1973. *Indenture at Nuzi.* Yale Near Eastern Researches, 5. New Haven and London: Yale University Press.

Falkenstein, A. 1956/7. *Die neusumerischen Gerichtsurkunden, 1–3.* Abhandlungen der Bayerischen Akademie der Wissenschaften, philologisch-historische Klasse, Neue Folge Heft 39, 40, 44. München: Verlag der Bayerischen Akademie.

Garelli, P. 1963. *Les Assyriens en Cappadoce.* Paris: Librairie Adrien Maisonneuve.

——. 1965. Tablettes cappadociennes de collections diverses, II. *RA* 59:19–48, 149–176.

——. 1987. Une tablette de la couche Ib de Kaneš. In *Language, Literature and History. Philological and Historical Studies presented to Erica Reiner*, ed. F. Rochberg-Halton. Pp. 107–114. American Oriental Serries vol. 67. New Haven: American Oriental Society.

Günbattı, C. 1989. Ev satışı ilgili beş Kültepe tableti ve bunlardan çıkan bazı sonuçlar. *Belleten* LIII/206:51–60.

Hirsch, H. 1969. Akkadisch (altassyrisch) *mazzāzum*, "Pfand, Verpfändung." *WZKM* 62:52–61.

Ichisar, M. 1981. *Les archives cappadociennes du marchand Imdilum.* Recherche sur les grandes civilisations, Cahier no. 3. Paris: Éditions A.D.P.F.

Kennedy, D.A., and P. Garelli. 1960. Seize tablettes cappadociennes de l'Ashmolean Museum d'Oxford. *JCS* 14:1–22.

Kienast, B. 1975/6. Bemerkungen zum altassyrischen Pfandrecht. *WO* 8:218–227.

——. 1984. *Das altassyrische Kaufvertragsrecht.* FAOS Beiheft 1. Stuttgart: Franz Steiner.

——. 1989. The Old Assyrian *be'ūlātum. JCS* 41:86–95.

Koschaker, P. 1911. *Babylonisch-assyrisches Bürgschaftsrecht.* Leipzig: Teubner.

Kraus, F.R. 1967. Briefschreibübungen im altbabylonischen Schulunterricht. *JEOL* 16:16–39.

Larsen, M.T. 1967. *Old Assyrian Caravan Procedures.* Istanbul: Nederlands Historisch-Archeologisch Instituut.

——. 1976. *The Old Assyrian City-State and its Colonies.* Mesopotamia 4. Copenhagen: Akademisk Forlag.

——. 1977. Partnerships in Old Assyrian Trade. *Iraq* 39:19–146.

—— and Eva Moller. 1991. Five Old Assyrian Texts. In *Marchands, diplomates et empereurs. Études sur la civilisation mésopotamienne offertes à Paul Garelli*, eds. D. Charpin et F. Joannès. Pp. 227–252. Paris: Éditions Recherche sur les Civilisations.

Lewy, H. and J. Lewy. 1967. Old Assyrian *subrum. HUCA* 38:1–15.

Lewy, J. 1937/8. Old Assyrian Documents from Asia Minor. *Archives d'Histoire du Droit Oriental* 1:1–18; 2:11–142.

——. On Some Institutions of the Old Assyrian Empire. *HUCA* 27:1–79.
Lutzmann, H. 1976. *Die neusumerischen Schuldurkunden.* Teil 1. Heidelberg: Selbstverlag.
Matouš, L. 1969. Der Streit um den Nachlass des Puzur-Aššur. *ArOr* 37:156–180.
——. 1976. Zur Bürgschaft in der Handelskolonie Kaniš. *WO* 8:206–210.
——. 1979. Verkauf des 'Hauses' in Kaniš nach I 568. *ArOr* 47:33–39.
Michel, C. 1991. *Innāya dans les tablettes paléo-assyriennes*, I–II. Paris: Éditions Recherche sur les Civilisations.
——. 1995. Validité et durée de vie des contrats et reconnaissances de dettes paléo-assyriens. *RA* 89:15–27.
Rosen, B. 1977. *Studies in Old Assyrian Loan Contracts.* Unpubl. Dissertation Brandeis University. Ann Arbor: University Microfilms 77–22.287.
Skaist, A. 1994. *The Old Babylonian Loan Contract.* Ramat Gan: Bar-Ilan University.
Stol, M. 1983. *Een Babyloniër maakt schulden.* Inaugural lecture. Amsterdam: Free University.
Teissier, B. 1994. *Sealing and Seals on Texts from Kültepe kārum Level 2.* PIHANS 70. Istanbul: Nederlands Historisch-Archeologisch Instituut.
Ulshöfer, A.M. 1995. *Die altassyrischen Privaturkunden.* FAOS Beiheft 4. Stuttgart: Franz Steiner.
Veenhof, K.R. 1972. *Aspects of Old Assyrian Trade and its Terminology.* Studia et Documenta ad Iura Orientis Antiqui Pertinentia, X. Leiden: E.J. Brill.
——. 1978. An Ancient Anatolian Money-Lender. His Loans, Security and Debt-Slaves. In *Festschrift Lubor Matouš*, I, ed. B. Hruška and G. Komoróczy. Pp. 279–311. Budapest: Eötvös Loránd Tudományegyetem, Okori Történeti tanszék.
——. 1987. "Dying Tablets" and "Hungry Silver". Elements of Figurative Language in Akkadian Commercial Terminology. In *Figurative Language in the Ancient Near East*, ed.
M. Mindlin et al. Pp. 41–75. London: University of London, School of Oriental and African Studies.
——. 1991. Private Summons and Arbitration among the Old Assyrian Traders. *Bulletin of the Middle Eastern Culture Center in Japan* 5:437–460.
——. 1994. Miete. C. Altassyrisch. *RLA* 8:181–184.
——. 1995a. "In Accordance with the Words of the Stele": Evidence for Old Assyrian Legislation. *Chicago-Kent Law Review* 70:1717–1744.
——. 1995b. Kanesh: An Assyrian Colony in Anatolia. In *Civilizations of the Ancient Near East*, ed. J.M. Sasson. Vol. II. Pp. 859–871. New York: Scribners.
—— 1995c. Old Assyrian *iṣurtum*, Akkadian *eṣērum* and Hittite GIŠ.HUR. In *Studio Historiae Ardens. Ancient Near Eastern Studies Presented to Philo H.J. Houwink ten Cate on the Occasion of his 65th Birthday*, eds. Th.P.J. van den Hout and J. de Roos. Pp. 311–332. PIHANS 74. Istanbul, Nederlands Historisch-Archeologisch Instituut.
——. 1995/6. The Old Assyrian *hamuštum* Period: A Seven-day Week. *JEOL* 34:5–26.
——. 1997a. "Modern Features" in Old Assyrian Trade. *JESHO* 40:336–366.
——. 1997b. Old Assyrian and Ancient Anatolian Evidence for the Care of the Elderly. In *The Care of the Elderly in the Ancient Near East*, ed. M. Stol and S.P. Vleming. Pp. 119–160. Studies in the History and Culture of the Ancient Near East XIV. Leiden: E.J. Brill.
——. 1997c. Two Marriage Documents from Kültepe. *ArAnat* 3:357–381.
——. 1999a. Silver and Credit in Old Assyrian Trade. In *Trade and Finance in Ancient Mesopotamia. (MOS Studies 1). Studies on the Economy of Ancient Mesopotamia*, I, ed. J.G. Dercksen. Pp. 55–84. PIHANS 88. Istanbul: Nederlands Historisch-Archeologisch Instituut.

——. 1999b. Redemption of Houses in Assur and Sippar. In *Munuscula Orientis Antiqui. Festschrift Johannes Renger*, eds. B. Böck, C. Cancik-Kirschbaum and T. Richter. Pp. 599–616. Alter Orient und Altes Testament 25. Münster: Ugarit-Verlag.

——. 2000. Archives of Old Assyrian Traders. In *Archives and Archival Traditions. Concepts of Record-Keeping in the Ancient World*, ed. M. Brosius. Study of Ancient Documents. Oxford: Oxford University Press (forthcoming).

THE MIDDLE ASSYRIAN PERIOD

Kathleen Abraham – Bar-Ilan University

I. Introduction

The principal category of security attested in the Middle Assyrian period, both in official and private context, is pledge. It coexisted with other forms of charging the debtor's property and various mechanisms to compel the debtor to pay or to satisfy the creditor in some other way.

The main characteristics of the institutions of pledge (*šapartu*) and other property liens (e.g. *kattû*) in the Middle Assyrian period were studied by P. Koschaker.[1] However, since Koschaker's study several new legal texts from the Middle Assyrian period have been published[2] and earlier published ones have been organized in archives[3]

[1] Koschaker 1928: 96–131. He discussed the following matters: the kind of goods that are given in loan (p. 92), the kind of legal document in which loans and debts are recorded (pp. 92–94), interest (pp. 94–95), the term of the loan (pp. 95–96); possessory pledge (pp. 96–98), hypothecary pledge (pp. 98–99), substance of the creditor's right in the debtor's property (full proprietary right, right of seizure, rules regarding the sale of pledged property; pp. 99–102), modes of recovering payment out of the pledge (pp. 102–111), other forms of lien on the debtor's property (pp. 117–118) or person (pp. 118–124), and the relation between the various forms of security (pp. 111–116 and 124–131). Koschaker's study was based on approximately sixty loan documents (cf. Koschaker 1928: 117 n. 1).

[2] In 1981 Saporetti counted 194 private contracts that were either formulated as loans from A to B, or imply the existence of such loans and other obligations (120 from *KAJ*, 4 from *KAV*, 16 from Tell Billa (abbreviated Bi), 36 from Tell Al Rimah (abbrev. TR), 6 from the Louvre (abbrev. AO), 8 from VAS 19 and VAS 21 (abbrev. MARV; note that ARu 53 = VAS 21 31), one from Tell Fakhariyeh (abbrev. OIP), and three more texts from Assur published at different places. For a survey of MA legal and administrative documents in general, from the capital Assur and the administrative centres across the Assyrian empire in Iraq and Syria, see Saporetti 1970 Vol. II: 261–369 (Assur), Saporetti-Freydank 1979: 225–228 (Assur), Pedersen 1985, 1986 and 1998 (Assur), Finkelstein 1953 (Tell Billa), Laessøe 1959 (Tell Bazmusian), Saggs-Wiseman 1968: 197–205 (Tell Al-Rimah), Güterbock 1979 (Tell Fakhariyeh), Machinist 1982 (Tell Amuda), Ismail 1982 and Harrak 1987: 136–137 (Tell Ali), Machinist 1982: 79 n. 30 and Harrak 1987: 175–176, 195, 204 (Tell Fray), Röllig 1984 and Cancik-Kirschbaum 1996a–b (Dur Katlimmu).

[3] Recently, many of the loan documents from Assur have been studied in their appropriate archives. These were archives of (wealthy) Assyrian families with strong

so that not only the legal but also the socio-economic background of the texts has come to light.

The new texts and the new insights obtained from the archival analysis of previously known texts make it necessary to reassess the nature of Middle Assyrian instruments of security, and in particular, the nature of the Middle Assyrian pledge (*šapartu*). The material basis for such a reassessment was laid between the years 1978–1981 by Saporetti in two articles on the Middle Assyrian private loan documents.[4] These articles collect all the then available texts pertaining to loans and debts from the Middle Assyrian period. Several new texts are to be added to Saporetti's list, mostly from official archives.[5] The focus of his study was on typology and terminology. Accordingly, the study was essentially "technical" and did not address the basic problems that arise from the texts, such as the legal status of the property given in pledge or the social position of the lenders and the borrowers and their relation to the palace and the rural administration.

The present article is an attempt to analyze the available evidence on security both from a legal and a socio-economic point of view, with an emphasis on the institution of pledge. The discussion is preceded by a brief survey of the available source material.

II. The Sources

Since pledges are a means of securing obligations the textual evidence on pledges for any period is in the first place to be looked for in documents recording obligations (Germ. *Verpflichtungsurkunden*,

governmental links and they show the role of private families in the administration of the rural provinces. For details, see Saporetti 1979 and 1982: a list of all the Assur texts that are treated in DSC 1–3 is found in DSC 3: 195; a list of the loans is found in DSC 1: 10 and DSC 3: 2, 40, 70–71; for details on the loans granted by members of family A in the second generation see DSC 1: 44–45 and 59; in the third generation see pp. 77–78 and 103; for details on the loans granted by the other families see DSC 3: 32–33 and 39; 66 and 69; 94–95 and 96–97. Another private family archive is discussed by Postgate 1988 (catalogue of the texts is found on pp. xxx–xxxiii). The loan documents from Tell Billa and Tell Al-Rimah also belong to family archives. On MA archives from Assur in general, see Pedersen 1985, 1986 and 1998.

[4] Saporetti 1978–1979 and 1981.

[5] To Saporetti's list (Saporetti 1981: 39–41) add the following texts: AO 19229, KAJ 118 and YBC 12860 (loans); KAJ 112, 119, 262, *Urad-Šerūa* 5, VAT 17888, VAT 17889, VAS 19 23 (obligations other than loans in promissory notes); KAJ 103, 106, 133, 143, 162, 170 (related to KAV 211), 268, 310, 315, TR 2039, *Urad-*

Schuldurkunden). In the Middle Assyrian period there are two types of documents that record obligations, the loan document and the promissory note.

First, there is the document of the type "Object has been borrowed by D(ebtor) from C(reditor)," followed by the obligation "D will pay back." These are loan documents in the strict sense of the word (Germ. *Darlehensurkunden*) because they record an obligation that arises from a true loan, i.e. a transaction in which a thing is given by one person, called the creditor, to another, called the debtor, for the latter's use and enjoyment, but under the condition that such thing or its equivalent be returned by the borrower at some later date.

In the Middle Assyrian period this type of document, namely the loan document *strictu senso*, is the only one used to record loans, and it has the following basic scheme: 1) description of the borrowed object, which is mostly corn or the medium of payment, i.e. lead[6] or silver, but occasionally bricks, animals and harvesters could also be borrowed; 2) introduction of the creditor by means of the formulation *ša* (*qāt*) C, or *ištu* C; 3) receipt (of the loan) by the debtor using slightly different phrases: D *ilqe*, *ina muḫḫe* D *ilqe*,[7] or *ša muḫḫe* D *ilqe*; 4) obligation of repayment (*iddan*) with or without a fixed date; 5) additional clauses which define the details of the loan, such as the modes of recovering payment at foreclosure or the existence of pledge, antichresis, interest, or a lien over the debtor's property. For a classified list of all the Middle Assyrian loan documents that are known to me, see Appendix A.[8]

Second, there is the obligation document of the type "Object, which is due to C from D, D will pay back." These documents are strictly speaking not loan documents but promissory notes (alias debt notes: Germ. *Verpflichtungsscheine*), although they share some of the

Šerūa 60, 76?, VAS 19 51, and YBC 12861 (references to obligations in various documents); as well as several contracts which are loosely related to the subject of loans and other financial obligations: KAJ 102, Bi 11, 26?, KAJ 92, 109, 113, *Urad-Šerūa* 33. Two texts were discussed by Saporetti but not indexed: for KAJ 82 see Saporetti 1978–1979: 75, and for TR 101 see ibid.: 90.

[6] For AN.NA = "lead" see Freydank 1982b: 74 n. 27.

[7] In TR 110 and 2913 the verb *ilqe* is lacking but this is most probably due to the scribe's negligence.

[8] The texts in Appendix A are ordered according to their place of publication which has the advantage of showing the archival distribution of the loan documents.

formulary with loan documents and may refer to an obligation arising from a loan.[9] Promissory notes are typically used when an obligation originating in a transaction other than a loan is converted into an obligation of loan (hence "fictive loan"), for instance in the case of a purchaser indebted to the seller for the purchase price. The original obligation (to pay the balance of the purchase price) is converted into an obligation of loan by the drawing up of a document of indebtedness, using loan terminology (*ina muḫḫe, ina pān*), and by the stipulation of a date for repayment (*inamdin, iddan*).

In the Middle Assyrian period promissory notes are occasionally used to record true loans, especially official loans[10] but their main use is to record fictive loans. Accordingly, financial liabilities of various types other than loans are found in the Middle Assyrian promissory notes, for instance, the obligation to pay *šulmānu*,[11] to pay outstanding debts of temple offerings,[12] to pay for the marriage gift,[13] to reimburse for a lost object,[14] to distribute rations among workers or prisoners of war,[15] to perform agricultural work and to deliver or

[9] So, for instance, in the NB period where the *u'iltu* or "promissory note" with its standard formulation "Object *ša* C *ina muḫḫi* D . . . *inamdin*" is the common type of document used to record loans (see Petschow 1956: 9–24). Cf. the formulation of OA and NA documents of obligation.

[10] Promissory notes that record a true loan are listed in Appendix B. Most loans listed in Appendix B are government loans, i.e. loans that were granted by official organs (e.g. KAJ 74, 82, 123; note the use of *ina qāt* D instead of *ina muḫḫe* D), usually to individuals representing their village or farmstead in times of hardship, e.g. KAJ 91 (so Postgate 1988: 131–132, 143–145), KAJ 101 and VAS 19 47. In order to make it clear that true loans are being recorded and not some other kind of obligation, the scribe may add the phrase "this grain (etc.) he received on exchange (*ana puḫe ilqe*)," i.e. "as a loan" (so in KAJ 91 and VAS 19 47, see further Postgate 1997: 164–165).

[11] E.g. Bi 24, KAJ 48, KAJ 49, KAJ 51, KAJ 54, KAJ 56, KAJ 72, KAJ 73, KAJ 75, KAJ 76, KAJ 89, KAJ 90, KAJ 91 (so Finkelstein 1952: 77 n. 1 and 8, and Saporetti 1978–1979: 82, but see previous note for a different interpretation), KAJ 93, KAJ 94, KAJ 95 (so Finkelstein 1952: 77 n. 1, and Postgate 1988: 13; but see below note 16 for a different opinion), KAJ 98, KAJ 100, TR 129, TR 2028, TR 2903, *Urad-šerūa* 5.

[12] E.g. VAT 17888 and VAT 17889, published by Ismail 1968.

[13] OIP 79: 89 No. 5.

[14] E.g. KAJ 128.

[15] E.g. KAJ 107 = 117, 119, and 319 from Urad-šerūa's archive discussed in Postgate 1988: nos. 63, 28, and 64. Perhaps also TR 2045, although the context is broken, but lines 12'–14' resemble KAJ 107 lines 13–15 (loan for distribution) and VAS 19 23 lines 10–12 (loan for work assignment). A person, often an official himself, receives ("borrows" in the terminology of the documents, *ina muḫḫe*; cf. Bi 7 and 8 where we actually have *maḫir* instead of *ina muḫḫe*) products from the royal storehouses to be distributed by him (*ušaddan*) to prisoners of war or workers. Note

manufacture goods.[16] They contain a statement of indebtedness (*ina muḫḫe*) and a statement of obligation (*iddan e.a.*). Upon fulfillment of the obligation the debtor "may break his tablet" (*ṭuppūšu iḫappi*). Promissory notes recording fictive loans are commonly found in official archives.[17] In addition to recording true or fictive loans, promissory notes may record the renewal of a debt after an interim settlement of accounts.[18]

It is important to distinguish between both types of documents,—the loan document and the promissory note—, because they differ not only in their formulary, distribution, and moment of obligation,[19]

---

that Bi 7, 8 and some of the Urad-Šerūa texts may also be interpreted as orders to collect debts (not to distribute rations), depending on the translation of the verb *ušaddan*, see Finkelstein 1953: 125 and Saporetti 1978–1979: 87 *versus* Postgate 1988: 57 (regarding KAJ 119). Note also the inconsistency between the Postgate's translation of *ušaddan* "he shall collect" and his comment on the verb as referring to a distribution in the cases of KAJ 107 = 117 and KAJ 319. See further, note 161 below.

[16] In these contracts certain commodities are given to persons who are usually either craftsman or herdsman for a specific task (e.g. to herd, to produce a specific artifact), for instance, *napḫar* x *emmerū ša* C *ša ana* D *ana ra'ê tadnūni ina ūme errišušūni iddan ṭuppūšu iḫappi* (KAJ 127), or *emāru . . . ša* C . . . *ina muḫḫe* D *alaḫḫene ana ṭe'āne tadnāšu iṭe''an iddan u ṭuppušu iḫappi* (KAJ 318). Additional examples of work agreements established by means of a fictive loan and formulated as a promissory note are, KAJ 99, 108, 111, 112?, 129, 130, 134, VAS 19 67 (see Saporetti 1978–1979: 62–63, 83–85) and VAS 19 23 (see Postgate 1988: 158). Work assignments may be implied in the transaction recorded in KAJ 107, 319 (obligation to bake bread from the flour that was issued for distribution, so Postgate 1988: 158–161), KAJ 315 (Postgate 1988: 91–92), KAJ 95 and Bi 10 (so Saporetti 1978–1979: 74–75, 84, n. 35 and 40. Different opinion held by Postgate 1988: 13 according to whom KAJ 95 is to be interpreted against the background of a *šulmānu* payment). Note further in this connection examples of work contracts from temple archives (see Freydank 1992: 276–321). In these documents the creditor is always the temple official in charge of the administration of offerings (*rabi ginâ*) who gives ("lends") products from the temple offerings to various persons; the latter have to deal with these products in various ways, e.g. boatmen who transport the products, or craftsmen who have to process the products (e.g. brewers, oil-pressers, bakers). For work contracts which are not formulated as fictive loans but as simple receipts of material for production, see e.g. Bi 25, KAJ 124, 131 or TCL 9 59.

[17] It is often hard to know whether the loan was private or governmental. The *iḫappi*-clause is insufficient evidence: see further Machinist 1982: 92 n. 108.

[18] E.g. KAJ 80, 112, 120, and 262?, cf. KAJ 122 (Deller-Saporetti 1970b: 307–308), debt-novation after a change in debtors. For the procedure of settling accounts (*nikkassu ṣabātu*), see Postgate 1986: 34–35. It is to be kept separated from the procedure known as *ṭuppu ṣabātu*, on which see below p. 25.

[19] In the loan document the obligation to pay the debt is created at the moment at which the creditor gives and the debtor receives the object of the loan—so that this type of documents has as its operative part "O has been borrowed by D from C. . . . he will pay back." On the other hand, in the promissory note the obligation is created at the moment at which the document itself was drawn up, and the

but also in their manner of securing recovery of the debt. Only obligations arising from the transaction of a loan were secured by charging the debtor's property, albeit not necessarily so, because there are true loans without such security, as we will see below. Obligations arising from transactions other than loans never mention property as security; they are secured only very rarely and by means other than charging the debtor's property.[20]

As pointed out above, loan documents are the major source for evidence on loans in general, and pledges in particular, but references to debts and pledges are found, as a matter of fact, in a variety of contracts from the Middle Assyrian period. Thus, references to loans, debts, and sometimes also pledges, can be found in receipts, sales of real estate, sales of title deeds to credit, annulments of debts, interim settlements of accounts, renewals of debts and miscellaneous undertakings. This evidence is summarized in Appendix C, with the pledged loans highlighted by an asterisk following the number of the text.

Summarizing the available evidence on debt and security from the Middle Assyrian period, one can distinguish between four categories of sources: 1) loan documents *stricto sensu*, 2) promissory notes formulated similar to loans but recording obligations other than loans, 3) references to loans, debts, pledges and debt notes in contracts of various kinds, 4) the collection of Middle Assyrian Laws. Security are found in sources 1), 3) and 4). The discussion below on security for loans in the Middle Assyrian period and on the nature of the Middle Assyrian pledge (*šapartu*) is based on the evidence from sources 1) and 3) only.

III. Typology

In order to understand the problems underlying a study of security for loans in the Middle Assyrian period it is important to further differentiate between the types of true loans that existed in this period. The different types of loans that existed in the Middle Assyrian

operative section of this kind of document is typically "O which is due to C from D, D will pay back." The promissory notes lack the basic element in which the debtor acknowledges receipt of the borrowed commodity (MA *ilqe*).

[20] See further below.

period depended on the specific conditions of each loan. There were long-term and short-term loans, and loans for which no date of repayment was fixed. There were loans of tin, silver, corn, harvesters, plots of land, animals, bricks, bows or a combination of two or more of these commodities. There were interest-bearing loans, loans without interest, and loans with default interest (Germ. *Verzugszinsen*).[21] Various obligations could be imposed on the debtor in addition to the obligation to pay the loan back and various means were developed to pressure the debtor to pay when the repayment date had passed.

Saporetti in his analysis of the Middle Assyrian private loan documents distinguished between thirteen types of loans. He collected the texts for each type arranging them chronologically. He analyzed their characteristic clauses and paid special attention to formulaic variants. His classification has to be modified at various points.

Our classification of the basic types of Middle Assyrian true loans, in Appendix D, is based on the following two criteria: 1) whether or not the loan had been secured by any means (*šapartu, kattû* or other instruments), and 2) the kind of obligations that the creditor imposed on the debtor, especially those obligations that were to take effect in case of delinquency or insolvency. The texts pertaining to each type of loan are listed (following Saporetti's classification in two periods) and subsequently an outline of structure and content of the relevant type is given. The classified data in Appendix D show that some loans were secured by pledge (*šapartu*), others by a lien over all or certain assets (no technical term), and still others by a type of property or personal lien known as *kattû* (= types 1–3). Occasionally, we meet a cumulation of security. Some loans were granted on the condition that the debtor render a service to the creditor, usually one that was related to the harvest, in addition to his obligation to pay off his debt before a certain date (= type 4). In contrast, there were loans in which no execution was made upon the debtor or his property until the date of repayment had expired (= type 5), so that the creditor had hardly any profit during the basic term of the loan. In a few cases it is unclear what gain the creditor might have expected during the basic term of the loan or thereafter (= type 6). In contrast, in two cases the creditor took full advantage of the loan by

[21] Koschaker 1928: 94–96. According to Koschaker all short-term loans bore interest whereas long-term loans provided for antichretic pledge instead of interest.

not only holding a pledge in his possession but also obliging the debtor to provide for harvesters at harvest time and pay interest if he failed to pay back the loan (= KAJ 11 and 29 s.v. type 1). In three other loans the creditor may have enjoyed a share in the profits from the debtor's business venture, but even if not, he was protected from the debtor's insolvency by a statement regarding the latter's financial reliability as well as a *kattû*-lien on his property (= KAJ 32, 37 and 39 s.v. type 1).

Clearly, pledge (designated as *šapartu*) was not the only means to protect the creditor against the loss of his capital; there existed in the Middle Assyrian period two other forms of lien on the debtor's property. First, there is a type of lien that is expressed in terms similar to those of pledge (use of the same verbs *iṣabbat* and/or *ukâl*, and expressions such as *kīmū ṣibtāte* and *kī našlamte*), but from which the term *šapartu* "pledge" is remarkably absent.[22] Since the texts do not give any other technical term to refer to this type of lien, we will call it, for convenience sake only, the "*ukâl*-lien."[23] The *ukâl*-lien could take effect already from the onset of the loan (like pledges), or only after the debt had matured. Secondly, there is a kind of lien on the debtor's assets known as *kattû*.[24] This type of lien is never part of the operational section of the loan document but is always mentioned at the end of the document, before the witnesses; it therefore seems to have been a subsidiary kind of liability. The latter is especially clear in the many cases where the loan was granted on condition that the debtor be financially reliable,[25] as well as in those three cases where the *kattû*-lien stands in addition to a pledge (KAJ 16 and 65) or an *ukâl*-lien (VDI 80:71).[26]

---

[22] Consequently, it is better to keep this kind of lien separated from the kind of lien known as pledge (*šapartu*). For a different opinion, see, Saporetti 1966: 278 with regard to Bi 5: even without *kī šaparte* to be interpreted as establishment of a pledge. See also Saporetti's classification of MA private loan documents: he classifies the texts which lack the phrase *kī šaparte* together with pledged loans, without comment (Saporetti 1978–1979).

[23] The examples are put together in Appendix E under paragraphs 1–3 (E.1; E.2; E.3).

[24] Saporetti 1978–1979 and 1981: *passim* simply translates *kattû* "garanzia" with no comments. CAD K s.v. *kattû* translates "(asset serving as) security" which is its meaning in the MA documents, whereas in Babylonian legal context it exclusively refers to a person, a "guarantor." Schorr 1932: 772 distinguishes between the *šapartu* "Faustpfand" and the *kattû* "Haftung" usually of real estate, and this theory has been fully developed by Koschaker 1928: 117–118 and 125 (*kattû* = Vermögenshaftung). The noun is derived from the OA verb *katû* (*katā'u*), see Von Soden 1957: 131f.

[25] As is stated in *rakis*-clause; see below.

[26] The examples of *kattû*-liens are collected in Appendix E under paragraph 4 (E.4).

Among the approximately one hundred private loan documents from the Middle Assyrian period thirty-six are secured by the prior arrangement of a pledge (*kī/ana šaparte*),[27] twenty by a subsidiary lien on various parts of the debtor's property (*kattû*),[28] thirteen by still another form of property lien which could be established either during the basic term of the loan or at its foreclosure (*ukâl*),[29] and three by two kinds of property lien.[30] Additional evidence on pledges and *ukâl*-liens is found in sale contracts and annulments of debts (see Appendix C.3 and C.4). The choice between the possible ways of securing a loan must have depended on the conditions under which the loan was made, and on the socio-economic circumstances of both debtor and creditor. In this respect, an archival study of loans may produce interesting results.

It appears that security for loans, in particular in the form of pledge (*šapartu*-loans), was common in four cases. First, security characterizes long-term loans where the pledge is antichretic instead of interest (type 3);[31] second, security is typically found in short-term loans where the charged asset(s) will be sold to the creditor (type 2). Third, we occasionally find a security instrument in loans with default interest which were granted for short periods of one to thirteen months,[32] or till harvest time (type 1). And fourthly, *kattû*-security is typically found in loans which also contain the *rakis*-clause[33] and which are sometimes explicitly linked to financing a business trip.[34]

Still, in many cases[35] there was no preliminary arrangement whereby the debtor's property was charged to secure the loan. Delinquency, in those cases, was met by various measures which will be discussed

---

[27] AO 19229, ARu 53, Bi 2, 3, 4, 4a, KAJ 11, 13, 14, 17, 18, 19, 20, 21, 22, 23, 25, 27, 28, 29, 30, 31, 36, 53, 58, 60, 61, 63, 66, 67, 70, 96, 141, TR 2052, 3007, 3021. The occurrence of pledge in KAJ 23 and 141, however, is not certain because the tablets are broken at the relevant passage.

[28] ARu 16, KAJ 32, 34, 37–47, 50, 69, 71, 85, 87, VAS 19 19.

[29] Lien on a field of the debtor during the basic term of the loan in AO 19228, Bi 5, KAJ 12, KAJ 24, VAS 19 20; fields in VAS 19 36. Particular or general lien after expiry of the basic term of the loan in KAJ 35, KAJ 26, KAJ 64 = 68, AO 21380, KAJ 101, TR 3022, and TR 104?.

[30] KAJ 65: pledge of an ox and a general *kattû*-lien; KAJ 16: pledge of a field, a house and a threshing-floor, and a *kattû*-lien on a field, a house, sons and daughters; VDI 80:71: *ukâl*-lien on a threshing-floor as well as a general *kattû*-lien.

[31] Probably also VDI 80:71, see more below on pp. 18–19, 20, and 22–23.

[32] TR 3021: two years.

[33] KAJ 32, 34, 37, 38, 39, 40, 41, 42, 43, 44, 45, 46, 47, 69, 71; ARu 16.

[34] So KAJ 32, 37 and 39.

[35] As against Koschaker 1928: 117 n. 1.

in more detail below. Security for loans, whether pledge, *ukâl*-lien or *kattû*-lien, is remarkably lacking, for instance, in those cases where the debtor had agreed to perform certain agricultural services for the creditor under threat of penalty (= type 4),[36] and in governmental loans (see s.v. type 6). It is also absent from the loans listed under type 5: the lien on the debtor's assets that is provided for in these loans was not a preliminary arrangement to secure the repayment of the loan, but rather a means of penalizing the defaulting debtor. It should be noted that in the latter two types of loan the debtor did not have any obligation vis-à-vis the creditor except for the obligation to pay back the loan before a certain date.

It is often hard to say why in certain cases a loan needed to be secured by pledge or lien whereas in others, in which the same conditions for repayment seem to have existed, no security had been claimed by the creditor. We may cite three examples to illustrate this point. Loans with the accrual of interest after the date of repayment (= type 1) were sometimes secured by pledge, *kattû*-lien or both pledge and *kattû*-lien; These loans were mainly short-term, for one to seven months, or until harvest time, and only rarely for longer periods, namely for either twelve,[37] thirteen[38] or twenty-four months.[39] However, such short-term loans could also be made without any apparent form of security (= type 5.1). Another example of such discrepancy is found in two type 1 loans as opposed to the loan of type 5.6. In KAJ 11 and KAJ 29 (= type 1) the debtor had to pay back the borrowed tin and seven harvesters within six months; if he failed to do so, he was to pay interest and deliver harvesters for reaping, probably in addition to the ones he had borrowed and not yet given back. The loan that is recorded in TR 112[40] (= type 5.6) was made under very similar conditions. And yet, while the loans in KAJ 11 and KAJ 29 were secured by pledges, the loan in TR 112 was not secured by any means. Finally, there is the case of loans in which the creditor was granted the right to acquire an item from

[36] The only exception at stake is TR 3022, but it is to be noted that the lien on the debtor's assets which was provided for in this case, was nevertheless postponed until after default on the loan. Consequently it functioned as a means of penalizing the defaulting debtor rather than as a means of securing the repayment of the loan.

[37] KAJ 18, 25, 28, 70.

[38] KAJ 65.

[39] TR 3021.

[40] Loan to be repaid at harvest time.

the debtor's property in order to satisfy his claim of repayment. In some instances this right was secured by a pledge (Germ. *Verfallspfand*) or a particular lien already from the onset of the loan (= type 2), in other cases, the creditor had no such security and had to satisfy his claim from whatever property was available at the time the debt matured (= types 5.2, 5.3, 5.4, 5.5).

Finally, as for the lack of security in obligation documents from the public sector it should be noted that creditor and debtor often worked closely together, the debtor being the employee or subordinate of the creditor. Their mutual acquaintance may explain why liabilities could exist between them without security. This point is illustrated by e.g. KAJ 120.[41] When both sides did not know each other well enough the creditor may have required recommendations, as for instance in KAJ 118 where private individuals received straw, probably as a loan, from the palace but only after the steward of their household personally made the request (*ana šipirte*) to the representative of the palace.[42]

IV. Guarantor and Joint Ability

The institution of guarantor, which is well attested in the OA and NA period, does not seem to have played an important role in the MA period. We find some evidence that points in this direction in only a few administrative documents from the public sector, and possibly in one private loan.[43] None of them use the OA and NA technical term for guarantor: *bēl qātāte*. KAJ 224,[44] for instance, is a list of eleven goat-skins, each followed by the name of an individual, who probably had to supply the listed item. However, only one of these individuals is mentioned at the end of the document as being responsible for ensuring the total delivery of the goat-skins: *pāḫat šallume* PN Governor of GN *naši*, "PN, Governor of GN, bears the liability for paying in full" (lines 13–17).[45] The responsibility for full

[41] See Postgate 1988: 62.

[42] On this document, see further below at notes 156 and 161. See also Postgate 1988: 52. Similar cases of official recommendations are recorded in *Urad-šerūa* 33, Bi 11 and 26, see Postgate 1986: 26, 28–29, and below in Appendix C.2.

[43] For the private loan (AO 21380) see below, note 177.

[44] Cf. *Urad-šerūa* 69.

[45] For the expression *pāḫat šallume* see AHw 1145 s.v. *šalāmu* D 7. As for Bi 10,

repayment is borne by Ninuāyu in KAJ 92,[46] an unwitnessed receipt of sheep by the latter from an official. Ninuāyu is called *mušallimānu* (lines 9–10), i.e, "the one responsible for full repayment (in this case)," whereas in other similar cases we may assume that other persons were liable.[47] In still another document the person who receives corn from the governor is also responsible for the clearance of this corn, whatever that may have meant (*pāḫat še'i* [. . .] *annê zakkue* PN *naši*, Bi 11 lines 14–16).[48] A different kind of responsibility is mentioned in VAS 19 47[49] which records a series of separate loans of corn, animals and harvesters from the government granaries to individuals representing their family or village.[50] The "responsibility for depositing the (borrowed) corn on the heap," however, is borne by one individual only, who is also among the debtors and whose seal is found on the tablet: *pāḫat še'um ana karme tabāke Tūra-Adad naši* (lines 55–56).[51] Finally, a guarantor may be found in KAJ 171.[52] The father of Mardukiya had borrowed a horse from "the sons of Iabšah," and Mardukiya had to meet the debt. Since he did not have a horse available he took one from "the administrative sphere (*ina pitte*)" of a third party (namely Išme-Ninurta). In order to indemnify the latter he handed over a slave instead of the horse. The role played by Išme-Ninurta may have been the one of guarantor, although the text does not explicitly say so and other interpretations are possible.[53]

The *rakis*-formula has been interpreted as granting the creditor security by means of the debtors' joint liability[54] but this may be doubted as far as the MA evidence is concerned. In OA and OB contracts the *rakis*-clause is clearly a clause regarding joint responsibility of the debtors because it always occurs in loans that were granted to more than one debtor. The repayment of the borrowed commodity was bound (*rakis*) to that person of the debtors who was

---

the document is too fragmentary to determine the context in which the expression occurs.

46 Cf. *Urad-Šerūa* 65.

47 Postgate 1988: 162 and CAD M 256.

48 For the expression *pāḫat . . . zakkue* see AHw 1507 s.v. *zakû* D 8a.

49 Cf. *Urad-Šerūa* 56.

50 One loan is to a palace farmer.

51 On Tūra-Adad see Postgate 1988: 142–143.

52 Cf. *Urad-Šerūa* 49 and Koschaker 1928: 113–114.

53 Postgate 1988: 105 maintains that the horse which the father of Mardukiya had borrowed was forfeited for an unknown reason to the public sector.

54 This is the *communis opinio*; bibliography in Saporetti 1978–1979: 70. Add CAD $Š_1$ s.v. *šalmu* mng. 2a-2' pp. 259–260.

financially sound (*šalmu*) and available at the due date ("reliable", *kēnu*).[55] In other words, if one debtor proved to be insolvent, the other(s) had to pay the whole debt. However, in Middle Assyrian contracts a *rakis*-formula occurs mostly in loans with only one debtor so that the interpretation of "joint liability" is questionable. It is, therefore, generally assumed that since the obligation to pay the debt lay on this one and only debtor, the creditor could require proof of his financial reliability: "(repayment of) Lent Object relies on his being financially sound and reliable" (*ina muḫḫe šalmēšu u kēnēšu* Lent Object *rakis*).[56] Moreover, the fact that the *rakis*-formula is immediately followed by the *kattû*-formula shows that if the debtor claimed to be insolvent or was not available at the due date the creditor was allowed to seize his house and field, occasionally also his sons or children. An alternative interpretation of the Middle Assyrian *rakis*-formula has been offered by Saporetti.[57] In his opinion, the repayment of the loan depended on the business trip's financially successful outcome (lit. "its being sound" *šalmēšu*) and the reliable distribution of its profits (lit. "its being reliable," *kēnēšu*).[58] In other words, the loan had been granted under two conditions: that the business trip which was financed by the loan would yield the expected profits, and that these profits would be honestly distributed between the creditor and the debtor. If the trip did not turn out successfully, the creditor could recover his money from the debtor's property that had been charged (*kattû*).

Finally, a reference to joint liability is perhaps attested in a fragmentary passage in KAJ 118. The latter document records the receipt of straw from the palace by four different individuals (lines 1–14). The receivers were probably obliged to repay the straw at harvest time (lines 15–17) and could then break their tablet (line 18: *i-ḫap-pi-ú* ?). The only word that can be read in the last line of the document (line 19), before the witnesses, is the word "mutually" and this may imply a reference to joint responsibility of the "debtors".[59]

---

[55] OA formula *ina qaqqad šalmēšunu u kēnēšunu rakis*. cf. OB formula, Skaist 1994: 231–237. For the interpretation of *kēnu* as "available at the due date", see Veenhof in this volume.

[56] The MA *rakis*-formula is difficult to translate and is in fact left untranslated in the dictionaries (CAD and AHw) s.v. *šalmu* and *kīnu*.

[57] Saporetti 1978–1979: 69–71 ("Ad 7").

[58] Saporetti 1978–1979: 71.

[59] So Postgate 1988: 50–52.

V. Instruments of Security

The discussion below focusses on *šapartu*-pledges and *ukâl*-liens because they are the better attested forms of security in the Middle Assyrian period. The clause which states their establishment as well as other clauses in the contracts, such as the redemption clause, provide us with enough information to undertake a study of their nature and function. In contrast, very little can be said about the *kattû*-lien because the contracts describe their existence only very briefly.

Several problems arise when defining the legal nature and function of security in the Middle Assyrian period. First, it is often difficult to ascertain whether the security was given to the creditor at the moment that the loan was contracted (possessory) or remained with the debtor until the loan was repaid (hypothecary). Secondly, it is not always clearly stated in the documents whether the encumbered asset(s) functioned as a substitute payment for the borrowed object(s), or rather as security; and even if it was security for the loan, it is difficult to tell whether it secured the entire loan or only its interest. Moreover, it is possible that the encumbered asset(s) served other purposes than securing the repayment of a loan, as for instance, enabling the creditor to have access to his debtor's property for many years.

We must start with a closer examination of the kind of property that served to secure the loan. A lien on all of the debtor's assets is likely to have been hypothecary; similarly, taking the debtor's slave or a member of his family as pledge is likely to have been possessory so that the creditor could enjoy the pledged person's labor force. However, one cannot be too strict in this matter because a lien on the debtor's real estate may be hypothecary as well possessory, depending on many more factors than just the kind of property at stake. Pledging all of the debtor's assets was rare; it is attested in less than one-fourth of the cases: only eight out of the thirty-eight pledged loans regard all of the debtor's (unencumbered) assets.[60] Charging

[60] A general pledge ("all of his unencumbered assets," *mimmūšu zakua*) is attested in Bi 2, 3, 4, 4a, KAJ 29, TR 2052; the pledge of some specific real estate and/or "all his (other) assets" (*mimmūšu*) is found in KAJ 58 and 67. It is possible that a pledge of the debtor's field(s), house(s), sons and daughters (KAJ 61 and 66) in reality amounted to a general pledge. Two loans are broken at the relevant passage (KAJ 23 and 141). All the other pledged loans regarded the debtor's field (*passim*), or his field together with other real estate such as his threshing-floor, his orchard,

all of the debtor's property in a form other than the *šapartu*-pledge was extremely rare in the case of *kattû*-liens (three out of twenty-three attestations),[61] and slightly more common in the case of *ukâl*-liens (three out of fourteen attestations).[62] Furthermore, pledge of real estate clearly prevailed over pledge of persons. One could pledge members of one's family, such as a son (KAJ 17; cf. the *kattû*-lien on the debtor's sons in KAJ 41), wife (KAJ 28, 31, 60), or children (KAJ 61, 66; cf. the *kattû*-lien on the debtor's children in KAJ 16 and KAJ 46), or one's sister and her daughter (TR 3021). It is remarkable that except for a few examples none of the texts mentions the pledge of slaves; I know of only two examples of pledged slaves.[63] It could either mean that the property of slaves in private hands did not play an important role in Assur in the period under discussion, or rather that slaves and other movable property were used as pledge but did not require any specific documentation to prove ownership.[64] Moreover, it should be kept in mind that the normal sale of slaves could in fact represent irredeemable conveyances of pledges.[65] There is only one example of the pledge of an animal (KAJ 65).

---

his house or his farmstead (*passim*). For details see Appendix A. For the pledge of persons and animals, see below. As for the kind of property that served as pledge according to the few conveyance texts which refer to pledged property: a 20 *iku* field was pledged to secure a loan of 27 2/3 minas tin (KAJ 163), 36 minas tin (KAJ 163), and 20 2/3 homers corn (KAJ 165). A 10 *iku* field was pledged to secure a loan of 30 minas tin (KAJ 150, sold for 1 talent 40 minas tin), and the same amount of field together with a farmstead, orchard, threshing-floor and well secured a loan of 36 minas tin and 3 homers corn (KAJ 162, sold "for the full price"). A slave and children had been pledged to secure a loan according to KAJ 170 and were later sold for 5 talents tin. Houses secured a loan of 4 homers corn (annulled in TR 3001) and one of 3 talents tin (annulled in TR 3002). Finally, a loan of 27 2/3 minas tin for which a field had been pledged is annulled in KAJ 142.

[61] KAJ 65: "all his unencumbered assets" (*mimmūšu zakua*), and similarly in VDI 80:71 and VAS 19 19: "his remaining belongings" (*bašīšu (u) bušīšu*). All other cases of a *kattû*-lien regard the debtor's field and house; three texts also include the debtor's children (KAJ 16, 41 and 46).

[62] AO 21380 and TR 3022: "all his unencumbered assets" (*mimmūšu zakua*); similarly KAJ 101: "his field, his house, all his unencumbered assets (*eqelšu bēssu mimmūšu gabba zakua*)." All other cases of an *ukâl*-lien concern the debtor's field (*passim*) or threshing-floor (VDI 80:71). Two texts are broken at the relevant passage (KAJ 26 and TR 104).

[63] In the loan KAJ 53 and in the sale documents KAJ 170 (+ KAV 211); a third example may be KAJ 168 if we follow Koschaker's interpretation (but see more on KAJ 168 below).

[64] Cf. Postgate, 1976: 47.

[65] On the pledge of persons in the MA period see Koschaker 1928: 97–99;

The problem of defining the legal nature and function of the Middle Assyrian pledge and *ukâl*-lien has generally been addressed by focussing on terminology. Appendices E and F present the different formulations that are found in the texts to refer to the existence of a pledge (Appendix F) or *ukâl*-lien (Appendix E) for each type of loan.[66] From this chart we can obtain the following information: the technical term for "pledge"; the verbs used to describe the act of charging the debtor's property, holding property as security and/or serving as security; and adverbial expressions that specify the function of the charged property vis-à-vis the loan. We can then continue by scrutinizing the content of the clauses that describe the conditions of the loan, and examine how this information can help us determine the nature of the Middle Assyrian pledge and *ukâl*-lien.

The term for pledge that is used in Assyia in all periods is *šapartu*, which is derived from the root *šapāru* "to send."[67] Such a derivation may indicate that pledges were originally mobile goods which were "sent" to the creditor to be in his possession.[68] In reality, however, the same term, *šapartu*, refers to different types of pledges.

The term *šapartu* may refer to possessory pledges as well as hypothecary pledges. The first type is generally regarded as the older form of pledge preceding the development of hypothec, but theoretically both could have co-existed in a given period. This seems also to have been the case in the Middle Assyrian period. Indeed, antichretic use of the pledge, as is provided for in the loan contracts of type 3, proves the existence of possessory pledges, whereas pledges consisting of *mimmūšu zakua* "(all) his unencumbered property" (e.g. Bi 2, 3, 4 and KAJ 29) proves the existence of hypothecary pledges.[69] A creditor can enjoy the use of charged property only if he possesses the property in question, and when all the assets of a debtor are being charged it is obvious that the creditor did not take pos-

106–107, 177–178; Korošec 1964: 160–162; Cardellini 1981: 169–172 and Chirichigno 1993: 72–77 and *passim*.

[66] The statement of pledge in KAJ 23 and 141 is not preserved.

[67] *AHw* 1170 (*šapartu*), 1170–1171 (*šapāru*); CAD Š$_1$ 428–430 (*šapartu*), 430ff. (*šapāru*). Eichler 1973: 88–95.

[68] Koschaker 1928: 96–97. Veenhof, however, correctly points out in this volume that the basic notion of the verb *šapārum* is "to manage (by order, letter), administer, govern" and a pledge is therefore something over which the creditor has power of disposition.

[69] The same is true for *ukâl*-liens, e.g. AO 19228 (antichresis), AO 21380 and TR 3022 (general lien).

session of the property at the time of the loan, but had only the vested right to satisfy his claim from whatever property of the debtor was otherwise unencumbered. In many cases, however, it is difficult to ascertain whether the Middle Assyrian *šapartu* or *ukâl*-lien was given to the creditor at the moment the loan was contracted (possessory pledge) or remained with the debtor until the loan was repaid (hypothecary).

Different verbs may be used to refer to the act of charging property as pledge or *ukâl*-lien.[70] The verbs *šakānu, ṣabātu, kullu, ušābu/šūšubu* and *eterrušu* are used in the following combinations: *kī šaparte ṣabātu* "to take as a pledge", *kī* (or *ana*) *šaparte šakin* "to be placed as a pledge/to be pledged", (*kī/ana šaparte*) *kullu* "to hold (as pledge)", *šūšubu* "to be made to stay (in the creditor's house) as pledge".[71] It is also possible to have a combination of two verbs: (*kī šaparte*) *ṣabātu kullu* "to take and hold (as a pledge)", (*kī šaparte*) *kullu eterrušu* "to hold (as a pledge) and cultivate", *kī šaparte nasāqu ṣabātu* "to choose and take as a pledge." The most elaborate formula is found in KAJ 27 and KAJ 35 where three verbs are used (*nasāqu, ṣabātu/leqû* and *kullu*).

Some of these verbs are indicative of the nature of the security, whereas others are not. Indeed, verbs like *ušābu/šūšubu* and *eterrušu* no doubt refer to antichretic security, which were in the creditor's possession from the onset of the loan and used by him as the equivalent of interest.[72] In contrast, verbs like *kullu* "to hold" and *ṣabātu* "to take" with the creditor as the acting party, do not say much about the actual nature of the security.[73]

The verb *nasāqu* proves that in certain cases the creditor had the right to select from the debtor's property those items he wanted as

---

[70] Cf. CAD Š$_1$ s.v. *šapartu*. Note that CAD's subdivision of the entry *šapartu* is misleading: many examples cited under paragraph b) "referring to holding a pledge or serving as a pledge" actually refer to the act of pledging itself—because they are found in that part of the contract that records the pledging of property. Consequently, the examples are to be subsumed under CAD's paragraph a) "referring to the act of pledging." AHw orders the text material regarding *šapartu* chronologically.

[71] Cf. *kī šaparte ušbu/ušbat* "to stay as pledge" to refer to a person who serves as a pledge.

[72] So explicitly said in AO 19228 with respect to an *ukâl*-lien: *kīmū ṣibtāte . . . ukâl etanarraš.*

[73] According to Koschaker *iṣabbat* means "he will take possession"; in other words, the creditor will have the pledge in his possession only in the future. The "present tense" of the verb, in Koschaker's opinion, shows that the pledge was hypothecary. When exactly the creditor is to take possession of the pledge, i.e, either before or after maturity of the loan, is unclear (Koschaker 1928: 99).

security for the loan.[74] The creditor could also explicitly be denied this right, so apparently in VDI 80:71 lines 11–12.[75] A certain flexibility in selecting property to be used as security is also reflected in the clause found in KAJ 61 lines 19–22: "if he (the creditor) cannot gain full compensation from his (the debtor's pledged) fields and houses, he will gain full compensation from his sons and daughters."[76]

Four adverbial expressions used in the statement of security help define the function of the security in the loan. The encumbered asset(s) may have been "*in full compensation for*" (*kī našlamte*) the lent object, or "instead of" (*kīmū*) the lent object. The precise legal implications of these two expressions, however, are open to discussion. More illuminating are the following two expressions because they highlight the antichretic character of the security: the first one indicates that the profits which the creditor is to obtain from his use of the encumbered property are "instead of (*kīmū*) interest for the lent object"; the other expression stresses the fact that the encumbered property or persons have been made to dwell "in the house" (*ina bēt*) of the creditor, thereby implying the latter's right to use the property or persons.

The precise legal meaning of the above mentioned term *našlamtu* is not clear. The word is known from Middle Assyrian loans only. It is translated "security" by the CAD,[77] but this is doubtful. Since *našlamtu* is derived from the root *šalāmu* which in the context of security means "to gain full satisfaction for one's loan from the encumbered property,"[78] it is possible that when property was charged *kī našlamte* for the borrowed capital a full compensation for the loan was to be gained from it. It was, therefore, similar in meaning to the expression *kīmū*.[79]

---

[74] So in KAJ 14, 27 (pledges) and 35 (*ukâl*-lien). See also CAD N_2 21 mng. 1 and AHw 753. Different interpretation by Koschaker 1928: 99.

[75] See further Saporetti 1978–1979: 36 with bibliography.

[76] CAD $Š_1$ s.v. *šalāmu* p. 218. This clause comes immediately after the clause that states the pledge of a field. In KAJ 58 lines 19–25 a similar clause is found. See also Koschaker 1928: 107 and 112.

[77] CAD N_2 65. Cf. AHw 760 "Ausgleichszahlung?."

[78] CAD $Š_1$ s.v. *šalāmu* mng. 6 and AHw s.v. *šalāmu* G mng. 7a., and MA examples cited there.

[79] The similarity between both expressions was already pointed out by Koschaker 1928: 112–113, who compared it with NA *kūm*. See also Saporetti 1978–1979: 35 who regards *kī našlamte* and *kīmū* as interchangeable.

It would be wrong to conclude from the use of the expressions *kī našlamte* and *kīmū* that the charged property were substitute payments for the borrowed capital and not security, even if semantically they seem to point in the first direction. If certain property were to stay with the creditor "in lieu of (*kīmū*)" the borrowed capital, i.e. as a substitute payment, it would follow that the debtor had no more liabilities vis-à-vis this property after having delivered it,[80] and had no obligation to return the capital but only possessed a right to redeem his property. The loans with the phrases *kī našlamte* and *kīmū*, however, do not allow for such conclusions for various reasons. First, in all these loans the debtor still had the obligation to pay back the capital of the loan. Second, the redemption clause, which is found in most of these loans,[81] makes redemption of the encumbered property dependent on the full repayment of the debt and its interest by the debtor; this proves that the security was not applicable to the amortization of the loan or its interest. Third, the existence of a *kattû*-lien on the debtor's property in addition to the pledge in KAJ 16 and 65, or in addition to an *ukâl*-lien in VDI 80:71 in order to secure the repayment of the debt shows that the pledge or *ukâl*-lien could not have been in lieu of the debt. Consequently, the Middle Assyrian pledge and *ukâl*-lien were basically security, even when the terminology of certain loans may still reflect the older nature of the lien as a substitute payment.[82]

In most loans the debtor had the right to redeem his encumbered property either upon repayment of the borrowed capital sum, or after he repaid both the borrowed capital and the interest incurred by the loan.[83] Appendix G shows in which loan documents a clause of redemption is attested as well as the way this clause is formulated.[84] The technical term that is commonly used for "to redeem"

[80] Note that MA loan documents do not have a risk clause. Such a clause is attested in the NA period and states that the debtor is liable for the death or loss of the pledge. See Radner 1997: 373–4.

[81] The only loans *kī našlamte*/*kīmū* which lack a redemption clause all provide for the sale of the pledge upon maturity of the loan. See below.

[82] Against Koschaker 1928: 112–113; 124 and 134–135 who maintains that the Middle Assyrian *šapartu* was still basically a substitute payment. Other scholars have pointed out that already in the Middle Assyrian period a development toward security pledge was taking place, as can be seen from certain specific clauses in the contracts: Petschow 1956: 75–77 and n. 226.

[83] Koschaker 1928: 106–108; 112 n. 2.

[84] For the reconstruction of a redemption clause in TR 3007 see Saporetti 1978–1979: 18, but doubtful.

is the verb *paṭāru* "to free" but a few texts use the general verb *leqû* "to take." The former can mean that the debtor was entitled to clear ("free") his encumbered property from any legal claims by the creditor, but it could also have a more "physical" meaning, namely that the debtor had to release ("free") his encumbered property from the hands of the creditor. Similarly, the verb *leqû* could mean either to free the encumbered property in a legal sense, or to take it (back), physically speaking, out of the hands of the creditor. If so, the redemption clause is direct evidence of the possessory character of the redeemable security: being held in possession by the creditor, the debtor had to "take" his security back, or to "free" it from the creditor's hands. It is possible that in some cases the creditor gained possession of the encumbered property only after foreclosure.[85]

The presence or absence of the redemption clause in a given loan document follows a certain pattern. A redemption clause is the rule in loans with antichresis (type 3),[86] and is frequent in short-term interest-bearing loans (type 1). In contrast, a redemption clause is typically absent from loans with sale of the encumbered asset(s) (type 2),[87] on the one hand, and loans in which all of the debtor's property was charged,[88] on the other hand. A redemption clause is also lacking in a few loans of type 1,[89] especially in those of the later period.[90]

Consequently, important information on the nature of the security may be derived from the redemption clause. It is not coincidental that all documents with general liens, for instance, lack a redemption clause, and that all documents with antichretic liens do have such a clause. Since the general liens were hypothecary, the charged property remained in the debtor's possession; consequently, there was no need to "release" or "redeem" the property from the

---

[85] Cf. Koschaker 1928: 106; and see below.

[86] As well as those loans where the use of the verbs *šūšubu* or *eterušu* points to antichresis: KAJ 70, KAJ 58, KAJ 21 (all type 1 loans). For the exceptional cases KAJ 16 and 20 see below.

[87] It is possible but not at all certain that VDI 80:71 and KAJ 66 are exceptions insofar as they provide for the sale of the pledge but also for the possibility of redemption. See further below.

[88] AO 21380, Bi 2, 3, 4, 4a?, KAJ 29, 67, 101, TR 2052 and 3022. For the exceptional cases KAJ 61 and 66 see below.

[89] KAJ 16, 29, 67.

[90] Bi 2, 3, 4, [4a]?, KAJ 31 and TR 2052. On the lack of a redemption clause in certain loan documents see also Koschaker 1928: 106 n. 4.

creditor's hands. The collateral to this reasoning is that a redemption clause was essential to protect the interests of the debtor when the security was possessory. It is, accordingly, not surprising to find a redemption clause in all but one of the secured loans of type 3.[91] These were all long-term loans, or loans for an unspecified period of time with the charge of property in lieu of interest. This charged property, therefore, was held and used as antichresis by the creditor from the onset of the loan. Consequently, it was not self-evident that the debtor will be able to take back the property he had given as a security for the loan once he had paid off his debt. It was, therefore, essential to include a redemption clause in this type of loan, as well as in all the other cases in which the property given as security was held antichretically by the creditor.

It would, of course, be an oversimplification of the facts if we categorically maintained that the occurrence of a redemption clause in the loan document is evidence for the possessory character of the security, whereas the lack of the clause is evidence for the hypothecary character of the security. As applicable as this rule may be in most cases, there are still exceptional or remarkably different cases. KAJ 61 records a loan that is secured by a pledge of all of the debtor's assets but the pledge is redeemable, whereas in all other cases of a general lien a redemption clause is lacking. If the pledge in KAJ 20 was indeed antichretic[92] the lack of a redemption clause is exceptional when compared with the other cases of antichretic pledge, which were all redeemable.[93] The only clear example of a non-redeemable antichretic pledge is attested in KAJ 16. The creditor had antichretic use of the debtor's field, house and threshing-floor, but it is not said that the debtor could redeem this property from the hands of the creditor upon repayment of the capital and interest. Moreover, there also existed a lien (*kattû*) on the debtor's field, house, son and daughter. As for KAJ 66 the matter cannot be decided: Saporetti[94] reconstructs a redemption clause in lines 11–12, but comparison with the other loan documents shows that a redemption

[91] For KAJ 20 see below.

[92] This may be doubted because there is no explicit statement in this respect.

[93] Koschaker 1928: 95 n. 4 and 106 n. 1 assumed that there was a redemption clause in KAJ 20. However, at the place where we can expect the clause in question (in lines 13ff.) there is hardly space for such a reconstruction: 13. [*ša*] D 14. [C] 15. [*ú-ka-al*] 16. [*a-na*] É *d*[*u-un-ni-šu*] . . .

[94] Saporetti 1981: 16.

clause is not found in this type of loan. VDI 80:71 is difficult to categorize in one or the other type of loans. It shares with type 2 loans the possibility of pledge sale but in every other respect it differs from type 2 loans and resembles type 3 loans. It is a long term loan, the pledge is "instead of interest"—hence antichretic—, and redeemable. If interpreted as a type 2 loan the redemption clause in VDI 80:71 would be extraordinary in the light of the rule that sold pledges were irredeemable. Finally, it is noteworthy that in KAJ 31 the debtor would lose his wife if he defaulted, failing to pay off his debt in time. According to Koschaker the lack of the redemption clause in this document, therefore, was most probably due to the scribe's negligence.[95]

The debtor had the right to redeem his property given as security for the loan by paying back the capital sum as long as the basic term of the loan had not expired. A defaulting debtor, on the other hand, could only under certain specific circumstances redeem his property. In the pledged loans of type 1, for instance, the debtor had to pay not only the capital sum but also the accrued interest in order to redeem his pledge.[96] The provision that the debtor would have to pay interest in addition to the capital sum in order to redeem his pledge seems to contradict another provision of such loans, namely that the accrual of interest will take place only if the debtor fails to pay his debt at the fixed time. It follows from the latter provision that the debtor could redeem his pledge by paying only the capital, without interest, as long as the date for repayment had not expired. We may, therefore, assume that the obligation to pay interest existed only if the debtor had failed to pay off his debt within the fixed time.[97] Before foreclosure of the loan the debtor could redeem his pledge, if necessary, by returning the borrowed capital without interest, even if the contracts do not explicitly say so. The silence of the contracts on this point is understandable because not in all cases was it necessary to redeem the pledge before the due date. Indeed, in those loans in which the pledge was not antichretic,[98] there was

---

[95] Koschaker 1928: 106 n. 4.

[96] KAJ 11: the borrowed tin, its interest, and the harvesters. The latter probably referred to the seven harvesters who had been borrowed (line 7) as well as to the unspecified number of harvesters which the debtor had to supply in case of default (lines 11–12).

[97] Cf. Aynard-Durand 1980: 18.

[98] All loans of type 1 with pledges, except for KAJ 16, 21, 58 and 70 which are antichretic.

no need to redeem the pledge before foreclosure of the loan if we assume that the pledge was hypothecary and hence not in the creditor's possession. Only at foreclosure would the pledge become possessory and needed to be redeemed. The latter was possible only if the debtor paid the borrowed capital and the interest, since the accrual of interest had taken effect. It is the latter case which is explicitly regulated by the contracts.

It was impossible for the debtor to redeem his property after foreclosure in the loans of type 3 and in VDI 80:71 (see s.v. type 2), all being long term loans with antichretic use of the encumbered property in lieu of the interest, because the property was then either sold or the status quo was to be continued. AO 19228, for instance, describes the following procedure: a) after eight years the debt matures and the debtor has to pay the tin in order to redeem his encumbered property (lines 15–17); b) if the debtor does not have the necessary tin to repay his debt, he can sell the encumbered property to the creditor (lines 18–20);[99] c) if the debtor does not pay the tin nor sells the property, the status quo is extended for another period (*kī pānītišūma . . . ukâl*, lines 21–23). A similar procedure is depicted in VDI 80:71: if the debtor paid his debt within four years, he was allowed to "take" back his threshing-floor, i.e. his encumbered asset (lines 13–15); if not, the threshing-floor was to become the creditor's property without the possibility of redeeming it (lines 16–20).[100] KAJ 13 is less elaborate but clearly states that "after six years he will repay completely the borrowed tin and redeem his field," (line 27). The other loans of the type 3 lack such specifications and it is therefore not clear from them whether or not the debtor could redeem his property also after the debt matured.

Finally, in loans of type 2, which stipulate sale of the encumbered property to the creditor after the date for repayment has passed, the debtor could not redeem unless he had paid the borrowed capital (*qaqqadu*) within the agreed period of time.

The fact that the debtor had to return the entire value of the loan in order to free his property proves that Middle Assyrian pledge

---

[99] This proves that the creditor did not enjoy full possession over the property that he held as security. It was still the debtor who had ownership thereof: he could sell the encumbered field, in which case AO 19228 allows the creditor to buy it (lines 18–20). Moreover, the debtor could, theoretically at least, give the field to another creditor as security, but practically speaking, such an act by the debtor is prohibited according to AO 19228 line 24.

[100] More on VDI 80:71 below.

and *ukâl*-lien were not applicable to the amortization of the loan. At most the charged property substituted for interest, but in those cases in which capital and interest had to be paid before redemption, even this was not the case and the pledge or *ukâl*-lien, therefore, were no more than a (general) security for repayment of the loan.

VI. Maturity and Default

If the loan was not paid back at the agreed time, the creditor could recover his capital by means of a sale from the debtor's assets. In the optimal case the loan had been secured by some form of lien from the outset under the condition that upon default the charged assets were to become the permanent property of the creditor, without the possibility of redemption.

In the Middle Assyrian period this procedure (known in German as *Verfallspfand*) is attested in AO 19228 and the loan documents of type 2 only, and can, therefore, not have been general practice.[101] In addition, the existence of *Verfallspfand* is implied by those sale documents in which property that had been pledged as security for a debt is sold to the creditor in order to satisfy his claim to payment of the debt.[102] Sporadic references to *Verfallspfand* are also found in some annulments of debts.[103] It almost always concerns real estate.[104]

The clause regulating the transfer of the encumbered property to the creditor's ownership contains formulations which are reminiscent of the sale formulary. The formulation found in KAJ 27, lines 16–21, may serve as a representative example: *edannu ettiqma eqelšu* (= Pledged O) *uppu laqi tuāru u dabābu laššu šīm eqlēšu maḫir apil zaku eqelšu uzakka ina ašal šarre imaddad* "if the term (for repayment) expires, his field is (considered) acquired and taken (into possession).[105] There is no contesting (the transaction). He (= the debtor) has received the price of

[101] Cf. Koschaker 1928: 102–105.

[102] KAJ 150 (Koschaker 1928: 102 n. 2 and 103–104), KAJ 162 and KAV 211. Probably also KAJ 157, so Saporetti 1978–1979: 77 and 1979: 46–47.

[103] KAJ 142 (Koschaker 1928: 102 n. 2), TR 3001 and TR 3002 (although the nature of the pledge in the latter two texts cannot be determined because the texts are too laconic).

[104] The only exception is KAJ 66 in which the debtor pledged his field, house, threshing-floor, well, sons and daughters; in short, all his property, and all this will become the creditor's property if the debtor fails to pay within the time limit.

[105] For the expression *uppu laqe* see Postgate 1976: 14–15.

his field, (and) he is paid off (and) quit. He (= the debtor) shall clear his field (from claims by third parties), (and) measure it according to the king's rope."

The transfer of ownership over the encumbered property did not take place automatically with expiry of the set term for repayment. It was to be accompanied by several legal steps: the debtor had to clear the encumbered object from claims by third parties, a conveyance text had to be drafted before the king, the creditor had to reimburse the debtor for the difference between the market value of the encumbered property and the value of the debt, and even the king was sometimes called upon to smooth out problems between the debtor, who was the previous owner, and the creditor, who was to become the new owner (so in KAJ 170 + KAV 211). These legal steps belong to the law of sale, and consequently, the practice of *Verfallspfand* had already developed into the more sophisticated practice of "pledge sale" (German *Verkaufspfand*).[106] This development must have been the result of certain economic and social changes which strove to protect the debtor's interests.[107]

In the description of the act of charging property as security at the beginning of the loan documents with *Verfallspfand* (type 2 loans) it is often specified that the property was charged *kīmū* "instead of" the borrowed object, or *kī našlamte* "as full compensation for" for the borrowed object. Although these expressions remain ambiguous, some light is thrown on their meaning if we take into account that the charged property was to be used as a payment for the loan (a *Verfallspfand*); in other words, was in lieu of the entire loan and not only in lieu of the interest to be paid.

One document of type 2, namely VDI 80:71, needs special attention because it is a borderline case between type 3 and type 2 loans. This document provides as follows: the debtor was to pay back "the capital of the (borrowed) corn" (*qaqqad še'im*, line 6) after four years, whereas the interest was covered by encumbering a threshing-floor (lines 7–11).[108] If the debtor paid his debt within four years (4 *šanāte ušallam še'am imaddad*), he was allowed to "take" back his threshing-floor (*adaršu ilaqqe*, lines 13–15); if not, the threshing-floor was to become the creditor's property without the possibility of redemption

[106] Cf. Koschaker 1928: 103–104. Petschow 1956: 120 n. 370 and 130 n. 395g.
[107] Petschow 1956: 121 n. 376.
[108] The meaning of the following line (line 12) is unclear.

(lines 16–20). The loan that is recorded in this document clearly belongs to type 2 because of the *Verfallspfand* mentioned in lines 16–20. We would expect a *Verfallspfand* to secure the entire loan, but the text states that the debtor's threshing-floor was given "instead of the interest" (*kīmū ṣibtāte*) only (lines 7–11), a feature characteristic of loans of type 3. The problem arises: if the pledge was indeed in lieu of the interest only, how had repayment of the capital sum been secured? The solution to this problem perhaps lies in the fact that this contract provides for an additional security in the form of a *kattû*-lien on the remaining belongings of the debtor (line 21: *kattê še'im bašīšu bušīšu*). Consequently, it seems to me that the interest was secured by the encumbered threshing-floor, whereas repayment of the capital of the loan was guaranteed by a general *kattû*-lien. In addition, it is to be noted that this was a long-term loan and that the creditor enjoyed the use of the debtor's threshing-floor, which he held (*ukâl*) in lieu of interest, during these eight years. VDI 80:71, therefore, belongs to the loans of type 2 because of the *Verfallspfand*, and to the loans of type 3 because of the long-term antichretic use of the encumbered asset.

In addition to the secured loans of type 2 and AO 19228 there are some loans which were not secured by a pledge or any other form of lien, but nevertheless provided for the transfer of ownership over some of the debtor's property to the creditor upon default (types 5.3 and 5.4). The clause regarding the transfer of the debtor's property to the creditor's ownership is formulated in a manner similar to the clause regarding the transfer of pledged property to the creditor's ownership in loans of type 2: both use the verbs *uppu laqi*.[109] The creditor's claim to satisfaction for his loan from a sale was limited to specific assets. He was to choose from the debtor's property and pick out particular items (only in KAJ 35; *inassaq ilaqqe*) which were then charged (*ukâl*) for sale to the creditor's benefit (*uppu laqi*).[110]

If sale was not provided for in the contract, the creditor could proceed against the delinquent debtor in various ways but did not necessarily recover the capital. In most cases the creditor put pressure on the debtor by requiring the accrual of interest. This is attested in the loans of types 1 and 5.1 as well as in several type 4-loans.

[109] KAJ 26, 35 and 64 = 68: these loans without the preliminary arrangement of security are considered by Koschaker (1928: 102 n. 2) as evidence of *Verfallspfand*.

[110] For the details regarding the formula, see Appendix E.3.

A second possibility was by creating a general lien. This is the case in loans of type 5.2 and in TR 3022 (type 4). They contain a clause which resembles the clause found in the loans of types 5.3–4 regarding the transfer of some or all of the debtor's property to the creditor at foreclosure but significantly differ from the latter because they lack the essential phrase *uppu laqi*. Moreover, they concern all of the debtor's unencumbered property. The verbs used in these clauses are (*iṣabbat*) *ukâl*, which, as we saw above, are typically used to describe the creation of a lien. Consequently, these texts provide for the establishment of some kind of general lien on the debtor's property, not during the basic term of the loan but at its maturity, upon default. Thirdly, the debtor could be pressed to pay after the date of repayment had expired by the combination of the accrual of interest and a general lien (type 5.5), or the accrual of interest and the obligation to supply a harvest or harvesters (s.v. type 1; and type 5.6).[111]

No real sanction existed for the delinquent debtor in the loans of type 3. If the debtor failed to pay, the state of prolonged antichresis was extended for another couple of years. Occasionally, the debtor could be asked to sell an item from his property, as is shown by AO 19228 (see above), but it was no more than an option to be decided by the debtor. If he preferred neither to pay nor to sell, the status quo was maintained. The creditor must have gained satisfaction in a different way, which will be examined in the next paragraph after we have considered two more issues that are related to the collection of debts upon default.

The creditor could send someone to collect the debts from his debtors, probably upon default. This practice gave rise to a special kind of contract, which is especially frequent in official context.[112] These contracts start with listing the content of one or more document(s) (e.g. 1 *ṭuppu ša* 26[?] *emmerē*... *ša ina muḫḫe* D *šaṭrutūni*, KAJ 115: 2–5), stating that this/these document(s) had/have been given to an agent of the creditor for collection (*ana šaddūni tadnā*/*tadnat*(*ā*)). The agent shall collect the debt(s) and give (*ušaddan iddan*) the proceeds to the creditor and then he may break his tablet (*u ṭuppūšu iḫappi*).[113]

[111] Also KAJ 52 of type 4 but without interest.
[112] See below Appendix C.5.
[113] Cf. the receipts Bi 9 (1 *ṭuppu ša x anneke ša* C *ša ina muḫḫe* D *šaṭrutūni ana* PN *ana šaddūne tadnat ša pī tuppe šuāte* C *maḫir*), Bi 13 (*ana pî ṭuppe našpirte ša* C *maḫir*),

It is not known how the agents made the debtors pay their debts, and whether any force was used to make the debtor pay.

Finally, Saporetti[114] maintained that if the debtor claimed insolvency the authorities were called upon by the creditor to help him collect his debt. Saporetti's theory is based on his interpretation of the idiom *ṭuppu ṣabātu*, literally "to seize the tablet." According to him it refers to a procedure of debt collection[115] that was initiated by the creditor and audited by the court. The procedure led to the drawing up of a "seized tablet" (a *ṭuppu ṣabittu*), which is understood by Saporetti as a kind of court order pressing the insolvent debtor to pay. Saporetti's interpretation, however, cannot be accepted. In fact, the procedure known as "to seize the tablet" (*ṭuppu ṣabātu*), and its result, the "seized tablet" (*ṭuppu ṣabittu*), have been much debated and still remain open to discussion.[116] The scribe may "seize" the tablet, meaning that he "keeps the tablet in an archive" (Johns), "holds the tablet while writing it" (Jas); "executes" it while preparing a witnessed and sealed document (Postgate); or the creditor may "seize" the tablet, meaning that he collects the obligation recorded in it with or without court approval (Zaccagnini and Saporetti); or a neutral third party, who may or may not be the scribe, "seizes" the tablet, meaning that he "takes it into safekeeping" (CAD, Parpola), until the agreement that is recorded in it is realized, the purchase price eventually paid, or the borrowed object actually delivered (Radner).[117] At all events, the MA *ṭuppu ṣabittu* clearly served the creditor as proof of the loan or other obligation, even if the exact procedure behind it remains uncertain. It still remains to be explained when or why a creditor needed such a proof.[118]

---

and TR 3016 ([1 *ṭupp*]*e* x *anneke ša ekalle* [. . .] *ša* C *ša ina muḫḫe* D PN *ana šipirte ša* C *maḫir*).

[114] Saporetti 1978–1979: 87–89.

[115] Cf. Zaccagnini 1997: 208, but refuted by Radner 1997: 76 n. 392 and 393; 90 n. 491.

[116] For a recent survey of the problem with bibliographic references, see Radner 1997: 89–90.

[117] Radner: 90–91. See also Radner's interpretation of KAJ 83: Lulāyu borrowed corn from Aššur-aḫa-iddina but the corn had not been delivered. Ištar-kidinni is charged by Aššur-aḫa-iddina to go and deliver the corn to Lulāyu. Upon delivery he is to "seize the tablet", i.e. he is to keep the debt note, that had already been drawn up, in safekeeping so that Aššur-aḫa-iddina will have proof of his loan.

[118] See Radner's suggestion, Radner 1997: 91–92.

VII. Other Measures to Satisfy the Creditor

In the Middle Assyrian period various procedures were developed to grant the creditor some advantage from his loan other than reimbursement, sometimes involving instruments of security. First, the creditor could gain from the loan by using the debtor's services in agriculture. Indeed, in many loan documents the creditor granted the loan on condition that the debtor extend a helping hand during the harvest (= type 4),[119] or manufacture a garment for him (KAJ 77 s.v. type 4). Pressure was put on the debtor by prescribing a penalty for non-performance of the service during the basic term of the loan. Moreover, failure to pay back the loan in time would bring upon the debtor additional sanctions by the accrual of interest or the demand of another harvest. In one case we hear of a subsidiary general *ukâl*-lien on the debtor's assets as a means of forcing the debtor to pay his debt, but the lien was to take effect only after the basic term of the loan had expired (TR 3022).

Second, at times the creditor was more interested in a prolonged use and enjoyment of the debtor's property than in the actual repayment of the loan. The pledge or lien in these cases did not so much serve to secure repayment of the loan as to grant the creditor usufruct rights over the debtor's property. This practice is attested in the loans of type 3. These were long-term loans or loans for an unspecified period of time with antichretic use of the pledge or *ukâl*-lien in lieu of interest. Since the creditor held the debtor's property "instead of interest" (*kīmū ṣibtāte . . .* C *ukâl*),[120] no interest had to be paid (*annuku ṣibta lā īšu . . .*,[121] or *še'um/annuku ana ṣibta lā illak*[122]).[123] He was interested in the use of the debtor's property for his own profit[124] over

[119] Cf. Koschaker 1928: 108ff. and Lautner 1936: 22–26.

[120] So explicitly stated in Bi 5 and AO 19228. In VAS 19 20 the creditor holds the debtor's field "instead of" (*kīmū*) the twenty bows which he lent the debtor.

[121] KAJ 13 and AO 19228.

[122] KAJ 30 and Bi 5.

[123] A clause pertaining to antichresis is lacking in KAJ 17 and 20 but these documents are nevertheless to be considered as reflecting loans of type 3 for the following reasons: 1) they are long-term loans; 2) they do not provide for interest which could be interpreted as equal to providing for antichresis instead of interest, found in the other long-term loans; 3) KAJ 17 has the redemption clause (*ipaṭṭar*), also found in the other long term loans.

[124] Note, however, that Durand interpreted the verb *etenarraš* as referring to a duty of the creditor, namely to maintain the pledged field(s), rather than a right, namely to enjoy the produce of the field (see Aynard-Durand 1980: 6 and 8).

many years or even as long as he wished. The debtor had the right to redeem his pledge after having paid his debt (except for KAJ 20). It is possible that the short-term loans in which the pledge was to be sold to the creditor in case of default reflect similar interests.[125] These were loans of tin or corn with the encumbrance of a field,[126] which the creditor was entitled to buy if the debtor failed to pay back the loan within four to six months.[127]

In KAJ 32, 37 and 39 (all type 1 loans) the loan had been granted to finance a business trip and the creditor must therefore have enjoyed at least a share in the profits, although the texts do not explicitly say so.[128] The other loans of the same type do not mention any business journey but they contain a statement regarding the debtor's financial reliability and are secured by a *kattû*-lien so that the creditor could reckon on recovery of his money even if the business venture did not turn out successfully.[129]

Finally, it remains unclear to me how the creditor could possibly get his loan repaid or gain from it in the loans of type 6 and the governmental loans,[130] because the contracts do not provide for any security, sanction or profit.

VIII. A Socio-Economic Analysis of Middle Assyrian Security

More knowledge of the socio-economic situation in Assyria in the Middle Assyrian period[131] would, no doubt, enable us to understand

---

[125] Type 2 loans. Problematic in this respect is only KAJ 66 because it would mean that the creditor was to acquire not only the debtor's field, house, threshing-floor and wells, but also his sons and his daughters; unfortunately the date for repayment is broken. For the similarity between VDI 80:71 and long-term antichretic loans of type 3 see above. VAS 19 36 is too fragmentary.

[126] A threshing-floor and an orchard in KAJ 63.

[127] Only KAJ 24 is for a little longer, namely for one year.

[128] KAJ 32: (silver) *ištu* C D *u tappaūšu ēṣūtu u mādūtu ana tapūtte ana ḫarrān* GN? *ilqeū*, "D and his partners borrowed silver from C for a joint business trip to GN." KAJ 39: (silver) *ištu* C *ina muḫḫe* D *ilqe ana ḫarrāne ša* GN, "D borrowed (silver) from C for a business trip to GN" (Cf. CAD H 110). In both cases the debt is to be repaid *ina erēb ḫarrāne*(*šunu*), "upon the return of the(ir) caravan." Cf. KAJ 37 where the debtor *ana urḫi* MN *ḫarrānēšu uppašma annaka u ṣibassu iḫīaṭ* "will make a business trip until the month MN and (then) pay the tin and interest on it" (cf. CAD E 208).

[129] See above.

[130] See, however, notes 181–182 below.

[131] Postgate 1971 and Garelli 1967.

better the social environment in which loans (including secured loans) were granted. In particular it would tell us about: the social position of the lenders and their relation to the government (palace); the social position of the debtors and the organization of the rural communities; the social conditions which led to the granting or taking of loans. However, a comprehensive survey of the socio-economic situation in Assyria in the Middle Assyrian period is beyond the scope of the present paper. The following discussion is limited to a choice of texts that contain evidence on the socio-economic conditions of some of the loans. In particular they inform us of the circumstances that could lead to debt slavery or other forms of servitude.

When economic hardship hit a person, his family or his village, he could either borrow corn from government stocks or enter in the service of a wealthy individual. Two texts from Urad-Šerūa's archive show the practice of granting loans, from government stocks, to the rural population in their times of need.[132] A recurring phrase in these texts brings out the fact that the loans were made for the benefit of the borrower's family or village in times of hardship: in KAJ 101 the person borrows the corn so that "he will maintain his household in the absence of any of his own" (*bēssu uballiṭ ina lā šuāte*, lines 12–13); similarly, in VAS 19 47 the borrower takes the corn and gives it to the member(s) of his village "in the absence of any of his own" (*ina lā šuāte*, lines 15–17).[133] The texts show the economic distress of the northern rural communities outside the capital Assur in years of low rainfall and consequent crop failure. As Postgate pointed out in his commentary on nos. 55–56 these were not cases of individual improvidence, but a general agricultural crisis forcing families and entire villages to borrow by the threat of starvation. Moreover, they show that the government could take advantage of the general agricultural crisis by granting the loans under what seem to be harsh conditions.[134] The debtors had not only to repay the corn and a

---

[132] KAJ 101 (= *Urad-Šerūa* 55) and VAS 19 47 (= *Urad-Šerūa* 56). See also Aynard-Durand 1980: 41 and n. 50.

[133] KAJ 91 is similar to KAJ 101 and VAS 19 47 in so far that it concerns the loan of corn, animals and harvesters from an official. It differs from the other two documents in so far that it does not specify that the borrowed commodities were taken from government stocks (*ša pit/pitte ḫašīme*) and were to be given to the family or village of the borrower in view of their destitution (*ina lā šuāte*). Cf. Postgate 1988: 143–144.

[134] So Postgate 1988: 145.

hundred percent interest on it within a fixed time,[135] but also, so it seems, to put the harvesters who were borrowed to work at harvest time, and to herd the borrowed sheep. Moreover, the borrower in KAJ 101 had to charge "his field and his house, all his unencumbered assets (*mimmūšu gabba zakua*)" as security for the loan.

Economic hardship may also have been the reason for the loan in KAJ 46. This loan was interpreted as a "charity" loan by Koschaker[136] since the loan was granted to the debtor "for his support" (*ana usītīšu*)[137] and did not bear interest. In contrast, Saporetti believes that the loan was granted to help finance some commercial activity.[138]

As for the phenomenon of debt slavery, there is plenty of evidence from the archives that were reconstructed by Saporetti in DSC 1 and 3. The archives show how once wealthy land-owning families gradually became impoverished, even to the point that family members had to be given in pledge but could not be redeemed.[139] The presence of the original loan documents with the statement of security in the archives of the creditor proves that the loans had not been paid back and consequently the encumbered property or persons had not been redeemed. It seems that, in general, many of the loans in the Middle Assyrian private archives have not been repaid, and the documents were probably kept in the creditor's archive because of the security mentioned—especially when it involved real estate, as was actually the case in most secured loans. It is also possible that in some cases the documents of unpaid loans were kept in the archive to be given for collection (e.g. in Urad-Šerūa's archive).

Additional evidence on debt slavery may be found in KAJ 102, KAJ 167 and KAJ 7, although the interpretation of the latter two

[135] The repayment clauses concern "the corn and its equal amount (*mitḫāršu*)": KAJ 91 lines 21–25 and KAJ 101 lines 14–15. VAS 19 47 lines 26–28 are too fragmentary. For *mitḫāru* see CAD M$_2$ 137 (mng. 1c) "equal amount (as fine for a debt past due)," but note that this cannot apply to KAJ 91 and 101 because the *mithāru* is to be paid before expiry of the due date. For the expression *ana mitḫār* (repayment of the loan "in the same amount," i.e. without interest) in the loan TR 3013 see Saporetti 1978–1979: 29.

[136] Koschaker 1928: 95.

[137] AHw 1437b s.v. *usātu* "Hilfe, Unterstützung".

[138] Thus he understands the expression *ana usītīšu* (Saporetti 1978–1979: 68).

[139] E.g. Members of family L who took loans from family A during four generations (recorded in ARu 53, KAJ 11, 12, 14, 26, 29, 53, 61, 63, 79 = 166, 157, 161, 163, and 165), see more Saporetti 1979: 20–21 and 32–33.

texts is open to discussion. KAJ 102 regulates the transfer of ownership of the son of PN to PN_2 and includes the renunciation by PN_3 of his rights over the transferred person. PN_2 was probably the creditor to whom PN had pledged his son. This son was later sold to PN_2 in order to pay back the loan. PN_3 may have been another creditor of PN still waiting for the repayment of his loan.[140] KAJ 167 and KAJ 7 recount the release from servitude of an "Assyrian" woman who had been taken in by someone (*lequ͂*, KAJ 167 line 4) in order to be saved from famine or some other calamity (*ana baluṭ u leqe*, KAJ 167 line 4).[141] The status of this woman has been much discussed. According to Koschaker and Garelli she had been "taken" (*leqe*) as pledge to secure a debt;[142] consequently, the texts would be evidence for the redemption of pledged persons from debt slavery in the Middle Assyrian period. According to other scholars the woman had been taken in as adoptee (so Oppenheim and the CAD),[143] or as a ward out of an act of charity by a wealthy individual (so Durand).[144] In the course of time she was released from her state of servitude (*ina amūtīša uzakkīši*, KAJ 7) by a third person who gave a substitute person as ransom (*ipṭēru*, KAJ 167, KAJ 7). She married the person who released her. The latter was an *ālāiu* of Amurru-nāṣir, which meant that he had to serve Amurru-nāṣir in one way or the other. The woman acquired her husband's status and both were to serve Amurru-nāṣir.[145]

Finally, one may also look in KAJ 168 for evidence on debt slavery. The text is formulated as a loan,[146] but was interpreted by

---

[140] See Postgate 1988: 66.

[141] Re-edited by Saporetti 1982: 55–57 and 144–145 (Family C).

[142] Koschaker 1928: 107. Garelli 1967: 13.

[143] Oppenheim 1955: 73–74.

[144] Aynard-Durand 1980: 23–25.

[145] About the status of *ālāiu* ("villagers") we also hear in AO 20154 (Aynard-Durand 1980: 19–27). This text is a manumission document in which three brothers (ll. 1–5), who have the status of *ālāiu* (ll. 6–8), release themselves (*ina migrat <raminīšunu> ipṭīrīšunu ana* PN *ittanū*, ll. 9–13). The text does not specify how the release was effected (unlike KAJ 167 which mentions a substitute). The text, thereupon, states that the former master of the brothers assumed responsibility for their release from the status of *ālāiu* (*[p]āḫat <ištu> [aḫ]hē z[akkue]* PN *n[aši]*, ll. 14–16).

[146] Judging from the following structure: Seal of debtor—Object of loan (tin)—Statement of loan (*ša* C *ina muḫḫe* D *il*$_5^!$*-ti-qí-ma*)—Purpose of the loan (*annuku anniu ana šīm* 1 *sinnište tadnašu*)—Clause stating that *sinništa uballaṭu*—Reimbursement of the debtor if the market value of the woman was higher than the value of the debt (*šīm sinništēšu isassiū reḫte annekēšu ilaqqi*). Postgate 1988: 120–121 reads ^{uru}*ti-qi-ma* in line 9 instead of Durand's reading *il*$_5^!$*-ti-qí-ma*.

Koschaker[147] as an example of the sale by auction of a pledged bondwoman upon default. In contrast, Durand[148] understood the text as a loan of silver (ll. 1–9) to help finance the purchase of a woman (ll. 10–12) on condition that the purchased woman serve the creditor (l. 13). The creditor, Uqur-abi, did not fix a date for repayment nor did he demand any security for the loan. Instead "he (Uqur-abi) will let the woman live" (l. 13) which, according to Durand, meant that the woman was to serve Uqur-abi. The latter could also sell the woman (l. 14) but would then have to reimburse his debtor for any difference in value (l. 15). Still other interpretations have been proposed by Oppenheim[149] and Postgate.[150]

As pointed out above, the reason for a person's impoverishment and state of servitude was not necessarily indebtedness. Other reasons must be considered, such as famine as the result of drought and failing crops,[151] as well as certain developments in the pattern of land tenure.[152] The gradual growth of latifundia in the Middle Assyrian period was often at the expense of smaller landholdings. Small farmers were deprived of their means of living and were hardly able to make both ends meet unless they entered into the service of the landed gentry. They may have stayed on their original farm but had now become part of a growing group of poor agricultural workers in the service of others, also known as "villager of so-and-so" (*ālāiu*).

[147] Koschaker 1928: 97 n. 5 and 105.
[148] Aynard-Durand 1982: 25 n. 29.
[149] Oppenheim 1955: 74.
[150] Postgate 1988: 122. I do not understand how Mušallim-Marduk could at the same time be the seller of the bondwoman and the debtor of part of the purchase price, as Postgate seems to suggest in his comment on the text.
[151] So Aynard-Durand 1980: 23 n. 24 with respect to KAJ 167.
[152] So Aynard-Durand 1980: 26–27 and n. 32 with respect to the status of *ālāiu*.

Abbreviations

ARu	M. David and E. Ebeling. Assyrische Rechtsurkunden. *Zeitschrift für vergleichende Rechtswissenschaft* 44 (1929): 305–381.
Bi	Texts from Tell Billa. See Finkelstein 1953.
DSC	Data Sets. Cuneiform Texts. See Saporetti 1979 and 1982.
MARV	Mittelassyrische Rechtsurkunden und Verwaltungstexte. See Freydank 1976 and 1982a.
OIP 79	Texts from Tell Fakhariyeh. See Güterbock 1979.
TCL 9	G. Contenau. *Contrats et lettres d'Assyrie et de Babylonie.* Musée du Louvre. Département des antiquités orientales. Textes cunéiformes 9. Paris: P. Geuthner, 1926.
TR	Texts from Tell Al Rimah. See Saggs-Wiseman 1986.
Urad-Šerūa	Texts from the archive of Urad-Šerūa. See Postgate 1988.

Bibliography

Aynard, M.-J., and J.-M. Durand. 1980. Documents d'époque médio-assyrienne. *Assur* 3: 1–54.

Cancik-Kirschbaum, E.C. 1996a. *Die mittelassyrischen Briefe aus Tall Šēḫ Hamad.* Berichte der Ausgrabung Tall *Šēḫ* Hamad/Dur-katlimmu, Band 4. Berlin: D. Reimer.

——. 1996b. Addenda und Corrigenda zu BATSH. *NABU*: 65–68.

Cardellini, I. 1981. *Die biblischen "Sklaven"-Gesetze im Lichte des keilschriftlichen Sklavenrechts.* Bonner Biblische Beiträge 55. Koenigstein/Ts.-Bonn: P. Hanstein.

Chirichigno, G.C. 1993. *Debt-Slavery in Israel and the Ancient Near East.* Journal for the Study of the Old Testament. Supplement Series 141. Sheffield: Sheffield Academic Press.

Deller, K. and C. Saporetti. 1970a. Documenti medio-assiri redatti per annullare un precedente contratto. *OrAn* 9: 29–59.

——. 1970b. Documenti medio-assiri redatti a titolo di ricevuta dietro parziale adempimento di un debito. *OrAn* 9: 285–314.

Eichler, B. 1973. Indenture at Nuzi. The Personal *tidennūtu* Contract and its Mesopotamian Analogues. Yale Near Eastern Researches 5. New Haven: Yale University Press.

Finkelstein, J.J. 1952. The Middle-Assyrian *šulmānu*-Texts. *JAOS* 72: 77–80.

——. 1953. Cuneiform Texts from Tell Billa. *JCS* 7: 111–176.

Freydank, H. 1976. *Mittelassyrische Rechtsurkunden und Verwaltungstexte* I. Vorderasiatische Schriftdenkmäler der Staatliche Museen zu Berlin 19 (Neue Folge 3). Berlin: Akademie Verlag.

——. 1982a. *Mittelassyrische Rechtsurkunden und Verwaltungstexte* I. Vorderasiatische Schriftdenkmäler der Staatliche Museen zu Berlin 21 (Neue Folge 5). Berlin: Akademie Verlag.

——. 1982b. Fernhandel und Warenpreise nach einer mittelassyrischen Urkunde des 12. Jahrhunderts v.u.Z. In *Societies and Languages of the Ancient Near East: Studies in Honour of I.M. Diakonoff*, ed. M.A. Dandamayev et al. Pp. 64–75. Warminster: Aris & Phillips.

——. 1992. Das Archiv Assur 18764. *AoF* 19: 276–321.

Garelli, P. 1967. Le Problème de la "féodalité" assyrienne du XVe au XIIe siècle av. J.-C. *Semitica* 17: 5–21.

Güterbock, H.J. 1979. In *Soundings at Tell Fakhariyah.* The University of Chicago. Oriental Institute Publications 79. Publication of tablets on Pp. 186–190. Chicago: The University of Chicago Press.

Harrak, A. 1987. *Assyria and Hanigalbat.* Hildesheim: G. Olms.

Ismail, B.Kh. 1968. Fünf mittelassyrische Texte aus Assur. *Sumer* 24: 17–38.

——. 1982. Informationen über Tontafeln aus Tell Ali. Studien. In H. Klengel (ed.), *Gesellschaft und Kultur im alten Vorderasien.* Schriften zur Geschichte und Kultur des Alten Orients 15. Pp. 117–120. Berlin: Akademie Verlag.

Jankowska, N.B. 1962. Un nouveau document juridique assyrien. (In Russian). *Vestnik Drevnei Istorii* 80/2: 67–74.

Korošec, V. 1964. Keilschriftrecht. In *Handbuch der Orientalistik* 1/3. Pp. 49–218. Leiden: E.J. Brill.

Koschaker, P. 1928. *Neue Keilschriftliche Rechtsurkunden aus der El-Amarna Zeit.* Abhandlungen der Sächsischen Akademie der Wissenschaften zu Leipzig, Philologisch-historische Klasse 39/5. Leipzig: S. Hirzel.

Lautner, J.G. 1936. *Altbabylonische Personenmiete und Erntearbeiterverträge.* Studia et Documenta ad Iura Orientis Antiqua 1. Leiden: E.J. Brill.

Laessøe, J. 1959. The Bazmusian Tablets. *Sumer* 15: 15–18.
Machinist, P. 1982. Provincial Governance in Middle Assyria and Some New Texts from Yale. *Assur* 3: 65–101 and Plates I–IV.
Oppenheim, A.L. 1955. "Siege-Documents" from Nippur. *Iraq* 17: 69–89.
Pedersen, O. 1985. *Archives and Libraries in the City of Assur. A Survey of the Material from the German Excavations.* Band I. Acta Universitatis Upsaliensis, Studia Semitica Upsaliensia 6. Uppsala: Almqvist & Wiksell.
——. 1986. *Idem.* Band II.
——. 1998. *Idem.* Band III.
Petschow, H. 1956. *Neubabylonisches Pfandrecht.* Abhandlungen der Sächsischen Akademie der Wissenschaften zu Leipzig, Philologisch-historische Klasse 48/1. Berlin: Akademie Verlag.
Postgate, J.N. 1971. Land Tenure in the Middle Assyrian Period: A Reconstruction. *BSOAS* 34: 496–520.
——. 1976. *Fifty Neo-Assyrian Legal Documents.* Warminster: Aris & Phillips.
——. 1986. Middle Assyrian Tablets: The Instruments of Bureaucracy. *AoF* 13: 10–39.
——. 1988. *The Archive of Urad-Šerūa and his Family. A Middle Assyrian Household in Government Service.* Roma: Editore Roberto Denicola.
——. 1997. Middle Assyrian to Neo Assyrian: The Nature of the Shift. In *Assyrien im Wandel der Zeiten,* ed. H. Hauptman and H. Waetzoldt. Pp. 159–168. Heidelberger Studien zum Alten Orient 6 (= CRRAI 39). Heidelberg: Heidelberger Orientverlag.
Radner, K. 1997. *Die neuassyrischen Privatrechtsurkunden als Quelle für Mensch und Umwelt.* State Archives of Assyria Studies 6. Helsinki: The Neo-Assyrian Text Corpus Project.
Röllig, W. 1984. Preliminary Remarks on the Middle-Assyrian Archive from Tell Schech Hamad/Dūr Kattlimu. *AAAS* 34: 158, 189–194.
Saggs, H.W.F. and D.J. Wiseman. 1968. The Tell Al Rimah Tablets, 1965–1966. *Iraq* 30: 154–205.
Saporetti, C. 1966. Intorno a VDI 80 (2/1962) 71. *Or* 35/3: 275–278.
——. 1970. *Onomastica medio-assira.* 2 vols. Studia Pohl 6. Roma: Biblical Institute Press.
——. 1978–1979. I prestito nei documenti privati dell'Assiria del XIV e XIII secolo. Parte I. L'analisi dei testi. *Mesopotamia* 13–14: 5–90.
——. 1979. *Assur 14446: La famiglia A.* (= Cybernetica Mesopotamica. Data Sets: Cuneiform Texts 1). Malibu: Undena.
——. 1981. I prestito nei documenti privati dell'Assiria del XIV e XIII secolo. Parte II. I testi in trascrizione. *Mesopotamia* 16: 5–41.
——. 1982. *Assur 14446: Le altre famiglie.* (= Cybernetica Mesopotamica. Data Sets: Cuneiform Texts 3). Malibu: Undena.
Saporetti, Cl. and H. Freydank. 1979. *Nuove attestazioni dell'onomastica medio-assira.* Incunabula Graeca 74. Roma: Ateneo & Bizziri.
Schorr, M. 1932. Review of *ARu. OLZ* 12 (1932): 771–773.
Skaist, A. 1994. *The Old Babylonian Loan Contract: Its History and Geography.* Bar-Ilan Studies in Near Eastern Languages and Culture. Ramat-Gan: Bar-Ilan University Press.
von Soden, W. 1957. Zum akkadischen Wörterbuch. 88–96. *OrNS* 26: 127–138.
Zaccagnini, C. 1997. On the Juridical Terminology of Neo-Assyrian and Aramaic Contracts. In *Assyrien im Wandel der Zeiten,* ed. H. Hauptman and H. Waetzoldt. Pp. 203–208. Heidelberger Studien zum Alten Orient 6 (= CRRAI 39). Heidelberg: Heidelberger Orientverlag.

APPENDICES A–G

APPENDIX A[1]

List of Middle Assyrian Loan Documents

	OBJECT LENT	PLEDGE (*šapartu*)	SET TERM	PROPERTY LIEN (*ukâl*, without *kī šaparte*)	PROPERTY LIEN (*kattû*)
AO 19228	1? t 20 m tin		8 years	fld	
AO 19229	38 1/2 m tin	h	6 months		
AO 20153	8 em 5 su corn		harv.t.		
AO 20156	5 su corn		in month X		
AO 21380	cow		2 months	*mimmūšu zakua*	
ARu 16	2 1/2 m silver		12 months		flds, hh
ARu 53	[x] em corn	[x] *iku* fld	6 months		
Bi 1	3 em corn, 3 *iku* 3 *kumāni* fld		harv.t.		

[1] Abbreviations: ch = children (DUMU.MEŠ); d = daughter (DUMU.MÍ); dd = daughters (DUMU.MÍ.MEŠ); em = homer (ANŠE) = ca. 100 liters; fld = field (A.ŠÀ); flds = fields (A.ŠÀ.MEŠ); h = house (É); harv. = harvesters (harv.t. = at harvest time); hh = houses (É.MEŠ); m = mina (MA.NA); *qû* = qa ($SILA_3$); s = son (DUMU); sh = shekel (GÍN) = ca. 6–8 grams; ss = sons or children (DUMU.MEŠ); su = *sūtu* (BÁN); t = talent (GÚ.UN) = ca. 30 kilograms; tr.f. = threshing-floor (*adru*); w = wife (DÁM).

	OBJECT LENT	PLEDGE (*šapartu*)	SET TERM	PROPERTY LIEN (*ukâl*, without *kī šaparte*)	PROPERTY LIEN (*kattû*)
Bi 2	x + 30 m tin	*mimmūšu* [*zakua*]	1 month		
Bi 3	12 em corn	*mimm*[*ūšu zakua*]	harv.t.		
Bi 4	[x] corn	*mimmūšu zakua*	harv.t.		
Bi 4a	[x] corn	*mimmūšu zakua*	[. . .]		
Bi 5	[x] em corn		unspecified	[x] *iku* fld (or [*kī šaparte*] in lines 17–18 ?)	
KAJ 11	12 m tin, 7 harv.	5 *iku* fld	6 months		
KAJ 12	17 m tin		4 months	5 *iku* fld	
KAJ 13	40 m tin	9 *iku* flds	6 years		
KAJ 14	1 t 5 m tin	20 *iku* fld	6 months		
KAJ 16	12 1/3 m. tin	fld, h, tr.f.	6 months		fld, h, ss, d[d]
KAJ 17	1 t tin	s	upon request		
KAJ 18	36 m tin	20 *iku* fld	12 months		
KAJ 19	10 m tin	1 *iku* fld	1 month		
KAJ 20	20 m tin	farmstead (*dunnu*)	5 years		
KAJ 21	10[+ x] m tin, [x]? 5 em corn	fld, tr.f., orchard, [. . .]	[. . .]		
KAJ 22	2 t 2 m tin	⌈. . .⌉	3? months		
KAJ 23	6 m tin	[. . .]?	[x +] 1 months		

	OBJECT LENT	PLEDGE (*šapartu*)	SET TERM	PROPERTY LIEN (*ukâl*, without *kī šaparte*)	PROPERTY LIEN (*kattû*)
KAJ 24	1 t 30 m tin		12 months	50 *iku* fld	
KAJ 25	1 t tin	10 *iku* fld	12 months		
KAJ 26	2 t 26 m tin		6 months	⌈. . .⌉	
KAJ 27	16 m tin	x + 2 *iku* fld	6 months		
KAJ 28	1 t 6 m tin, 10 [+ x] em corn	w	12 months; harv.t.		
KAJ 29	10 m tin, 10 harv.	*mimmūšu zakua*	6 months		
KAJ 30	1 t tin	[x +] 5 *iku* fld	[x +] 1! month!		
KAJ 31	10 m tin	w, fld, h	[x] months		
KAJ 32	2/3? m silver		upon return		flds, hh
KAJ 33	2 m tin		7 months		
KAJ 34	1 t 6 m tin		13 months		fld, h
KAJ 35	[x t] 28 m tin		[. . .]	30 *iku* fld	
KAJ 36	[x] t [x +] 5 m tin	[. . .] flds	7 months		
KAJ 37	25 m tin		1 month?		fld, h
KAJ 38	6 m tin		2 months		fld, h
KAJ 39	2 2/3 m silver		upon return		flds, hh
KAJ 40	19 5/6 m tin		7 months		fld, h
KAJ 41	1 t 6 m tin		7 (+ 1)? months		fld, ss, h
KAJ 42	[x] tin		[x] months		fld, h
KAJ 43	11 m tin		6 months		fld, h

	OBJECT LENT	PLEDGE (*šapartu*)	SET TERM	PROPERTY LIEN (*ukâl*, without *kī šaparte*)	PROPERTY LIEN (*kattû*)
KAJ 44	4 2/3 m 8 sh silver		6 months		fld, h
KAJ 45	9 m tin		3 months		fld, [h]
KAJ 46	[x] + 7 m tin		upon request		fld, h, ss, dd
KAJ 47	5 m silver, 100 em corn		unspecified		flds, hh
KAJ 50	[x +]? 30 m tin		10 months		fld, h
KAJ 52	1 t 4 m tin		5 months		
KAJ 53	15 1/2 m tin, 1 em 9 su corn	slave, farmstead (*dunnu*)	6 months		
KAJ 58	[x] em 8 su corn	[x] *iku* fld, or h + *mimmūšu*	[. . .]		
KAJ 59	3 em corn		[. . .]		
KAJ 60	2 em 6 [+ x *qû*] corn	w	7 months		
KAJ 61	⌈3⌉ em corn	flds + hh, or ss + dd	11 [+ x] months		
KAJ 62	10 em 5 su corn		harv.t.		
KAJ 63	1 em 6 su corn	tr.f., orchard	5 months		
KAJ 64 = 68	12 em corn		5 months	[x *iku*] fld	
KAJ 65	17 em corn	ox	13 months		*mimmūšu zakua*

	OBJECT LENT	PLEDGE (*šapartu*)	SET TERM	PROPERTY LIEN (*ukâl*, without *kī šaparte*)	PROPERTY LIEN (*kattû*)
KAJ 66	5 em corn	fld/h/tr.fs/ well/ss/dd	[. . .]		
KAJ 67	16 em corn	[fld], h, *mimmūšu*	6 months		
KAJ 69	2 em 6 su corn		harv.t.		fld, h
KAJ 70	1 em corn	w	12 months		
KAJ 71	1 em 2 su corn		harv.t.		fld, h
KAJ 77	2 em corn		harv.t.		
KAJ 78	2 em [corn]		harv.t.		
KAJ 81	1 em corn, 2 *kumāni* fld		harv.t.		
KAJ 85	12 em corn		5 months		fld, hh
KAJ 86	250 bricks		12 months		
KAJ 87	1200 bricks		9 months		fld, h
KAJ 88	[x] ewes, their lambs		1 month		
KAJ 96	1 cow	2? [+x? *iku*] fld	6 months		
KAJ 97	1 ewe, her lambs, her wool		upon request		
KAJ 141	[x] m tin	[. . .]?	1 month		

	OBJECT LENT	PLEDGE (*šapartu*)	SET TERM	PROPERTY LIEN (*ukâl*, without *kī šaparte*)	PROPERTY LIEN (*kattû*)
TR 104	15 em corn		harv.t.	[. . .] (lines 19–20)	
TR 110	1 t 10 m tin		2 months		
TR 112	[x] m tin, [x em] corn, [x] harv.	harv.t.			
TR 2021 + 2051	1 ax (*ulmu*)		upon return		
TR 2052	[. . .]	*mimmūšu zakua*	[. . .]		
TR 2907?	a *šarpu*		3 months		
TR 2913	10 m tin		1 month		
TR 3007	34 em corn	flds, hh	harv.t.		
TR 3013	1 em corn		harv.t.		
TR 3014	2 em corn, 8 harv.		harv.t.		
TR 3015	20 em corn		harv.t.		
TR 3021	1 t 10 m tin	D's? sister + her daughter	2 years		
TR 3022	3 em corn		harv.t.	*mimmūšu zakua*	
TR 3036	[. . .]		[. . .]		
YBC 12860	5 em corn, 5 *iku* fld		harv.t.		
VDI 80:71	[x] em corn		4 years	tr.f.	*bašīšu bušīšu*

	OBJECT LENT	PLEDGE (*šapartu*)	SET TERM	PROPERTY LIEN (*ukâl*, without *kī šaparte*)	PROPERTY LIEN (*kattû*)
VAS 19 19	6 m tin	—	6 months		*bašīšu u bušīšu*
VAS 19 20[2]	20 bows		2 years	[x] *iku* fld	
VAS 19 36	[x +] 2 1/2 m tin		[. . .]	50 *iku* fld [. . .], orchard, tr.f. [. . .]	

[2] Note that the formula of this contract slightly deviates from a standard loan.

APPENDIX B

List of Middle Assyrian Promissory Notes Recording Loans[3]

	OBJECT LENT	SET TERM	SECURITY OR GAIN FOR THE CREDITOR
KAJ 74	1 em corn	harv.t.	(none)
KAJ 82	8 em corn	upon request	(none)
KAJ 91	130 em corn, 50 sheep, 50 harv.	6 months	100% interest
KAJ 95	1 cow	unspecified	(none)
KAJ 101	150 em corn, 70 sheep, 70 harv.	5 months	100% interest; *ukâl*-lien on fld, h, and *mimmūšu gabba zakua*
KAJ 118[4]	40 bales of straw	⌜harv.t.⌝	[. . .] joint liability[?] (line 19)
KAJ 123	2 grinding slabs	unspecified	(none)
TR 110	1 t 10 m tin	2 months	default interest
TR 2913	10 m tin	1 month	default interest
VAS 19 47	large amounts of corn, sheep, harv.	4 months/unspecified	

[3] For different interpretations of TR 110 and TR 2913 see also above note 7; of KAJ 91 see also notes 10 and 11; and of KAJ 95 see also above notes 11 and 16.

[4] Instead of *ina muḫḫe* D the document has D *maḫrū* (line 14). See also note 161 above.

APPENDIX C

References to Obligations in Various Contracts

C.1. Receipts[5]

The basic formula of the receipts is as follows: Commodity *ša* (*qāt*) D C *maḫir*, or Commodity *ša* (*ina*) *muḫḫe* D (*šaṭrutūni*) C *maḫir*. The reason for the debt, a loan or some other obligation, is usually not specified.[6] Several of the payments were made in accordance with a credit note (*ša pî ṭuppe ṣabitte*, VAS 19 8), or had to be deducted from the credit note(s) (*ina ṭuppāte ṣabtāte . . . ukarrû*, TR 100).[7]

C.1.1. Receipts of part of the debt:
Texts: AO 20155, KAJ 143, TR 100, TR 101, TR 102, TR 2039, TR 2057, TR 2058, TR 2062 + TR 2905, TR 2065, TR 2069 + TR 2908, TR 3016, VAS 19 8, VAS 19 51.

C.1.2. Receipts of the entire debt:
Texts: Bi 9, Bi 13, Bi 14 (fragm.), KAJ 104.

C.1.3. Receipts of the purchase price:
In these documents the debt clearly resulted from a purchase (not a loan):
Texts: KAJ 144, KAJ 145, KAJ 159, KAJ 244.

C.1.4. Receipts of a reimbursement for the loss of borrowed objects:
Texts: TR 2015, TR 3011.

---

[5] Most texts assembled by Saporetti 1978–1979: 86–90. For the texts under C.1.1 see also Deller-Saporetti 1970b, and Postgate 1986: 15 (TR 2039 and 2905), and 19 (VAS 19 51).

[6] Only in VAS 19 8 do we clearly have the repayment of part of a loan and its interest.

[7] On the *ukarrû*-clause, see Postgate 1986: 15 and 19. On the *ṭuppu ṣabittu* see above.

C.2. Administrative debt notes, memoranda, and inventories[8]

Texts: An administrative debt note is not a real legal document but rather a note recording the issue of agricultural products or animals from government stocks (e.g. *ša ekallim*, *ša pitti ḫašīme*) by (*ša*/*ša qāt*) an official to (*ina muḫḫe*) another official (or individual); sometimes the reason for the disbursement is specified, namely for distribution as rations among prisoners of war or workers: KAJ 103, 106 (*ana kurummat . . . tadin/tadnaššu*), KAJ 133, YBC 12861;[9] cf. KAJ 120 lines 18–20. Such notes may explicitly be called "memoranda" (*ana lā mašā'e šaṭir*), e.g. KAJ 255, 268. For an inventory listing dozens of debts, see e.g. KAJ 310.

C.3. Sales[10]

C.3.1. Sale of a previously pledged field:

Texts: KAJ 150*, KAJ 162*, KAV 211* (+ KAJ 170); probably cf. KAJ 157 (= DSC 1: 46–47).

C.3.1. Sales of credit-notes:

These contracts record the sale of tablets by creditors for the full amount of the debt; the advantage to the purchaser is presumably the expected interest on the loan.

Texts: KAJ 79 = 166, KAJ 161, KAJ 163*, KAJ 165*

C.4. Annulments of Debt-notes[11]

Texts: Bi 18, Bi 19, KAJ 142*, TR 115, TR 2061, TR 3001*, TR 3002*, TR 3012, VAS 19 38, *Urad-Šerūa* 60 and 76$^{?}$.

---

[8] For the texts see Postgate 1988 and Machinist 1982: 6–8.

[9] Similar issues by officials can also be formulated as receipts from the point of view of either the receiver (PN *maḫir*, e.g. Bi 7, 8, 11$^{?}$; KAJ 92, 118), or the giver (*ana* PN *tadin/ittidin/iddinūni*; or PN *ittiši*, e.g. KAJ 113, 109, AO 19229 lines 19–23; *Urad-Šerūa* 33, Bi 26$^{?}$). It is possible that some of these receipts were actually government loans (e.g. KAJ 118). In addition, disbursements for further distribution can also be formulated as promissory notes stating the receiver's obligation to distribute the "borrowed" products (see above note 15).

[10] Texts assembled by Koschaker 1928: 103–105 (KAJ 150 and 168), 42–43 (sale of credit-notes); Saporetti 1978–1979: 75–76 (KAJ 150), 76–77 (sale of credit-notes); and Saporetti 1982 (KAJ 162, KAV 211 and KAJ 170). For the relevant passages in KAJ 163 and 165 see also Postgate 1986: 34 and n. 51.

[11] Deller-Saporetti 1970a.

C.5. Undertakings to collect debts[12]

Texts: KAJ 110, KAJ 114, KAJ 115.

C.6. Miscellaneous

KAJ 83[13] is formulated as a promissory note: a certain amount of corn has been borrowed by PN_1 from PN_2. The main part of the contract concerns the undertaking of PN_1 to deliver the corn to a third party (PN_3) and draw up a loan contract with him. Lines 17–22 stipulate the conditions of the loan to PN_3.

[12] See above.

[13] See Koschaker 1928: 166 no. 19; Postgate 1988: 41–43 and Idem 1970: 147.

APPENDIX D

Typology of the Middle Assyrian Loan Documents

TYPE 1: Secured Loans with Default Interest

Texts: Period 1 (37 texts): KAJ 11, 18, 19, 21, 22, 23, 25, 28, 29, 36, 53, 58, 60, 61, 67, 70, 96, 141 (pledge); KAJ 34, 37, 38, 39, 40, 41, 42, 43, 44, 45, 46, 47, 50, 69, 85, 87; ARu 16; VAS 19 19 (*kattû*-lien); KAJ 16, 65 (pledge + *kattû*-lien)

Period 2 (11 texts): AO 19229 (eponym unknown), Bi 2, 3, 4, 4a, KAJ 31, TR 2052, 3007, 3021 (pledge); KAJ 32, 71 (*kattû*-lien)

Structure:

1 Seal of debtor (optional)
2 Object lent
3 Statement of loan
4 Expiry date (1–13 months or till harvest time)[14]
5 Default clause (interest)[15]
6 *rakis* clause about debtor's solvency (only in specific *kattû*-liens)
7 Statement of security
8 Redemption clause (optional)
9 Clause specifying to whom exactly the debt should be repaid (optional)
10 Clause granting the creditor the right to choose from which property to satisfy his claim (optional)

---

[14] Except for TR 3021: 2 years; Other stipulations are: "Till the return of the caravan" (*ina erēb ḫarrāne*, KAJ 32, 39; cf. KAJ 37 *ḫarrānēšu uppašma*); "Upon demand" (*ina ūme errišušūni*) (KAJ 17, 46).

[15] In KAJ 11 and 29 the debtor had to pay interest and to deliver harvesters. In KAJ 50 the debtor may choose to reap the creditor's field instead of paying interest, but if he fails to reap so that the creditor has to hire harvesters, the debtor pays a fine in tin.

TYPE 2: Secured Loans with Sale of the Encumbered Asset(s)

Texts: Period 1 (9 texts): ARu 53, KAJ 14, 27, 63, 66 (pledge); KAJ 12, 24 (*ukâl*-lien); VDI 80:71 (*ukâl*- + *kattû*-lien); VAS 19 36 (*ukâl*-lien$^{?}$)

Structure:
1 Seal of debtor
2 Object lent
3 Statement of loan
4 Expiry date (4–6 months)[16]
5 Statement of Security
6 Default clause (Sale of the pledged/encumbered object)

TYPE 3: Secured Loans with Antichresis instead of Interest

Texts: Period 1 (4 texts): KAJ 13, 17, 20 (pledge); AO 19228 (*ukâl*-lien)
Period 2 (2 texts): KAJ 30 (pledge); Bi 5 (pledge or *ukâl*-lien); cf. VAS 19 20 (*ukâl*-lien)

Structure:
1 Seal of debtor
2 Object lent
3 Statement of loan
4 Expiry date (all long-term loans)[17]
5 Statement of security
6 Statement of no-interest

---

[16] Except for KAJ 24: 1 year; and VDI 80:71: 8 years.

[17] The term of the pledged loan in KAJ 30 is uncertain: Saporetti 1981: 12 reads in line 9 [*ana* x +] 1$^{!}$ ITU$^{!.ḫi}$ SAG$^{!}$.[D]U. KAJ 17 leaves the matter open to the will of the creditor, i.e. repayment "upon demand" (*ina ūme errišušūni*); Bi 5 does not seem to have a statement regarding the length of the loan.

7 Redemption clause (not in KAJ 20)
8 Default clause (only in AO 19228)

TYPE 4: Loans with extra obligations upon the debtor, usually under threat of penalty. Additional penalty upon default.

Texts: Period 1 (1 text): KAJ 52
Period 2 (8 texts): Bi 1, KAJ 62, 77, 81, TR 3014, 3015, 3022, 3036.

Structure:
1 Seal of debtor (optional)
2 Object lent[18]
3 Statement of loan
4 Expiry date
5 Description of the obligation;[19] and breaking of the debt note (optional)
7 Default clause:[20] additional penalty (usually interest)[21]
8 Upon failure to fulfill the extra obligation: penalty[22]

---

[18] Note that in some contracts the debtor also received harvesters from the creditor (TR 3014, Bi 1, and KAJ 81); cf. KAJ 11 and 29 (type 1), TR 112 (type 5), and the promissory notes KAJ 101 and VAS 19 47.

[19] The following obligations are attested: 1) to reap (creditor's) field(s) (*ina turēze eqla eṣṣid*, Bi 1, KAJ 81; or *eqla ina turēze eṣṣid*, TR 3014; cf. the partial receipt AO 20155); 2) to weave? a garment instead of interest *kīmū ṣibte* (O) (a commodity) D *ina bētēšu* [*imaḫḫis*]*su*? *u ana* C *inaddin*-[*š*]*u*? C [. . .] *inaddin*, KAJ 77, cf. Postgate 1988: 126–127); 3) to provide harvesters to the creditor at harvest time: x *ēṣidē ina turēze illak*, KAJ 62, TR 3015, 3036; TR 3022: *x ēṣedē*; 4) to deliver a harvest (from the debtors' field ?!) instead of interest (*kīmu ṣibat anneke annê bilat* 5 iku *eqle ina adre še'am u tibna ana* C *inaddinū*, KAJ 52, cf. KAJ 50 s.v. type 1).

[20] I.e. upon failure to repay the loan at the fixed date.

[21] Interest (Bi 1, KAJ 62, 81, TR 3014, 3015); another harvest (KAJ 52); general *ukâl*-lien (TR 3022); broken (TR 3036; KAJ 77).

[22] Obligation to give the creditor a harvest like the one he would have harvested had he been given the harvesters in time, or had the debtor reaped the fields (*bilat eqle inašši/umalla/iddan*). No penalty in KAJ 52. Reconstruction of relevant passage in TR 3014 by Durand 1980: 31 n. 39. Broken in KAJ 77.

TYPE 5: Loans with no sanction before default.[23]

Texts: Period 1 (6 texts): KAJ 26, 33, 35, 64 = 68, 86, TR 104
Period 2 (10 texts): AO 20156, 21380, KAJ 59, 78, 88, TR 110, 112, 2913, 3013, YBC 12860.

Structure:

1 Seal of debtor (optional)
2 Object lent
3 Statement of loan
4 Expiry date
5 Default clause

5.1. accrual of interest (AO 20156, KAJ 33, 59, 78, 86, 88,[24] TR 110, 2913, 3013; cf. KAJ 83 lines 17–22)
5.2. lien on all the assets of a guarantor[25] (AO 21380; cf. KAJ 101)[26]
5.3. sale of an item from the debtor's encumbered assets (KAJ 35; KAJ 64 = 68)
5.4. accrual of interest and sale of an item from the debtor's encumbered assets (KAJ 26 but fragmentary)

---

[23] TR 2907 may belong to this type of loan but the text is too fragmentary to know the context of the obligation that is recorded in it. Cf. Saporetti 1978–1979: 83.

[24] KAJ 88 is exceptional. At the beginning of the document (lines 10–14) it is stated that the debtor had to return not only the ewes lent and their lambs but also their wool within a specific period of time; in other words, it seems that the debtor had to pay back capital (i.e. ewes + lambs) as well as interest that accrued during the basic term of the loan in the form of wool. If he failed to do so, he was to pay (additional?) interest which this time consisted of paying for the costs of "pasturing, assisting in labour, and shearing" (lines 15–18). However, at the end of the document (lines 19–21), when speaking of breaking the tablet upon repayment, it is stated that the repayment included the lent ewes only. One wonders what happened to the obligation to pay back the lambs and to render the extra services (i.e. the "interest").

[25] Note that it is not the person who took the loan whose property is being charged, but a third party. In Machinist's opinion this arrangement reflects "the well-known Middle Assyrian institution of community (*ālu*) responsibility for the activities of its members . . ." (Machinist 1982: 99–100).

[26] For a possible prosopographical link between KAJ 101 and AO 21380 see Aynard-Durand 1980: 40.

5.5. accrual of interest and apparently also the creation of a property lien (TR 104)[27]
5.6. accrual of interest and the performance of an obligation that is related to the harvest (TR 112, YBC 12860)[28]
6 Clause specifying to whom exactly the debt should be repaid and breaking of the document upon repayment (both optional)

TYPE 6: Loans without any apparent gain for the creditor

Texts: Period 2 (3 texts): AO 20153, KAJ 97,[29] TR 2021 + 2051, cf. the promissory note KAJ 95 and the government loans KAJ 74, 82, and 123.[30]

Structure:
1 Seal of debtor (optional)
2 Object lent
3 Statement of loan
4 Expiry date
5 Breaking of tablet upon repayment

[27] TR 104 lines 19–20 are very fragmentary; a sale is not excluded, hence TR 104 may be similar to KAJ 26, see s.v. 5.4.

[28] In YBC 12860: obligation to return the borrowed field at the beginning of the harvest time, or to hand over the produce of the field to the creditor. In TR 112: obligation to provide harvesters to creditor at harvest time (*ina turēze ēṣidē illak*); if the debtor fails to fulfill the latter obligation he will have to give a harvest like the one the creditor would otherwise have harvested: [*edannu*] ⸢*e*⸣*tti*[*qma*] *še'um u annuku ana ṣibte šumma ēṣidē ina* ⸢*tu*⸣ [*rēze*] *lā ittalak* . . . (TR 112 14–17). We must assume (cf. Saporetti) that the standard formula as it is attested in KAJ 11 and KAJ 29 (see type 1) has been much abbreviated by the scribe of TR 112: *edannu*] ⸢*e*⸣*tti*[*qma*] *še'um u annuku ana ṣibte* <*illukū*> <*ina turēze ēṣidē illak*> *šumma ēṣidē ina* ⸢*tū*⸣[*rēze*] *la ittalak* . . .

[29] Probably, the creditor enjoyed the debtor's herding services. We may assume that the debtor had to look after the ewe by, for instance, pasturing her (cf. KAJ 127: *emmerū ša* C *ša ana* D *ana ra'ê tadnūni*), or "pasturing her and assisting her in labour; (as well as) shearing her" (so KAJ 88: *ina muḫḫešu iri''a u ullada' ibaqqan*, ll. 17–18).

[30] In the government loans KAJ 91, 101 and VAS 19 47, the palace must have enjoyed the debtor's herding and harvesting services: Postgate 1988: 144. This would have been in addition to interest.

APPENDIX E

Terminology of Property Liens other than Pledge in the Middle Assyrian Loan Documents

E.1. Creation of a particular *ukâl*-lien during the basic term of the loan

kīmū ṣibte/ṣibtāte	(O lent)	(field)	(C) *ukâl*	(Bi 5, = long-term antichretic loan)
kīmū ṣibte/ṣibtāte	(O lent)	(field)	(C) *ukâl etanarraš*	(AO 19228, = long-term antichretic loan)
kīmū ṣibtāte	(O lent)	(threshing-floor)	(C) *ukâl*	(VDI 80/70, with sale of charged asset at foreclosure)
kī našlamte	(O lent)	(field)	(C) *ukâl*	(KAJ 12, with sale of charged assets at foreclosure)
kīmū	(O lent)	(field)	(C) *ukâl*	(VAS 19 20, = long-term antichretic loan)
kīmū	(O lent)	(field)	(no verb)	(KAJ 24, with sale of charged assets at foreclosure)
		(fields)	⌈C⌉ [*ú-k*]*a-al*	(VAS 19 36, lines 5'–10', with sale of charged assets at foreclosure in lines 11'–14', but very fragmentary)

E.2. Creation of a general *ukâl*-lien upon default

when the debt matures	*mimmūšu zakua ša* PN C	*iṣabbat ukâl*	(AO 21380)
when the debt matures C	*mimmūšu zakua*	*iṣabbat ukâl*	(TR 3022)
when the debt matures	*eqelšu bēssu mimmūšu gabba zakua*	*iṣabbat ukâl*	(KAJ 101, promissory note)
when the debt matures C		x x x ⌈i⌉-*ṣa?!-bat* x x	(TR 104, lines 19–20)

E.3. Sale from the debtor's encumbered assets upon default

when the debt matures (Real Estate)	*inassaq ilaqqe* [Real Estate]	*ša* D C	*ukâl uppu laqi* . . .	KAJ 35
when the debt matures [. . .]			[*uppu*] *laqi* . . .	KAJ 64 = 68
when the debt matures [. . .]		⌜C⌝ ⌜*ukâl*⌝ ?	⌜*uppuat laqiat*⌝ . . .	KAJ 26

E.4. The ***Kattû***-lien

ka-te	(O lent)	(O encumbered)	(KAJ 34, 38, 40, 41, 42, 43, 46, 47, 50, 69, 71, VAS 19 19, VDI 80:71)
ka-tu/tù/tu$_4$	(O lent)	(O encumbered)	(ARu 16, KAJ 16, 32, 44, 45, 65, 85, 87)
ka-[*te/tu*]	(O lent)	(O encumbered)	(KAJ 39)
[*ka-te/tu*]	(O lent)	(O encumbered)	(KAJ 37)

APPENDIX F

The Terminology of Pledge (šapartu) in Middle Assyrian Loan Documents and Other Legal Documents

F.1. The statement of pledge in short-term loan documents with default interest (= loans of type 1)

	kī šaparte (O pledged)	(KAJ 31; TR 3007)
	kī šaparte (O pledged) *šakin*	(AO 19229)
	kī šaparte (O pledged) (C) *ukâl*	(KAJ 11, 18, 19, 22, 29, 60, 61, 67; TR 2052, 3021)
	kī šaparte (O pledged) (C) *iṣabbat*	(Bi 2)
	kī šaparte (O pledged) (C) *iṣabbat ukâl*	(KAJ 53, 96; Bi 4, 4a)
	kī šaparte (O pledged) *ina bēt* C *šēšub*	(KAJ 16)
kī našlamte (O lent)	(O pledged) *ana šaparte šakin*	(KAJ 25, 36)
kī našlamte (O lent)	*kī šaparte* (O pledged) (C) *iṣabbat ukâl*	(Bi 3)
kī našlamte (O lent)	*kī šaparte* (O pledged) (C) *ukâl*	(KAJ 28, 65)
kī našlamte (O lent)	*kī šaparte* (O pledged) (C) *ukâl etanarraš*	(KAJ 21, 58)
kī našlamte (O lent)	*kī šaparte* (O pledged) *ina bēt* (C) *ušbat*	(KAJ 70)

F.2. The statement of pledge in loan documents with pledge sale (= loans of type 2)

	kī šaparte (O pledged)	(C) *ukâl*	(KAJ 63)
	kī šaparte (O pledged) *inassaq iṣabbat*	(C) *ukâl*	(KAJ 14)
kīmū (O lent)	(pledged O) *kī šaparte*	(C) *ukâl*	(ARu 53, KAJ 66)
kī našlamte (O lent)	(O pledged) *inassaq iṣabbat*	(C) *ukâl*	(KAJ 27)
	(O pledged) *kī šaparte*		

F.3. The statement of pledge in long-term loan documents with antichresis (= loans of type 3)

	kī šaparte	(O pledged)	(C) *ukâl*	(KAJ 17, 20)
	kī šaparte	(O pledged)	(C) *ukâl etanarraš*	(KAJ 13)
	kī šaparte	(O pledged)	(C) *iṣabbat ukâl*	(KAJ 30)
kīmū ṣibte/ṣibtāte (O lent)	[*kì šaparte*]?	(O encumbered)	(C) *ukâl*	(Bi 5)

F.4. References to pledged property in other legal documents

1 *ṭuppu ša* (O lent) *ša muḫḫe* D *šaṭrutūni*	(O pledged)	*ina pîša*	*kī šaparte šaknūni*	(KAJ 163, sale of debt notes)
1 *ṭuppu ša* (O lent)	(O pledged)	*ina pîša*	*kī šaparte ša muḫḫe* D	
napḫar 3 *ṭuppātu ša* C	(Os pledged)	*ina pî ṭuppāte šināti*	*kī* [*šaparte* . . .]	
	(O pledged)	*ina pî ṭuppe šiāti*	*kī šaparte šaknū*	(KAJ 165, sale of debt notes)
	(O pledged)	*ša ṭuppe ša* (O lent) *ša* C	*kī šaparte šēšubūni*	(KAJ 150, sale of pledged O)
napḫar 2 *ṭuppāte ša kunuk šarre*!		*kīmū* (O lent)	*ina bīt* C *ana šaparte šaknā*	(KAJ 162, sale of pledged O)
	(Os pledged . . .		*ša kī šaparte* [*ina bītišu*] *šēšubūni*	(KAV 211, sale of pledged O)
	(O pledged)	*ina pîša*	*kī šaparte . . . šaknūni*	(KAJ 142, annulment of debt)
	(O pledged)	*kī šaparte adi 5 šanāte . . . šaknāni*		(TR 3001, annulment of debt)
	(O pledged)	*ina libbiša*	*šaṭrāni*	(TR 3002, annulment of debt)

APPENDIX G

The Redemption-Clause in Middle Assyrian Loan Documents

G.1. Upon repayment of borrowed capital and any possible interest (in loans of type 1)

ina ūme	(O lent) *ṣibtātēšu iḫiṭṭūni*	(his pledge/ (O pledged)	*ipaṭṭar*	(KAJ 18, 22, [23], 25, [36], [141], TR 3021)
ina ūme	(O lent) *ṣibtātēšu imaddudūni*	(O pledged)	*ipaṭṭar*	(KAJ 58)
ina ūme	(O lent) *ṣibtātēšu iddunūni*	(his pledge/ (O pledged)	*ipaṭṭar*	(KAJ 21, 28, 53, 60, 70)
ina ūme	(O lent) *ṣibtātēšu iddan*	(O pledged)	*ipaṭṭar*	(KAJ 61)
ina ūme	(O lent) *ṣibtātēšu imaddudūni*	(O pledged)	*ilaqqe*	(KAJ 65)
ina ūme	(O lent) *ṣibtūtēšu ēṣide iddunūni*	(O pledged)	*ipaṭṭar*	(KAJ 11)
<*ina ūme*>	*gurrata buqūna u tūlitta idd*[*unūni*]	(O pledged)	*ipaṭṭar*	(KAJ 96)
	(O lent) *u ṣibtātēšu iḫīaṭ*	(O pledged)	*ipaṭṭar*	(KAJ 19)
	(O lent) *u ṣibtātēšu iddan*	(O pledged)	*ipaṭṭar*	(AO 19229)
	(O lent) u *ṣibtātēšu ina* (Place) *imaddad*	(O pledged)	*ipaṭṭar*>?	(TR 3007)

G.2. Upon repayment of borrowed capital (in loans of type 3 and VDI 80:71) Possibility of Pledge Sale after Default without Right of Redemption

ana x *šanāte qaqqad*	(O lent) *imaddad*	(Encumbered asset)	*ilaqqe*	(VDI 80:71)
x *šanāte ušallam*	(O lent) *iḫīaṭ*	(asset encumbered)	*ilaqqe*	(AO 19228)
x *šanāte ušallam*	(O lent) *iḫīaṭ*	(pledge)	*ipaṭṭar*	(KAJ 13)
ina ūme	(O lent) *iḫiṭṭūni*	(pledge)	*ipaṭṭar*	(⌈Bi 5⌉, KAJ 17, 30)
ina ūme	(O l[ent) . . .]	(asset encumbered)	*ipaṭṭar*	(VAS 19 20)

NUZI

Carlo Zaccagnini – Istituto Universitario Orientale (Naples)

Before attempting a brief sketch of the pertinent Nuzi evidence, a preliminary theoretical and methodological remark is in order. Whenever analysing and commenting on ancient Near Eastern "law codes"—as a whole or in single points of detail—on juridical institutions and legal practices attested in the millennial history of pre-classical civilizations, we should be well aware that a substantial gap exists between our contemporary "Western" juridical categories—as variously elaborated, in the course of some 2,500 years, by the scholarly reflection of countless jurists—and those attested in the ancient Near East. It is a well-known fact that in Mesopotamia (and adjacent or peripheral regions) no theoretical work on juridical categories and principles ever seems to have been undertaken or even attempted (cf. among many others Zaccagnini 1988; Pintore 1976). This state of affairs is by no means confined to the sphere of law but concerns the entire conceptual world of the ancient Near Eastern civilizations.[1]

With reference to the "Western" juridical categories and speculative frameworks mentioned above, a further source of possible misunderstanding should be pointed out. In very rough terms, two substantially different theoretical and methodological approaches can be observed in past and present studies of ancient Near Eastern law and juridical institutions: the former uses the conceptual categories of the Roman law tradition, ultimately going back to the monumental synthesis of Justinian's *Corpus Iuris Civilis*; the latter derives from the English Common Law tradition. As is well known, the two systems exhibit quite distinctive and at times divergent features, a

---

[1] There is hardly need to quote here the provocative but highly stimulating essay of Frankfort, H. et al., *The Intellectual Adventure of Ancient Man. An Essay on Speculative Thought in the Ancient Near East* (Chicago 1946: The University of Chicago Press), translated into Italian with the title, significantly, *La filosofia prima dei Greci* (Torino 1966: Einaudi).

This paper is a result of a joint research project "Merchants and politics in the ancient world" which I direct at the IUO-Naples with the financial support of the Italian Ministry of Universities (MURST).

fact which has, or can have, considerable bearing on any interpretation of other sets of juridical systems, institutions and legal procedures. This is certainly the case with the Mesopotamian and related Near Eastern documentary heritage, especially as concerns the broad field of private law.

With specific reference to the topic of security for loans, there is hardly any need to recall here the epochal contributions of P. Koschaker and H. Petschow. The Nuzi evidence, which is particularly rich and intriguing, has been tackled by a vast number of scholars, including Koschaker himself and E. Cassin, E.A. Speiser, H. Lewy, B.L. Eichler, M. Müller and the present writer. This is certainly not the place to speculate on the different juridical backgrounds that have supported the various and often conflicting reconstructions offered by these and other researchers whose contributions are to be found in the pertinent literature. At any rate, it is easy to perceive the serious difficulties that have been encountered by the various attempts to offer a coherent and "modern" interpretation of the ancient Near Eastern practices of securing loans.

It will suffice here to call attention to the contract of antichresis, of Graeco-Roman and modern times, which has been adduced as the most appropriate term of comparison for a widespread type of contract, stemming from Mesopotamian, Syrian, and other peripheral private archives from the Ur III period until neo-Babylonian times. In them, a person or real estate is handed over to the creditor(s) as security for a loan and more specifically in usufruct in place of interest on the capital lent. In fact, close scrutiny of the textual evidence reveals that, despite their standardized and apparently unequivocal formulations, the real substance of these contracts can hardly be reconciled with the features, scope and limits of classical antichresis. In this regard, the case of Nuzi "antichretic" contracts (*ṭuppi tidennūti*) is very instructive: Eichler's exhaustive and penetrating investigation of personal *tidennūtu* (Eichler 1973) and later studies of the same legal transaction on the one hand, and investigations of the evidence pertaining to real-estate *tidennūtu* on the other have underscored noteworthy divergences between apparently identical (or closely similar) types of contract.[2] I will return to this point later on.

[2] Cf. *inter alia* Zaccagnini 1975: esp. 194–201; Zaccagnini 1976; Zaccagnini 1979: esp. 7–13. The unpublished Ph.D. diss. of Jordan, G.D., *The Land-Field tidennūtu Transaction at Nuzi* (Hebrew Union College 1986) was not available to me. Jordan

On a more general level, it can be noted in passing that, according to ancient Roman doctrine, which is still largely shared by modern Western juridical thought, security for debt is of two kinds: real (i.e. property) and personal (i.e. obligations). The former include pledge (*pignus*), hypothecary pledge (*hypotheca*) and antichresis; the latter include the surety (*fideiussio*).[3] However, this schematic arrangement should only be considered as an approximate attempt to compare similar but not identical juridical institutions and legal systems, whose respective historical backgrounds and developments are to a considerable extent independent of one another. It goes without saying that more serious problems are encountered in the study of the ancient Near Eastern evidence. It therefore seems advisable to analyse and evaluate the relevant documentation by concentrating on its substantial content without forcing it into inadequate schemes of interpretation.

The rich corpus of Nuzi loan contracts (*ḫubullu*) has been sufficiently investigated (cf. Owen 1970; Wilhelm 1992: esp. 9–23 with the comments of Zaccagnini 1997) and the basic features of this type of legal transaction have been ascertained. Individual or multiple loans, with or without interest, could be secured by one or more sureties, i.e. persons who guaranteed fulfilment of the debtor's obligation in its entirety. Movables or real estate are not attested as security in *ḫubullu*-contracts; on the other hand, they occur in another type of Nuzi contract (the *ṭuppi tidennūti*) which, at least on a formulaic level, is patterned on the scheme of antichretic arrangements. Some features of these contracts that are relevant to the present discussion will be dealt with below.

According to the terminology of the Nuzi loan contracts (*ḫubullu*), the person(s) who assume obligation to stand surety for the full repayment of a debt are qualified *māḫiṣ pūti* (lit.: "striker of the forehead"). Whatever interpretation might be envisaged for this technical term,[4] it is important to point out the distinctive features that characterize

1990—presumably a short résumé of his dissertation—represents a first provisional attempt to single out and evaluate the basic economic features of this type of Nuzi transaction. Besides total disregard of the previous literature, the author's methodology and reasoning are not entirely convincing.

[3] Note, however, that, according to modern doctrine, antichresis is often considered to belong also to the sphere of personal security.

[4] Cf., with all due reservations, the now dated contribution of Cassin 1937: esp. 154–59.

the functional role of the *māḫiṣ pūti*.[5] Save for a very few exceptions, sureties only occur in multiple loans in which every single co-debtor assumes full liability to the creditor: the standard formulation of the clause is "one man is surety for another man (*awīlu ana awīli māḫiṣ pūti*)," followed by the repayment obligation which concerns the entire amount of the loan: "whoever of them is present will pay x (= the total amount of the debt) in full" (*mannummê (ša) ina libbišunu ašbu x* (*ana* PN [= the creditor]) *umalla*). In addition to this clause, many loan documents exhibit a further suretyship clause, whereby one or two co-debtors act as *māḫiṣ pūti* (note the variant writing MA.U) for the fulfilment of the obligation.[6] It is not entirely clear what the exact function of these additional sureties might have been, given that the documents in any case foresee the full mutual responsibility of each debtor for the entire group of co-debtors: all that can tentatively be suggested is that these loans were not only secured by a general *fideiussio* shared by each and every single debtor but, more specifically, by one or two of them as additional and final surety for fulfilment of the obligation.[7]

As mentioned before, individual loans, as a rule, were not secured by sureties. I will briefly dwell on the isolated and at times problematic occurrences of a personal security supporting *ḫubullu*-contracts entered into by single debtors. HSS IX 68 (= Wilhelm 1992 no. 200) is an interest-bearing barley loan contracted by Prince

[5] Note that the Nuzi documents attest to the sporadic occurrence of suretyship outside the sphere of loan agreements: cf. e.g. JEN 263 (exchange of fields); JEN 155 (lawsuit).

[6] For the abbreviated writing MA.U = *māḫiṣ pūti* see Fadhil 1983: 175–76; Deller 1984: 95, and Wilhelm 1992: 18 with n. 10. The functional and procedural aspects of the Nuzi joint responsibility clause in multiple loan contracts have been surveyed by Wilhelm 1992:16–18, on the basis of the rich evidence provided by the Shilwateshup archives (cf. the remarks of Zaccagnini 1994: esp. 30–34). In this context I offered a new interpretation of the standard neo-Assyrian joint responsibility clause (*ša karmūni ušallam*) and further proceeded to a comprehensive analysis of the other neo-Assyrian occurrences of the verb *karāmu*, as attested in non-juridical documents (ibid.: 37–42). For a different view, see Jas 1996: 84, who could not take into account the arguments and conclusions of my article, and cf. Radner 1997: 168 with n. 889. Moving from Jas' standpoint, an alternative unitary interpretation of the neo-Assyrian verb *karāmu* has been proposed by Fales forthcoming. I will comment on these contributions elsewhere.

[7] Wilhelm's suggestion (Wilhelm 1992:18) that the function of these sureties, selected from the group of co-debtors, was "die Exekutionsbereitschaft aller Schuldner zu garantieren und dem Gläubiger *den säumigen Schuldner* [italics mine] auzuliefern" is not convincing.

Shilwa-teshup with PN: PN_2, the administrator of Shilwa-teshup's household, is surety (*māḫiṣ pūti*) for PN's repayment of his debt. The memorandum HSS XIII 404 records an amount of various goods that are the balance still charged to PN; the same PN is surety (*māḫiṣ pūti*) for PN_2. Despite the conciseness of the document, it seems clear that PN's obligation to an unrecorded creditor derives from a guarantee previously provided by PN in favour of PN_2.

HSS IX 17—a difficult text (cf. Cassin 1937: 159–160 and the comments of Zaccagnini 1979a: 11)—records an outstanding obligation (i.e. the delivery of a fine choice maid or else 10 shekels of refined gold) due by PN to Shilwa-teshup, as final accounting from a previous contract.[8] A third party stands surety for PN's obligation.

An interesting but not entirely clear agreement is recorded in HSS XVI 238. A quantity of barley belonging to two people is handed over to PN in GN; the same PN will give back the same amount of barley in GN_2. The recipient(s) and the date of PN's delivery are not mentioned. The contract is witnessed by three people, one of whom is surety (*māḫiṣ pūti*) for PN; interestingly enough, the same PN is surety for his own(!) obligation. Both persons, as is the rule in the Nuzi suretyship clauses, seal the clay tablet. It may well be that this agreement is not a *ḫubullu*-contract (without interest charged to the debtor): no mention is in fact made of the technical term ur_5.ra (= *ḫubullu*). Nonetheless, the joint personal responsibility for the "debtor's" performance, which is shared by the "debtor" himself and a third party, is noteworthy.

A number of long-distance trade agreements concluded between Nuzi private entrepreneurs and merchants represent a special case. The merchants are either palace dependants or more or less independent tradesmen also operating on behalf of the palace administration.[9] These trade agreements, some of which are patterned on *ḫubullu*-contracts, most often include a suretyship clause in which one person stands surety for fulfilment of the merchant's obligation towards the financing party. Since I have already dealt with the topic in

---

[8] Possibly a trade agreement: cf. Zaccagnini 1979a: 11 n. 39.

[9] Cf. Zaccagnini 1977: esp. 178–85, with the detailed comments of Maidman 1980: 187–89. Additional textual material, which entirely confirmed my 1977 sketch of the Nuzi long-distance trade organization, both as concerns the palace and private sectors, has been made available and commented on by Morrison 1993: 95–114 ("The Family of Pula-hali and the Merchants"); Maidman 1993: 18–35; Wilhelm 1996: 361–64 (no. 28. *aladumma epēšu* "begleichen; kaufen" [text EN 9/2 292]).

some detail (Zaccagnini 1977: esp. 180–188), it is not necessary to comment again on this matter.

Another type of debt agreement, widely attested in Nuzi private archives, concerns loans of various amounts of different commodities (primarily barley) that are handed over to individuals for a fixed or indefinite length of time: as security for repayment of the capital sum and in compensation for accruing interest, persons or land (most often fields) are put at the creditor's disposal. In both cases the creditor will benefit: either from the work of the persons given as security or from the usufruct of the land owned by the debtor. In the unique legal terminology of the Nuzi documents, these agreements are labelled as *ṭuppi tidennūti* and the security itself is termed *tidennu*.[10] In spite of the still unclear etymological explanation of the term, the substance of these contracts has been sufficiently elucidated, on the basis of an internal analysis of the Nuzi textual evidence and by comparison with analogous Near Eastern sources.[11] Broadly speaking, the *tidennūtu* contracts can be interpreted as loans secured by 1) individuals, including the debtor himself, or by 2) parcels of land belonging to the debtor, that are either 1) physically transferred or 2) put at the creditor's disposal in accordance with the well-known antichretic mechanism. Movables other than human beings are never handed over as security.

As was intimated above, the personal and real estate *tidennūtu* contracts only apparently correspond to "classical" antichresis, for reasons that need not be repeated. Suffice it to say that, despite the apparently strict similarity between the formulaic patterning of Nuzi *tidennūtu* and ancient or modern antichretic obligations, the former agreements *de facto* represent a form of alienation of persons or land to third parties, in compensation for an outstanding obligation. This substantial aspect of the *tidennūtu* contracts is clearly revealed by those instances in which the agreed duration of the "antichretic" arrange-

---

[10] This term exclusively concerns persons: I only know of two occurences in which *tidennu* refers to fields: HSS XIII 171: 1–2 and HSS V 66: 8 (cf. AHw, p. 1362b): both texts belong to the archives of Shilwa-teshup. As an incidental remark, I would like to point out the extremely interesting evidence provided by the former text, a short memorandum which records 41 homers of *tidennu* fields and 13.8 homers of fields *ša mārūti*: there is little need to stress the significance of this datum, which to my knowledge has never been duly appreciated, for any inquiry concerning the vexed question of the nature, functions and possible relationships of the *tidennūtu* and *mārūtu* institutions—a subject that cannot be dealt with here.

[11] Cf. Eichler 1973, and the additional bibliography quoted above n. 2.

ment is decades and even the entire life of the person handed over as security (cf. Zaccagnini 1976: 197), and is further confirmed by the penalty clauses that expressly forbid repayment of debts before expiry of the fixed term (ibid.: 196–197). Note, for that matter, that the Nuzi texts only provide two cases of cancellation of real estate *tidennūtu* contracts, after repayment of the debts (AASOR XVI 67 and EN 9/1 181). I do not know of any cancellation of personal *tidennūtu*.[12]

In his extensive and detailed survey of Mesopotamian analogues to the Nuzi *tidennūtu* institution, Eichler (1973: 88–95) has reviewed the evidence of the Middle Assyrian *šapartu* contracts.[13] The object of the *šapartu* ("pledge") could be persons, goods of various kinds and land. According to CAD Š I's reading (p. 429a) of HSS XIII 259: 5, this document would represent the sole occurrence of a *šapartu* (= *tidennūtu* [?])-contract in the entire Nuzi archival corpus.[14] The text reads as follows: "PN <will give> PN_2, in the month MN, a maid—2 cubits and 1 *kimṣu* tall—as his pledge (*a-na ša-pá-ar-te-šu*); if PN does not hand her over to PN_2, there will be a compensation (for her wages) (*uriḫul-ša*)" (lines 1–8).[15] It goes without saying that the antecedents of HSS XIII 259 are totally unknown to us: it would be a matter of sheer speculation to hypothesize the existence of a previous loan (*ḫubullu*) contracted by PN, who now finds himself unable to repay his creditor (= PN_2), or to venture any other alternative explanation. Be that as it may, the arrangement of HSS XIII 259 is entirely consistent with those of the Nuzi personal *tidennūtu* agreements.

Special attention is merited by some personal *tidennūtu* contracts in which an additional surety (*māḫiṣ pūti*) is included to secure the obligation: the wording of these clauses exhibits noteworthy variants.

TCL IX 10 (cf. Eichler 1973: 126–127) records a loan of 30 minas of copper from PN_2 to PN, who will remain in PN_2's house as *tidennu*, in order to perform the harvest-work of PN_2. When he has completed

[12] A few documents record the cancellation of debts (*ḫubullu*): see e.g. EN 9/2 326; 9/2 348; 9/3 465; 9/3 412 (?).

[13] An extensive list of the Old, Middle and neo-Assyrian occurrences of the term *šapartu* can be found in CAD Š I, pp. 428a–430b.

[14] Note, for that matter, that HSS XIII 259 belongs to the Shilwa-teshup archives, as do the other two documents mentioned above in n. 9.

[15] For the meaning and function of *uriḫul* cf. Eichler 1973: pp. 21–25 and the comments of Zaccagnini 1976: 193–95.

his work obligation, PN shall give back the 30 minas of copper and then go free. After the usual penalty clause imposing a payment of one mina of copper for each day of absence from work, the contract adds that PN_3 stands surety for PN and for (repayment of) the copper (due by the same PN): "Therefore, if PN dies or disappears, then PN_2 [= the creditor] may seize PN_3 and he shall pay the copper in full" (lines 19–23).

JEN 306 (cf. Eichler 1973: 129) records a loan of 10 homers of barley in favour of PN, who remain in PN_2's house for ten years. PN_3 stands surety for PN: "If PN departs from work for a single day, PN_3 shall pay one mina of copper per day. If PN_3 and PN [note the inversion of the sequence as between the main debtor and the surety] violate the agreement, they [i.e. each of them, individually responsible for the entire obligation] shall pay (a fine of) one mina of silver" (lines 11–17).

EN 9/2 152 (SMN 2102: cf. Eichler 1973: 128–129) records a loan of 29 minas of bronze in favour of PN and PN_2—two brothers—one of whom (= PN_2) is to stay in the creditor's house for four years and perform service. Both brothers share joint responsibility for compensation in the event of PN_2's "hiding" from his service: the standard amount of the fine is one mina of copper per day. Two people [PN_3 and PN_4] stand surety for the two brothers: "If they cannot find them [i.e. the two brothers = PN and PN_2], then PN_5 [= the creditor] can seize PN_3 and PN_4 [= the sureties]".

To all appearances, these additional personal securities who are included in the personal *tidennūtu* contracts, have different functions. At all events, they serve as further security for the implementation of the creditors' rights, which are recorded in the standard format of these transactions. The first object of the suretyship always concerns the regular and uninterrupted performance of the *tidennu*'s work. In addition, in TCL IX 10 the surety also assumes responsibility for repayment of the debt; in JEN 306 a surety is provided in case of breach of contract. It is difficult, not to say impossible, to ascertain what might have been the reasons that induced the contracting parties to include these additional suretyship clauses: we can only surmise that the particular backgrounds of these agreements, albeit totally unknown to us, prompted the inclusion of the above clauses, in addition to the personal security offered by the *tidennu*.

In this connection, a unique and enigmatic case is recorded in AASOR XVI 29 (cf. Eichler 1973: 129–130): PN, a weaver, declares:

"I am a *tidennu* of ᶠPN and there is no surety (*māḫiṣ pūti*) for me. Therefore, of my own free will, I have cast myself into bondage (*ramanīma ramanī ina šeršerrēti iddanni*) . . . If I raise a complaint against ᶠPN concerning my bondage, I shall pay (a fine of) [1 mina of gold] and 1 mina of silver to ᶠPN" (lines 3–14). Any tentative interpretation of this document is seriously hampered by its conciseness and by the lack of any comparative evidence, at least as concerns the Nuzi archives. In the light of what we know about the legal and formulaic features of the personal *tidennūtu*-contracts, I will limit myself to offer the following comments. PN's self-qualification as *tidennu* implies that his compulsory work as a weaver derives from an earlier debt contracted with ᶠPN either by PN himself or, less likely, by another party. As a consequence of this obligation, PN entered ᶠPN's house where he started to work as a weaver; we have no clue as to whether the "antichretic" arrangement was of fixed or indefinite duration. The latter possibility looks unlikely since, in such cases, the standard arrangements foresee termination of contract if and when the debtor—be he the *tidennu* or a third party—repays the creditor the amount of the loan; until that time, the *tidennūtu* mechanism operates in full, i.e. the *tidennu* goes on working for his creditor. On the contrary, if the original *tidennūtu* contract was of fixed duration, we could hypothesize that the deadline had expired (or was about to expire) and that PN was unable to repay his (or someone else's) debt. PN's statement about the absence of any surety for his *tidennu* obligations vis-à-vis ᶠPN would then derive from an intervening death, disappearance or whatever other kind of non-availability of a *māḫiṣ pūti*, originally involved as personal security in a previous *tidennūtu* contract. As an alternative hypothesis, one could suggest that, upon expiration of the deadline for repaying the debt and consequent releasing of PN from his *tidennu* services, the debtor(s)—be they the same PN or any other person acting as his surety—were unable to fulfil their obligation. While underscoring the great uncertainty of the above attempted reconstruction of the totally unknown prehistory of AASOR XVI 29, it seems worthy of notice as the unique occurrence of an evolution from the personal status of *tidennu* to that of a (permanent) slave.[16]

[16] Aside from AASOR XVI 29, the frequent occurrences of the term *šeršerrātu*

I will now comment on two *tidennūtu* contracts which include an additional real estate security: in these cases too, the documents make use of the technical term *māḫiṣ pūti*, a term that normally only refers to persons acting as sureties for someone else's obligation.

EN 9/1 265 (SMN 1598: cf. Eichler 1973: 127) is a personal *tidennūtu*, whereby PN enters PN_2's house as security (*tidennu*) for a debt that he has contracted with PN_2. The same PN assumes responsibility in case of failure to perform his work obligations: the standard fine (*uriḫul*) is set at one mina of copper per day. An additional real estate security is added: "Thus (declares) PN: 'If I die or disappear, my 6 ho[mers of field] . . . shall be my surety (*ana iâši māḫiṣ pūtia*); PN_2 may take hold (*ukâl*) of them in lieu of the silver'" (lines 16–25). The meaning and implications of this clause deserve some comment. First of all, the exceptional use of the technical term *māḫiṣ pūti* with reference to land should be pointed out: to my knowledge, the only other occurrence of such a usage in the Nuzi texts is recorded in AASOR XVI 30, for which see below. On a substantive level, although the (real estate) surety is meant to cover the risks of PN's death or disappearance—and not his failure to work—the question nonetheless arises what is the real meaning of the "silver" mentioned in the above clause: does it refer to the penalty to be paid as a consequence of temporary or indefinite absence from work, or does it also include the amount of the loan? The latter option seems more probable, especially considering that the death of the *tidennu per se* excludes any continuation of his personal services for the benefit of the creditor; there is no mention of substitutes who might take over his work. On the other hand, it would appear that the real estate security appended to this contract operates according to the well-known mechanisms of real estate *tidennūtu*,[17] with the obvious yet significant implication that other people (probably PN's relatives) were still involved with the management of the family estate.[18]

in the Nuzi texts always concretely refer to "chains, fetters, shackles": cf. CAD Š II, p. 321. Interestingly enough, our text does not make use of the term *ardu* (ir), lit., "slave" (but also "palace official, dependent, etc.").

[17] The possibility that this real estate "is to serve as the object of a potential future foreclosure by Party C [= PN, debtor]", as proposed by Eichler 1973: 29, is only a guess, especially since we do not have any conclusive evidence suggesting that the Nuzi personal and real estate *tidennūtu* operated in the same way as the Middle Assyrian *Verfallspfand*.

[18] If we accept the above tentative explanation of the real-estate security clause

AASOR XVI 60 (cf. Eichler 1973: 127–128)—another personal *tidennūtu*—closely resembles the wording of EN 9/1 265, but includes a further security clause: PN contracts a loan from ᶠPN and enters her house in order to perform a ten years' *tidennūtu* service, at the end of which, upon repayment of his debt, he will be released. As usual, the penalty for neglecting work is set at one mina of copper per day, to be paid by the same PN. Two additional persons are provided as security by PN, who declares:

> "If I am not present, ᶠPN may seize (*iṣabbat*) my sons and daughters and wife." They shall restore in full the silver [i.e. the amount of the debt] and his hire (for a replacement) (*uriḫul*) to ᶠPN. The buildings of PN are sureties (*māḫiṣ pūti*) for PN (lines 25–30).

In the light of the comparable evidence of EN 9/1 265, I draw attention to the following peculiarities exhibited by the security clause in AASOR XVI 60: PN's family members are explicitly involved as joint sureties for repaying the debt and/or compensating for PN's absence from work. Their physical "seizure" (*ṣabātu*) by the creditor—unlike the "taking hold" (*kullu*) of real estate, as recorded in EN 9/1 265—means that PN's wife and children will (temporarily) act as substitutes for PN's *tidennu* work, and/or that they will become ᶠPN's property definitively when ultimately it is determined that PN has failed to absolve his obligation. In the absence of any additional details, it is impossible to ascertain how the real estate security was meant to work: in principle, one could either suggest that the "buildings" could be the object of another *tidennūtu* contract or, less likely, that they might simply be forfeited by PN.[19]

A different case is illustrated by EN 9/1 194 (SMN 2622), a real estate *tidennūtu*: PN and PN_2 (two brothers) give one homer of field

---

in EN 9/1 265, and proceed to an overall evaluation of this document, we may gain significant insights concerning the crucial issue of Nuzi (and, more generally, ancient Near Eastern) features of land ownership, pledge and alienation with respect to economic emergencies suffered by peasant family units. I have already repeatedly dealt in some detail with this subject: see e.g. Zaccagnini 1979: esp. 14–27; Zaccagnini 1984a; Zaccagnini 1984b; etc.

[19] Cf. above, n. 16. Eichler 1973: 29 points out that "the difficulty in distinguishing between the role of his [i.e. PN's] family and that of his é^hi^ warrants the interpretation of é as household rather than estate," thus implying that "Party D's [= PN] second statement would then be a recapitulation of his first declaration." Eichler's arguments are worthy of consideration but his conclusion—i.e. PN's wife and children = PN's household—are by no means convincing.

to PN_3 as security for a loan of barley and wheat, to be repaid after three years. A third party (PN_4) stands surety (*māḫiṣ pūti*) for PN and PN_2 and for the field (lines 17–18). The first object of the suretyship is clear, also in the light of the parallel evidence that has been discussed above. On the other hand, it is difficult to specify the nature and function of PN_4's guarantee of the *tidennu* field, also because it cannot be meant as a security against possible prior encumbrances of the land (the clear title clause in lines 13–14 is personally assumed by PN and PN_2).

The above evidence reveals the complexities and the still open questions raised by the overall system of Nuzi security institutions and legal procedures, especially if they are analysed from the viewpoint of other ancient and modern juridical frameworks—a point that I have tried to underscore at the beginning of my paper. I will conclude by offering some comments on the extremely meagre and by no means clear evidence provided by a few lawsuits dealing with personal security attached to loan contracts: as far as I know, only two lawsuits are of particular interest for the present matter at issue.

EN 9/1 400, a badly damaged and difficult text, concerns the judicial settlement of a defaulted debt (*ḫubullu*), amounting to 16 shekels of silver, contracted by PN with PN_2, father of PN_3. PN_4, who had stood surety for PN (PN_4 *pussu ša* PN *ašar* PN_2 *imḫaṣ* [lines 8–10]), will be responsible for PN's delivery of his wife and children (?) to PN_3, son of the original creditor. To all appearances, PN's default on his debt implied the handing over of his family to the creditor (PN_2) and, later on, to the creditor's son (PN_3). In accordance with well-known Nuzi practice, we can surmise that the new obligation would take the form of a personal *tidennūtu*. The functional role and personal liabilities of the surety (PN_4) are anything but clear and I refrain from any further speculation.

A different and again difficult case is recorded in AASOR XVI 73. PN suits PN_2 and declares: "I am not indebted (*ḫubullāku*) to PN_2, but he threw me into jail (?) (*sīḫu*)[20] and for two days I have been in jail (?)" (lines 4–6); the judges summoned PN_2 who declares: "PN stood surety for my debtor and I (!) threw him into prison" (lines 10–12: PN lú *ḫubullia pūta imtaḫaṣmi u ina usurti iddīšumi*). Following a negative declaration issued by the only witness produced by PN_2,

[20] Cf. CAD Š, p. 242b; AHw, p. 1040b.

and PN_2's subsequent refusal to take an evidentiary oath, PN_2 lost the case and was condemned to pay a fine of one ox for having thrown PN in jail (?). The evidence of the above court procedure is indeed remarkable and would require extensive comment; I shall only draw attention to two points. First, and most important, the ambivalence—or, in other terms, the semantic extension—of the technical term *ḫubullu* (line 5: *ḫabālu* D stative; line 10: *amēl ḫubulli*), which unquestionably refers both to the original debtor's obligation and to the accessory personal security provided by the surety; in the second place, the unique occurrence in the Nuzi texts of imprisonment of a surety—albeit for only two days—following his failure to perform the substitutive obligation incumbent on him in his role of *māḫiṣ pūti*.

I hope that the above synthetic sketch of the complex and still partly obscure topic of security for debt, as resulting from the rich evidence of Nuzi private archives, can represent a useful starting point for future research and discussion, also in a wider historical perspective which should include the Northern Mesopotamian and Syrian documentary corpora of the Late Bronze Age.

Bibliography

Cassin, E. La caution à Nuzi. *RA* 34: 154–68.

Deller, K.-H. 1984. Akkadische Lexikographie: CAD M. *Orientalia* 53: 72–107.

Eichler, B.L. 1973. *Indenture at Nuzi: The Personal tidennūtu Contract and its Mesopotamian Analogues*. Yale Near Eastern Researches 5. New Haven: Yale University Press.

Fadhil, A. 1983. *Studien zur Topographie und Prosopographie der Provinzstädte des Königsreichs Arraphe*. Baghdader Forschungen 6. Mainz am Rhein: Verlag Phillip von Zabern.

Fales, F.M. [Forthcoming.] Neo-Assyrian *karāmu*: A Unitary Interpretation. In *Studies L. Cagni*. Napoli: Istituto Universitario Orientale.

Jas, R. 1996. *Neo-Assyrian Judicial Procedures*. State Archives of Assyria Studies 5. Helsinki: The Neo-Assyrian Text Corpus Project.

Jordan, G.D. 1990. Usury, Slavery, and Land Tenure: The Nuzi *tidennūtu* Transaction. *ZA* 80: 76–92.

Maidman, M. 1980. Review of *XIII Rencontre Assyriologique Internationale*. *BO* 37: 185–89.

——. 1993. Some Late Bronze Age Legal Texts from the British Museum: Problems of Context and Meaning. In *Law, Politics and Society in the Ancient Mediterranean World*, ed. B. Halpern and D.W. Hobson. Pp. 66–69 (Text 5: BM 17604). Sheffield: Sheffield Academic Press.

Morrison, M. 1993. The Eastern Archives of Nuzi. In *SCCNH* 4: 3–130.

Owen, D.I. 1970. *The Loan Documents from Nuzu*. Unp. Ph.D. diss., Brandeis University.

Pintore, F. 1976. La struttura giuridica. In *L'alba della civiltà* I, ed. S. Moscati. Pp. 417–511. Torino: UTET.

Radner, K. 1997. *Die Neuassyrischen Privatrechtsurkunden*. State Archives of Assyria Studies 6. Helsinki: The Neo-Assyrian Text Corpus Project.

Wilhelm, G. 1992. *Das Archiv des Šilwa-Teššup, 4. Darlehensurkunden und verwandte Texte*. Wiesbaden: Harrassowitz.

——. 1996. Nuzi Notes. In Studies on the Civilization and Culture of Nuzi and the Hurrians 8, ed. D. Owen and G. Wilhelm. Pp. 361–64. Bethesda: CDL Press.

Zaccagnini, C. 1975. The Yield of the Fields at Nuzi. *OA* 14: 181–225.

——. 1976. Osservazioni sui contratti di "anticresi" a Nuzi. *OA* 15: 191–207.

——. 1977. The Merchant at Nuzi. *Iraq* 39: 171–89.

——. 1979. The Price of the Fields at Nuzi. *JESHO* 22: 1–31.

——. 1979a. Les rapports entre Nuzi et Hanigalbat. *Assur* 2/1: 1–27.

——. 1984a. Land Tenure and Transfer of Land at Nuzi (XV–XIV Century B.C.). In *Land Tenure and Social Transformation in the Middle East*, ed. T. Khalidi. Pp. 79–94. Beirut: American University of Beirut.

——. 1984b. Proprietà fondiaria e dipendenza rurale nella Mesopotamia settentrionale (XV–XIV secolo a.C.). *Studi storici* 25: 697–723.

——. 1988. La formazione del diritto in Mesopotamia: codificazioni regie e consuetudine nel II millennio a.C. In *La formazione del diritto nel Vicino Oriente antico*, ed. G. Pugliese. Pp. 35–50. Roma: Edizioni Scientifiche Italiane.

——. 1994 [= 1996]. Joint Responsibility in Barley Loans of the Neo-Assyrian Period. *State Archives of Assyria Bulletin* 8: 21–42.

——. 1997. Review of Wilhelm 1992. *BO* 54: 402–406.

EMAR

Aaron Skaist – Bar-Ilan University

It is axiomatic that a person who lends money or goods expects to be repaid, whether in the Syrian town of Emar in the thirteenth century BCE or anywhere else in the world. However, sometimes a borrower, even a person of absolute integrity, may for some reason be unable to repay the loan when it is due. This paper will describe the various means that were available to the creditor in ancient Emar, located in North Syria at the bend of the Euphrates, to obtain his money or goods should the debtor default.

It must be noted at the outset that two different types of contract documents were used at Emar. They differ not only in their physical format—a long text which is usually referred to as Syrian type and a broad text which is referred to as Syro-Hittite—but also in the legal formulations employed by each type.[1] This fact has not yet found full expression in the rather meager amounts of analysis devoted to the legal texts from Emar. Actually, most of the corpus of security texts belong to the Syro-Hittite type; only a few belong to the Syrian type. In the current state of our knowledge it is difficult to determine if this is coincidental or whether there is some historical or social reason for it.

I. Pledge and Surety

A number of years ago Hoftijzer and van Soldt published an article[2] in which they surveyed the then available texts dealing with security for loans, which were discovered at Ugarit, Emar and Alalah level IV. They noted that none of the usual terms for pledge which are to be found elsewhere,[3] such as *mazzazānu*, or *šapartu*, or *maškanu*, occur in the Emar texts. They also noted that, in contrast to the

---

[1] Wilcke 1992: 115–141, nn. 33, 36, 41.
[2] Hoftijzer and van Soldt 1991: 189–218.
[3] Petschow 1956.

situation elsewhere in the ancient Near East where pledge is terminologically differentiated from surety, the texts from Emar (and Alalah IV), do not differentiate terminologically between the two types of security. The formulas employed in these texts to designate various types of security, whether pledge or surety, are all based on the term *qātātu*. It follows then that each text must be examined individually as to the type of security recorded therein. Hoftijzer and van Soldt did not offer any reason for this change in terminology from the usage of the rest of the Near East, nor did they deal with possible implications of such a change.

The six texts used by Hoftijzer and van Soldt to describe security for loans at Emar[4] are all of the Syro-Hittite type. Since then an additional number of *qātātu* texts from Emar have been published, all of them of the Syro-Hittite type[5] except for one which is Syrian,[6] so that we now have a corpus of fourteen *qātātu* texts from that site. The new material from Emar does not change the picture presented by Hoftijzer and van Soldt, that the Syro-Hittite texts from Emar designate both pledge and surety as *qātātu*.

Actually, in the Syro-Hittite texts from Emar the term for security is written either as a logogram or syllabically. The logogram employed is either šu or a compound en-šu.[7] Curiously this latter logogram occurs at Emar only in nominal sentences where it serves as a predicate.[8] In the verbal formulation, the term used for security is written either with the logogram šu[9] or is transcribed syllabically in Akkadian, as a form of the word *qātātu*.[10] When the term for security is used in a verbal clause it occurs mostly as the indirect object of different verbs, each verb used no doubt to reflect a different situation as will be mentioned below.

It should be noted that in the one Syrian type text from Emar,[11] the term for security is written logographically, šu-du$_8$-a, a logogram

[4] Emar VI 87; 88; 119; 209; ASJ 35; *Acta Sumerologica* 13 (1991), 335 (Text A).

[5] TBR 27; 34; 53; RE 58. It is not clear to me why Hoftijzer and van Soldt ignored Emar VI 77; 116; 121, which were already published when they wrote their study.

[6] Dalley 5.

[7] en-šu^{meš} Emar VI 87, 88; en^{meš}-šu$^{meš.ti}$ TBR 27; en^{meš}-šu^{meš} Emar VI 77, 119.

[8] This particular logogram occurs elsewhere only in Neo-Assyrian texts. See Radner 1997: 357.

[9] Emar VI 116: TBR 34.

[10] *Acta Sumerologica* 13 (1991), 335 (Text A); ASJ 35; RE 58; TBR 53.

[11] Dalley 5.

that appears at Alalah IV[12] and is standard in Lower Mesopotamia during the Old Babylonian period. In the text from Emar, šu-du$_8$-a is used to describe a guarantor. Nevertheless, in view of the paucity of Syrian security texts one cannot be certain if šu-du$_8$-a at Emar is limited to describe guarantors, as is the case in Old Babylonian texts, or if it also describes pledge as is the case at Alalakh IV. Finally, it should be pointed out that there is a text which clearly involves security for loans although it does not use any technical term for security.[13]

Hoftijzer and van Soldt limited their analysis of security at Emar strictly to those texts that contain the word *qātātu*. They did not consider the broader question of what means were available to the creditor to collect his debt in the case of default.

A credit transaction is composed of several stages. In the first stage an obligation is incurred. The second stage is the time when the obligation must be paid, and then there is a third stage which comes into play if the obligation to pay is not fulfilled. The second stage is not relevant for this study because if the loan is repaid on time then there is no need for any legal steps by the creditor.

Already in the first stage the creditor could take a pledge or demand that the creditor provide a guarantor. Both possibilities are reflected in the available texts.

Text ASJ 33, a Syrian type text, records the loan of two hundred shekels of silver. 1) 2 *me-ti* kù-babbar *ṣur-pu* 2) na$_4$ ^{uru}*e-mar*^{ki} 3) ki *še?-i?-ba-aḫ-li* 4) $^{\text{I⸢d}}$en⸣-*ka-bar* 5) *ù ì-lí-*^{d}*da-gan* 6) ^{I}*i-*[*d*]*í-*^{d}*da-gan* 7) dumu ^{d}[iš]kur-*a-bu* 8) é-*šu ù* dumu^{meš}-*šu* 9) šu ba-an-ti-meš. There are however, certain difficulties in this text. Who is debtor, who is creditor?

Ostensibly, the text is formulated according to the pattern of the Old Babylonian and Middle Assyrian loan texts, i.e. Object of loan, KI (from) the creditor, the debtor received (šu ba-an-ti). The verb šu ba-an-ti-meš in line 9 is plural, which would indicate that more than one person is the recipient of the loan. But if debtors are the subject of the verb šu ba-an-ti-meš, then line 8, é-*šu ù* dumu^{meš}-*šu* "his house and his sons," is problematic. The pronoun *šu* indicates that we are dealing with one person. Whose house, whose sons? If it refers to the creditor, then this line remains without a verb and has no meaning.

---

[12] AT 48; 49; 50; 70; 83; 84; 85. The word *qātātu* does appear in AT 4.
[13] ASJ 33.

The text concludes with a clause that provides for penalty interest if the loan is not repaid in eight years. 10) mu-8-kám kù-babbar ì-lá-e$^{!}$ 11) *ú-še-et-te-eq-ma* 12) máš *li-ṣa-ab* "he shall repay the silver in eight years; should the (time of payment) pass, he shall pay interest." This clause clearly indicates that there is only one debtor. We would thus translate lines 1–9: "*Idī-Dagan* (borrowed) two hundred shekels of silver according to the weight of Emar from *Šēī?-Baḫli*, *Belū-kabar* and *Ilī-Dagan*. They took his house and his sons." Whatever may have caused this deviation from the Old Babylonian and Middle Assyrian pattern it is clear that the house and sons of the debtor were taken as pledges. Though there is no specific technical term for pledge used in this text the wording of the text indicates that the pledge is quite probably possessory.

There are available five first stage Syro-Hittite texts in which the term for security is the logogram en-šu. One would normally expect this logogram to be exclusively a surety term as is the case in the Neo-Assyrian texts.[14] Yet, there are two texts, Emar VI 77: 3). . . . en^{meš}-šu^{meš}-*šú* 4) é-*šú ù* ^{I}*ad-da* [du]mu-*šu* . . . "his house and his son, Adda, are his en^{meš}-šu^{meš}," and Emar VI 87: 7) 5 gú-un na_4 *ga-bi-i* 8) *i-na* $na_4^{\text{meš}}$ *ka-a-ri* 9) *i-na* é *ša* ^{Id}kur-gal 10) *šak-na* en-šu^{meš} 11) *ša* 1 me 50 gín kù-babbar^{meš} "5 talents alum by the weight of the *kārum* is placed in the house of *Dagan-kabar* as en-šu^{meš} for 150 shekels of silver," in which the logogram en-šu is best understood as a term for a pledge. A house and alum are not likely to be guarantors. It should also be noted that in Emar VI 88, where family members—a sister-in-law or son—are the en-šu^{meš}, very likely reflects a pledge rather than a surety. So too TBR 27: 4). . . . *ù* ^{f}nin-*ki-mi* dam-*šú* en^{meš}-šu^{li}-*ši* 5) *ša* ^{f}*ḫu-da-ti i-na* iti *ša a-bi-e* 6) *la-qì* "*Ba'alat-kimī*, his wife (of the debtor), is en-šu of *Ḫudati*, in the month of *Abē* (she) was taken," quite probably describes a possessory pledge.

Only in Emar VI 119 is en-šu used as a term for a surety. The pertinent section reads: 6) . . . *ù* ^{I}*šur-ši*-^{d}kur 7) en^{meš}-šu^{meš} *i-na-an-na* 8) [š]e^{meš} *ša-a-ši a-na* [x x] x [x] x *ù* ^{I}*šur-ši*-^{d}kur 9) [*u*]*l-tal-li-mu* ". . . and *Šurši-Dagan* is en^{meš}-šu^{meš}; now that grain x-x-x-x-x and *Šurši-Dagan* will pay it." The text is partially broken but it is clear that as is specifically provided in line 8, *Šurši-Dagan*, who is en^{meš}-šu^{meš}, has to repay the loan. This logogram, en-šu, would then be a general term

[14] See Radner 1997: 357.

for security. It is used only as a predicate in nominal sentences as noted above, and its precise meaning depends on the context in which it is used.

There is one other text, Emar VI 205, that quite likely reflects the first stage, obtaining a loan. The precise nature of the transaction which led to the need for guarantors is not certain, for the beginning of the text is partially broken.[15] In this text the scribe used the regular Old Babylonian formula for assuming a guarantee: *qātātin leqûm*. The text is unusual in that we have here a rather rare situation where a second person serves as guarantor for the first guarantor. Thus 5) . . . ^{I}*lu-a-da* dumu *nu-ú-ri* pa$_5$ *ta-am-ni-tu*$_4$ 6) *qa-*[*t*]*a-ti-šu il-qè* "(for) *Luada*, the son of *Nūri*, from the irrigation district of Tamnitu, is the guarantor," (*qātātišu ilqe*) of *Buzeze*, the debtor. We then read 9) ^{I}*la-aq-ra-ʿu* dumu *kàr-bi* dumu *a-bi-te-ri* 10) ša ^{I}*lu-a-da* dumu *nu-ú-ri* 11) *qa-ta-ti il-qè* "Laqrau is the guarantor of Luada."

---

[15] According to Arnaud the beginning is to be reconstructed as follows:

1. ^{I}[*b*]*u-ze-zu* d[um]u *ḫa-b*[*i-t*]*i ki-i*[*r-ṣ*]*i-tu*$_4$ *q*[*á-du*] na$_4^{meš}$-*šu*
2. *a-na* 14 gín kù-babbar[^{meš} *a-na* ^{Id}iškur-u]r-sag dumu *zu-ba-la*
3. *a-*[*na q*]*a-*[*t*]*a-ti it-ta-*[*din-š*]*u*

"*Buzēzu* son of *Ḫabitu* delivered a ki [*irṣit*]*u* to[gether] with its stones? for 14 shekels of silver [to Iškur-ur]-sag son of *Zu-bala* [as *q*]*ā*[*t*]*ātu*." The text then goes on to provide that if *Buzēzu* flees then *Luada* is to be seized (*i*[*ṣ*]-*ṣa-ab-ba-tu*$_4$),

5\. . . . . ^{I}*lu-a-da* dumu *nu-ú-ri* pa$_5$ *ta-am-ni-tu*$_4$
6\. *qa-*[*t*]*a-ti-šu il-qè*

"(for) *Luada*, the son of *Nūri*, from the irrigation district of *Tamnitu*, is the guarantor" (*qātātišu ilqe*). We are then informed:

6\. . . . . *ur-ra-am še-ra-am*
7\. ^{I}*bu-zé-e-zu* kù-babbar *iš-tu qa*ʹ*-ti* ^{Id}iškur-ur-sag *i-ra-aš-ši*
8\. ìr-*ma ša* ^{Id}iškur-ur-sag *šu-ú-ut*

"If in the future *Buzēzu* will acquire silver from the hand of Iškur-ur-sag he is the slave of Iškur-ur-sag."

The text then concludes:

9\. ^{I}*la-aq-ra-ʿu* dumu *kàr-bi* dumu *a-bi-te-ri*
10\. *ša* ^{I}*lu-a-da* dumu *nu-ú-ri*
11\. *qa-ta-ti il-qì*

"*Laqrau* is the guarantor of *Luada*." We have here a rather rare situation where a second person serves as guarantor for the first guarantor.

The text as reconstructed by Arnaud is problematic. Why should *Buzēzu* provide property as *qātātu* for fourteen shekels of silver when it would appear from ll. 6ff. that he has not yet received the silver? Furthermore, if *Buzēzu* can provide some property as *qātātu* why should he agree to become a slave in exchange for fourteen shekels of silver?

As it now stands I cannot accept Arnaud's reconstruction. The few signs that Arnaud copied at the beginning of the text and the remainder of the signs in line 3 do not, in my opinion, in any way support his reconstruction.

What can a creditor do to collect a debt that is due him should the debtor default? There are a good number of texts that deal with the third stage: failure or inability of the debtor to repay the loan. There are at least four options available to the creditor.

I. If there are guarantors, the creditor can claim the debt from the guarantors. There are two specific examples from Emar, both Syro-Hittite type texts.

According to text *Acta Sumerologica* 13, p. 335 text A, PN [*ša*] dumu ^{I}*Ši-mi-da-ri ṣa-bit* "PN, the guarantor (*qātātu*) of the sons of *šimidari* was seized" and paid of the debt of the sons of *šimidari*. The text concludes with a clause recording mutual agreement between the creditor and the guarantor not to raise claims against each other.

The second text, Emar VI 116, records that: 1) ^{I}*ba-ba dumu* ìr!-dingir^{meš} ^{Id}u-en dumu en-gal šeš-*šú* 2) 5 gín kù-babbar^{meš} "*a* ^{I}*a-ḫi-*^{d}kur dumu ^{d}kur-gal šu$^{\text{meš-}ti}$-*šú ṣa-bít* "*Baba*, son of *Abdi-ilī*,—*Ba'al-bēlī* son of *Belū-kabar* (is) his brother—was seized as guarantor (šu$^{\text{meš-}ti}$) for five shekels owed to *Aḫī-Dagan*, son of *Dagan-kabar*. The formula *qātātu ṣabit* in these two texts is best understood not as a physical act of seizing the guarantor but as a symbolic action placing him under the obligation to pay the loan.

Curiously, according to Emar VI 116, the guarantor paid the debt, not with his own property but with 4) . . . ha-la-*šú ša* ^{d}u-en šeš-*šú* 5) *ma-la it-ti* šeš-*šú* dumu^{meš} *im-ma-ri i-kaš-ša-ad-šú* "the share of *Ba'al-bēlī*, son of *Belū-kabar*, which he will receive together with his brother(s), the sons of *Immaru*."[16] This property is apparently the assigned share of *Ba'al-bēlī* son of *Belū-kabar* which has not yet been apportioned, so that *Baba* has some say in how to use the property. The text concludes with the stipulation that whoever among the sons of *Immaru* will raise claims will pay five shekels of silver to the creditor and take the property. In this case the transferred property is redeemable upon payment of the original debt.

The right of regress of the guarantor who paid the debt is recorded in text Emar VI 121. The situation is as follows: *Ḫimāši-Dagan*, son

[16] Though *Baba* and *Ba'al-bēlī* are referred to as brothers they do not have the same father. *Baba* is the son of *Abdi-ilī*, whereas *Ba'al-bēlī* is the son of *Belū-kabar*. The property is described as that "which he will receive together with his brother(s), the sons of *Immaru*." In all likelihood the property in question belongs to that social group at Emar known as "brothers." See Bellotto 1995: 210–228.

It is noteworthy that in text TBR 5, a sale deed, one of the neighbors is a *Baba* son of *Immaru*. Could this be the same person as Baba, the son of *Abdi-ilī* of Emar VI 116?

of *Abba* could not pay his debt and one *Milki-Dagan*, son of *Ahī-Dagan* paid it. *Ḫimāši-Dagan* then became a slave of *Milki-Dagan*. However, line 13ff. provides that 13) *šúm-ma* kù-babbar^{meš} *ša* šu^{ti}-*šú i-na-din!* 14) kù-babbar téš-bi *li-din* "if the silver of his guarantor (šu^{ti}-*šú*) will be paid, he shall pay double." As the only person who can be in a position to release *Ḫimāši-Dagan* upon payment of the money is *Milki-Dagan*, it seems obvious that *Milki-Dagan* must be the guarantor referred to in this clause. In other words the text records the fact that *Milki-Dagan*, the guarantor, paid the debt of *Ḫimāši-Dagan* and recovered his money by taking *Ḫimāši-Dagan* as a debt-slave.

TBR 82, a Syrian type text, records a somewhat similar situation to that recorded in Emar VI 121. One brother pays the debts of another brother and takes the house of the debtor in lieu of the debt. However, the one who paid the debt is nowhere referred to as guarantor of the debtor though it is possible that he was so described in the original loan text. The text stipulates that when the debtor returns to his city and pays the debt to his brother, he will receive back his house.

There are a number of other texts which record the fact that a third party paid the debt of the debtor. There is nothing in these texts that indicates that the one who paid the debt was a guarantor. Nevertheless, according to these texts one who paid the debt now becomes the new creditor of the debtor. There is similarity to the right of regress of the guarantor as found in Emar VI 121, where we are informed that the one who paid the debt was a guarantor, not in the payment clause where it could logically be expected to be mentioned, but only in the redemption clause. The original creditor is not a factor in these texts.

In all of these cases the debtor entered some form of servitude under the new creditor, i.e. the one who paid of his loan. There are three texts which record the payment by *Zu-Aštarti* son of *Aḫī-malik* of the loan of an insolvent debtor. In one case (ASJ 36) the debtor becomes a slave of *Zu-Aštarti* forever. There is no mention in this text of the possibility that the debt-slave can be released. Another text (Sigrist 1) provides that the debtor and his family become the slaves of *Zu-Aštarti*. If someone raises claims against them, i.e. the debtor and his family, the one raising claims is to pay double the amount of the loan, and can then take them. This seems to be an oblique way of providing for their release. In the third text (ASJ 37) the debtor, a woman, declares that in a famine year *Zu-Aštarti* paid her debt and kept her alive. The fact that the debtor entered the service of *Zu-Aštarti* is not explicitly stated but is to be deduced from the clause at the end of the document which provides that if someone raises claims against the debtor, he shall pay one servant girl to *Zu-Aštarti*, and may take the debtor.

In text Emar VI 86, one *Zu-Dagan* declares that *Dagan-tali'*, kept him alive in a famine year and paid his debt. He then declares that as long as he is alive he will serve *Dagan-tali'*. If, however, he wishes to leave the house of *Dagan-tali'*, he is to pay 10 shekels of silver (4 times the amount of the loan) and may go wherever he pleases.

In another text, RE 10, the debtor *Ḫemiya*, son of *Aḫī-malik* declares there was no one to serve him, so that he took *Bēlu-qarrād* son of *Itūr-Dagan* to serve him (*a-na pa-la-*⌈*ḫi*⌉ *-ya él-te-qa-an-ni*) and that *Bēlu-qarrād* paid his debt. Though the text is technically not an adoption text it contains the usual clauses found in adoption texts providing in this case for the inheritance of the debtor's property by *Bēlu-qarrād*.

Text TBR 25 records the declaration by a person that in the year that the TAR-W/U surrounded the city he could not pay his debt and that *Arwu* saved him from starvation. Though it is not specifically stated in the text, it is clear from the final clause that the debtor was in some manner of servitude to the creditor. The final clause provides that if the debtor wishes to leave the house of the creditor he is to provide a person and only then may he leave.

RE 58 is unusual in that it records the declaration of the one who paid the loan whereas the other texts contain declarations by the debtor. *Zadamma* paid the debts of *Benti*: 6 . . . *ù* ^{I}*be-en-ti* dumu *i-túr*-^{d}kur 7) é-*šú ù* dam-*šú* 8) *a-na qa-ta-ti ša* 20 gín kù-babbar^{meš} 9) *a-na* ^{I}*za-dam-ma* dumu *ip-qí*-^{d}kur 10) *il-ta-kán* "Now *Benti*, son of *Itūr-Dagan* has consigned his house and his wife as *qātāti* for 20 shekels." The debtor was required to consign his wife and house as *qa-ta-ti* for the new obligation. *Qātātu* in this text is hardly likely to be a surety, for a house cannot serve as surety though it can serve as a pledge. It is best to see *qātātu* in this text as some sort of pledge.

A nearly identical situation is described in ASJ 35. *Yašur-Dagan* paid the debts of *Itūr-Dagan* and took him as *amēlūti* (= antichretic pledge). The wife of the debtor together with his son and house *a-na qa-ta-ti il-ta-kán* "he has consigned as *qātātu*." It is difficult to see the wife and son of a debtor, who is himself an antichretic pledge because he cannot pay his debt, serving as guarantors for the debt.

Note that in both cases *qātātu šakānu* is used when the debtor provides the *qātātu.*

There are available two texts which are in reality testaments but which contain references to the payment of loans. In both texts a woman, *Ba'alat-kimī*, declares that her husband paid off the debts of *Yakmu-Dagan* (TBR 28) and *Nana-Dagan* (TBR 29), and in both cases the husband received two houses in return for paying the loan of a debtor. *Ba'alat-kimī* gave the houses to her son. Both texts contain the proviso that if someone should claim the houses he is to pay double and take them.

II. Another option open to the creditor was to distrain members of the family of the debtor in order to force the debtor to pay the loan of which there are several examples. In TBR 26, the creditor seizes the wife of the debtor. The woman, of her own free will, then sells herself into slavery to a third party, *Bulalu*, son of *Arwu*. The text concludes with a clause providing that if a claimant should appear a number of people who are listed in the text are to satisfy the claim whereas *Bulalu* is free of claims.

In another case, TBR 34, the creditor holds the wife and three sons of the debtor *ki-i-mu* kù-babbar-*šu u-ka-al* "(The creditor) detains on account of his silver." The debtor, 4) . . . *i-na-an-na* ^{I}*ṣa-al-mu* 5) *a-na* šu$^{\text{meš.}\textit{ti}}$ *ša* dam^{meš}-*šu* dumu^{meš}-<*šu*> *i-te-ru-ub* 6) dam-*šu* dumu^{meš}-*šu ul-te-ṣi* "Now *Ṣalmu* entered as *qātātu* for his wife (and) his sons. His wife and his sons shall go out (free)." The use of the term *ukâl* and *ulteṣi* with regard to the wife and son of the debtor is a clear indication that they were in some way under the control of the creditor.[17] As the debtor in this case substitutes (lit., enters) for his wife and child it appears that the term *qātātu erēbu* in this text very likely means to become a pledge the nature of which is not clear (antichretic pledge?).

III. Another option open to creditor was to sue the debtor in court. There are available two such texts: TBR 84 and TBR 36. In TBR 84 one *Aštartu-Līt* sued *Karbu* for the debt which *Karbu* owed his cousin, one *Galalu*, and lost the suit. In TBR 36 one *Uginu* sued *Abī-Šaggar* and his brother *Abba* for debts that their father owed to *Uginu*. *Abba* denied any connection with the debt but was sued by his brother, who won the suit. The judge then ruled that *Uginu* must

---

[17] See *kullu* in CAD K p. 511, for examples of the term *kullu* with the meaning "to control."

take an oath that the money was due him, which he did. As the brothers apparently did not have the necessary cash they paid the debt with various parcels of property.

IV. Another likelihood that must be taken into account is the possibility that the creditor and debtor may reach some agreement as to the payment of the debt. Thus in Emar VI 123, we are informed that the debtor could not pay his loan and so sold his house for the exact sum of his debts to his creditors.

Another rather interesting text is TBR 74. The woman *Dāda* declared that she has no one to serve her (*ša i-pal-la-ḫa-an-ni i-ia-nu*) and so adopted one *Bēlu-qarrād*, who apparently borrowed from her in a famine year, as her son with the right to inherit from her in return for serving her. Nothing is said about repaying the loan.

There remains one text which relates to debt payment but whose precise classification is not certain. In RE 90, a Syrian text, we read: 15) ^{giš}kiri$_6$-geštin ḫa-la 16) *ša* ^{I}*pa-ra-i* dumu *ia-ṣú* 17) *aš-ra-nu-ma* 18) ^{I}*ì-lí-a-bi ki-i* 19) 5/6 ma-na kù-babbar *ṣa-bi-it!* 20) *ša* 5/6 ma-na kù-babbar 21) *a-na* ^{I}*ì-lí-a-bi i-n*[*a*]*din* 22) *ù* ^{giš}kiri$_6$-geštin *li-il$_5$-qè* "*Ilī-abu* seized the vineyard, the inheritance portion of *Para'u*, son of *Yaṣu* in the same place (as the first vineyard) in lieu of 5/6 mina of silver. Whoever pays *Ilī-abu* 5/6 mina of silver shall take the vineyard." It would appear that the property taken by *Ilī-abu* was taken in lieu of the payment of the debt due him. It is not clear if the property was originally pledged for a loan or if *Ilī-abu* seized the property because the debtor had no other means of paying the debt.

Finally, there is a house sale text, TBR 53, which contains a *qātātu* clause. The text contains a price clause as well as a clause against revocation of the sale. This is followed by a list of witnesses. The text concludes with the following clause: 23) *ù qa-ta-ti ša* é *an-ni-i* 24) a-šà^{meš}-*šu i-na* edin-na 25) ^{I}*ki-it-ta i-ṣa-bat* "Now the *qātātu* of this house, his field in the plain, Kitta (the buyer) shall seize." The description of the field as *qātāti* is a clear indication that in this case *qātātu ṣabātu* is not a surety formula. In contrast to *qātātu ṣabit* of Emar VI 116 and *Acta Sumerologica* 13, p. 335 text A, it is highly likely that the verb *ṣabātum* "to seize" is to be taken literally.

It is very probable that the field served as a hypothecary pledge protecting the buyer should the seller fail to deliver the house. Though this text is formulated as a cash sale, as are most other Syro-Hittite sales, we have here an indication that the price was not always paid at the time of the sale.

II. Antichresis

The antichretic pledge is in reality a possessory pledge though its purpose is to guarantee the payment of the interest. There can be little doubt that antichresis was known to the people of Emar, for the institution was used in many regions of the ancient Near East. The problem is to find documentation of this institution at Emar.

There are a number of texts, all of the Syro-Hittite type, which record that a person is taken as lú^{meš}-ú-lu-*tu* (*amēlūtu*) because of a debt.[18] These *amēlūtu* texts can be grouped into different categories. Texts ASJ 35 and Emar VI 77, both noted above, record the taking of a person as *amēlūtu* in exchange for repaying the loan of the debtor. Now in ASJ 35, although the one who takes the person as *amēlūtu* is not specifically referred to as guarantor, the fact that the text records the list of creditors to whom the silver was paid and does not include the one who paid the debts is indicative that the one who paid was not the original creditor.[19] In both texts the *amēlūtu* also provided subsidiary guarantees, his wife, son and house, which in ASJ 35 is specifically described as en-šu, which we suggested above were possibly hypothecary pledges. There is then a clear distinction between *amēlūtu* and *qātātu.*

A second group of texts record changes in the relationship of the *amēlūtu* and his creditor. In TBR 39 and TBR 40 the debt of the *amēlūtu* is cancelled and he is then adopted by the creditor, who also gives him a wife.[20] Emar VI 117 and Emar VI 16 (only a portion of the debt is cancelled in this text) record an arrangement whereby the debtor is required to serve the creditor and his wife as long as they live. The arrangement is similar to that of adoption except that the clauses against breach of the agreement are not those of the usual adoption agreement.

---

[18] The usual formula is lú-ú-lu *ša* n kù-babbar. ASJ 10A reads: *a-na* lú-ú-lu—*ti ki-i-mu-u* n kù-babbar ⸢*aš*⸣-*bu*. ASJ 35 reads: *ki-i* n kù-babbar *a-na* lú-ú-lu-*ut-ti al-ta-qè-šu*. The Akkadian equivalent of lú^{meš}-ú-lu-*tu* is *amēlūtu* which the dictionaries CAD and AHw translate as "retainers," which fits so far as I can see in the Middle Babylonian contexts where this term appears but does not fully express the usage at Emar.

[19] One cannot be certain that he was guarantor or someone to whom the debtor turned in his extremity.

[20] See also TBR 74 for another example of debtor being adopted by creditor.

Only text *Acta Sumerologica* 10, p. 173 text A, provides a clear indication that *amēlūtu* transaction is an antichretic arrangement. Three persons, *Dudu* and his two sons, become *amēlūtu* in exchange for one hundred and five shekels and forty grains of silver. We are then informed that *Dudu* paid forty shekels of silver of the outstanding loan. As a result *Dudu* was freed, but his two sons remained in the house of the creditor for the remaining 65 shekels and forty grains of silver. The text then stipulates that when *Dudu* repays the rest of the silver, i.e. the remaining 65 shekels and forty grains of silver, the tablet will be broken.

The payment clause is followed by another clause which apprises us that Dudu stayed in the house of the creditor and was freed from nine months' servitude. We are further informed that when *Dudu* will pay the remainder of the loan he is to provide one of his sons to the creditor and 9 itu^{meš} kin^{meš} *i-ṣa-bat* "9 months work he (the son) will perform."

The nine months of work that the son must perform cannot be related to payment of the balance of the loan, for only upon payment of the outstanding silver is the debtor to provide a son to work for the creditor. It must then reflect the balance of the interest that was not yet paid on that portion of the loan, the forty shekels that was paid, and led to the release of the father.

The means by which a creditor could obtain his money from a defaulting debtor are many and variegated. Apart from securities for loans such as guarantors and pledges of various types the creditor could also avail himself of legal steps to obtain the repayment of a loan. Though there is no definite example of the foreclosure of a pledge, the fact that there are examples of guarantors paying a loan is a good indication that pledges were also forfeited.

Abbreviations

ASJ	A. Tsukimoto. Akkadian Tablets in the Hiryama Collection: *ASJ* 12 (1990) 177– 259 (nos. 1–16, *ASJ* 13 (1991) 275–333 (nos. 17–42), *ASJ* 14 (1992) 289–310 (nos. 43–50).
Dalley	S. Dalley and B. Tessier. 1992. Tablets from the Vicinity of Emar and Elsewhere. *Iraq* 54: 83–112.
Emar VI	D. Arnaud. 1985–87. *Recherches au pays d'Aštata. Emar VI. Textes sumeriens et accadiens.* Tomes 1–3. Paris: ERC.
RE	G. Beckman. 1966. *Texts from the Vicinity of Emar in the Collection of Jonathan Rosen.* HANEM 2. Padua: Sargon srl.
Sigrist	M. Sigrist. 1993. Seven Emar Tablets. In *kinattūtu ša dārâti. Raphael Kutscher Memorial Volume.* Pp. 165–187. 165–184. *Tel Aviv*, Occasional Publications, No. 1. Tel Aviv: Institute of Archaeology.
TBR	D. Arnaud. 1991. *Textes syriens de l'âge du bronze récent.* Aula Or. Suppl. 1. Barcelona: Editorial Ausa.

Bibliography

Bellotto, N. 1995. I LÚ.MEŠ *aḫ-ḫi-a*. *AoF* 22: 210–228.
Hoftijzer, J. and W. van Soldt. 1991. Texts from Ugarit concerning Security. *UF* 23: 189–218.
Petschow, H. 1956. Neubabylonisches Pfandrecht. Abhandlungen der Sächsischen Akademie der Wissenschaften, Philologisch-historische Klasse 48, 1. Berlin: Akademie-Verlag.
Radner, K. 1997. *Die neuassyrischen Privatrechtsurkunden als Quelle für Mensch und Umwelt.* SAAS VI. Helsinki: The Neo-Assyrian Corpus Project.
Wilcke, C. 1992. AḪ die "Brüder" von Emar, Untersuchungen zur Schreibtradition am Euphratknie. *Aula Orientalis* 10: 115–141.

ISRAEL

Tikva Frymer-Kensky – University of Chicago

I. Introduction

The Biblical rules of credit do not reflect an economy in which money is borrowed for entrepreneurship or speculation. On the contrary, loans are seen as a device by which the poor stave off disaster. As a result, they are mentioned with a positive valence.

> (If you have a poor man among your kin . . . do not harden your heart.) Indeed, open your hand and lend, lend (*hʿbṭ tʿbyṭnw*) enough to meet his shortfall. (Deut. 15:7–8)

> Do not withhold good from those in need when you are able. Do not say to your neighbor, "Go away and come back another time, I will give it to you tomorrow." (Prov. 3:27–30)

> Those who are gracious to the lowly are blessed. (Prov. 14:21)

Nevertheless, despite the high esteem in which loans are mentioned, it is clearly much better to be a creditor than a debtor, and the ability to be one is a mark of divine blessing.

> The Lord your God will bless you as he said and you will lend (*hʿbṭt*) to many nations and you will not borrow (*tʿbṭ*). (Deut. 15:6)

Israel may have had a system of commercial credit to finance trading ventures, and may have facilitated borrowing such sums by providing for equitable rates of interest, but the loans that are mentioned in the Bible are not part of a commercial credit system; they are subsistence loans to ameliorate dire poverty. Such poverty was expected as a permanent part of social reality (Deut. 15:11), and credit was to be extended as a social obligation, to support others in the community. For this reason, it could not be an opportunity for the lender to make money by charging interest:

> When you lend money to my people, to the poor who are with you, do not be as a *nôšeh*-creditor: do not impose interest on him. (Exod. 22:24)

The prohibition of interest applies both to money subtracted from money lent at the time of the loan or to money that had to be paid over the amount lent when the loan became due.[1]

> If your fellow weakens, and comes under your hand, you "make him strong" and support him as a landless inhabitant (resident alien). And let him live with you. Do not take interest either before or after, fear God and let your brother live with you. (Lev. 25:35–37)

Despite the necessity poor men have to borrow and the social obligation to lend money to them, Jeremiah indicates that the *nôšeh*, the "creditor," was not a beloved figure.

> I have not been a creditor, nor does anyone hold a debt on me, but they all curse me. (Jer. 15:10)

The creditor may have been beloved when he lent money, but he was hated when it came time to collect. The prophet Amos is particularly upset at those who collect loans from people who do not have a monetary surplus: "Because you exact a levy of grain from him (the poor man)" (Amos 5:11). The term *nôšeh* might be used for one who lent with interest (Exod. 22:24) but even a permissible loan by a *nôšeh* probably had some means to coerce payment, some form of security for the loan.

II. Secured Loans

1. *Terminology*

Creditors were not to take advantage of a fellow's poverty by charging interest for loans, and the ideal Israelite simply gave the poor what they needed:

> He has not wronged anyone, he has not taken a pledge or acquired anything improperly; he has given his bread to the hungry and clothed the naked. He has kept his hand back (from taking from) the poor man and has not taken advanced or accrued interest: he has followed my rules and obeyed my laws. (Ezek. 18:16)

[1] On interest see Neufeld 1955: 355–412; Gamoran 1971: 127–134; Gordon 1982: 406–426. On loans in Israel, see Seeligmann 1978: 183–205 (Hebrew) and 209–210 (English absract); and Rasor 1993–94: 157–192.

The ideal creditor simply gave, but in the real world, people could not be expected to risk all or part of their own property if loans were defaulted, and two institutions protected the creditor: pledges and third party security.

The biblical law collections do not include a law that calls for and defines pledges, but we know about the institution from laws that excluded objects that could not be pledged and limited the mode of seizure. There are two possible pledges, the possessory pledge (pawn) which the borrower deposits with the lender from the moment of the loan, and the hypothecary pledge, which remains in the borrower's possession unless he defaults on the loan. There are also two different Hebrew words used, *ḥabol* and *ʿaboṭ*. It is not a simple matter to differentiate them. They are not distributed by the sources, since Deuteronomy uses both terms, and they do not seem to line up neatly between the two types of pledges. The verbs are clearer: the verb from *ʿaboṭ* can mean simply "to lend": the verb is used in the positive injunction to help a poor person; the verb from *ḥabol* means "to seize."

If either one of these terms means a possessory pledge, then lending would not only be cruel at collection, as Amos points out, but even at inception. The amounts borrowed were tiny. People were living close to the edge of utter destitution; the pledges offered were the very last items a person would give up, literally "the cloak from off his back." It seems inconceivable that either Exodus or Deuteronomy would envision a situation in which the borrower was deprived of his cloak (at least in the daytime) from the moment that he borrowed money. It does not seem likely that *ʿaboṭ* could be urged as a positive expression of community support if the verb meant to take the poor man's last possession in the very act of lending him money. For this reason I would suggest that neither term refers to a true possessory pledge, and both refer to a situation in which the loan is due and about to be defaulted. The two terms would refer to the same act, but carry a different valence: *ḥabol* means the object seized in default and *ʿaboṭ* the equivalent, or at least substitute, for the loan.

There is narrative evidence for a "pledge" that was given as a deposit until the debt was paid. In Genesis 38, Judah offers the disguised Tamar an *ʿerabôn* as a guarantee that he will pay her for the sex. The term *ʿerabôn* may be a technical term for such a deposited pledge, distinguished from both *ḥabol* and *ʿaboṭ*. The story's pledge might not be applicable for debts, for there is no real debt here, just payment owed for services rendered. Moreover, Judah's *ʿerabôn* has nothing to do with poverty law and subsistence credit. In addition, the *ʿerabôn* in question, Judah's staff and seal, may not have had the monetary value of the promised kid, and may have been deposited more as a method of identification. Judah's decision to let her keep them rather than to keep searching for her may indicate that they did have some independent value.

The prayer in Ps. 119:121–22 offers another use of this root *ʿrb*:

> I have done righteousness; do not give me to my oppressors. Guarantee good for your servants; let evil ones not oppress me.

The root implies an obligation, and this verse may give the reason that *ʿarbeni*, "be obligated for me" comes to mean "be good to me," in much the same semantic development of the English, "be obliged."

2. *Protection of debtors*

The institution of pledges is dangerous and easily abused. To prevent untrammeled exploitation, the laws provide that certain objects are unpledgeable. These are objects that provide for life's basic necessities, like a millstone or a widow's garment.

> You cannot take the garment of a widow in pledge. (Deut. 24:28)

> You cannot take a millstone in pledge for then you take a life in pledge. (Deut. 24:6)

Moreover, borrowers could not have unlimited use of those articles that could be pledged. The poor man's cloak, the last object likely to leave his possession, was to be returned at night when he might need it for protection from the cold.

> If you take your fellow's garment in pledge, return it by evening. (Exod. 22:25)

> If he is a poor man, you cannot lie on the items you have seized from him. When the sun comes down, return the "pledge" to him. He will lie in his garment and bless you and it will be a righteous deed for you. (Deut. 24:12)

Moreover, to prevent creditors from humiliating the poor, and to prevent them from taking whatever they might like, the law also provided that a creditor could not trespass when he came to seize the pledged object (most probably at the time of default on debt). Even then, the creditor had to wait for the debtor to give him the object.

> If you have extended credit to your fellow, for any debt you may not come into his house to seize the object to be seized. Stand outside, and the man whose creditor you are will bring the "pledge" (*ʿaboṭ*) out to you. (Deut. 24:20)

Despite these rules, there were serious abuses. "Unpledgeable items" were taken, and garments were not returned.

> They stretch themselves out at every altar on garments taken in pledge. (Amos 2:8)
>
> They drive the orphan's ass, take the widow's ox in pledge. (Job 24:3)

Improper creditors might also refuse to return items even after the debt was paid.

> He doesn't return the seized item (*ḥbl*). (Ezek. 18:12)

And the good one and the repentant sinner are noteworthy that he does return it.

> He does return the debt with its pledge (*ḥablato ḥob yašib*). (Ezek. 18:7)
>
> The sinner returns the pledge (*ḥabol yašib*). (Ezek. 33:15)

Evil creditors might even seize items when there was no debt due (*ḥinam*). This is the indictment that Eliphas hurls at Job.

> For you seized from your brother for nothing, stripping the clothes off the naked. (Job 22:6)

This is also the complaint of the worker in a letter that has survived from Meṣadhašaviahu from the seventh century BCE. In this letter the worker complains that his supervisor seized his cloak for nothing, that he was innocent (*nqyty*).[2]

A final note comes from the prophet Amos, who is very upset about the transfer of wealth from the poor to the rich during his time. To him, collecting a debt—even without interest or without a pledge—is improper. If the debtor does not have surpluses with which

[2] See the inscription "A Letter from the Time of Josiah," translated by W.F. Albright, in Pritchard 1969: 568–569.

to acquire silver to pay off the debt, Amos would have the creditor not collect (Amos 5:11).

3. *Sureties*

This institution is not mentioned in the laws, but can be inferred from Proverbs which advise people not to stand surety for a non-family member. The risks are so great that Proverbs advises people to run, not walk, and beg to get out of their guarantee.

> My son, if you have stood surety for your fellow, struck the palm for an outsider, you are snared by your own words, trapped by what you have said. Do this my son and save yourself, for you have fallen into your neighbor's power. Go grovel and importune your fellow—give your eyes to no sleep, your eyelid no rest. Save yourself like a gazelle from a hand, like a bird from the hand of a trapper. (Prov. 6:1–3)

> It goes ill for one who stands surety for an outsider; the one who hates "strikings" (of the palm) is secure. (Prov. 11:15)

> Someone without sense strikes the palm, stands surety before his fellow. (Prov. 17:18)

> Don't be one who "strikes the palm," who stands surety for debt; if you do not have (the wherewithal) to pay, he (the creditor) will take your bed from under you. (Prov. 22:26–27)

The narrative in Gen. 44 seems to refer to a similar institution, though not in a legal context. Judah has stood surety to his father that he would bring Benjamin home. He therefore offers to stay with Joseph so that Benjamin can go home. In this case Judah would not be a pledge or security—he is offering to be taken in slavery instead of Benjamin.

III. Results of Delinquency

The results of delinquency are easily inferred from the warnings and limitations. The property of the borrower could be seized, as could the property of anyone who stood surety for the debt.

> Take his garment, for he has stood surety for an outsider; on behalf of a foreign woman seize from him. (Prov. 27:13)

> Take his garment, for he has stood surety for an outsider; on behalf of foreigners seize from him. (Prov. 20:16)

> Don't be one who "strikes the palm," who stands surety for debt; if you do not have (the wherewithal) to pay, he (the creditor) will take your bed from under you. (Prov. 22:26–27)

A curse wishes this fate on enemies:

> Let the creditor seize everything he has,
> Let outsiders plunder all his wealth,
> Let no one show mercy to him,
> Let no one be gracious to his orphans. (Ps. 109:11–12)

Not only mobilia, but land could be forfeit. The prophets describe "latifundization" in which large estates were formed, almost certainly through foreclosure on debts or forcing distress sales to pay the debts. This process may have begun early, for Judg. 11:3 relates that Jephthah's army was composed of "empty ones," a term that probably means people emptied of their property, landless. The army of David in 1 Sam. 22:2 also contained "everyone who has a creditor," people who were avoiding paying their debts, people who probably had already lost their land and were now running for their lives.

Family members could also be seized as debt slaves:

> They grab the fatherless from the breast, seize the child of the poor. (Job 24:9)

> Who is my creditor to whom I have sold you? (Isa. 50:1)

Two narratives discuss this situation. In 2 Kgs. 4: 1–7, an old miracle story about Elisha, the prophet, Elisha encounters a desperate woman who has nothing left, who "cries out" that "the creditor is coming to take my two children as slaves." Elisha cannot stop the pauperization of the peasantry and the resultant debt slavery; the best he can do is miraculously increase the woman's small stock of oil so that she can sell it and pay off her creditors (*mikri . . . wešalmi ʾet nišyek*(*i*)). Neh. 5:1–5, from much later, demonstrates how serious matters could become, for the people cry out to their brother Jews that matters have become dire. Some have eaten up their produce; some have set their fields and houses as security in order to eat in the famine; some have borrowed money for their fields. As a result, "We now take control ("conquer") over our sons and daughters to be slaves, and some of us have already had our daughters captured; we have no power and our fields and vineyards belong to others."

The end of the road is sale of self into debt slavery. The Hebrew Slave portions of the laws might refer to distrained or delivered children, but another of the Elisha stories, 2 Kgs. 6:1–7 may reflect how men might become slaves themselves. In this story, the disciples were cutting timber, and an iron axe head fell into the water. The disciples were distraught because it was a borrowed axe, so Elisha miraculously made the axe float so that it could be retrieved. The implication is that the disciple would have been in serious trouble if he could not return a borrowed item, most probably becoming a slave.

IV. Remediation

Both the above narratives involve formal complaints, *ṣeʿaqah*, and both are followed by action for remediation. "Outcry", *ṣeʿaqah*, is a formal demand for such action, and Exod. 22:25 warns that a person whose garment you do not lend back will cry out to God to remedy the situation, or at least to avenge the outcryer. A similar warning is given in Deut. 15:9 for the person who refuses to lend money near the sabbatical year.

There were two forms of remediation: individual and collective.

1. *Individual redemption of land* (*geʾulah*)

Geʾulah is the right to buy back land when the original seller sells it. The advantage of the sale is that it keeps land in the family, but the law might not have required the redeemer to return the land to the original seller. The original sale of land may have been a disguised distraint, disguised because distrained land is returnable when debt is paid, but sold land would be considered alienated for good. But even in sale, there is a right of redemption in which both the seller and his kin could buy back land. We can assume that they would be allowed to buy it back at the amount for which it was sold, because the right of redemption would be meaningless if buyers had to pay full value to buy back land which had been sold in distress, possibly sold for less than its worth.

The narrative evidence for this practice is in Jer. 32:6–15, in which Jeremiah's cousin asked him to buy land "for you have the redemption right to buy" or "for you have the right of inheritance and redemption, buy it for yourself." Jeremiah bought it for seven shekels.

We do not know if this was the correct price or a bargain distress sale.

More narrative evidence comes from Ruth 4. Boaz made an agreement with Ruth to be the redeemer and to marry her. Naomi is selling Elimelech's land, which she still held the right to sell even though Elimelech had both abandoned it and died, along with his sons. Boaz publicly informed the next of kin that he could buy the land. There would, however, be a child through Ruth who would ultimately inherit it. The kinsman opted out, and Boaz took over. In this case the advantage to Naomi was that she could maintain a connection with both the land and with Ruth despite the sale. Otherwise, as far as land is concerned, Naomi would receive the same no matter who was the redeemer.

2. *Individual redemption of persons*

Individual redemption is described in Leviticus 25:

> If a resident alien has prospered, and your kin in trouble comes into his control . . . he shall have the right of redemption even after he has given himself over. One of his kinsmen shall redeem him, or his uncle or his uncle's son or anyone of his family who is of his own flesh shall redeem him, or, if he prospers, he may redeem himself. (Lev. 25:17)

In this case, he reckons the amount of labor he has performed and pays back the amount left until his purchase price is paid up.

Such redemption is not mentioned if a person becomes the slave of Israel, because of the automatic release prescribed for Hebrew slaves in the seventh year in Exod. 22:21–27, Deut. 15:12–18. The laws call for individual release seven years after enslavement.

3. *Collective redemption of debts*

The seventh year was also to be the occasion for the remission of debts. From Deuteronomy, it seems that the remission was supposed to work by the calender and collectively, rather than individually from the time the debt was incurred.

> Take care that . . . you shouldn't say "the seventh year, the Shemittah year is coming" and look evilly upon your poverty-stricken brother

> and not give him. He will call upon God and it will be your sin. (Deut. 15:9)

Narrative evidence for this comes from Neh. 10:32, after the restoration from Babylon. The people made a formal agreement to follow certain teachings: no intermarriage, no buying on Sabbath, and no collecting any debt in the seventh year. Since the first two provisions were subjects of considerable discussion in Israel, it would seem that this provision might also be new. Deuteronomy shows that it was not new to Nehemiah's time, but in Nehemiah, perhaps it was given a more regularized legal status by formal agreement.

4. *Dror: Mass Remission of Debts and Release of Slaves*

This institution, well known in Mesopotamia, was also known in Israel. Two stories relate its occurrence. In Jer. 34:13–16, King Zedekiah made a pact with the people to release their Hebrew slaves.[3] Jeremiah reports that this was in accord with the rule of the seventh year that had been promulgated after the redemption from Egypt, but was not followed. Even in this instance, the people released their slaves, but then promptly re-enslaved them.

The second story is from the time of the Restoration in Neh. 5:6–13. Nehemiah relates the outcry of the people who had fallen into debt and whose daughters were already debt-slaves. Nehemiah censured the creditors: the people had bought back Jews from the slavery among the nations, and now they were enslaving them themselves. Nehemiah demanded that they give them back their fields and abandon the claims that they were pressing for silver, grain and wine. The creditors swore an oath to return everything and not demand anything, and did so.

5. *Jubilee: Regularized Dror*

Lev. 25:8–12 proclaims a *dror* at a regular, fixed interval, every 50 years. This idea had a long history in post-Biblical Israel, but it is

[3] See Sarna 1973: 143–147; Kaufman 1984: 277–86.

not known whether it was every put into practical effect, either before or after the Babylonian Exile.[4]

V. Conclusion

The Biblical system of secured poverty loans, debt slavery and debt remission, redemption, release and Jubilee all reveal a legal system devising means to cope with one of the harsh realities of the socio-economic system of the ancient world. As sons divided their father's patrimony after his death, the plot of each farmer became smaller with each generation. Eventually these plots of land were economically marginal, and minimally valid. In a bad harvest year, with too little rainfall or devastation by crop pests, the owners of marginal plots could begin to go under. They would borrow money to last until harvest and would then find the repayment of the loan too burdensome to bear. They would pawn various articles and send their children to work as debt slaves, but even this would not be enough, for many would keep sinking lower, would incur even more debt, and would lose their land to their creditors or to those who could buy it with money gained from commercial ventures. The impoverished peasants could then become slaves as the wealthier owners gained more land and greater riches. Left to its own devices, the agricultural "market" would create a great gap between the landowners and the poor, and the poor would become increasingly destitute. Biblical law respects private property, and lets this process continue to a high degree, intervening to regulate matters only when the poor are at the very edge of total deprivation, arranging that they can at least keep their garment at night. The law also takes account of the inexorability of the economic process by leveling the playing field by remitting debts in the seventh year and releasing slaves after their seventh year. Debt easement, general release and Jubilee further set the economic clock to zero by returning all land to its original owners in addition to freeing the slaves and canceling debts. It is in this context of the increasing impoverishment of the poor and the widening gap between poor and rich that secured loans are mentioned. By minimizing the risk of losing money lent

[4] See Weinfeld 1982: 491–519; *id.*, 1990: 38–62; Westbrook 1991: 36–57; Amit 1992: 47–59.

to another, the law allows people who are marginally better off than their neighbors to help them with minimal fear that default of the loan will topple them from their slightly higher rung on the economic ladder. The encouragement to lend money was a short term relief for the needy, but it did not provide a long lasting solution and may ultimately have exacerbated the poor man's predicament. Moreover, lending back a garment to a poor man is a long way from true social justice. These two failings of Israel's system of poverty loans and their securing are what so upset the prophet Amos.

Bibliography

Albright, W. 1969. A Letter from the Time of Josiah. In *Ancient Near Eastern Texts Relating to the Old Testament*, ed. J. Pritchard. 3rd ed., pp. 568–569. Princeton: Princeton University Press.

Amit, Y. 1992. The Jubilee Law—An Attempt at Instituting Social Justice. In *Justice and Righteousness: Biblical Themes and their Influence*, ed. H.G. Reventlow and Y. Hoffman. Pp. 47–59. JSOT Supplement Series 137. Sheffield: JSOT Press.

Gamoran, H. 1982. Biblical Law against Loans on Interest. *JNES* 30: 127–134.

Gordon, B. 1982. Lending at interest: Some Jewish Greek and Christian Approaches, 800 BC–AD 100. *History of Political Economy* 14: 406–426.

Kaufman, S. 1984. A Reconstruction of the Social Welfare System of Ancient Israel. In *In the Shelter of Elyon*, ed. G. Ahlström. Pp. 277–86. Sheffield: Sheffield Academic Press.

Neufeld, E. 1955. The Prohibitions against Loans at Interest In Ancient Hebrew Law. *Hebrew Union College Annual* 26: 355–412.

Rasor, P. 1993–94. Biblical Roots of Modern Consumer Credit Law. *Journal of Law and Religion* 10: 157–192.

Sarna, N. 1973. Zedekiah's Emancipation of Slaves and the Sabbatical Year. In *Orient and Occident*, ed. H. Hoffner. Pp. 143–147. AOAT 22. Kevelaer: Butzon & Bercker.

Seeligmann, I.L. 1978. Lending, Pledge and interest in Biblical Law and Biblical Thought. In *Studies in Bible and the Ancient Near East presented to Samuel E. Loewenstamm on his Seventieth Birthday*, eds. Y. Avishur and J. Blau. Pp. 183–205 (Hebrew) and 209–210 (English abstract). Jerusalem: E. Rubenstein.

Weinfeld, M. 1982. "Justice and Righteousness" in Ancient Israel against the background of social reforms in the Ancient Near East. In *Mesopotamien und seine Nachbarn: Politische und Kulturelle Wechselbeziehungen im Alten Vorderasien vom 4. bis 1. Jahrtausend v. Chr.*, vol. 2, eds. H. Nissen and J. Renger. (RAI 25). Pp. 491–519. Berlin: Dietrich Reimer.

——. 1990. Sabbatical Year and Jubilee in the Pentateuchal Laws and their ancient Near Eastern Background. In *The Law in the Bible and its Environment*, ed. T. Veijola. Pp. 38–62. Goettingen: Vandenhoeck and Ruprecht.

Westbrook, R. 1991. *Property and the Family in Biblical Law*. JSOT Supplement Series 113.

THE NEO-ASSYRIAN PERIOD

Karen Radner – Ludwig-Maximilian University of Munich

I. Prolegomena

In the neo-Assyrian period, tablets of the so-called contract type[1] are used to record obligations between two parties. The formulation of these texts is abstract; a certain sum, not a concrete object, is described as owned by the creditor (*ša* PN) and held by the debtor (*ina pān* PN).[2] The origin of the obligation is of no importance and hence rarely ever mentioned. Possible reasons for the existence of the obligation are actual loans of money, grain or animals, debts of all kind including fines, overdue taxes and temple offerings as well as contracts to supply work, to deliver or to manufacture goods. In the following, I will employ the term "obligation document" (Germ. *Obligationsurkunde*) to denote these texts; the term "loan document" (Germ. *Darlehensurkunde*) is consciously avoided.

Although the origin of the obligation is usually not mentioned explicitly, it can be inferred from the context in certain cases. Postgate has suggested that the presence of the enigmatic clause *ina pūḫi našû*, literally "to take as a replacement" and attested both in neo-Assyrian and Middle Assyrian obligation documents,[3] indicates that the obligation arose from a true loan.[4] However, final proof of this attractive and, at least to the present writer, plausible theory has yet to be established.

[1] Postgate 1976: 32. Texts of the contract type are either written on a horizontal tablet enclosed in a sealed envelope or, more rarely and mostly in the case of debts of grain, on a sealed triangular lump of clay formed around a knotted string. All texts have to be sealed by the debtor. On the format see Postgate 1976: 4, Postgate 1997: 160f., 167, Radner 1995: 68–70 and Radner 1997a: 25–32.

[2] On the formulation see Postgate 1976: 35 and Postgate 1997: 168.

[3] See Postgate 1988: 130 for the Middle Assyrian evidence.

[4] Postgate 1976: 37; compare Ponchia 1990: 57 with n. 62 and also Kwasman 1986: 210. The latter sees "an opposition between the *ina pūḫi* procedure and a regular system of controlled distribution of rations," basing his conclusions on the evidence of the letter ABL 871 = SAA 1 105.

Note that there is evidence that the clause could be omitted: While it is featured in the envelope or inner tablet of two texts it is missing in the matching parts of the document.[5] This seems to indicate that the *ina pūḫi našû* clause was not considered to be an indispensable part of the operative section of a document. Therefore, documents without this clause may also represent true loans, if we accept Postgate's theory, making it virtually impossible to separate the loans from all other obligations.

II. Prior Arrangement

In the neo-Assyrian period, debts were a matter that did not concern individuals, but households.[6] When a man incurred debts he could pledge or even sell his wife, his children and his slaves into debt slavery. On the other hand, the head of a household was responsible for debts incurred by members of his household.

The death of a debtor was of little consequence to his creditors as his heir was responsible for settling the debts. As his universal successor, the heir took over the deceased's rights and obligations as a whole. This is made clear in a Kalḫu adoption document which specifies the adoptee's status as the principal heir should there ever be additional sons: "He will enjoy his inheritance share with them [i.e. his hypothetical brothers]; he will go to (perform) the *ilku* duty with them; he will settle his [i.e. the father's] debts and he will claim

---

[5] (a) ND 3444 (dated to the post-canonical eponymy of Zababa-erība; unpublished, cf. Wiseman 1953: 143; thanks to Dr. C.B.F. Walker I was able to see this and other texts from Kalḫu which are currently kept in the British Museum in 1995): The inner tablet of ND 3444 reads: ^{1} 6 gín kù.babbar ^{2} *ša* ^{PNd}utu-man-pap ^{3} *ina* igi ^{PN}*ur-di* ^{4} *ina* 4-*tú-šú* gal-*bi* (date and six witnesses), whereas the envelope reads: ^{1} [na$_{4}$.kišib ^{PN}*ur*]-*di* ^{2} ⌈du⌉[mu ^{PN}*lu-šá-ki*]*n* ^{3} 6 [gín kù.babbar] ^{4} [*š*]*a* ^{PNd}utu-man-pap ^{5} [*ina*] igi ^{PN}*ur-di* ^{6} [*ina*] *pu-u-ḫi i-ti-ši* ^{7} *a-na* 4-*tú-šú* gal-*bi*. (b) ADD 3 (last edition: SAA 6 263) and ADD 26 (last edition: SAA 6 262): ADD 26 is a later copy of the now lost envelope of ADD 3, s. Radner 1997a: 43. The inner tablet, ADD 3, reads: ^{1} 1 ma.na kù.babbar *ina ša* uru.*gar-ga-*[*mis*] ^{2} *ša* ^{PN}sanga-^{d}15 ^{3} *ina* igi ^{PN}*a-du-na-iz* ^{4} *ina pu-u-ḫi i-ti-ši* ^{5} *a-na* 4-*ut-ti-šú i*-gal-*bi* (date and three witnesses), whereas the copy of the envelope reads: ^{1} na$_{4}$.kišib ^{PN}*a-du-na-i-zi* ^{2} 1 ma.na kù.babbar *ina ša* uru.*gar-ga-mis* ^{3} *ša* ^{PN}sanga-^{d}15 ^{4} *ina* igi ^{PN}*a-du-na-iz* lú*.*šá-mut-qi-ti-šú* ^{5} *a-na* 4-*ut-ti-šú i*-gal-*bi* (date and six witnesses).

[6] See VAT 5605 = VAS 1 97 = Jas 1996: no. 20 = Radner 1997b: 125ff., a judicial document regarding a lawsuit of Ilu-lē''i against Urdu-Nanaia "concerning the debts of his household" (*ina* ugu *ḫi-bi-il-tú šá* é).

payment for the debts due to him [i.e. his father]."[7] In a similar vein, the postscript of a document concerning the division of the paternal inheritance between the two sons of Šumma-Aššūr states: "They will settle the debts of the household of the father jointly."[8] Where a debtor left no (or no grown-up) sons, his wife was liable to pay back his debts.[9]

In order to secure a debt two means were at the disposal of the creditor: suretyship and pledge.[10] Both are well attested. Suretyship is documented in 67 cases known to me and pledge is attested in 89 cases. In three cases, a debt was secured by both methods.[11]

The sum for which the creditor demanded security varied considerably. In the case of silver debts secured by a surety, the smallest attested amount is four shekels of silver,[12] the highest is 1200 shekels of silver.[13] Clearly, it was not the size of the debt but the reliability of the debtor that determined whether security was deemed necessary.

1. *Suretyship*[14]

As in the Old Assyrian period, the neo-Assyrian term for surety is *bēl qātāte* (en šu.2.meš). Note that the complete form of the clause, PN *bēl qātāte ša* [sum owed], relates the surety to the debt, not the

---

[7] ND 5480 (unpublished; see the quotes in Postgate 1982: 307).

[8] VAT 20350 = Fales and Jakob-Rost 1991: no. 28 l. h. e. 1f.: *ḫa-bu-li ša* é ad *qa-ni* [2] *a-ḫi-ši* sum-*nu*.

[9] See Radner 1997a: 162 and note especially the evidence on badly abused widows in the letter VAT 9326 = KAV 197: 25–37 from Assur, see Postgate 1974a: 363–367 and Fales 1997: 39f. Note the four marriage documents which explicitly protect the wife from the consequences of her husband's business dealings (see n. 65) and compare the marriage document ADD 307 = Kwasman 1988: no. 214: [r. 12] pab 3 lú.*ur-ki-ú*.meš [13] *ša* mí ta igi *sa-ar-te* šu.2-*ṣib-ti ḫa-bul-li* [14] *šá kar-me-u-ni šu-ú* lú.*ur-ki-ú* "Altogether three 'back-ups' for the woman against fraud, theft and debt. He who is present will be the 'back-up'."

[10] Radner 1997a: 357–390 for a detailed discussion.

[11] From Assur: VAT 20341 = Fales and Jakob-Rost 1991: no. 31: the debt is 23 homers of barley; SÉ 104 = Jursa and Radner 1995/96: 93f.: the debt is 27 homers of barley. From Kalhu: ND 2078: the debt is 30 shekels of silver (unpublished; cf. Parker 1954: 33 and Radner 1997a: 359 and 379).

[12] ND 2089 (unpublished; cf. Parker 1954: 35).

[13] ADD 5 = SAA 6 26.

[14] See Radner 1997a: 357–367 for a discussion of suretyship in the neo-Assyrian period.

debtor.[15] Mention of the surety does not have a specific location in the obligation document; it is usually featured after the operative section before the date and the witness list, but sometimes also in the witness list or at the very end of the text. Sureties are not only attested in obligation documents, but occasionally also in judicial documents and in sale documents. The latter attestation proves that although the sale documents are phrased as if the transaction were always a cash sale, delivery and payment could be separated in time.[16]

Usually, a single surety was agreed on, but up to three men[17] are attested in this function. In the case of obligations with several debtors, suretyship was quite common and usually one of the debtors acted as surety for the others.[18] In this context it may be necessary to stress that joint debtors could pay back their shares individually.[19]

If the debtor were unable to pay the debt at maturity the surety was to satisfy the claims of the creditor in his stead. To signify that the surety assumes responsibility, the phrase *qātāte ša* [debtor] *issu qātāte* [creditor] *maḫāṣu*, lit., "to strike the hands of the debtor out of the hands of the creditor," is used.[20]

A judicial document from Assur demonstrates that the surety had the right of regress and could demand reimbursement from the debtor after paying off the creditor.[21] Nevertheless, acting as somebody's

[15] See Radner 1997a: 361 and already Ungnad in Friedrich, Meyer, Ungnad and Weidner 1940: 54 and Jakobson 1974: 52.

[16] Radner 1997a: 361.

[17] VAT 8643 and VAT 20782; ADD 1165 = Kwasman 1988: no. 231.

[18] For attestations see the table in Radner 1997a: 359f. and 361 with n. 1977.

[19] Such a case is attested with ADD 134 = SAA 6 70, dated to 29–vi–686, and ADD 135 = SAA 6 72, dated to vii–685. The first text documents that Nabû-nūru-nammir, Lā-tubāšanni-ilu and Sabutānu owe barley to Baḫiānu; the second text is a receipt stating that Sabutānu and Lā-tubāšanni-ilu have paid back their debts whereas Nabû-nūru-nammir has not yet paid: [1] 1 anše [PN]*ṣa-bu-ta-a-nu* [2] 1: [PN]*la-tu-ba-šá-a-ni*-ding[ir] [3] pab 2 : še.pad.meš [4] *a-na* [PN]*ba-ḫi-a-ni* [5] *ú-sa-li-mu* [r. 1] [PNd]pa-zálag-*nam-mir* [2] *la ú-šal-lim* "One homer: Sabutānu, one homer: Lā-tubāšanni-ilu; altogether two homers of barley they have paid back to Baḫiānu. Nabû-nūru-nammir has not (yet) paid." Compare also VAT 9323 = KAV 45 = Fales and Jakob-Rost 1991: no. 4: [1] ⌈ta*⌉ šà še.in.nu [2] *ša* [PN]*pa-qa-a-na-aš-šur* [3] [PN]*da-da-ḫi ḫab-ba-lu-ni* [4] [PN]*da-da-ḫi* ḫa.la-⌈*šú*⌉ [5] *ú-sa-lim* "Dāda-aḫḫē paid back his share of the straw which Paqa-ana-Aššūr (and) Dāda-aḫḫē owed."

[20] See Radner 1997a: 362–367 for a discussion of the seven attestations; for the Aramaic equivalent of the phrase, see most recently Lipinski 1998: 39–44.

[21] VAT 5606 = VAS 1 96 = Jas 1996: no. 28 = Radner 1997b: 129ff.: [1] *de-e-nu ša* [PNd]utu-pap [2] ta* [mí]uru.4*-dingir-*ḫa-mat* mí-*šú* [3] *ša* [PN]*sa-na-a-nu* ta* [PNd]pa-su dumu-*šá* [4] pap 2 ta* šà uru *ša* dumu.mí man [5] *ina* ugu *ḫi-bil-te-šú ina* ugu

surety meant taking a considerable risk. Therefore only a person closely related to the debtor would be willing to take on this responsibility. In one case, VAT 20396, the motive of the surety is obvious: it is the son who stands surety for his father.[22] However, due to the conciseness of the documents we are usually at a loss as to the exact relations between debtor and surety.

2. *Pledge*[23]

As in Old and Middle Assyrian periods, the neo-Assyrian term for pledge is *šapartu*.[24] This nominal form is based on *šapāru* "to send," making it likely that the term was originally coined for the possessory pledge of movable objects.[25] *šapartu* is usually used in the phrase [object] *ana šaparti šakin* "[object] is placed as a pledge" or, in the case of people, alternatively [person] *ana šaparti kammus* "[person] dwells as a pledge (in the creditor's house)"; more rarely, the phrase [object] *šapartu* "[object] is the pledge" is attested.[26] Note that the

níg.ka$_9$.meš-*šú* ^{6} *ig-ru-u-ni ma-a* 1 ma.na kù.babbar ^{7} [*ina*] ugu-*ḫi-ki aḫ-te-bil* $^{l.e.\ 8}$ *ma-a* ta* é lú.sag *ša* man ^{9} *ú-se-ṣa-ku-nu ma-a* šu.2.meš-*ku-nu* $^{r.\ 10}$ *ša* 50 anše še.bar *ša* giš.apin *ša* gu$_4$ ^{11} 12 1/2 ma.na kù.babbar *a-taḫ-ṣa* ^{12} ^{mí}4*-dingir-*ḫa-mat* ^{PNd}pa-su *iq-ṭí-bi-u* ^{13} *ma-a ina ku-um* níg.ka$_9$.meš *an-nu-te* ^{14} *ni-pa-laḫ-ka* ^{mí}4*-dingir-*ḫa-mat* ^{15} ^{PNd}pa-su ^{mí}en-zu ^{mí}nin-*la-mur* ^{16} ^{mí}di^{-mu}-*i-tú* pap 5 zi.meš *a-na* ^{PNd}utu-pap ^{17} *i-pal-lu-ḫu man-nu ša ina še-er-te* ^{18} *ina li-di-iš lu* šeš-*šá lu* lú*.gar-*nu-šá* ^{19} *de-e-nu* dug$_4$.dug$_4$-*u-ni* níg.ka$_9$.meš *an-nu-te* $^{u.e.\ 20}$ ⌈*a-na*⌉ ^{PNd}utu-pap ⌈sum⌉-*an* un.meš *ú-še-ṣa* ^{21} záḫ *ina* ugu *ra-me-ni-šú-nu* "Lawsuit which Šamaš-nāṣir brought against Arbail-ḫammat, the wife of Sanānu, (and) against Nabû-erība, her son, altogether two (persons) from the town of the king's daughter, concerning his debt (and) his property. (Šamaš-nāṣir spoke) as follows: "I owed one mina of silver because of you. I let you (2pl) leave the house of the king's eunuch. I stood surety for you (2pl) with fifty homers of barley, a plough (and) an ox (worth) 12 1/2 minas of silver." Arbail-ḫammat (and) Nabû-erība said as follows: "We will serve you instead of this property." Arbail-ḫammat, Nabû-erība, Bēl-lē'i, Bēssī-lāmur, Šulmītu, altogether five persons will serve Šamaš-nāṣir. Whoever it is who will bring a lawsuit, tomorrow (or) the day after tomorrow, either her brother or her prefect, shall give this property to Šamaš-nāṣir (and) shall let the people leave. They are liable for (their) flight."

[22] VAT 20398 = Fales and Jakob-Rost 1991: no. 46.

[23] For a discussion of pledge in the Neo-Assyrian period see Koschaker 1928: 96–116, Postgate 1976: 47–54 and Radner 1997a: 368–390.

[24] AHw 1170, CAD Š/I 428–430, Koschaker 1928: 96–116 and Eichler 1973: 88–95.

[25] Koschaker 1928: 96. Occasionally, variants of *šapartu* are attested: *šapattu* in VAT 9695, *šipartu* in ADD 64' *šipirtu* in A 1055+1070 and *šapru* in ADD 72.

[26] Radner 1997a: 371f.

Babylonian term *maškanūtu*[27] is attested once in a judicial document from Assur in the phrase *ana maškanūti šakānu* "to place as a pledge."[28]

Persons and real estate were most commonly used as pledges, but also a donkey and a piece of furniture[29] are attested in this function. Obligations could be pledged in the form of legal documents. In one case the pledging of the entire property of the debtor is attested.[30]

In order to pledge an object it was necessary that the debtor hold the possessory title to the object, that the debtor and the creditor come to terms about the nature of the pledge and that an obligation existed which was to be secured by the pledge. With the fulfilment of the obligation the pledge had to be restored to the debtor.

The creditor benefited in two ways from a pledge. Prior to the maturity of the obligation the pledge served as security for the debt. The pledge was potentially an actual substitute for the debt as the creditor had a right to satisfy his claims from it at maturity. Upon creation the pledge could either be handed over to the creditor (possessory pledge) or remain in the possession of the debtor (hypothecary pledge). The hypothecary pledge could be claimed at the maturity of the obligation in order to satisfy the creditor's claims.

The more common type was the possessory pledge. This is clear whenever the verb *kammusu* "to dwell" is used in the pledge clause in the case of the pledging of a person. In one case the text even explicitly states that the pledged person will live in the house of the creditor.[31] Note that it was the debtor who bore responsibility if the pledged person died or fled.[32] The possessory nature of the pledge

---

[27] A nominal form based on *šakānu* "to place," see AHw 627 *sub maškanūtu* 1., CAD M/I 374 *sub maškanūtu* and CAD Š/II 127 *sub šakānu* 1. o.

[28] VAT 19500, see Radner 1997a: 369 for an edition.

[29] Radner 1997a: 390.

[30] ADD 66 = SAA 6 97, cf. Postgate 1976: 53.

[31] ADD 71 = SAA 6 295: 3 mu.an.na.meš [*ina* é] *ú-šab* "He will live [in the house] for three years"; compare also the case in VAT 19500 [see n. 28]: ^{1} *de-e-nu ša* ^{PNd}pa-nun-dingir.meš ^{2} ta* ^{PNd}pa-numun-aš ^{3} dug$_4$.dug$_4$-*u-ni ma-a* ⸢*a-na*⸣ *ma-aš-ka-nu-tú* ^{4} 1 mí dumu.mí-*šá ina* é-*ka ta-sa-kan*. "Lawsuit which Nabû-etel-ilāni brought against Nabû-zēru-iddina. He stated: 'A woman and her daughter you placed as a pledge in your house'."

[32] Radner 1997a: 373–375 on the risk clause *šumma mētu šumma ḫalqu ina mê ina šamni ina ṣēri ina zuqāqīpi ina muḫḫi bēlišu* Creditor *ṣarpušu idaggal*: "If he (i.e. the pledged person) dies (or) flees (according to the sworn testimony of the creditor) by means of water, oil, snake (or) scorpion, his master is liable. The creditor will see his silver." For this provision compare the use of *dagālum* in Old Assyrian in the same context, see K. Veenhof's contribution in this volume.

is also evident whenever the debtor's right to "bring out" (*uṣû* Š) the pledged object is stated in the redemption clause.[33]

The creditor had the right to use the pledge and take its fruits, such as crops in the case of the pledge of a field.[34] In exchange for the right to use the pledge the creditor could waive interest on the debt: in eleven documents the pledge is explicitly stated to be antichretic in nature (*kūm rubbê* "instead of interest").[35] An explicit case of right to use is attested with the pledging of a house; it is stated in the document that the creditor will live in the pledged house for five years.[36] Pledge of land is closely connected with lease.[37] In the latter case, the land served as an antichretic pledge, the "rent" received by the owner in reality being the sum lent by the lessee.[38]

The debtor could redeem the pledge upon payment of the debt. However, if the debtor failed to satisfy the creditor, the latter kept the pledge in his possession. Four or possibly five documents show[39] that the pledge was forfeited; these texts contain clauses which explicitly declare the pledge to be the property of the creditor in the case of default. In some texts the pledge is said to be given instead of (*kūm*) the debt.[40] This makes it clear that the pledge was considered a substitute for the obligation and that the creditor could not demand further compensation from the debtor.[41] If the debtor was to have the option to redeem a pledge once forfeited the right was accorded in a special clause, the redemption clause, in the document.[42]

---

[33] Radner 1997a: 375–377.

[34] Radner 1997a: 368f. for a detailed discussion.

[35] Radner 1997a: 370f.

[36] TIM 11 17: 5 mu.an.na.meš *ina* šà-*bi uš-šab*.

[37] Postgate 1976: 29–32 and Radner 1997a: 384–389.

[38] Radner 1997a: 385.

[39] ADD 67 = Kwasman 1988: no. 413, ADD 72 = SAA 6 272, ADD 79 = Kohler and Ungnad 1913: no. 130 and VAT 8893 = Deller, Fales and Jakob-Rost 1995: no. 121, probably A 2427 where where the clause is abbreviated: urudu.meš nu sum; see Radner 1997a: 377.

[40] ADD 58 = SAA 6 81, ADD 59 = SAA 6 91, ADD 60 = SAA 6 317, ADD 63 = Kwasman 1988: no. 18, ADD 64 = SAA 6 245, ADD 71 = SAA 6 295 (for a complete transliteration see Radner 1997a: 243 n. 1288), ADD 1154 = SAA 6 268 and A 1055 + 1070 (unpublished).

[41] Koschaker 1928: 112.

[42] Radner 1997a: 375–377.

III. Delinquency

"Slave, listen to me." "Here I am, sir, here I am."
"I am going to make loans as a creditor."
"So make loans, sir, [make loans.]
The man who makes loans as a creditor—his grain remains his grain, while his interest is enormous."
"No, slave, I will by no means make loans as a creditor."
"Do not make loans, sir, do not make loans.
Making loans is like loving [a woman;] getting them back is like having children.
They will eat your grain, curse [you] without ceasing,
And deprive you of the interest on your grain."

(Dialogue of Pessimism ll. 62–69)[43]

As stated in this popular text, obtaining repayment of a debt could be as hard as giving birth to a child. If a debtor claimed to be unable to pay back his debts, what measures were at the disposal of the creditor to compel payment?

The action taken depended very much on the relationship between debtor and creditor. If the debtor was of equal social status to the creditor or of even higher status, the creditor could face many more difficulties in asserting his right to receive his money back than if the debtor was of lower status.

1. *Persistency*

As the possibility that a debtor was not actually out of funds but just unwilling to pay was always to be reckoned with, the creditor might wish to make sure that there was in fact no money available. The simplest way to do so was of course just to ask, if necessary, again and again.

Persistency is probably the only method which Salmānu-[. . .], in all probability a merchant in the king's service (*tamkāru*), had at his disposal. He was in the rather delicate position of being a creditor of Sargon II. The king owed him the impressive sum of 570 minas of silver and when Salmānu-[. . .] had earlier used the opportunity

[43] Translation by Lambert 1960: 149. The passage survives in two neo-Assyrian copies of the text from Assur and in one copy from Ashurbanipal's library in Nineveh, cf. Lambert 1960: 143 (a, b, D).

of an audience with the king to ask for his money, Sargon had turned him down. Salmānu-[. . .] claimed that he needed the money himself in order to satisfy his own debtors; the king, however, who had used Salmānu-[. . .]'s money to finance the construction of his new residence city Dūr-Šarrukēn, was not inclined to repay his debts before the building work was completed. Salmānu-[. . .] was apparently not content with this information; after finding out that other merchants had already been paid back their debts, he wrote a letter[44] to the king urging him again to return his money to him.

> (4–r. 12) The king, my lord, told [me]: "Until the work at Dūr-Šarrukēn is completed nobody will pay back your debts (*ḫa-bul-li-k*[*a*])!" They have pa[id back] the credit (*nisḫu*) for (that part) of Dūr-Šarrukēn which has (already) been built to the (other) merchants, but nobody has [remembered] me! 570 minas of silver with [my seal] and due this year have not been repaid as yet. When the king, my lord, bestowed gold and pre[cious stones] onto me I told the king, my lord, that my father was much indebted to Ḫar[. . .], Ḫuziri and [. . .]. After my father('s death) I paid half of [his debts], but now their sons [are telling me]: "Pay us the debts that [your] father owes our fathers!" As soon as Dūr-Šarrukēn has been [completely] bu[ilt], the king, my lord, [will . . .] to the house [. . .] and pay back the debts to [. . .].

2. *Going to court*

If the creditor lost his patience with the debtor who would not pay he could go to court. Indeed, most legal texts from the Neo-Assyrian period documenting court proceedings[45] deal with lawsuits.[46] Usually, the parties and additional witnesses were asked to give statements, thus forming the basis for the judge's decision. A good example is a record of litigation from the goldsmiths' archive in Assur:[47]

> Lawsuit which Nabû-zēru-iddina brought against Zērūtî on account of the silver of the city of Laḫīru. They brought the lawsuit before the mayor Sîn-dūrī (who decided): If Iadi'-il comes (and) states: "Zērūtî will pay back the silver which they have fired"[48] (or) if Iadi'(-il) states:

[44] ABL 1442 = SAA 1 159; cf. also Deller 1987: 16ff.
[45] The hitherto published documents pertaining to lawsuits have been published in Jas 1996; more of these texts have been collected in Radner 1997/98: 379–387.
[46] Cf. also Otto 1998: 278f.
[47] VAT 8656 = Jas 1996: no. 19 = Radner 1999: no. 35.
[48] *ṣarāpu*, a method for refining silver.

> "Zērūtî has (already) paid back the silver," there will be judicial peace between them. Whoever contravenes, may Aššūr (and) Šamaš be his adversaries in court. (Date and four witnesses.)

Apparently, Zērūtî owed money to Nabû-zēru-iddina. The mayor who was serving as the judge decreed that the solution of the case depended on a future statement of Iadi'-il who was obviously not available at the time of the trial; however, two possible statements of his were anticipated, both of which would result in a resolution of the argument between Nabû-zēru-iddina and Zērūtî: Iadi'-il would either testify that Zērūtî had already paid back the debt or else that he intended to do so. Clearly, the debt was expected not to be settled in Assur, but somewhere else, in all likelihood in Laḫīru. As apparently neither the plaintiff nor the judge could easily check whether the debt had been paid or not, the word of Iadi'-il who seems to have been on the spot would have to be accepted. From another text from the same archive[49] we know more about the relationship between Nabû-zēru-iddina and Iadi'-il. The two men and a certain Zīzî had entered a business partnership on account of "3 1/2 minas of silver of the city of Lahīru." The receipt which is sealed by Iadi'-il certifies that Nabû-zēru-iddina paid his share to Iadi'-il in full. It is clear that Iadi'-il was a business partner of Nabû-zēru-iddina and that his statement therefore could be trusted.[50]

However, lawsuits concerning debts could also call for an oath to be taken or an ordeal to be performed.[51]

The goal of the court was always to find a compromise between the disputing parties. Thus the creditor would sometimes accept less than the original sum as the result of the ruling of the judge.[52]

[49] CT 33 17 = Postgate 1976: no. 40; see also Deller 1987: 20ff. Envelope: "Seal of Iadi'-il son of Halimusi. 3 1/2 minas of silver of the city of Laḫīru which Zīzî, Nabû-zēru-iddina (and) Iadi'-il have taken on credit. Nabû-zēru-iddina has completely paid back his share to Iadi'-il. If anybody should sue Nabû-zēru-iddina, Iadi'-il shall pay (the sum in question) tenfold. (Date and four witnesses.)" Inner tablet: "[3] 1/2 minas of silver of the city of Laḫīru which <Zīzî,> Nabû-zēru-iddina <(and) Iadi'-il> have taken on credit. Nabû-zēru-iddina has completely <paid back> his share to Iadi'-il. If anybody should reduce (the receipted sum) for Nabû-zēru-iddina, Iadi'-il shall pay (the sum in question) tenfold. (Date and two witnesses.)"

[50] For another case of witnesses' statements in court in a lawsuit regarding a debt see ADD 101 = Jas 1996: no. 53.

[51] See TH III 908e = Friedrich, Meyer, Ungnad and Weidner 1940: no. 106 = Jas 1996: no. 24, MAH 20613 = Scheil 1925: 147 = Postgate 1976: no. 48 = Jas 1996: no. 46 and VAT 5604 = VAS 1 101 = Jas 1996: no. 55 (see Radner 1997b: 134 for a new copy and 121ff. for an edition).

[52] See CTN 3 31 = Jas 1996: no. 9 and TH III 1160 = Friedrich, Meyer, Ungnad and Weidner 1940: no. 107 = Jas 1996: no. 10.

3. *Appeal to the king*

A creditor whose debtor would not pay his debts could appeal to the king,[53] just like everybody else who found himself wronged. As witnessed by a letter addressed to Sargon II, this method was used by an unidentified high official in a remote northern province, probably a governor. In his letter the author complains about one of his debtors who does not show the slightest intention to repay his debts, not even obeying the king's direct orders to do so.[54]

> (r. 1'–11') I [was informed] by my lord the king's court: "He [sha]ll pay your debts to you, as much as he ow[es to you]!" (But) he did not heed the king's word (*abat šarri*) and did [n]ot pay my debts to me. From the moment I appealed to the king, my lord, he has been killing and robbing my lord the king's subjects, wherever he sees them; he has been laying waste to the king's roads. I cannot leave my house; he is talking about killing me!

If the plaintiff's word is to be taken at its face value, not paying his debts is to be counted among his debtor's minor offences. The first appeal to the king clearly did not do the plaintiff any good as the debtor simply ignored the king's orders; worse still, he took vengeance upon his creditor for complaining to the king by starting to wreak destruction upon his province. Using all the methods also favoured by medieval robber-barons and modern-day terrorists, such as murder, robbery and ambushing, the debtor is clearly a man with considerable manpower at his disposal. Therefore, he must have either been a rival Assyrian official, possibly of a neighbouring province,[55] or a member of the local gentry. We do not know about the outcome of the dispute but clearly the Assyrian king could hardly tolerate open disregard of his orders. Therefore we can suppose that the king would have taken measures to guarantee that the delinquent acted according to the king's directions.

In spite of the limited success that appeal to the king had in the present matter, calling in the king would have ended a dispute concerning an unpaid debt quite effectively in most cases.

---

[53] For the institution of the appeal to the king see Postgate 1974b: 417–426; Postgate 1980: 180–182 and Garelli 1989: 45.

[54] ABL 463 = SAA 5 260.

[55] Problems between the officials of neighbouring provinces are attested, see, AO 4506 = TCL 9 68 = SAA 5 81, a letter by Aššūr-zēru-ibni to his colleague ("brother") Nergal-ēṭir concerning his quarrels with the governor of Ḫalziatbar.

IV. Insolvency

If a debtor was unable to repay, the problem could be resolved in two very different ways. Either the debtor had to find alternative ways to satisfy the creditor, by asking another party for financial aid or by entering into debt slavery in the creditor's household, or the debt could be cancelled by external intervention. The king was in the position to declare all debts null and void by proclaiming a debt remission. However, the debtor could only hope for such a *deus ex machina* act as he had no means of knowing about such a decision beforehand.

1. *Measures to satisfy creditors*

If a debtor found himself unable to repay his debts he had to look for a way to solve the problem as quickly as possible. Interest rates ranged between 33 percent and 12.5 percent, with 25 percent being the standard rate, although no interest at all could be charged at times. However, when the debtor failed to pay back the debt within the agreed time a penalty interest rate which was much higher than the original became applicable. Quite frequently, double the original debt had to be paid. Therefore it was in the debtor's own interest to settle his debt as soon as possible.

Note that at least sometimes a debtor could pay back his debts in instalments.[56]

1.1. *Calling in debts*

Some texts document how debtors sell off their property or demand payment for obligations due to themselves in order to raise money to find a way out of an insolvency.

The author of a private letter found in Assur, Nabû-uballissu, who was then staying in Nineveh, asked Kallutu, his mother, and Qarruru, probably his brother, to tell a certain Kiṣir-Nabû to sell some don-

[56] VAT 9703 = Fales and Jakob-Rost 1991: no. 90. The debtor of a sum of eight shekels of silver is to pay four shekels in the month of Ulūlu, i.e. next month, and the other four shekels after the harvest, i.e. in two months' time (the document was written in the month of Ābu).

keys in order to raise money to pay back a debt incurred by Nabû-uballissu. The rest of the money was to be sent to him in Nineveh.[57]

A document from Dūr-Katlimmu[58] bears witness to another way to satisfy a creditor, by pressing one's debtors to meet their obligations in order to get enough money to pay off one's own debts. A certain Kēnî was required to deliver a certain slave woman to Nineveh. That woman was the property of Sukki-Issār who seems to have had acquired her earlier from Kēnî. If Kēnî failed to produce the woman in time he was to pay double the amount that Sukki-Issār owed Nabû-mār-šarri-uṣur (obviously to Sukki-Issār):

> Seal of Kēnî son of Tilakusu. Should Kēnî be not present in Nineveh on the 25th of Šabāṭu (xi.) together with Sukki-Issār son of Marduk-šimanni concerning Abī-dimrī, the slave woman of Kēnî, whom he (i.e. Sukki-Issār) gave to Kēnî for the tanned leather, should he not enter (Nineveh and) should he not bring the slave woman, Kēnî shall give double as much as Sukki-Issār owes to Nabû-mār-šarri-uṣur.

As we are lacking the context, we do not know how and if the dealings between Kēnî and Sukki-Issār and between Sukki-Issār and Nabû-mār-šarri-uṣur were connected beyond the involvement of Sukki-Issār. It seems likely, though, that Sukki-Issār was making Kēnî meet his claims in the first place in order to satisfy his own debtor Nabû-mār-šarri-uṣur.

1.2. *datio in solutum*

If a debtor had no ready cash available to cover his debts he could also try to satisfy his creditor's claims by offering him property as alternative payment.

Hence Dāda-aḫḫē son of Erība-Aššūr and his nephews Aḫu-tabši and Marduk-ēreš sons of Kaqqadānu handed over the house of

---

[57] BM 103390:21–24: ^{PN}*ki-ṣir-*^{d}pa anše.níta.meš ^{22} *ḫa-an-nu-ti lid-din* ^{23} kù.babbar *liš-ši-a* ^{24} *ḫa-bul-le-ia lu-šal-lim* "Kiṣir-Nabû shall sell these donkeys (and) take the silver; he shall pay back my debts"; copy: Fales 1983: 253 no. 13, edition: Deller 1986: 21–27 *and cf.* Neumann 1997: 281–293.

[58] DeZ 5662 = SH 86/8975 I 145: ^{1} na$_4$.kišib ^{PN}gin-*i* ^{2} *a* ^{PN}*ti-la-ku-su* ^{3} *šum-ma ina* u$_4$-25 *ša* itu.zíz ^{4} ^{PN}gin-*i la kar-me ina* ⸢nina⸣.ki (sealing) ^{5} ta ^{PN}*sùk-*^{d}15 dumu ^{PNd}šú-ḫal-*a-ni* ^{6} *ina* ugu mí.ad-*dim-ri* géme-*šú* $^{\text{l. e. 7}}$ *ša* ^{PN}gin-*i ša a-*⸢*na*⸣ ^{PN}⸢gin⸣-*i* ^{8} sum-*u-ni ina* ⸢duḫ.ši⸣ ^{9} *šum-ma la e-ru-{ub}* géme *la ú-ba-la* ^{10} *a-mar ša* ^{PN}*sùk-*^{d}15 $^{\text{r. 11}}$ *a-na* ^{PNd}pa-a-lugal-pap *iḫ-ḫa-bíl-u-ni* ^{12} ^{PN}gin-*i e-ṣip* sum-*an* (date [post-canonical eponymy of Dādî]; eight witnesses; Aramaic inscription).

Erība-Aššūr as payment for a debt of thirteen minas of silver according to a document from Assur.[59] Another text from Assur documents how Lišēru gave a house, his inheritance share, to Nabû-biqur to clear his debt.[60]

Another way of satisfying a creditor is the action the debtor Ubru-Aššūr took in order to cover his debt of thirty shekels of silver. He handed over his daughter Aḫāt-abiša to his creditor Zabdî "instead of his debt."[61]

An insolvent debtor could also hand over legal documents to his creditor in order to pay off a debt, as witnessed by a document from Ḫuzirīna.[62] A clause at the end of the document stipulates that even if the creditor receives a multiple of the original debt the debtor will have no claims.

> One mina four shekels of silver (and) fifty homers of barley, debt of Issār-emūqāia at the disposal of Šarru-lū-dāri son of Rēšū'a. Instead of the debt he (i.e. Šarru-lū-dāri) paid a document concerning fields, another concerning a house (and) two documents concerning silver to Issār-emūqāia. Judicial peace is between them. Whoever will break the

[59] VAT 14451 = Fales and Jakob-Rost 1991: no. 1: 6–10 (dated to 653 BCE): é ad-*šú-nu a-na gi-mir-te-šú* ^{7} *šá* ^{PN}su-*aš-šur* ad-*šú-nu* ^{8} *ku-um* 13 ma.na kù.babbar ^{9} *ḫa-bu-li šá* uru.šà.uru-*a-a* ^{10} *i-ta-nu e-gir-te ú-ta-ri-qu* "They gave the house of their father in its entirety, (the house) of Erība-Aššūr, their father, instead of 13 minas of silver, the debt of the men of Libbi-āli (i.e. Assur). They have crushed the debt document."

[60] VAT 9758 (dated to 648 BCE): na$_4$.kišib ^{PN}*l*[*i-še-ri* a NN] ^{2} é ḫa.la *šá* [^{PN}*li*]-⸢*še*⸣-[*ri a-na*] 3 ^{PNd}ag-*bi-qur ḫa-bu*-[*li-šu*] ^{4} *ú-šal-lim i*-[*ti*]-⸢*din*⸣ "Seal of L[išēru son of NN]. He paid his debt (with) a house, the inheritance share of Lišēru, to Nabû-biqur."

[61] ADD 86 = Kwasman 1988: no. 401 (dated 652 BCE): $^{1'}$ ⸢^{mí}nin⸣-ad-*šá* dumu.mí-*s*[*u*] $^{2'}$ ⸢*ša*⸣ ^{PN}suḫuš-*aš-šur* $^{3'}$ ⸢*ú*⸣-*piš-ma* ^{PN}*za-ab-di-i* $^{4'}$ ta igi ^{PN}suḫuš-*aš-šur* $^{5'}$ ⸢*ku-um*⸣ 30 gín.meš kù.babbar ⸢*il*⸣-*q*[*í*] $^{6'}$ ⸢*šá*⸣ ^{PN}*za-ab-di-i šá* AN [x x x] $^{7'}$ ⸢*ku-um*⸣ *ḫa-bul-le-e*-⸢*šú*⸣ $^{8'}$ dumu.mí-*su a-na* ^{PN}*zab-di*-⸢*i*⸣ $^{9'}$ ⸢*it*⸣-*ti-din* mí *šu-a-tú* $^{10'}$ ⸢*za*⸣-*ar-pat* [*la*]*q-qí-at*.

[62] S.U. 51/44 = Finkelstein 1957: 139 (copy), 141–143; cf. Deller 1965: 469. According to the copy and edition the text is not dated; however, as only the right edge of the tablet would be inscribed according to the copy, it is likely that the date is to be found at the left edge (which normally would be inscribed before the right edge was used). As the present whereabouts of the text are unknown (probably it is kept in Ankara) this theory cannot be checked against the original. ^{1} 1 ma.na 4 gín kù.babbar ^{2} 50 anše še.pad.meš ^{3} *ḫa-bul-lu*$_4$ *šá* ^{PN}15-á-*a-a* ^{4} *ina* igi ^{PN}man-*lu-dà-ri* a ^{PN}sag-*u-a* ^{5} *e-gér-tú šá* a.šà.meš ki.min *šá* é ^{6} 2 *e-gér*.meš *šá* kù.babbar ^{7} *ku-mu ḫa-bul-lu*$_4$ ^{8} *a-na* ^{PN}15-á-*a-a* ^{9} ⸢*ú*⸣-<*sa*>-*sal-lim* $^{l. e. 10}$ ⸢di⸣-*m*[*u ina ber-te*]-⸢*šu-nu*⸣ ^{11} *man-nu ša* ⸢*ina ur*⸣-*kiš* ^{12} *i-ba-la-kàt-u-ni* $^{r. 13}$ ⸢^{d}⸣30 ^{d}nin.<gal> ^{d}⸢im⸣ ^{14} *lu-u* en-*de-ni-šú* $^{15-21}$ seven witnesses; sealing $^{l. h. e.}$ sealing $^{r. h. e. 22}$ *šum*$_4$-*mu* ^{PN}15-á-*a-a* ^{23} 1* gú.un kù.babbar šàm$^{?}$ ^{24} [^{PN}man-*lu-d*]*à-ri la* ⸢dug$_4$$^{?}$⸣.

> contract in the future, may Sîn, Nikkal (and) Adad be his adversaries in court. (Even) if Issār-emūqāia (received) a talent of silver as price, Šarru-lū-dāri shall not sue.

1.3. *Third party aid*

If a debtor was unable to pay a debt he might appeal to a hitherto uninvolved party for financial aid. We may almost certainly suppose that a debtor unable to satisfy his creditor might try to take on a loan from another party. However, a person known to be in financial difficulties would have trouble finding someone to borrow money from. Relatives and personal friends were probably the first the debtor would turn to; also former benefactors might seem to offer promising possibilities to help out.

Thus, the exorcist Urdu-Gula wrote a long letter[63] to his former employer Ashurbanipal, whom he had known since the latter's childhood, in order to alert him of the dire situation he found himself in since falling out of the king's grace several years earlier. Being deeply worried about his professional situation and his lack of a son, the acute reason for writing the letter was clearly the desperate state of his finances. He could not afford to replace the two animals he had used for transportation since they had died two years earlier. The three homers of land he had inherited from his father offered insufficient means to sustain himself and his household consisting of his wife and ten or eleven slaves, most of them women. His report culminated in a dramatic oath:

> (r. 26–29) By Anu, Enlil and Ea who are firmly implanted in the head of the king, my lord, I cannot afford as much as a pair of sandals or the wages of a tailor, I do not have a change of clothes (and) I owe a capital sum only some shekels short of six minas of silver!

We do not know whether the king took pity on Urdu-Gula and helped him out or not. However, just as debtors often succeeded in finding someone to act as a surety on their behalf we can certainly assume that in many cases somebody could be found who would step in financially when a debtor found himself unable to pay his debts.

---

[63] ABL 1285 = SAA 10 294.

Hence, we know that Bēl-tarṣi-ilumma, governor of Kalhu, settled substantial debts incurred by three men.[64] Unfortunately, the relationship between the governor and Urdu-Issār, Samāku and Ḫanana is unknown to us. It would be interesting to know whether it was personal or strictly professional. The fact that the governor is mentioned with his full title would seem to indicate the latter.

1.4. *Debt slavery*

Free-born persons could become slaves as the result of an unpaid debt incurred by themselves or by a family member.[65]

Such a person could enter the creditor's household in order to serve him for the rest of the debt slave's life.[66] However, the option to redeem the debt slave was usually reserved to whoever paid off the debt on his behalf; in the legal documents this is reflected by clauses using the terms *uṣû* Š or *paṭāru*.[67] A good example is the case of Nargî, who owed barley and an ox to the crown prince on whose behalf his governor Bēl-dūri acted. Unable to hand over the barley

---

[64] CTN 2 91 (dated 797 BCE): [1] *ḫa-bùl-li ša* [PN]ìr-[d]innin [2] lú.uš.bar *bir-me ša* [PN]en-lal-dingir-*m*[*a*] [3] lú.gar.kur uru.*kal-ḫi ú-šal-li-mu-ni* (list of creditors) [13] pab 23 lú.meš-*e* [14] en [*ḫ*]*a-bu-ul-li ša ṣu-bar-šú-nu* [15] [*i*]*š-ka-nu-ni* (list of debts) [r. 12] pa[b] 53 1/2 ma.na ⌈ud⌉.ka.⌈bar⌉.m[eš] *ḫa-bùl-li* [13] [PN]en-lal-*ṣi*-dingir-*ma* lú*.gar.kur uru.*kal-ḫi* [14] *ú-šal-li-mu-*⌈*ni*⌉ (witnesses and date) "Debt of Urdu-Issār, weaver of multi-coloured garments, which Bēl-tarṣi-ilumma, governor of Kalḫu, paid back. (List of creditors), altogether 23 men, the creditors who impress their fingernails (as a sealing). (List of debts), altogether 53 1/2 minas of bronze, debt which Bēl-tarṣi-ilumma, governor of Kalḫu, paid back." Similar is the less well preserved CTN 2 90 (dated 803 BCE) regarding a debt of Samāku and of Ḫanana which Bēl-tarṣi-ilumma, governor of Kalḫu, paid back as well.

[65] Note the clauses in four marriage documents which explicitly protect the wife from the consequences of her husband's business dealings; see Radner 1997a: 158f on CTN 2 247 and ND 2316 from Kalḫu, TIM 11 14 from Nineveh and A 2527 from Assur, and 170f on ND 2316 from Kalḫu.

[66] ADD 76 = Kwasman 1988: no. 324 (dated to 654 BCE): [1] *ku-um* kù.babbar [2] [mí]gašan-ki-*ia* géme [3] *ša* mí. *šá-kín-te* [4] *a-na* [mí]*sin-qi*-15 [5] *a-di bal-laṭ-u-ni* [6] *ta-pal-làḫ-šu* "Instead of the silver Bēlet-issē'a, slave woman of the *šakintu*, will serve Sinqi-Issār as long as she lives."

[67] See also Postgate 1976: 28f on what he terms "restricted conveyances" of persons. In this context it should be noted that in a number of sale documents from Assur the possibility that the seller would try to release (*paṭāru*) the sold property by announcing his intention to do so is explicitly excluded. Attestations in published texts from Assur: Fales and Jakob-Rost 1991: no. 33 r. 3: *ma-a* é-ad-*ni ni-paṭ-ṭar*; Fales and Jakob-Rost 1991: no. 34:15f: *ma*-[*a* un.meš] [16] *a-paṭ-ṭar*; Fales and Jakob-Rost 1991: no. 53 r. 3f.: *ma-a* l[ú] [4] *a-paṭ-ṭar*; Fales and Jakob-Rost 1991: no. 61:17f.: *ma-a* ⌈géme⌉ [18] *a-paṭ-ṭar*; Deller, Fales and Jakob-Rost 1995: no. 76:20: *ma* lú *a-*⌈*pa*⌉-[*ṭar*]; Deller, Fales and Jakob-Rost 1995: no. 99:25: *ma-a* a.šà.g[a *a*]-*paṭ-*

and the ox, Nargî had to agree to serve (*palāḫu*)[68] Bēl-dūri. Upon settlement of the debt Nargî's debt-slavery in Bēl-dūri's household would end.[69]

> 32 homers five seah of barley (and) one draught-ox of the crown prince under the charge of Bēl-dūri, governor of the crown prince, at the disposal of Nargî of the town of Balāṭu. He will serve Bēl-dūri instead of the barley (and) the ox. Whenever somebody brings the barley and the ox (!) he will redeem the man.

Quite frequently the fine imposed on the convicted party in a trial could not be paid and instead the culprit entered into debt-slavery in the victim's household. Hence Aḫu-la-amašši, who had stolen an ox from the house of Nabû-šarru-uṣur and who was sentenced to replace that ox "was seized instead of his fine." On the day that he brought the ox, Aḫu-la-amašši would go free.[70] Similarly Nabû-tariṣ, slave of Ṣapānu, who had abducted four slaves of Šangû-Issār, was convicted to pay a fine of 210 minas of copper. Unable to produce the money he had to enter into debt-slavery—his master could free him by paying the money to Šangû-Issār.[71] The convicted Hānî "was taken together with his people and his land" as he could not raise

ṭar; Deller, Fales and Jakob-Rost 1995: no. 109:17: *ma-a* lú ⌈*a-paṭ*⌉-*ṭar*; Deller, Fales and Jakob-Rost 1995: no. 126 r. 1': [*ma-a* m]í [*a-p*]*aṭ-ṭar*; Deller, Fales and Jakob-Rost 1995: no. 132 r. 3: *ma-a* mí *a-*⌈*paṭ-ṭar*⌉; Ahmad 1996: no. 2:23: *ma-a* ìr *a-pá-ṭar*; Ahmad 1996: no. 3:16: *ma-a* ìr *a-pa-a-ṭár*; Ahmad 1996: no. 7:21: *ma-a* mí *a-paṭ-ṭar*; Ahmad 1996: no. 11:20: *ma-a* géme *a-paṭ-ṭar*. Attestations in unpublished texts from Assur kept in the Vorderasiatisches Museum, Berlin: VAT 8232 r. 2f.: [*ma-a* un.meš *šú-a-te*] ^{3} *a-pa-ṭar*; VAT 8270:17: *ma-a kaq-qí-ri a-pa-ṭar*; VAT 8274:16: *ma-a* šám *a-paṭ-ṭar*; VAT 8280:13: *ma-a* mí *a-pa-ṭar*; VAT 9137:12f.: *ma-a* mí ^{13} *a-pa-ṭar*; VAT 9778:12: *ma-a* mí ⌈*a*⌉-[*pa-ṭar*]; VAT 9838 r. 1': ⌈*ma-a*⌉ giš.s[ar *a-pa-ṭar*]; VAT 19495 r. 2f.: *ma-a* ⌈mí⌉ [*šú-a-tú*] ^{3} *a-paṭ-*⌈*ṭar*⌉; VAT 19511 r. 5: ⌈*ma-a*⌉ é *a-paṭ-ṭar*; VAT 20351:12: *ma-a* lú *a-pa-ṭar*; VAT 20688 r. 1: *ma-a* m[í *a-pa-ṭar*]; VAT 21000 r. 3: [*ma-a*] é *a-paṭ-ṭar*. No examples for this clause are known from other sites.

[68] On *palāḫu* see Radner 1997a: 199 with n. 1045.

[69] ADD 152 = Kwasman 1988: no. 73 (dated to 658 BCE): ^{1} 32 anše 5-bán še.pad.meš ^{2} 1 gu$_{4}$.níta *ša* giš.*ta-lak-te* ^{3} *ša* dumu man *ša* šu.2 ^{PN}en-bàd ^{4} lú*.en.nam *ša* dumu man ^{5} *ina* igi ^{PN}*nar-gi-i ša* uru.*ba*$^{!}$*-la*.meš ^{6} *ku-um* še.pad.meš *ku-um* gu$_{4}$.níta ^{7} *a-na* ^{PN}en-bàd *i-pa-làḫ-šú* ^{8} *ša-niš ša* še.pad gu$_{4}$.meš ^{9} *ú-še-rab-a-ni* ^{10} lú *ú-še-ṣa*.

[70] ADD 160 = Jas 1996: no. 14: 11–13 (dated to the post-canonical eponymy of Mušallim-Aššūr): *ku-um sa-ar-te-šú* ^{12} *ṣa-bit ina* u$_{4}$*-me ša* gu$_{4}$.níta *ú-še-rab-a-ni* ^{13} *ú-ṣa*.

[71] ADD 161 = Jas 1996: no. 44: 7–9 (dated to 679 BCE): *man-nu* 2-me 10 ma.na urudu.meš ^{8} *a-na* ^{PN}sanga-^{d}15 *id-dan-u-ni* ^{9} ìr-*šú ú-še-ṣa* "Whoever gives 210 minas of copper to Šangû-Issār will bring out his slave." Clearly, it is Nabû-tariṣ's master Sapānu who has the option to redeem his slave.

the fine of 300 sheep and the blood money, he was sentenced to pay for stealing sheep from the crown prince's flock and slaying his shepherds.[72] Upon payment of the fine and the blood money Hānî could be freed.[73] Note that nothing is said about whether his people and his land could be redeemed or not.

Being liberated from the creditor's household does not necessarily imply that the released person was his own master again. Quite the contrary, the released debtor had to serve his liberator until the latter's claims were satisfied. A good example is the case of Mannu-kī-Inurta from Nineveh.[74] Together with his wife and daughter, this heavily-indebted man was kept in debt-slavery by his creditor, an anonymous merchant. Ṣalmu-šarri-iqbi paid Mannu-kī-Inurta's debt to the merchant and thus freed the family. To cover the interest of the sum which Ṣalmu-šarri-iqbi paid on their behalf they had to serve him. The possibility existed that somebody might release Mannu-kī-Inurta and his family by satisfying Ṣalmu-šarri-iqbi's claims.

> [Seal] of Mannu-kī-Inurta. [Ṣalmu-ša]rri-iqbi gave [x minas of sil]ver, his (i.e. Mannu-kī-Inurta's) debt, to the merchant. (Thus) he released Mannu-kī-Inurta, his wife Arbail-šarrat (and) his daughter, together three souls, from the merchant. They will serve Ṣalmu-šarri-iqbi instead of the interest on the silver. (Whoever it is), either his (i.e. Mannu-kī-Inurta's) governor [or the mayor of] his [to]wn, who [gives] the silver [with the interest to] Ṣalmu-šarri-iqbi will redeem [the people].

A similar case is documented in another fragmentarily preserved text. Lū-šakin and his wife were released from their creditor Nabû'a's household by a man whose name is unfortunately not preserved in the remaining part of the tablet. The unknown benefactor satisfied Nabû'a by paying 70 minas of copper to him. In turn, Lū-šakin and his wife had to serve him for the rest of their lives. If somebody

---

[72] ADD 164 = Jas 1996: no. 1: 6–10 (dated to 680 BCE): ^{PN}*ḫa-ni-i* ^{7} *a-di* un.meš-*šú a-di* a.šà.meš-*šú* ^{8} *ku-um* 3-me udu.meš *a-di sa-ár-ti-ši-na* ^{9} *ku-*(*um*) úš.meš *ša* lú.sipa.meš ^{10} *na-ši* {*na*}.

[73] ADD 164 = Jas 1996: no. 1 r. 5f.: ^{PN}*ḫa-ni-i* $^{\text{r. 6}}$ *ú-še-ṣa*.

[74] ADD 85 = Kohler and Ungnad 1913: no. 656 (date lost): ^{1} [na$_4$.kišib] ^{PN}*man-nu-ki-i-*^{d}ma[š] ^{2} [x ma.na kù].babbar *ḫa-bu-li-š*[*u*] ^{3} [^{PNd}nu-m]an-*iq-bi a-na* lú.dam.gà[r] ^{4} *i*[*d-di*]*n* ^{PN}*man-nu-ki-i-*^{d}maš ^{mí}4*.dingir.ki-man-*ra*[*t*] ^{5} mí-*šú* dumu.mí-*su* (unused seal space, showing that the text is a later copy of the original sealed tablet, see Radner 1997a: 40ff.) ^{6} pab 3 zi.meš ta* igi lú.dam.gàr *ip-ta-ṭar* ^{7} [*k*]*u-um ru-bé-e šá* kù.babbar *a-na* ^{PNd}nu-man-*iq-bi* ^{8} [*i-p*]*a-lu-ḫu-šú lu-u* lú.gar-*nu-šú* $^{\text{l. e. 9}}$ [*lu-u ḫa-za-nu* ur]u$^{?!}$- *šú ša* kù.babbar $^{\text{r. 1}}$ [*a-di ru-bé-e a-na*] ^{PNd}nu-man-dug$_4$.ga $^{\text{r. 2}}$ [*id-din-u-ni* un.meš *ú*]- *še-ṣa*. For the restoration of l. 9 compare ADD 77 = Kohler and Ungnad 1913: no. 133:8 (see below).

paid off the anonymous benefactor Lū-šakin could be released. This option does not seem to have existed for his wife.[75]

> He released [Lū-šakin (and) FN, his wife, from] the city of Kalhu, altogether two so[uls, from] Nabû'a. [Instead of the 70 minas] of copper they will [ser]ve him as long as they live. Tomorrow or the day after tomorrow, [or sometime in the fu]ture, should either the brothers [of Lū-š]akin, his people, [his gov]ernor, his prefect or the [may]or of his city come forward and [. . .], he will pay 70 minas of copper [to PN] and he will redeem the man.

The case of a family which was first released by their surety from debt-slavery in the household of their creditor and later had to serve the surety to cover his expenses has already been discussed above.[76]

All these persons had to serve their liberators for life unless released by somebody else. The only case I know of in which a person's service to his liberator was restricted to a certain period of time is documented in a judicial text from Assur.[77] Nabû-šallim-aḫḫē was kept in slavery by a woman, in all probability his creditor. His two brothers (or possibly colleagues)[78] brought a lawsuit against the woman in order to free him. Upon payment of 35 shekels of silver they had Nabû-šallim-aḫḫē released from fetters and in turn he was to serve his brothers for three years.

> Lawsuit which Bēl-šumu-iškun (and) Nabû-mušabši brought on account of Nabû-šallim-aḫḫē against the woman Bānia in the presence of the Governor of Assur. They stated: "Why do you hold our brother in slavery?" They paid half a mina five shekels of silver (and) released him from his fetters. Instead of the silver he will serve them for three full years. (Date and witnesses.) He has (already) served Bēl-šumu-iškun for the first month.

---

75 ADD 77 = Kohler and Ungnad 1913: no. 133 (date lost): [^{PN}*lu-šá-kín* FN mí-*šú ša*] uru.*kal-ḫi* pab 2 z[i.meš]$^{2'}$ [ta igi] ^{PNd}ag-*u-a ip-ta-aṭ-ra* $^{3'}$ [*ku-um* 70 ma.na] urudu.meš *a-di* ti-*ú-ni* $^{4'}$ [*i-pal-l*]*a-aḫ-šú ina šir-ti i-li-diš* $^{5'}$ [*ina ma-te*]-*e-ma lu-u* šeš.meš-*šú* $^{6'}$ [*ša* ^{PN}*lu-š*]*á-kín lu-u* un.meš-*šú* $^{7'}$ [*lu-u* lú*.e]n.nam-*su lu-u* lú*.gar-*šú* $^{8'}$ [*lu-u a-za*]-*nu* uru-*šú il-la-kan-ni* $^{9'}$ [x x x x]-*šú-ni* 70 *ma.na urudu.meš* $^{10'}$ [*a-na* PN] *i-da-an* lú *ú-še-ṣa*.

76 VAT 5606, see n. 21.

77 BM 103206 = Jas 1996: no. 16 (dated to 653 BCE): *de-e-nu šá* ^{PN}en-mu-gar ^{2} *ša* ^{PNd}pa-*mu-šab-ši* ^{3} (*ina*) ugu ^{PNd}pa-di-pap.meš ^{4} ta ^{mí}*ba-ni-ia ina* igi lú*.gar.kur ^{5} *id-ba-bu-u-ni* ^{6} *ma-a a-ta-a* pap-*u-ni* ^{7} *a-na* ìr-*a-nu-te ta-kab-ba-*⌈as⌉-*šú* ^{8} 1/2 ma.na 5 gín kù.babbar ^{9} *i-ta-nu* ta šà urudu.meš-*šú* ^{10} *ip-t*[*a-aṭ*]-*ru-niš-šú* ^{11} ⌈*ku-um* kù.babbar⌉ 3 mu.an.na.meš ⌈itu⌉.meš-*ni i-pa-làḫ-šú-nu* (date and witnesses) ^{21} itu *pa-ni-u* ^{22} *ina* igi ^{PN}en-mu-gar ^{23} *i-te-te-zi*.

78 Note that *aḫu* "brother" was also used in the sense of "colleague." Nevertheless, the relations between the three men would still be very close if they were all

Note that normally, if a person was released from debt slavery by a member of his original household, there was no need to stress the obligation of the redeemed to serve his benefactor as it was implicitly the duty of any member of the household to serve the household's head. Thus, a document from Nineveh dealing with the release of Nabû-rēḫtu-uṣur, the nephew of Mukīn-aḫḫē, by his uncle simply states:[79]

> Mukīn-aḫḫē has given one mina of silver according to the royal mina to Nabû-iqbi (and) Nurtî. He has released Nabû-rēḫtu-uṣur, the son of his brother, and cleared him from claims.

Similarly, when Ṭāb-Bēl redeemed his sister Api' and her son Pāšî according to a text from Assur by paying thirty shekels of silver to Biša', no mention is made of Api''s and Pāšî's obligation to serve Ṭāb-Bēl.[80]

> Ṭāb-Bēl weighed out thirty shekels of silver of his inheritance share, gave them to Biša' (and) released Api', his sister, and Pāšî, the son of his sister, from the hands of Biša'.

2. *Mechanisms for the discharge of debts*

Like the kings of the Old Babylonian period, the neo-Assyrian king could proclaim a remission of debts, called (*an*)*durāru*. By doing so, debtors were freed from all their obligations towards their creditors and all debt slaves were released.

The proclamation of a debt remission served the interest of the debtors, but caused discomfort for the creditor. Therefore it comes as no surprise that three texts bear witness to the fact that sometimes creditors required a clause to be inserted which preserved their rights in case of a debt remission. Two texts from eighth-century Kalḫu and one document from seventh-century Nineveh contain such

---

members of the same guild. A number of guilds is attested in Assur. Best known are the guilds of the goldsmiths, the bakers and the *ḫundurāiē*.

[79] TIM 11 18 (dated to 669 BCE): inner tablet: 1 ma.na kù.babbar *ina ša* man [2] [PN]gin-pab.meš [3] *a-na* [PNd]ag-*iq-bi* [4] *a-na* [PN]*nu-úr-ti-i* [5] *i*[*t*]-*ti-din* [PNd]pa-*re-eḫ-tú*-pab [6] dumu pab-*šú ip-ta-ṭar* [7] *ú-zak-ki*.

[80] VAT 20374 (dated to 666 BCE or to the post-canonical eponymy of Kanūnāiu): [7] 30 gín.meš kù.babbar *ša* ḫa.la-*šú* [PN]dùg.ga-en [8] *iḫ-ti-ia-aṭ a-na* [PN]*bi-šá-a*" *i-ti-din* [9] [mí]*a-pi-i*" nin-*su* [PN]*pa-ši-i* dumu nin-*šú* [10] ta šu.2 [PN]*bi-ša-a*" *ip-ta-ṭar-ra*.

clauses which protect the claims of the creditor or the buyer of what must be debt slaves.[81] The existence of these clauses is unequivocal evidence that contractual right was given priority over a debt remission.[82] However, unless the creditor had made sure to protect his rights beforehand, all his claims against the debtor had to be relinquished in the event of a debt remission. The proclamation of a debt remission was certainly not a routine matter and, as insurance clauses against debt remissions are rare, the creditor apparently accepted the risk normally.

It seems that the proclamation of a debt remission at least sometimes coincided with the beginning of a king's reign. This can be deduced from the dates of eight contracts from seventh-century Nineveh, Assur and Kalḫu which are said to have been set up after a debt remission.

A debt remission early in 680, at the time of Esarhaddon's accession to the throne:[83]

ii–680	text from Nineveh[84]
iii–680	text from Nineveh[85]
viii–678	text from Assur[86]

A debt remission late in 669, at the time of Ashurbanipal's accession to the throne:

[. . .]–669	text from Nineveh[87]

---

[81] The land lease ADD 629 = SAA 6 226 (dated to 676 BCE) from Nineveh stipulates that the creditor will recover his money in the case of a debt remission. The slave sale CTN 2 248 from Kalḫu (date lost but certainly eighth century) stipulates that the seller will return the price of the persons sold to the buyer in the case of a debt remission. The slave sale CTN 2 10 from Kalḫu (date lost but certainly eighth century) stipulates that the sold slave [would remain the property of the contractor (?)] should the king proclaim a debt remission. Note that the usual clause excluding litigation (s. Radner 1997a: 353–356) is missing in these two sales texts.

[82] Otto 1997: 50.

[83] The lasting impression of this debt remission is probably witnessed by ADD 629 = SAA 6 226 (dated to 676 BCE) from Nineveh with its insurance clause against a debt remission. Note that the proclamation of a debt remission for Assur is recorded in the inscriptions of Esarhaddon: Ass. A ii 27–iii 15, s. Borger 1956: 2f, cf. Otto 1997: 46.

[84] ADD 73 and 74 = SAA 6 260 and 259.

[85] ADD 113 = SAA 6 221.

[86] VAT 10491 (unpublished).

[87] ADD 310 = Kwasman 1988: no. 149.

Two debt remissions in the years after Ashurbanipal's reign, the first probably at the time of Aššūr-etel-ilāni's accession to the throne:

iv–629* (Parpola) or 624* (Reade)[88]	text from Kalḫu[89]
x–615* (Reade) or 612* (Parpola)[90]	text from Assur[91]
[. . .]–615* (Reade) or 612* (Parpola)	text from Nineveh[92]
date lost[93]	text from Assur[94]

A debt remission[95] was certainly seen as a benefit by most of the king's subjects and therefore an excellent token of the king's good intentions towards the country at the time of the assumption of his office. The observation gained from the legal texts matches the fact that Sargon II, after subduing Babylonia, proclaimed debt remissions for several of the Babylonian cities. Debt remissions for Dēr, Ur, Uruk, Eridu, Larsa, Kullaba, Kissik and Nēmed-Laguda are mentioned in the inscriptions of this king[96] while two letters refer to a debt remission in Babylon.[97] It seems that a remission of debts was not proclaimed for the whole country, but for specific cities. Thus, an inscription of Esarhaddon notes the proclamation of a debt remission for the city of Assur.[98]

---

[88] Eponymy of the palace scribe Nabû-šarru-uṣur. For recent suggestions for the sequence of the post-canonical eponyms see S. Parpola in Radner, ed. 1998: xviii–xx and Reade 1998: 256f.

[89] CTN 3 59.

[90] Eponymy of Šamaš-šarru-ibni.

[91] Assur 2 = Ahmad 1996: no. 2.

[92] TIM XI 3.

[93] The text is ceratinly of post-canonical date, cf. the prosopographical links with VAT 9686 = Deller, Fales and Jakob-Rost 1995: no. 92, dated to the eponymy of Nabû-sākip (629* according to Reade and 618* according to Parpola).

[94] VAT 9695 = Deller, Fales and Jakob-Rost 1995: no. 89.

[95] Possibly, a group of administrative texts listing debts found in Nineveh is to be placed in this context. The term *ḫabullu* "debt" is mentioned in ADD 815+ = SAA 7 30 ii 9', ADD 926 = SAA 7 34:3', 8' and ADD 923 = SAA 7 35 i 3; the texts SAA 7 27–29, 31–33 and 36–40 belong to the same category.

[96] "Große Prunkinschrift": 136f., s. Fuchs 1994: 229f. and 351; "Kleine Prunkinschrift des Saales XIV": 4, s. l.c. 75 and 307; "Schwelleninschrift Typ V": 6–9, s. l.c. 272 and 362; cf. Otto 1997: 45.

[97] ABL 387 = SAA 5 203, ABL 702 = SAA 10 169.

[98] Ass. A ii 27–iii 15, s. Borger 1956: 2f., cf. Otto 1997: 46.

Bibliography

Ahmad, A.Y. 1996. The Archive of Aššur-mātu-taqqin Found in the New Town of Aššur and Dated Mainly by Post-Canonical Eponyms. *Al-Rāfidān* 17: 207–288.

Borger, R. 1956. *Die Inschriften Asarhaddons, Königs von Assyrien.* Archiv für Orientforschung, Beiheft, 9. Graz: Selbstverlag des Herausgebers (E.F. Weidner).

Deller, K. 1965. Neuassyrisches aus Sultantepe. *OrNS* 34: 457–477.

——. 1986. Ein Assyrer tilgt Schulden. *Oriens Antiquus* 25: 21–27.

——. 1987. *tamkāru*-Kredite in neuassyrischer Zeit. *JESHO* 30: 1–29.

Deller, K., and F.M. Fales and L. Jakob-Rost, with contributions by V. Donbaz. 1995. Neo-Assyrian Texts from Assur. Private Archives in the Vorderasiatisches Museum of Berlin. Part 2. *State Archives of Assyria Bulletin* 9: 1–137.

Eichler, B. 1973. *Indenture at Nuzi.* Yale Near Eastern Researches, 5. New Haven: Yale University.

Fales, F.M. 1983. Studies on Neo-Assyrian Texts II: "Deeds and Documents" from the British Museum. *ZA* 73: 232–254.

——. 1997. People and Professions in Neo-Assyrian Assur. In *Assyrien im Wandel der Zeiten*, ed. H. Hauptmann and H. Waetzold. Pp. 33–40. Heidelberger Studien zum Alten Orient 6 (= CRRAI 39). Heidelberg: Heidelberger Orientverlag.

Fales, F.M., and L. Jakob-Rost, with two appendixes by K. Deller. 1991. Neo-Assyrian Texts from Assur. Private Archives in the Vorderasiatisches Museum of Berlin. Part 1. *State Archives of Assyria Bulletin* 5: 1–157.

Friedrich, J., and G.R. Meyer, A. Ungnad and E.F. Weidner. 1940. *Die Inschriften vom Tell Halaf.* Archiv für Orientforschung, Beiheft, 6. Berlin: Selbstverlag des Herausgebers (E.F. Weidner).

Finkelstein, J.J. 1957. Assyrian Contracts from Sultantepe. *Anatolian Studies* 7: 137–145.

Fuchs, A. 1994. *Die Inschriften Sargons II. aus Khorsabad.* Göttingen: Cuvillier-Verlag.

Garelli, P. 1989. L'appel au roi sous l'empire assyrien. In *Reflets des Deux Fleuves: Volume de mélanges offerts à André Finet*, ed. M. Lebeau and Ph. Talon. Pp. 45–46. Akkadica, Suppl. 6. Leuven: Peeters.

Jakobson, V.A. 1974. On Guaranty in Neo-Assyrian Law. (In Russian). *Palestinskij Sbornik* 25: 45–51.

Jas, R. 1996. *Neo-Assyrian Judicial Procedures.* State Archives of Assyria, Studies, 5. Helsinki: The Neo-Assyrian Text Corpus Project.

Jursa, M., and K. Radner. 1995/96. Keilschrifttexte aus Jerusalem. *AfO* 42/43: 89–108.

Kohler, J., and A. Ungnad. 1913. *Assyrische Rechtsurkunden.* Leipzig: Eduard Pfeiffer.

Koschaker, P. 1928. *Neue keilschriftliche Rechtsurkunden aus der El-Amarna-Zeit.* Abhandlungen der philologisch-historischen Klasse der Sächsischen Akademie der Wissenschaften, 39/5. Leipzig: S. Hirzel.

Kwasman, T. 1988. *Neo-Assyrian Legal Documents in the Kouyunjik Collection of the British Museum.* Studia Pohl, Series Maior, 14. Roma: Biblical Institute Press.

——. 1986. Three Notes: I. *nāmaru*, II. *a/lapp/bbānu*, III. *ina/ana pūḫi*. *Mesopotamia* 21: 209–212.

Lambert, W.G. 1960. *Babylonian Wisdom Literature.* Oxford: Oxford University Press.

Lipiński, E. 1998. Old Aramaic Contracts of Guarantee. In *Written on Clay and Stone: Ancient Near Eastern Studies Presented to Krystyna Szarzynska*, ed. J. Braun, K. Łyczkowska, M. Popko and P. Steinkeller. Pp. 39–44. Warsaw: Agade.

Neumann, H. 1997. Gläubiger oder Schuldner? Anmerkungen zu einem neuassyrischen Privatbrief. In Ana šadî Labnāni lu allik. *Beiträge zu altorientalischen und mittelmeerischen Kulturen: Festschrift für Wolfgang Röllig*, ed. H. Kühne, B. Pongratz-Leisten and

P. Xella. Pp. 281–293. Alter Orient und Altes Testament, 247. Kevelaer and Neukirchen-Vluyn: Butzon & Becker and Neukirchener Verlag.
Otto, E. 1997. Programme der sozialen Gerechtigkeit. Die neuassyrische (*an-*)*durāru*-Institution sozialen Ausgleichs und das deuteronomistische Erlaßjahr in Dtn 15. *Zeitschrift für Altorientalische und Biblische Rechtsgeschichte* 3: 26–63.
——. 1998. Neue Aspekte zum keilschriftlichen Prozeßrecht in Babylonien und Assyrien. *Zeitschrift für Altorientalische und Biblische Rechtsgeschichte* 4: 263–283.
Parker, B. 1954. The Nimrud Tablets, 1952—Business Documents. *Iraq* 16: 29–53.
Ponchia, S. 1990. Neo-Assyrian Corn-Loans: Preliminary Notes. *State Archives of Assyria Bulletin* 4: 39–60.
Postgate, J.N. 1974a. *Taxation and Conscription in the Assyrian Empire*. Studia Pohl, Series Maior, 3. Roma: Biblical Institute Press.
——. 1974b. Royal Exercise of Justice under the Assyrian Empire. In *Le Palais et la Royauté*, ed. P. Garelli. Pp. 417–426. Actes de la XIXème Rencontre assyriologique internationale. Paris: Geuthner.
——. 1976. *Fifty Neo-Assyrian Legal Documents*. Warminster: Aris & Phillips.
——. 1980. "Princeps Iudex" in Assyria. *RA* 74: 180–182.
____. 1982. *ilku* and Land Tenure in the Middle Assyrian Kingdom—A Second Attempt. In *Societies and Languages of the Ancient Near East: Studies in Honor of I.M. Diakonoff*, ed. M.A. Dandamayev *et al.* Pp. 304–313. Warminster: Aris & Phillips.
——. 1988. *The Archive of Urad-Šerūa and his Family. A Middle-Assyrian Household in Government Service*, Roma: Editore Roberto Denicola.
——. 1997. Middle Assyrian to Neo-Assyrian: the Nature of the Shift. In *Assyrien im Wandel der Zeiten*, ed. H. Hauptmann and H. Waetzold. Pp. 159–168. Heidelberger Studien zum Alten Orient, 6 (= Actes de la XXXIXème Rencontre assyriologique internationale). Heidelberg: Heidelberger Orientverlag.
Radner, K. 1995. The Relation Between Format and Content of Neo-Assyrian Texts. In *Nineveh 612 BC. The Glory and Fall of the Assyrian Empire*, ed. R. Mattila. Pp. 63–78. Helsinki: The Neo-Assyrian Text Corpus Project.
——. 1997a. *Die neuassyrischen Privatrechtsurkunden als Quelle für Mensch und Umwelt*. State Archives of Assyria, Studies, 6. Helsinki: The Neo-Assyrian Text Corpus Project.
——. 1997b. Vier neuassyrische Privatrechtsurkunden aus dem Vorderasiatischen Museum, Berlin. *Altorientalische Forschungen* 27: 115–134.
——. 1997/98. Review of Jas 1996. *Archiv für Orientforschung* 44/45: 379–387.
——. 1998 (ed.). *The Prosopography of the Neo-Assyrian Empire 1/I: A*. Helsinki: The Neo-Assyrian Text Corpus Project.
——. 1999. *Ein neuassyrisches Privatarchiv der Tempelgoldschmiede von Assur*. Studien zu den Assur-Texten, 1. Berlin: Deutsche Orient-Gesellschaft.
Reade, J.E. 1998. Assyrian Eponyms, Kings and Pretenders, 648–605 BC. *OrNS* 67: 255–265.
Scheil, V. 1925. Un contrat assyrien. *RA* 22: 147–149.
Wiseman, D. 1953. The Nimrud Tablets, 1953. *Iraq* 15: 135–160.

THE NEO-BABYLONIAN PERIOD

Joachim Oelsner – Friedrich Schiller University of Jena (em.)

I. Introduction[1]

As in the Old Babylonian period,[2] in the neo- and Late Babylonian period, at least up to the beginning of the Hellenistic age, the bulk of documents which have come down to us refer to loans. During the latter period there is a change in the character of the sources insofar as this kind of document is no longer attested after c. 300 BCE. Most of the later examples were written in the city of Babylon.[3]

After a gap of some centuries in the text tradition from the end of the Cassite period, the earliest neo-Babylonian documents concerning debts are dated to about 700 BCE. From then on there is a constant flow of documents for the following four centuries. Thousands of documents of this kind are preserved, so far only published in part. They refer to silver but also to commodities (e.g. barley) as being due.

In the neo- and Late Babylonian period, the instrument used in the overwhelming number of instances to record loans or debts was the promissory note (Germ. *Verpflichtungsschein*, Fr. *reconnaissance de dette*). This type of document is known from earlier periods (in the Old Assyrian period it was the most commonly used instrument), but in second-millennium Babylonia it is only rarely attested (e.g. BE 14 115—Middle Babylonian).

---

[1] The fundamental studies, which are still valuable today, are Koschaker 1911: 32–236 and Petschow 1956. See also Korošec 1964; Haase 1965.

[2] Skaist 1994: 11.

[3] See Oelsner 1995: 116 and nn. 57, 61; 119 and nn. 78ff. The latest examples of this type from Uruk are: VAS 15 2 and OECT 9 3 (both dated year 13 SE = 299/298). Documents for *imittu* of dates from Uruk are known to the year 16 SE, see Doty 1978: 67–69 (now add von Weiher, Uruk 5 308, 309, 311). For texts from Babylon see Oelsner 1971: 164 (*sub* A4), also CT 44 83; Strassmaier 1888: 129ff. no. 13 (new edition Oelsner 1995: 128–133). Regarding *imittu* "(Pacht-)Auflage" (AHw), "estimated yield" (CAD), see Petschow 1976–80: 68–73.

The neo-/Late Babylonian promissory note (*u'iltu*) is generally formulated as an abstract document; it is not stated why the debt arose. The basic structure is as follows:[4]

A. BRM 1 29 = San Nicolò 1951: no. 50
(Bel-ibni yr. 3 = 700/699)[5]

> x *uṭṭatu ša* PN_1 *ina muḫḫi* PN_2 *ina* ^{itu}MN x *uṭṭata qaqqada* PN_2 *ana* PN_1 *tanamdin* . . .
>
> x barley belonging to PN_1 charged against PN_2. In the month . . . x barley, the principal, PN_2 to PN_1 will give.

B. Actes du 8e Congrès International no. 3 = San Nicolò 1951: no. 51 (Asarhaddon yr. 4 = 677/676)

> x *kaspu ša* PN_1 *ina muḫḫi* PN_2 *ina qīt arḫi ša* ^{itu}MN *kaspa ana* PN_1 *inamdin kī lā ittannu arḫa* y *šiqil kaspu ina muḫḫi-šu irabbi*
>
> x silver belonging to PN_1 charged against PN_2. At the end of month . . . x silver PN_2 to PN_1 will give. If he does not give, (every) month y shekel silver against him will increase.

Use of the real contract (Germ. *Realvertrag*) as a credit document—characteristic in the neo-Assyrian sphere—is rare in first millennium Babylonia. It is not clear in which instances it was used instead of the promissory note, but we do not consider it necessary to postulate Assyrian influence.[6] A possible exception is some examples from Nippur during the Assyrian hegemony in the seventh century. Nevertheless, one may assume that the ancients had their reasons when they decided to use one or the other formulary. Its strucure is:

C. TuM 2/3 41 = San Nicolò 1951: no. 68
(Sin-šarra-iškun yr. 6 = 621/620)[7]

> x *kaspu ša* PN_1 *ina pāni* PN_2 *ina patê bābi kaspa ina qaqqadi-šu inamdin*
>
> x silver belonging to PN_1 at the disposal of PN_2. At the opening of the gate,[8] the silver in its principal he will give.

---

[4] See Petschow 1956: 10–24, also San Nicolò and Ungnad 1935: 192–195.

[5] The debtor is female.

[6] See San Nicolò 1938: 129; San Nicolò and Ungnad 1935: 192.

[7] TuM 2/3 42 = San Nicolò 1951: no. 69, dated a few days later, differs only slightly in respect of the amount of silver due and some orthographic variants.

[8] The time fixed for repayment presumes a siege: see Oppenheim 1955: 69–89.

That part of the debt notes which is never lacking is the statement that silver or some commodity belonging to the creditor is owed by the debtor (Germ. *Schuldklausel*). A repayment clause is the rule, but sometimes it is lacking (e.g. Moldenke II 2 = San Nicolò 1951: no. 52). In the examples given above no interest is mentioned. It could mean that there is no interest at all (A and B above) or that interest is charged at the standard rate (commodities: 25 percent; silver: 20 percent). If the debtor does not pay in time (B above), interest on the arrears is often stipulated.

There are further clauses, mostly concerning security for the loan. As in other regions and periods of the ancient Near East, there is personal security, i.e. suretyship (*pūt . . . našû*)[9] and real security, i.e. pledge (*maškanu*, abstract noun *maškanūtu*). A further clause may provide that another creditor is not allowed to take possession of the object given as pledge as long as the amount due has not been paid to the creditor (*rašû šanamma ul išallaṭ adi* creditor object *išallim*).

Before going into details, a remark on the nature and use of the promissory note is necessary. Where this type of document is used, the transaction is not always a loan. It is apparent that it is a formula which fits different needs and could be used for all types of obligations. The so-called *imittu*,[10] for example, is an agreement to deliver goods, while other cases have the character of a manufacturing contract.[11] Sometimes the exact nature of the juridical act cannot be identified. Furthermore, it should be noted that the term *u'iltu* also has the meaning "obligation" in general.[12]

With the inclusion of all the additional clauses, the elements of a promissory note are:[13]

1. Statement that the debtor is indebted to the creditor (examples A and B above)
2. Repayment clause, often mentioning the time and place for payment (A and B)
3. Interest and/or interest on arrears (B)
4. Joint liability if there is more than one debtor

[9] The term is analyzed by Malul 1988: 272–276.

[10] See n. 3 above and Ries 1976: 90–110.

[11] For example, if there are promissory notes referring to large quantities of bricks, one may assume that the contract is an order to make and deliver the product, not an ordinary loan. See also below Nabû-ušallim archive no. 17 O.

[12] Petschow 1956: 10 n. 23 (first paragraph).

[13] Petschow 1956: 71.

5. Suretyship
6. Pledge
7. *rašû* clause
8. Witnesses, place, date.

A single document may not contain all these elements.

II. Case Studies

The principal questions that arise in connection with security for debt are:

1) In which cases is there pledge?
2) When is there suretyship?
3) Why is there sometimes no security at all?

Another question that should be mentioned is, what kind of objects are given as pledges and who are the persons standing surety?

To illustrate these problems, we have selected three archives from the seventh century, all of which come from controlled excavations:

1. The archive of a person called Bēl-ušallim, from Babylon;
2. The Sin-uballiṭ archive, from Ur;
3. The Nabû-ušallim archive from Uruk.

1. *The Archive of Bēl-ušallim*

This collection of tablets (excavation number BE 38135, now in the Vorderasiatisches Museum, Berlin) consists of legal deeds, dated between Šamaš-šum-ukin year 8 and Kandalānu year 20 (= 660–628). The tablets were published by Jakob-Rost 1968: 39–62 and 1970: 58 (no. 11).[14]

There are 22 tablets that have been published or discussed. Most of them are promissory notes (13 in a reasonable state of preserva-

[14] = Babylon 12 in Pedersén 1998: 196 and n. 70. According to Jakob-Rost 1968: 39, part of the archive presumably came into the Iraq Museum, Baghdad. This remains unpublished. I thank Dr. Beate Salje, Director of the Vorderasiatisches Museum, Berlin, and Dr. Joachim Marzahn, of the same institution, for permission to collate the Berlin tablets.

tion) for silver, partly with and partly without pledge. In nearly all of them, as well as in some fragments and an *ina-pāni* contract (1968, no. 13), a certain Bēl-ušallim, descendant (i.e. member of the family) of Lēʿea acts as creditor. Only in no. 16 does he seem to be the debtor. In detail, the situation is as follows:

Simple promissory note without further conditions: nos. 1–4, 6: interest, but no repayment clause;

no. 5 and 1970, no. 11: loan without interest (no. 5: *ḫubuttūtu*), but repayment clause and interest on arrears.

Comparable are nos. 17 and 18: two debtors, but apparently without joint liability (on joint liability, see below).

The amount due varies between 15 shekels and 1 1/2 minas.

Promissory notes with pledge:

In nos. 7–12 there is a pledge introduced by: object *maškanu* (*ša* creditor) "... is pledge of the creditor." The following objects are used as pledge:

nos. 7 and 11: a person (personal name, but no specification—male or female slave of the debtor or one of his children?);

nos. 8–10, 12: landed property (8: land with date-palms,[15] 9 and 10: a field; 12: field and house).

There is a peculiarity in no. 12. There is no interest, but if the debtor does not pay in time, the amount which is due will be added to the share the creditor has in the *ḫarrānu* business venture that he and the debtor are running jointly.[16]

The amounts due are in the range of 10 to 40 shekels, i.e. they are often less than those of the above-mentioned documents without pledge. Perhaps this is due to the character of Bēl-ušallim's business activity, which seems to be in the realm of trade (*ḫarrānu* business).

[15] The traces of the sign at the end of l. 5 seem to be part of GIŠIMMAR; the traces at the beginning of the damaged section look like a Winkelhaken (I have seen the traces of an additional impression below, number sign 40 or 50?). The expected determinative GIŠ seems to be missing. Translate: "40/50 [date] palms." Regarding *bīt karāni* "vineyard" (l. 6) see CAD K 206. The measurements of the fields (nos. 9 and 12) read contrary to the publication GUR instead of IKU (what seems to be a Winkelhaken in no. 9 l. 7 is in reality a scratch).

[16] No. 13 (*ina pāni* formula) refers to a share in a *ḫarrānu* business venture too, but this is without relevance to the present discussion. On the *ḫarrānu* contract, see Lanz 1976.

In nos. 8–12 there is the so-called *rašû* clause: [lú]*rašû šanamma ina muḫḫi* object of the pledge *ul išallaṭ adi* creditor *kasap-šu išallim* "another (creditor) has no right to the pledge until the creditor is satisfied" (no. 9 variant: *manma ina muḫḫi ul išallaṭ*).

In no. 15 some particulars of the text are obscure because the tablet is damaged. But the formula *pūt . . . naši . . .* 1/2 *mina iturru* (ll. 5–8) makes it clear that this refers to a surety (comparable to UET 4 198 = San Nicolò 1951 no. 81 below).[17]

The fundamental elements of giving a pledge may be recognized in this archive. The next group of texts to be discussed provide us with insights into the use of suretyship.

2. *The Archive of Sin-uballiṭ, son of Sin-zēru-līšir*

In contrast to the previous archive, the owner of the documents is primarily the debtor, not the creditor. In addition to promissory notes, there are other kinds of legal documents, as well as letters and some lists.[18]

The tablets are dated from Nabopolassar year 2 to year 9 (= 624/23–617/16). If the place where the tablet was written is mentioned, it is Babylon or another settlement in Northern Babylonia. This means that Sin-uballiṭ lived there for some time and was engaged in business activities. This is confirmed by his letters.[19]

However, in UET 4 61 (written in Babylon), the silver is to be paid at Ur. The field given as pledge in UET 4 72 is situated at

[17] See Jakob-Rost 1968: 58 *sub numero*. No. 20 (upper part of an oblong tablet) differs from the other tablets. In addition it has nail marks on all edges (groups of three impressions). This speaks against a promissory note. The state of preservation of no. 21 does not permit reconstruction of its contents (approximately 2 lines broken at the top of the tablet, l. 4':]x *i-leq-qé*, rev. l. 1 end of the contract text before the witnesses: *ú-šal-lam*). Nos. 14 and 19 are also fragments of promissory notes (female debtor).

[18] E.g. lists of plants for magical purposes (UET 4 146–148). Excavation number U 17238 and—exclusively letters—U 17239. The tablets had been excavated in a dwelling house in Ur, see Pedersén 1998: 203–204 (Ur 3).

[19] Based on UET 4 183 (= Ebeling 1949: no. 318) l. 14. See also UET 4 186 (= Ebeling 1949: no. 321) l. 3. Ebeling drew the conclusion that Sin-uballiṭ was acting in Babylon as an official (*s/šukkallu*, see AHw 1264 s.v. A 10; CAD S 357, 9'). The commercial activities that can be seen in his legal documents and letters are restricted exclusively to the private sphere.

the same place. As in the Bēl-ušallim archive discussed above, there are loans without interest and others with interest but without any security, as well as some where pledge or surety to secure the loans is mentioned. In some tablets with the same excavation number persons other than Sin-uballiṭ act as contracting parties.

By content there are:

Loans without interest (*ḫubuttūtu*):

neither repayment clause nor interest on arrears: UET 4 61, 62;

repayment clause, but no interest on arrears: UET 4 63 (short term loan, dated to the 5th of the month, to be paid at the end of the month);

repayment clause as well as interest on arrears: UET 4 68,[20] 83;[21]

the same, but the term *hubuttūtu* is missing: UET 4 70;

other persons as debtor: UET 4 69, 71.

Promissory notes with interest, but repayment clause missing: UET 4 81, 82.

The amount of silver due varies from 6 shekels to 1 mina.

In addition, there are a number of loan documents that refer to a pledge. The circumstances vary. They will be arranged here according to the object given as pledge:

Female slave (*ṣeḫertu*)

With the exception of UET 4 73 (no interest, but not called *ḫubuttūtu*, with *rašû* clause; silver due: 1/2 mina), all the documents have stipulations regarding the use of the pledge:

74—the slave girl is at the disposal of the creditor (*ina pāni* PN *ušuzzat*), antichretic pledge—usufruct, no interest,[22] *rašû* clause; amount due 1 mina;

75—in case of delay in repayment an antichretic pledge is to be given, *rašû* clause lacking; amount due 25 shekels;

76—Iṣṣurtu, the wife of Sin-uballiṭ, becomes debtor instead of her husband and gives her slave girl as a forfeitable pledge; the creditor is obliged to add 10 shekels, *rašû* clause; amount due 1 mina;

[20] Regarding the amount of interest the text says: *akī kaspi ša ina muḫḫi Sin-etelli-ilī irabbû* "corresponding to the silver which increases against the account of Sin-etelli-ilī (he will give silver)" (ll. 7–10). This refers to another debt. Sin-etelli-ilī occurs several times as a business partner of Sin-uballiṭ.

[21] A further stipulation in l. 8f. is dubious (referring to another claim?).

[22] *ša kaspi ḫubulli-šu ianu u ša* PN (of the slave girl) [*i*]*di-šu ianu* . . . *adi* creditor *kasap-šu išallimu*.

77, 78, 79—a slave girl as antichretic pledge for part of the amount due (77, 78 half; 79 two thirds);[23] claim of interest for the remaining sum, no *rašû* clause; amount due 1 mina.

See also UET 4 89, formulated as a promise for payment. The legal transaction on which it is based is not evident, perhaps conveyance; slave girl as pledge; Sin-uballiṭ is witness; debtor and creditor are other persons.

UET 4 73, 74, 79 and 197 all belong to a single dossier. 197 refers to the restitution of a slave girl who had been given as a pledge. If she is returned at a fixed date, the creditor has to pay a daily hire to Sin-uballiṭ. Mention should also be made of UET 4 203, the self-pledge of a person.

Field

UET 4 72, 88—besides the pledge, interest is charged. The debtor is a person other than Sin-uballiṭ; both documents contain a *rašû* clause; amount due 1 mina and 55 shekels respectively.

Date-palm orchard

UET 4 87—*ina pāni* contract with interest; amount due 1/2 mina.

To be added are documents in which suretyship is mentioned: UET 4 80—promissory note (amount due 6 shekels) with claim of interest and an additional surety (l. 6: *māḫiṣ pūtu*[24] without any specification). UET 4 112 speaks of a surety guaranteeing payment for a debtor. Another example of suretyship is UET 4 198 (= San Nicolò 1951: no. 81): a number of persons guarantee to an official that somebody will not flee (in these last two examples Sin-uballiṭ is not among the contracting parties). There is a contract for establishing a *ḫarrānu* business in which one of the partners gives a guarantee in respect of the money invested (UET 4 56 = San Nicolò 1951: no. 48; Sin-uballiṭ is not mentioned in the text).

Pledge (of a slave girl as in the above cases) and suretyship are also mentioned in some letters of the Sin-uballiṭ archive (UET 4 174, 182, see also 184 = Ebeling 1949: nos. 310, 317, 31), but add nothing new.[25]

---

[23] To be read 2/3 in l. 4 instead 5/6 of the copy.

[24] The following sign (TAR?) makes no sense.

[25] Other documents of the Sin-uballiṭ archive (UET 4 113 and duplicate 114, 195, 196, 202) have no relation to the problems discussed here.

3. *The so-called Nabû-ušallim Archive*

32 cuneiform tablets, constituting an archive, were recovered from a dwelling house in Uruk (excavation number W 20032; published by Hunger 1970).[26] Most of the tablets are dated between 631 and 593; some are earlier (the oldest is no. 3, a prebend sale, dated 700).[27] The character of the archive—named after Nabû-ušallim, son of Bēl-iddin, the person most often mentioned as a contracting party—differs in one respect from those discussed so far. It gives a glimpse into the activities of persons active—as far as one can see—exclusively in the field of commerce and trade. Those involved are closely connected with the temples. Nevertheless they behave in their commercial activities as private persons. A considerable number of the contracts deal with bakers' prebends purchased by them. In addition Nabû-ušallim and his offspring who continued his commercial activities also managed lending operations. Mostly they are attested as creditors. If there are silver loans (varying from 6 shekels to 2 1/2 minas), a pledge is normally given. There is one exception: no. 17 D. Here two sons of Nabû-ušallim, i.e. brothers, act as creditor and debtor, and a third person is surety for part of the silver owed.[28] Pledges are also absent from commodity loans (no. 17 H: a loan of silver is to be repaid in dates according to the current price; no. 17 M and N: loan of barley; no. 17 O: bundles of reeds—if repayment is delayed, there is interest of 20 percent on the arrears, to be paid in the same commodity).

Objects given as pledge (normally with interest) are:

Slaves

rašû clause missing: no. 17 E (including the statement that there is neither interest nor rent for the slave, i.e. the pledge is antichretic;[29] no. 17 K (the work to be done by the pledged person is specified exactly).

---

[26] See also Kessler 1991: 55–62 (including remarks on the genealogy), van Dijk 1962: 41–43.

[27] Read Aššur-nādin-šumi (Brinkman 1972: 245, see also the copy). Other texts are dated Šamaš-šum-ukīn and Assurbanipal.

[28] It is probable, but not proven, that this person, Šuma-ukīn, is a brother of the two (see the genealogical table Hunger 1970: 174), as there also is another person with the same name but with another filiation (Hunger 1970: 271).

[29] *ša kaspi ḫubulli-šu ianu u idi-šu ianu adi* creditor *kasap-šu išallimu*. See also n. 22 above.

Prebends

rašû clause missing: no. 17 C (compensation for interest against *pappasu* "income"); no. 17 P (instead of interest the debtor is obliged to fulfil prebendary duties;[30] there is no interest to pay nor is there *utru* "income" from the prebend); no. 27;

rašû clause included: no. 19 and duplicate no. 20 (see also below); no. 25.[31]

Prebend and Hypothecary Pledge of Entire Property—mimmû ša āli u ṣeri (mala bašû) "whatever property there is in the city and abroad"

rašû clause included: no. 18 (in addition reference is made to an existing surety); no. 21 and duplicate no. 22 (neither interest nor *utru* "income" from the prebend).

Hypothecary Pledge of Entire Property

rašû clause missing: nos. 17 A, 17 G (for one year without interest, afterwards interest of 15%); nos. 17 I,[32] 17 L;

rašû clause included: nos. 17 B, 17 F,[33] 24,[34] 28 (interest on arrears).

If there is more than one debtor, joint liability is imposed (*pūt aḫameš našû*) in no. 19 and duplicate no. 20, but not in no. 27.

The possibility of litigation against a surety can be seen in no. 14. One may suppose that the prebend given as pledge was alienated without authority. Now the surety is made responsible for the loss.

Three archives of the seventh century have been analyzed. Most of the deeds refer to loans of silver. A few exceptions are preserved in the Nabu-ušallim archive. In the first and third group of texts the most frequently occuring person is the creditor, in the second it is the debtor. Regarding the giving of pledges all the texts are comparable. Securing the debt by surety occurs more rarely.

The quantity of material could be increased many times over by documents from other sites. I will add only a few texts that give additional information:

---

[30] Regarding the verb *resēnu* and the abstract noun *resinūtu* see McEwan 1981: 102–109. The meaning of the root *r s n* refers to the duties that are to be fulfilled by the prebendaries.

[31] The end of line 11 is damaged: *ūmē u mimma* . . .; possibly to be restored as *pappasu* or *utru*.

[32] The amount due was given by the father of the creditor to the father of the debtor for the purchase of a slave.

[33] The property pledged has been in the hands of the creditor for some years. This means that it is a pledge for an earlier debt too.

[34] The interest clause may be lost in the gap in ll. 4f.

In TuM 2/3 104 (= San Nicolò 1951: no. 80) a house is given as pledge. There is antichresis for two-thirds of the amount due (1 mina); for the balance, interest is charged at 20 percent.[35] The *rašû* clause in UET 4 84 (= San Nicolò 1951: no. 72) is curious, in that no pledge is mentioned in the text itself.[36]

Finally, mention should be made of UCP 9/I 2 (= San Nicolò 1951: no. 82, with surety) and VAS 4 5 (= San Nicolò 1951: no. 86). Possibly ll. 5–7 of the latter speak of making sure a person given as pledge is available.

To summarize, the basic types of loan documents and of security for loans characterisic of the neo- and Late Babylonian period already existed in the seventh century. From that time on they were used for centuries up to the Hellenistic period, even if there are some minor differences and developments in the formula over the centuries. If there are peculiarities, they arise from the special circumstances of the case, even if these are not mentioned in the texts. To the case studies given above some general remarks will now be added.

III. Types of Security

There were two ways, dating back to the earliest historical periods, for the creditor to secure his loan: suretyship and pledge.

1. *Suretyship*[37]

1.1. *Identity of the Surety*

1.1.1. Third party

This is the most common case. The surety sometimes had family or business connections with the debtor; otherwise, the relationship has to be determined separately in each document.

---

35 There is no stipulation for repair of the house (contrary to the later document Camb. 306 = Petschow 1956: 161 no. 4).

36 BM 74652 (= Weidner 1952/53: 37f., pl. III no. 2) is a sale of a person by himself. But presumably this does not arise from a loan, but from general economic distress caused by external circumstances.

37 Already Koschaker 1911, which will be summarized here, could base his study on a considerable number of documents, mostly of the sixth and fifth centuries. His

1.1.2. Joint liability[38]

If there is more than one debtor the loan clauses are normally followed by the words *ištēn pūt šanî naši* or, more rarely (e.g. Hunger 1970: no. 19 and duplicate no. 20), *pūt aḫameš našû* "they have joint liability for each other." There are only a few exceptions to this rule (e.g. Jakob-Rost 1968: no. 17 and duplicate no. 18). Sometimes another provision is added: *ša qerbi ušallam* "he who is the nearest shall repay" (e.g. TuM 2/3 no. 38 = San Nicolò 1951: no. 60) or the like (*ša qerbi iṭṭer*, Nbn. 375 and duplicate no. 619: *ša qerbi inandin*, Nbk. 138).

1.1.3. Self

In a number of documents a debtor stands surety for himself. This seems to be determined by the special circumstances of the contract.[39]

1.2. *Typology*[40]

There are two main types of suretyship attested in the sources. In the first, the guarantor has an obligation to produce the debtor (Germ. *Gestellungsbürgschaft*); in the second, he guarantees that the debtor will be present at the place of payment (Germ. *Stillesitzbürgschaft*).

Koschaker was of the opinion that in the neo- and Late Babylonian period suretyship guaranteed fulfilment of the legal transaction (Germ. *Erfüllungsgarantie*). The surety has an obligation to the creditor to ensure that the debtor will pay.[41]

---

results are still basic for all further investigation, even though his conclusions in respect of comparative law are no longer regarded as central. Important texts have been discussed by San Nicolò 1937 as well as Petschow 1951 and 1959. Another aspect that will not be considered here is guarantee against eviction in the neo-Babylonian documents of slave and animal sales, where the seller also gives a guarantee. See Petschow 1939: 55–79, and Koschaker 1911: 173–209.

[38] See Koschaker 1911: 87–103, 148–166, 209–236; for the Old Babylonian period, see Skaist 1994: 231–237.

[39] See the examples given by Koschaker 1911: 104–108.

[40] Generally following the results of Koschaker 1911. Regarding the problem of "debt and liability," see also Petschow 1956: 25–50.

[41] Koschaker 1911: 71. Originally there were gestures made by the body (e.g. the hands), if somebody binds himself to stand surety (analyzed by Malul 1988). In the first millennium these are only rarely mentioned (e.g. Evetts Ev.-M. no. 13 l. 13, analyzed by Koschaker 1911: 104–106). For a definition of suretyship in Roman law see Kaser 1971: 660, cited by Radner 1996: 357 and n. 1961.

2. *Pledge*

The fundamental study remains that of Petschow 1956. The documents published since do not change the picture.[42]

2.1. *Objects Pledged*[43]

2.1.1. Persons

Examples were given above of pledged male and female slaves. In addition, family members of the debtor were given, such as his wife or children, but only rarely.[44] Occasionally there are persons who give themselves as pledge.[45] *šīrkū* "oblates (of a temple)" are also mentioned in the texts as pledges. The persons given are always dependants.

2.1.2. Things

Animals and other movables are only rarely attested as pledges. Most often landed property is given (fields, gardens, houses, even if they had been leased), prebends (i.e. rights to temple income: see the Nabû-ušallam archive above). Silver and sums owing may also be pledged. Besides individual items, the debtor's entire property may be subject to a hypothecary pledge.

It is very difficult to see a relation between the amount due and the value of the pledged property. An investigation of the relative prevalence of both types is still lacking. It seems that it was dependent on the economic situation.

---

[42] The law of pledge in the Old Babylonian period was analyzed by Kienast 1978: 92–150. See also Skaist 1994: 202–230.

[43] For details see Petschow 1956: 57ff. and Index *sub* "Gegenstand des Pfandrechts" (p. 164).

[44] In the following example a debtor gives his son (*mār-šu*) as pledge:

x *kaspu šá* PN_1 *ina pān* PN_2 // *ul-tu ūmi* 1^{kam} *šá* ^{itu}x *ina* 1 *šiqli* 4–*tú ina muḫ-ḫi-šú i-rab-bi* // PN_3 *mār-šú maš-ka-nu šá* PN_1 // ^{lú}*ra-šú-ú šá-nam-ma a-na muḫ-ḫi ul i-šal-laṭ a-di* PN_1 *kasap-šú i-šal-li-mu* // (witnesses, scribe, date).

(Assurbanipal yr. 18 = 651/650; Langdon 1928: 322, 325 = San Nicolò 1951: no. 53). See also Dandamayev 1984: 137–156 (pledging of slaves), 157–180 (use of free persons and debt slavery).

[45] See Petschow 1956: 164 Index sub "Pfand/Selbstverpfändung." A characteristic late example is OECT 9 2 (re-edited by Oelsner 1995: 130–133), where a person and his family will work for 50 years in the household of their creditor.

2.2. *Nature of Pledge*

If the entire property is pledged it remains in the hands of the debtor, but the creditor has the right to take it. The same partly holds true for real estate which is given as pledge. Otherwise the pledge is put in the possession of the creditor. Examples can be seen in the archives analyzed above. Individual objects can be pledged with the right of usufruct (i.e. antichresis) or without right of use. In addition, automatically forfeitable pledge (Germ. *Verfallspfand*) is attested.[46]

The fact that forfeitable pledges in the neo- and Late Babylonian period were of minor importance led Petschow to the conclusion that the law of pledge in that period had undergone a development "von der reinen Sachhaftung zum Sicherungspfand."[47] In the private sector of the economy, suretyship seems to have been less important in this period as a means to secure loans than the various kinds of pledge.[48]

The importance of suretyship and pledge in the highly developed and complex law of the neo- and Late Babylonian period may be seen not only in the law of obligations but also in the area of litigation. That topic, however, is beyond the scope of the present study.

---

[46] See Petschow 1956: 57, 99ff. (§ 10 Generalhypothek, § 11 Das antichretische Pfand, § 12 Pfand mit Verfallvereinbarung) and *passim*.

[47] Petschow 1956: 147.

[48] Petschow 1956: 148 and n. 455 (suretyship in the temple economy).

Appendix

Some selected text examples for further study.

Seventh Century
1. UET 4 76 = Petschow 1956: 160–161, no. 3.
2. TuM 2/3 104 = San Nicolò 1951: no. 80.
3. UET 4 198 = San Nicolò 1951: no. 81.

Hellenistic Period
4. Arnaud 1987: 217–219 (L.83.6) = Oelsner 1995: 128–130.
5. OECT 9 2 = Oelsner 1995: 130–133.
6. Strassmaier 1888: 129ff. no. 13 = Oelsner 1995: 142–143.

Abbreviations

SE Seleucid era

Bibliography

Brinkman, J.A. 1972. Documents Relating to the Reign of Aššur-nādin-šumi. *Or.* 41: 245–248.

Dandamayev, M. 1984. *Slavery in Babylonia.* DeKalb: Northern Illinois University Press (translation of: Rabstvo in Babylonia. 1974. Moscow: Isdatelstvo "Nauka" [in Russian]).

Doty, T. 1978. The Archive of the Nanâ-iddin Family from Uruk, JCS 30: 65–90.

van Dijk, J. 1962. *Die Inschriftenfunde.* UVB 18. Pp. 39–61. Berlin: Gebr. Mann.

Ebeling, E. 1949. *Neubabylonische Briefe.* Abhandlungen der Bayerischen Akademie der Wissenschaften, Philosophisch-historische Klasse, Neue Folge Heft 30. München: Verlag der Bayerischen Akademie der Wissenschaften.

Haase, R. 1965. *Einführung in das Studium keilschriftlicher Rechtsquellen.* Wiesbaden: O. Harrassowitz.

Hunger, H. 1970. Das Archiv des Nabû-ušallim. *Bagh. Mitt.* 5: 193–304.

Jakob-Rost, L. 1968. Ein neubabylonisches Tontafelarchiv aus dem 7. Jahrhundert v.u.Z. *FuB* 10: 39–62.

——. 1970. Urkunden des 7. Jahrhunderts v.u.Z. aus Babylon. *FuB* 12: 49–60.

Kaser, M. 1971. *Das römische Privatrecht,* 2. Aufl. Handbuch der Altertumsw. X.3.3.–1. München: C.H. Beck.

Keßler, K. 1991. Das Archiv des Nabû-ušallim. In: *Uruk. Urkunden aus Privathäusern. Die Wohnhäuser westlich des Eanna-Bereichs, Teil 1.* Ausgrabungen in Uruk-Warka. Endberichte 8. Pp. 55–62. Mainz: Philipp von Zabern.

Kienast, B. 1978. *Die altbabylonischen Briefe und Urkunden aus Kisurra, I.* Freiburger Altorientalische Studien, 2. Wiesbaden: Steiner.

Korošec, V. 1964. *Keilschriftrecht.* Handbuch der Orientalistik, 1. Abt. Erg. bd. 3, Leiden: E.J. Brill.

Koschaker, P. 1911. *Babylonisch-assyrisches Bürgschaftsrecht.* Leipzig and Berlin: B.G. Teubner.

Langdon, S. 1928. Kandalānu and Ašurbanipal. *JRAS* 1928: 321–325.

Lanz, H. 1976. *Die neubabylonischen ḫarrânu-Geschäftsunternehmen.* Münchener Universitätsschriften. Juristische Fakultät. Abhandlungen zur rechtswissenschaftlichen Grundlagenforschung, Bd. 18. Berlin: J. Schweitzer Verlag.

Malul, M. 1988. *Studies in Mesopotamian Legal Symbolism.* AOAT 221. Kevelaer und Neukirchen-Vluyn: Verlag Butzon & Bercker/Neukirchener Verlag.

McEwan, G. 1981. *Priest and Temple in Hellenistic Babylonia.* Freiburger Altorientalische Studien, 4. Wiesbaden: Steiner.

Oelsner, J. 1971. Review of D.A. Kennedy, *Late-Babylonian Economic Texts* (CT 49) (London: British Museum 1968). *ZA* 61: 159–170.

——. 1995. Recht im hellenistischen Babylonien: Tempel—Sklaven—Schuldrecht—allgemeine Charakterisierung. In: *Legal Documents of the Hellenistic World.* Papers from a Seminar arranged by the Institute of Classical Studies, the Institute of Jewish Studies and the Warburg Institute, University of London, February to May 1986. Ed. M.J. Geller and H. Maehler in collaboration with A.D.E. Lewis. Pp. 106–148. London: The Warburg Institute, University of London.

Oppenheim, A.L. 1955. "Siege-documents" from Nippur. *Iraq* 17: 69–89.

Pedersén, O. 1998. *Archives and Libraries in the Ancient Near East 1500–300 B.C.* Bethesda: CDL Press.

Petschow, H. 1939. *Die neubabylonischen Kaufformulare.* Leipziger rechtswissenschaftliche Studien, 118. Leipzig: Verlag Theodor Weicher.

——. 1951. Ein neubabylonischer Bürgschaftsregress. *Tijdschrift voor Rechtsgeschiedenis/ Revue d'Histoire du Droit* 19: 25–57.
——. 1956. *Neubabylonisches Pfandrecht*. Abhandlungen der Sächsischen Akademie der Wissenschaften, Philologisch-historische Klasse 48, 1. Berlin: Akademie-Verlag.
——. 1959. Zum neubabylonischen Bürgschaftsrecht. ZA 53: 241–247.
——. 1976–1980. *imittu*. In: *Reallexikon der Assyriologie* 5: 68–73.
Radner, K. 1997. *Die neuassyrischen Privatrechtsurkunden*. State Archives of Assyria Studies 6. Helsinki: Helsinki University Press.
Ries, G. 1976. *Die neubabylonischen Bodenpachtformulare*. Münchener Universitätsschriften. Juristische Fakultät. Abhandlungen zur rechtswissenschaftlichen Grundlagenforschung, Bd. 16. Berlin: J. Schweitzer Verlag.
San Nicolò, M. 1937. *Zur Nachbürgschaft in den Keilschrifturkunden und den gräko-ägyptischen Papyri*. Sitzungsberichte der Bayerischen Akademie der Wissenschaften. Philosophisch-historische Abteilung, Jahrgang 1937, Heft 6. München: Verlag der Bayerischen Akademie der Wissenschaften.
——. 1938. Darlehen. In: *Reallexikon der Assyriologie* 2: 129.
——. 1951. *Babylonische Rechtsurkunden des ausgehenden 8. und des 7. Jahrhunderts v.Chr. 1. Hälfte* (Nos. 1–86). Abhandlungen der Bayerischen Akademie der Wissenschaften, Philosophisch-historische Klasse, Neue Folge Heft 34. München: Verlag der Bayerischen Akademie der Wissenschaften.
San Nicolò, M., and A. Ungnad. 1935. *Neubabylonische Rechts- und Verwaltungsurkunden*. Band I. Leipzig: J.C. Hinrichs'sche Buchhandlung.

DEMOTIC PAPYRI (664–30 BCE)[1]

Joseph Manning – Stanford University

A wise man who has a
mortgage gives service
for security
a demotic wisdom text

I. Introduction

Moses Finley, in a programmatic statement in his classic study of the ancient economy, argued that the use of accumulated capital in the Greco-Roman world took three principal forms: 1) purchase of land, 2) placing it out in short-term loans, and finally 3) placing it in a strongbox.[2] The first of these choices was the safest and the preferred one, given the ancient world's primitive economic institutions and fragmentary markets, and it was reinforced by the elite's attitude toward the use of wealth. In the predominantly agrarian economies of the ancient world, lending bridged a crucial gap between liquid capital and annual cycle of agricultural production. While Finley's great work explicitly excluded Egypt and the ancient Near East, economic institutions, if not attitudes, were much the same and I believe his rule applies equally well to the later part of ancient Egyptian history.

In the following paper I present an outline of the various security arrangements used in demotic Egyptian instruments of loan. I leave out of the discussion the law of the Greek papyri, which forms an increasingly important body of evidence for later Ptolemaic and Roman Egypt. Demotic is both a stage of the ancient Egyptian language and a script, a kind of cursive hieroglyphic which originated

---

[1] I thank Koen Donker van Heel and Hans-Albert Rupprecht as well as the editors of this volume for kindly reading and offering suggestions for improvement to this paper. Demotic texts are cited according to the system of Vleeming and Den Brinker 1993.

[2] Finley 1975 (reprinted 1999): 116.

in the Delta and spread throughout the country beginning in the seventh century BCE (in Middle Egypt by 664, in Thebes by 559 at the latest) as an instrument of political consolidation during the Saite reunification and reorganization of Egypt after the Nubian Kushite dynasty. In the south of Egypt, in particular at Thebes where we have the documentation, demotic replaced what is called, rather unfortunately I think, "Abnormal Hieratic." It was a gradual replacement of the older writing system in Egypt, although it is a phenomenon which we can follow within one family of scribes where the father wrote in the older hieratic script while his sons wrote in the new medium of demotic.[3] Demotic was originally a script for recording business and legal transactions; by the third century BCE, however, under the Ptolemies, demotic was used for a wide variety of texts, including inscriptions and literary texts.

I stress here that this study is but a brief outline—any full study of the practice of lending and the security arrangements to guarantee loans should consider the Greek papyri which record Egyptian practice, increasingly so after the third century BCE.[4] Just to be complete in this regard, an inclusion of the Aramaic papyri, and particularly of Aramaic loan words in demotic legal papyri, would also inform any thorough study since there is little doubt that there is a connection between Aramaic and demotic legal practice which would repay the effort.[5] It is important to note that while evidence is slight about lending and credit arrangements before the demotic papyri of the seventh century, lending may be traced back to the Old Kingdom.[6] Important changes in the structure of loans appear in demotic texts from the Persian period.[7] These include the stipulation that the contract was to be placed in to the hands of the creditor and that children could be taken to extinguish the debt of a parent.[8]

[3] Donker van Heel 1994; 1995: 48–71.

[4] See Rupprecht 1994: 118–21, for a survey of the Greek papyri. For studies of the law of Greek loan contracts, see Seidl 1962; 132–45; Rupprecht 1967; 1995; 1997.

[5] Porten 1986–1993; with the comments of Menu 1994 [1998]: 387. The exact relationship of demotic to Aramaic law has been hotly debated for years and it is not germane here to add to that debate.

[6] Menu 1973 [1982].

[7] Menu 1994 [1998]: 395–99, has recently published two important ostraca recording interest-free loans from the reign of Darius II which come from the Kharga oasis.

[8] "taken" in the sense that they were liable to a number of days' work to pay off the debt. So Menu 1994 [1998]: 390.

The written evidence of lending is very sketchy before the demotic material beginning in the late seventh century. The extent that lending, either of money or of grain, the two principal categories of loan in Egypt, was common we simply cannot say. Nor should we assume that lending was always documented. There is no reason, it seems to me, not to assume that there were more informal kinds of unwritten transactions, especially among lower-status individuals and within families and particular status groups. Such informal lending may have been, I believe, quite widespread and secured merely by personal reputation or by dint of a family's goodwill. To be sure, such goodwill played a part in some loans which were late in being paid back or were uncollectable.[9] As always with the demotic legal documentation, one must ask whether it documented the norm. Another point to consider, of course, is the survival of the evidence. Much of the published demotic material has been preserved in the form of private archives, archives that tended to preserve important family papers. Such documents as marriage contracts and land sales were regarded as crucial to preserve because they protected long-term property interests. Documents such as sales of animals and short term loan contracts would have been less likely to survive in family archives, given their more ephemeral importance, so any reckoning of the amount of transactions inferred from the surviving evidence is doomed to be an inaccurate reflection of the economic situation.

II. Terms Used in Loan Contracts

The demotic term for a legal instrument of loan was *sẖ n rʿ-wḫꜣ*, which may be translated "document of claim."[10] Thus in the conception of demotic law, a loan contract established a claim for the creditor against the debtor which was returned to the debtor upon the extinction of the debt. This claim is recorded in the loan agreement by the acknowledgement of the debtor:

wn mtw = k ḥḏ qt 9 r sttr 4 1/2
r ḥd qt 9 ʿn ỉỉr-n = y (n) rn n ḥḏ r-
dỉt = k n = y

---

[9] Pestman 1971: 21.
[10] Pierce 1972: 44–50; Pestman 1982: 93; Martin 1986: 170–71, n. 15.

> You have nine silver kite, making 4 1/2 staters,
> making nine silver kite still, against me, in the
> "name" of the money which you have given me.[11]

Several terms were used to connote the interest on the loan. These terms were *ḥw*, lit., "addition," or *ms.t*, formed from the demotic *ms* (Coptic ⲘⲎⲤⲈ) "to give birth." The phrase used in some loan contracts to express the notion of "principal + interest" was *ḏ3ḏ3 r ms.t*, lit., "head in addition to interest."[12] The word *šmw*, lit., "harvest tax" was used in loans in kind in which the "interest" or the payment in grain paid at the time of loan repayment was not included in the principal.[13]

By "security" I mean the use of personal property which served to guarantee to the creditor that the principal sum will be repaid. In earlier Egyptian practice, loans were normally secured through an oath taken in the name of a local deity by the debtor to repay the loan or be liable to beating and a fine of twice the borrowed amount. Third party security *may* have been used occasionally as a personal guarantee for a debtor and pledges, and "real securities," may also have been used.[14] In one text from the Ramesside period, a man took out a loan and promised:

> I will repay you for it (a jar of fat) in barley
> through the agency of this brother of mine after
> whom one has the right to pursue to unbind
> my obligation.[15]

In the small village world that was much of Egypt for most of its history, such a third party was no doubt known to both parties and his guarantee would be based upon his good "credit," his status as an upright person whose reputation was beyond reproach. Here "brother" no doubt meant "colleague" or "business associate." In demotic texts, third party guarantors who accepted liability for the performance of the debtor were indicated by the term "accept the hand" (*šp dr.t*) of the debtor.[16] The term for security in demotic

[11] P. BM Glanville 10525, 1 (284 BCE, Thebes).
[12] Erichsen 1954: 673.
[13] See the summary by Vandorpe 1998.
[14] Théodoridès 1971: 316.
[15] Ostracon Oriental Institute 12073. Cited by Théodoridès 1971: 315–16. Republished with further literature cited by Manning et al. 1989. Additional comments on this text in McDowell 1990: 180–82, Allam 1973: 73–76.
[16] Coptic ϢⲠ̄-ⲦⲰⲢⲈ, Crum 1939: 425a–b; Sethe and Partsch 1920: 70, 496–515.

Egyptian was *ỉwy.t*, and has been derived from an earlier word *ỉwꜣ* found in a papyrus from the New Kingdom.[17] In that text (P. Mayer A), which records an investigation of the robbery of the royal tombs in the Valley of the Kings during Dynasty 20, a slave was brought before the investigative commission and forced under torture to answer questions about one of the accused robbers, a brother-in-law, who had not been captured.

> Fourth month of summer day 17. Taking the testimony of the rest of the tomb robbers. Amun-khaw, son of Soped-mose, an ergastulum slave, was brought. He was brought as a *ỉwꜣ* for Pawero, son of Kaka. He was examined by beating. Making a twisting of his feet and hands. The oath-by-the-king, life, prosperity, health, was administered to him, not to speak falsehood. His statement was heard. The magistrates said, "As for the brother of his wife, don't bring him for him." He was dismissed and set at liberty.[18]

It was determined that this slave could not serve as a *ỉ wꜣ*, "hostage" to bring the accused to justice because he was not closely related to him. Thus the origin of the term is found in legal contexts where persons were seized as "pledges," made to stand in for another party's liability. The classical Egyptian word is related to the verbal root *ỉwꜣ* which means "to seize, take away." Thus it may be possible to posit an evolution at least in terms of the etymology of the word (and perhaps in terms of legal sophistication in the legal instruments involved), from physical substitution to pledge, which could take many forms. Any real model of this development, of course, is hampered by the fact that the evidence from earlier Egyptian legal history is meager in the extreme.

III. Types of Loans and the Development of Legal Clauses[19]

Documents of loan in demotic Egyptian are, along with the lease and sale of land, easily among the most common texts and the practice of lending was probably widespread in the later periods of

[17] Gardiner 1952: 111. See the discussion of the passage and other early examples of the term in Pierce 1972: 130–32.

[18] P. Mayer A, 3.7–9.

[19] Taubenschlag 1955; Pestman 1971; Vleeming 1991: 156–88; Donker Van Heel 1995: 229–35.

Egyptian history.[20] Loan transactions and the use of various security clauses are no doubt the most complex area of demotic law. Loan documents are unilateral real contracts which compel the borrower to restore to the creditor a thing borrowed within a fixed period of time.[21] The texts show a wide variety of terms for repayment and, as is the case in other types of demotic contract, the surface form of loan disguised other types of transactions.[22] For example, in loans secured by conditional sales, discussed below, if we had only the sale text, we would not know if the agreement was a real or a conditional sale.

Demotic loans fall into two broad categories, namely loans of money, and loans in kind, principally grain and, later, wine as well. In loans of money, the rate of interest is usually not specified. Some loans, between a father and son for example, may not have carried real interest. But since it is assumed that money had a cost, it is thought that the interest was simply included as a lump sum and listed together with the borrowed amount.[23] This is sometimes expressed by the phrase: *pꜣy = w ḥw ẖn = w*, "their addition is in them."[24] In some cases in early Demotic texts, the interest rate is specified and it is almost always quite high, 50 or 100 percent.[25] Bocchoris' reforms in the late eighth century BCE established a limit on the maximum collectable principal plus interest at twice the borrowed amount.[26] In the Ptolemaic period, the interest rate was reduced by government decree to a maximum of an annualized rate of 24 percent.[27] In certain cases, it appears that the payment ("addition," i.e. "interest") for seed loans in the Greek garrison town of Pathyris in Upper Egypt was not fixed at the time of the loan but was, rather, dependent on the crop yield at the time of the harvest.[28]

---

[20] See, for example, the register of loans from the village of Tebtunis in the Fayyum from the years 42–47 CE which records 369 loans. Cited in Pestman 1971: 28.

[21] Cf. Menu 1994 [1998]: 388–89.

[22] These include sale with deferred delivery.

[23] See Vandorpe 1998.

[24] Menu 1972 [1982]: 305–06.

[25] Loans at interest are first attested in Egypt during the New Kingdom and come from the artisan village of Deir el-Medina on the west bank of Thebes. In these loans, the normal interest rate paid was 50%. See further Menu 1994 [1998]: 389.

[26] Diod. Sic. I, 79.

[27] Mentioned in the petition P. Col. Zenon II 83 (245/244 BCE), cited by Seidl 1962: 135.

[28] See the detailed discussion of such loans in Vandorpe 1998: 1468.

Demotic texts are silent about the purpose behind loans. Most of them were probably either for one-time expenses, loans taken out for celebrations such as marriage and the like, or were loans taken out in anticipation of the new agricultural year or at the time of harvest. There may have been cases, however, where individuals were forced to borrow in order to live.[29] For the most part, the loans were generally small amounts of money or grain. There are some private archives from the Ptolemaic period which suggest that there were individuals who were engaged in the business of lending, probably not as a profession but as a result of having surplus capital. We do hear, however, of professional moneylending as well, at least in the Roman period.[30]

Demotic loans show a change in the contract language from Abnormal Hieratic texts which may well only reflect a difference in legal custom between the Delta and Upper Egypt.[31] In the Abnormal Hieratic texts, the loan contract begins with an acknowledgment of the debtor that he is in receipt of a certain commodity: "I have received X from you." In Early demotic loans, the contract opens: "You have X with me" or "You have given to me X." This latter clause is the standard acknowledgment of debt in Ptolemaic demotic texts as well and is similar to the acknowledgments of debt in the Greek papyri.[32]

Loans in the context of marriage agreements

One special category of loan which I will not treat here in depth consists of the items brought into the husband's house by the woman at the beginning of a marriage. These personal goods of a woman were considered to be deposits rather than loans since they could theoretically be claimed back at any time.[33] They were listed on a

[29] Such was thought to be the case of the soldier Dionysios son of Kephalas in Pathyris at the end of the second century BCE, who took out at least twenty loans over the course of a ten-year period. See further Pestman 1982. Recently Lewis 1983; 1986, has offered a radically different interpretation of this evidence.

[30] Schnebel 1933.

[31] There are clear differences in the contract language between texts from the Fayyum and texts from Upper Egypt. On the changes in phraseology between Abnormal Hieratic and demotic see Menu 1988.

[32] Seidl 1962: 133; Rupprecht 1967; Pierce 1972: Chapter five.

[33] Depauw 1997: 147.

separate sheet of papyrus as part of a certain type of marriage agreement and available to the husband for use. The husband promised to return these items or give an equivalent upon divorce, the whole agreement being secured by the entirety of the husband's property. In other types of loan arrangements, more specific security was used. It may be posited that the function of specific security was to guarantee loans to parties less well known to the lender, whereas loans within families could be secured by social pressure. In any case, this kind of arrangement is specific to the law of marriage.

IV. Types of Security

As in other systems of law, the use of security in loan agreements served as a means to satisfy the creditor that he will be repaid even if the debtor defaults on the loan itself. Demotic legal papyri show a variety of security arrangements ranging from third party guarantees to binding debtors to creditors by oath to the use of deposit and conditional sale contracts, liens and mortgages. Legal clauses of security were both embedded within loan contracts and written on separate instruments. I leave out of the discussion here the use of security in other legal contracts such as sale and lease and in the so-called "Cautionnements" or "Bürgschaftsurkunden" texts of the Ptolemaic period. These latter texts were third party guarantees of payment of a debt incurred in the operation of a monopoly, in tax farming, in some types of leases and performance bonds to guarantee that a worker in state business will appear in a specified place and do the work. All of these documents are attested within the limits of the third century and are a product of the Ptolemaic government's strategy of insulating itself from risk while trying to maximize revenues.[34] These documents are of the "double document" type written in epistolary style and are clearly a Ptolemaic administrative adoption of the old Egyptian legal tradition of third party guarantee.

The securing of loans falls into a few basic categories: 1) the conveyance or deposit of one or more items of value to the creditor in exchange for a sum of money or an amount of a commodity (this comes close to our modern institution of pawn); 2) The conveyance of a legal instrument as security; 3) the conditional conveyance of

[34] Sethe and Partsch 1920; DeCenival 1973; Depauw 1997: 137–38.

property ripening into real conveyance on default by the debtor. The last two are close variants. The difference, it seems, is that while in type 2 a legal instrument was conveyed to the creditor, in type 3 the legal instruments were not so conveyed.

In the first type of security, the use of a pledge or deposit, a specific item was turned over to the creditor at the time of the loan. Additionally, a separate document may have been drawn up in order to establish the rights of the creditor that served as evidence to legally claim the pledge:

> This *ʿrʿr*[35] together with this instrument which I have given to you are security for 16 artabae of wheat of regnal year 13; and I shall give you 32 artabae of wheat in the second month of summer of regnal year 14. If I do not give them to you by the above term, [then I am far from you with respect to this *ʿr*]*ʿr* together with this instrument which I have given to you as security (*ỉwy.t*).[36]

To the extent that it can be determined, there were no receipts issued for the debtor; the return of the pledge was a condition of repayment.[37] In at least one published example of a loan of grain, the creditor wrote at the end of the agreement that he had no claim on the debtor with respect to the loan agreement that the debtor had drawn up.[38] The debt had apparently been paid, the creditor acknowledges so and returns the loan agreement to the debtor. The legal agreements, of course, do not tell us anything about the interrelationship of repayment and reconveyance of the pledge. As in other private legal agreements in demotic, the transaction was oral and was witnessed by several persons whose names were recorded in the contract. Ultimately any breach would have been enforced by the mores of the local community and the social pressure of the witnesses. In certain cases, the creditor asked for deposits with a

---

[35] Clearly an object of value, written with a wood determinative. It appears to be related to a noun meaning "basket, measure of grain."

[36] P. dem. Adler 10, (102/101 BCE, Gebelein) Cited by Pierce 1972: 110.

[37] So Pierce 1972: 111.

[38] P. Philad. 16744 (96 BCE, Gebelein). The editor of the text, Chesire 1977, was uncertain why the text had two dating clauses, one at the beginning of the acknowledgement of debt, the other at the foot of the text, written after the creditor's statement. But the two dates must be tied to two separate statements, one the acknowledgement of debt by the debtor, the other, the removal of any claim by the creditor.

value higher than the loan amount. In these cases, a receipt *may* have been issued to the debtor but none of these receipts have survived.[39] In more complex loan agreements, however, disputes occurred when partial repayment of a loan triggered a demand for return of one of the pledges used to secure the loan. In this case it is clear that the pledges had been transferred at the time of the loan and indeed in most cases the pledge(s) remained with the debtor.[40] In early demotic cases, the creditor had a choice of pledges which he thought would extinguish the debt:

> . . . and you will take them [to you] because
> of them (scil. the money and interest)
> till [you have filled them with the
> above money and their interest].[41]

In the second type, the pledge took the form of a legal document, specifically, that of sale and withdrawal documents. In a typical demotic instrument of sale, there were two important legal sections, the acknowledgement of receipt of a sale price, and a quit-claim that the new owner had exclusive, unencumbered legal right to the property in question. The transaction required the use of specific clauses acknowledging the receipt of the satisfactory price for the item, the seller guaranteed to the buyer that they are the exclusive owner of the transferred item, all title deeds were conveyed to the new owner, and if any third party were to come against the buyer, the seller promised to repel them and swear an oath if necessary. In addition, the seller stated that he/she is "far" from the new owner with respect to any rights to the item being sold. In early demotic papyri, all of these legal clauses were incorporated in one text; in the Ptolemaic period, sale transactions had two separate documents, a "sale" (*sẖ n-ḏbꜣ ḥḏ*) and a "withdrawal" (*sẖ n wy*) and both of the texts had to be drawn up to effect a real sale.[42] These sale instruments served as legal title to the property, and at the time of sale all such documents drawn up concerning the property in the past were also con-

[39] Pierce 1972: 111.

[40] Donker van Heel 1995: 234. In the penalty clause of one early demotic loan, the debtor declares: "If I fail to give it to you (i.e. repay the loan) together with its interest, [you] have a claim on all the pledges that you want from me all, all."

[41] P. Loeb 48 + 49A (487 BCE, Hou) discussed in Vleeming 1991: 156–77.

[42] Depauw 1997: 140–43 with bibliography.

veyed to the new owner. It is apparent that a legal instrument of sale could be used to secure a loan.

In one complicated transaction documented in a papyrus from the early first century, a pledgee (Montemhet) acknowledged the receipt of several objects as a pledge. The man who made the pledge (Nechtmonthes) had agreed to redeem the pledged objects by a specified time (within about forty days).[43] The pledgee was required to maintain the value of the pledge during the time of the deposit ("The thing which will be missing from them . . . you will replace it."). If the pledgor redeemed the pledges, the pledgee was required to return the objects or an equivalent value in money. A document for the sale of priestly offices (consisting of in fact two sales recorded on the same sheet of papyrus) in which the pledgee was the seller and the pledgor was the buyer was also used as additional security for the redemption of the pledge.[44] In effect, the man giving the pledges became the purchaser of the emoluments if he failed to redeem his pledges by the specified time. What is not mentioned in the agreement, but in fact must have been a crucial aspect of the transaction, was a loan of money from pledgee to pledgor. In effect this borrowed capital would become the purchase price for the priestly offices.

[43] P. Berlin 3108 (98 BCE, Thebes[Djeme?]; = P. Survey 72), cited by Pierce 1972: 112–13. The fullest account of the text is to be found in Pestman 1993: 221–23. The objects on loan were apparently made of metal, although the readings of these words remains problematic. Among the objects was an *ʿkr*, a metal object of some kind (Erichsen: 1954, 74; Seidl: 1962, 138). Some scholars have suggested that the term *ʿkr* was a technical term that meant deposit, related to Semitic *ꜣkr*. But this has been rightly rejected by both Seidl and Pestman. The body of the text begins: *iw gm wʿ ʿkr r-ḥr = y iw = f ir sttr 9.t* . . . and translated by Pestman: "There are to be found in my keeping one *ʿkr*-vessel, which makes 9 staters, two *ʿš*-vases (ovens?) . . ." The opening here is difficult grammatically. I myself do not see, as Pestman 1993: 223 does, how *iw gm* . . . *r-ḥr = y* . . . can be the functional equivalent of *wn mtw = k* . . . *i͗ir-n = y*. *r-ḥr = y* ought to mean "against me" rather than "in my possession," which should be written *n-dr.t = y*. But without access to a photograph, I accept Pestman's provisional remarks and would hope to revisit this interesting text at some later date. I owe special thanks to Richard Jasnow who reviewed this difficult text with me.

[44] These instruments of sale are P. Berlin 3106 and P. Berlin 3139 (= P. Survey 70 + 71).

Montemhet ← Nechtmonthes

objects of value

conditional seller of emoluments → conditional buyer of emoluments

loan of money?

Fig. 1. The transaction of P. Berlin 3108.

The pledges to perform on the loan in this case were objects of value and legal instruments, conditional purchases, and in demotic this required the drawing up of sale document, a "document in exchange for money" (*sẖ n-ḏb³ ḥḏ*), which acknowledged that the seller had received the satisfactory price for the item(s) being sold, that the item sold was now in the possession of the buyer, that he will expel any third party claim to the property, that all other documents relating to the item are transferred to the buyer. Presumably, upon default of the loan, the "debtor" pledgor would be forced to draw up documents of withdrawal to complete the sale. Thus the "debtor" offered a promise of purchase as well as giving real security in the form of a deposit, creating in effect a cash lien, in exchange for a loan.

Similar to this second type of security was the surrender of title deeds to secure debt, creating a lien against the debtor's property. Title deeds were the records of sale and withdrawal of a piece of property which prove free and clear title to the property. At the time of a real sale the vendor was required to hand over to the purchaser all such "old and new documents" which proved clear title and the absence of any contingent private interest in the property.[45] In the case of a split title to property, the owner probably kept all of the previous documentation.

A conditional or suspended sale, that is, a debtor's promise to sell a specified piece of property in case of default, was another method of securing a loan. In this type of text, the debtor acknowledged the debt and promised to repay the debt by a fixed date. The document then continued with a conditional sentence: "If I do not repay

[45] The fundamental study is again that of Pestman 1983.

you by X date, you have satisfied my heart with the purchase price [of the pledged property]." The rest of the text is the standard language of the demotic sale contract:

> You have three (deben) of money, that is,
> fifteen staters, that is three (deben) of money
> still, against us, in the name of the money
> that you have given us. We will give it to
> you, up to year 26, the second month of *šmw*
> season, the last day (i.e. one month later).
> If we do not give it to you up to year 26,
> second month of *šmw* season, last day, you
> have caused our hearts to agree to the price
> of the house of the woman Taminis daughter of
> Phagonis . . . We have given it to you, it is yours . . .
> your house it is . . . No one, ourselves included,
> shall be able to exercise authority over it,
> except you, from today on, yours are its
> legal documents and title deeds, wherever they are . . .[46]

As Pestman has pointed out, the legal manual from Hermopolis (P. Mattha) in Upper Egypt, aids in our understanding of the Egyptian law on this point.[47] A hypothetical case is described in which a debtor has pledged a house by a conditional sale in order to secure a loan. The debtor subsequently sold his house to a third party. It is clear from the passage cited in the manual that clear title would pass to the new owner unless the creditor in the loan agreement objects by a process known in Egyptian law as "making a public protest" (*ỉr šʿr*). The title deeds must therefore have been kept by the debtor until the sale of the pledged house and the practice of conveying deeds through ὑπάλλαγμα was an Alexandrian and not an "Egyptian practice."[48]

Since these were conditional sales, a sales tax had to be paid but at a lower rate from the standard sales tax.[49] If the debtor defaulted, as was the case in P. Hauswaldt 18,[50] she had to draw up a document of withdrawal to complete the sale of the pledged property, in

[46] P. Philad. 15 (259 BCE, Thebes), 2–4, cited by Pestman 1983: 296–97.
[47] Pestman 1985: 300–01. For an updated edition of the manual, see Donker van Heel 1990.
[48] As claimed by Taubenschlag 1955: 275.
[49] The evidence for this sales tax comes from Greek dockets, is late and rather thin. See Pierce 1972: 114.
[50] 211 BCE, Edfu; Manning 1997: 170–79.

this case five plots of land.[51] As far as I know, pledged land was not posted as such, as was the case, for example, with the Greek *horoi*.[52] But such contracts were very likely registered in daybooks in the local notary office.[53] Successful repayment of the loan on time would have required the creditor to return the conditional sale text crossed out. There is no language in these conditional sales which provided for execution against the debtor's property and we therefore do not know how successful this kind of pledge was and what happened in the case of the refusal of the debtor to execute a withdrawal contract.

A problem of considerable significance regarding the execution or the conveyance of pledges is the question of the conveyance of the title in order to secure a loan by suspended sale. We are often at the mercy of vague language and incomplete records in many legal questions in demotic law, and so it is with the mention of security. A text from the second century would seem to provide the creditor with a right of claim against a debtor's property:

> I have given to you my house . . . as security for it (the debt) until I have paid it to you by the above term. If I do not pay it to you, you have a claim upon me to make for you an instrument of sale for my house, which is (specified) above, in the month after the month in question, necessarily (and) without delay.[54]

As Pierce points out, the interpretation turns on what the meaning of "give" is. According to the language of the contract here, there had not been a legal conveyance of the house. Was the debtor temporarily prevented from conveying the house used as a pledge until the loan was repaid? Or did the debtor give the right of inhabitation to the creditor during the length of the loan as a form of interest? As in other cases of "incomplete" conveyance to secure a loan, the creditor is vulnerable.

To solve this problem and to protect both debtor and creditor, Egyptian law developed an institution of trusteeship. In lieu of a

---

[51] More examples of this kind of arrangement are cited by Seidl 1962: 138, n. 3.

[52] Finley 1952.

[53] For one such text, see de Cenival 1987.

[54] P. BM 10425, 10–14, Second Century BCE. Cited and translated by Pierce 1972: 115.

debtor handing over title deeds to his creditor to secure a loan, a "letter of agreement" (*šʿ.t n hn*) could be drawn up by a notary before a third party "trustee" (*ʿrbṯ*).[55] In such an agreement, the debtor handed a deed to the third party in trust. If the debt was repaid on time, the trustee returned the deed to the debtor. If, however, the debtor defaulted on the loan, the trustee was obliged to convey the title deed to the creditor and the debtor had to forfeit any claim to the property whose title deed was conveyed to the creditor. In specific instances when we can be certain of the transaction involved, the title deeds which served as security were a sale (*sẖ n-ḏbꜣ ḥḏ*) and a cession (*sẖ n wy*) document, in effect, then, a real sale put into the hands of a third party. The sale was made complete by the conveyance of the title deeds to the creditor and the payment of the five per cent sales tax, a tax which had to be paid by the purchaser, or in this case the creditor, under the Ptolemaic regime.[56] In terms of the historical evolution of demotic security, this last type comes closest to a mortgage in that it was a real conveyance of property, but it was not fully so since there would not have been a real conveyance because it was only with the satisfactory payment of the transfer tax that a sale became effective. Mortgages *sensu stricto* took on a distinct and complex form and all texts of this type date to the early Roman period (first century CE).[57]

On the right side of this type of instrument a Greek text recording an acknowledgment of loan was written. On the top left hand side a demotic instrument of sale was recorded and to the left of this, the instrument of cession.[58] Below the demotic instruments a Greek sale text was written.[59] The debtor in the loan agreement was the seller in the sale and the sale took effect immediately. This kind of complex transaction may have occurred in the Ptolemaic period using separate documents, a Greek loan, a demotic sale to secure the loan and a cession of the property written out upon default.[60]

[55] Pierce 1972: 116–19. On *ʿrbt*, see Darnell 1990.

[56] On this *enkuklion* tax, see Pestman 1978; 1993: 353–59; Vleeming 1992.

[57] Pierce 1972: 119–21; Taubenschlag 1955: 272.

[58] In demotic real sales where both the sale and the cession document were written on the same day, the cession instrument was always written to the left of the sale.

[59] On the relationship of the Greek and demotic texts, see Pestman 1985.

[60] P. dem. Adler 15 and 20. The demotic sale is missing. See the discussion by Pierce 1972: 120–21.

In both these cases, what distinguishes this kind of arrangement from demotic conditional sales is the right of execution established for the creditor in the Greek loan text. As for execution, we must speculate as to the options open to the creditor. It may have been the case—the texts themselves are of no help here—that the creditor could accept the conveyance of the property to satisfy the debt or lay a claim to the whole of the debtor's property. Some forms of Greek security from the Roman period (ὑπάλλαγμα) offer this option, a right of execution against all of the debtor's property, and we have seen this in the early demotic loans as well.

Indeed this general liability of the debtor was in fact the usual way to secure debt in demotic agreements. This "paragraph of general security," as Pierce termed it, took the following form to secure loans and other agreements such as marriage contracts:

> All that is mine together with everything that I shall acquire is the security for the right of the instrument which is above.[61]

General security clauses in earlier demotic are more explicit in listing just what the options were:

> He shall have claim against me for the securities desired from me, each and every one, grain, land, male slave, female slave, cow, ass, silver, copper, clothing, oil, everything in the world that is mine; and he shall take them on account of it (scil. the debt) until he has recovered his money which is (specified) above together with its accumulated interest.[62]

While general execution against a debtor's property was at least a theoretical option in demotic law, execution against a person, and the extent of this option against heirs and other sureties for private debt is a problematic area of demotic securities. Whatever the veracity of Diodorus' statement that Bocchoris forbade debt slavery, it definitely existed in certain early demotic texts, although it never apparently involved the debtor himself.[63] In lists of property used to secure a pledge, the phrase "son or daughter" was added as a pos-

---

[61] P Lrookl. Pierce 1 (108 BCE, Memphis), 24–25, cited by Pierce 1972: 124.

[62] P. Berl. 3110 (= Malinine: 1953, text 5; 498 BCE), 7–8 cited by Pierce 1972: 126.

[63] Diod. Sic. I.79.

sible pledge. In Ptolemaic Egypt, personal execution is certainly attested for non-payment of debts to the Crown.[64] A Greek text from the mid-third century appears to confirm that this method of gaining satisfaction from a debt was re-instituted by the Ptolemies.[65] The question of the extent of the debtor's liability is raised by the general execution clause:

> This money which is (specified) above together with its accumulated interest will be on my head together with (those of) my children.[66]

Several interpretations of this clause have been offered. Some have suggested that the clause served as a means to ensure that the debt would continue past the debtor's death; others that it assured that the debtor and his heirs and perhaps any surety of his were generally liable for the debt; still others that it meant that heirs assumed responsibility for the debts. Pierce has concluded, based on the location of this clause just before the clause of general security of the debtor's property, that the clause established "liability of the debtor and of his sureties."[67] And finally, Vleeming has suggested the possibility that the clause served to prevent heirs from raising any objections to selling property to which they had a claim based on the right of inheritance in order to settle a debt.[68]

V. Conclusions

This paper has sketched demotic instruments of loan and the security of loans. It is far from comprehensive. Indeed, a comprehensive study of demotic loans and the social context of lending remain *desiderata.* In a country where liquid assets were lacking, lending would have served an important economic and social function. We do not often hear of problems in debt recovery, but it is safe to assume that it was a difficult business. In his study, Pierce concluded that

[64] The early demotic texts were discussed by Vleeming 1991: 173.
[65] P. Hibeh I, 34 (243/242 BCE)—a petition to the king concerning improper procedures arising from an illegal seizure of a donkey and subsequent imprisonment of the accused.
[66] P. dem. Berlin 3110 (498 BCE), 9 cited by Pierce 1972: 128.
[67] Pierce 1972: 129.
[68] Vleeming 1991: 171.

an evolution may be traced in demotic instruments from a promise to convey property in case of default to conditional and then absolute conveyance. These stages of conveyance may be documented, in the Ptolemaic and Roman periods, using the evidence of payment of the sales tax, from a promise to a written contract. Promises to convey of course carried no obligation to pay a sales tax. Conditional sales required a two percent tax, mortgages the full five percent tax.

The use of security in demotic Egyptian loan contracts took many forms. An evolution in the means used to secure loans *may* have occurred from the use of personal security to the use of more sophisticated legal instruments of contract. Whatever the means, though, the lack of enforcement of private agreements had always been a fundamental weakness in Egyptian law. I have not discussed the institution of lending in its economic history context and I have not been able to treat here the extent of lending markets in Egypt but this might reward further study and indeed one might suggest that as the economy became increasingly monetized after the fourth century BCE, money lending increased concomitantly. In Roman Egypt, most loans were transacted on a cash basis.[69]

Several problems, of course, remain. One of these is in the valuation of pledges. How was it determined how much land to pledge as security for a fixed money loan? Given the fragmentary markets, a plot may not have brought the desired amount to cover a bad loan, although if the land were kept by the creditor and made productive, one presumes that creditors got a good deal in non-performing loans secured by land. Loans never specified the value or the quality of the land under pledge.

[69] Foraboschi & Gara 1982.

BIBLIOGRAPHY

Allam, S. 1973. *Hieratische Ostraka und Papyri aus der Ramessidenzeit*. Tübingen: Im Selbstverlag des Herausgebers.

Cheshire, W. 1977. A new demotic loan from Gebelein. *Enchoria* 7: 51–54, pl. 9.

Darnell, J.C. 1990. A note on *ʿrb.t* (and *ꜣrb*/ⲁⲣⲏⲃ). *Enchoria* 17: 83–87.

De Cenival, F. 1987. Répertoire journalier d'un bureau de notaire de l'époque ptolémäique en démotique (P. dém. Lille 120). *Enchoria* 15: 1–9, pl. 1.

——. 1973. *Cautionnements démotiques du début de l'époque ptolémaïque (P. dém. Lille 34 à 96)*. Paris: Société d'Histoire du Droit. Collection d'histoire institutionelle et sociale.

Depauw, M. 1997. *A Companion to Demotic Studies*. Papyrologica Bruxellensia 28. Brussels: Fondation égyptologique Reine Élisabeth.

Donker van Heel, K. 1995. *Abnormal Hieratic and Early Demotic Texts Collected by the Theban Choachytes in the Reign of Amasis. Papyri from the Louvre Eisenlohr Lot*. Ph.D. diss., University of Leiden.

——. 1994. The lost battle of Peteamonip son of Petehorresne. In *Acta Demotica: Acts of the Fifth International Conference for Demotic Studies. Pisa, 4th–8th September 1993. Egitto e Vicino Oriente* 17: 115–24.

——. 1990. *The Legal Manual of Hermopolis*. Text and translation. Leiden: Papyrologisch Instituut.

Erichsen, W. 1954. *Demotisches Glossar*. Copenhagen: Ejnar Munksgaard.

Finley, M.I. 1975. *The Ancient Economy*. Berkeley: The University of California. Reprinted with a new foreword by Ian Morris, 1999.

Foraboschi, A., and A. Gara. 1982. L'economia dei crediti in natura (Egitto). *Athenaeum* 70: 69–83.

Gardiner, A.H. 1952. A Word for 'Representative', 'Substitute', or the Like. *Journal of Egyptian Archaeology* 37: 111.

Macdowell, A. 1990. *Jurisdiction in the Workmen's Community of Deir el-Medina*. Leiden: Nederlands Instituut voor het Nabije Oosten.

Malinine, M. 1953. *Choix de textes juridiques en hiératique <anormal> et en démotique*. Paris: Librairie ancienne Honoré Champion.

Manning, J.G. 1997. *The Hauswaldt Papyri. A Third Century Family Dossier from Edfu, Upper Egypt*. Würzburg: Gisela Zauzich Verlag.

Martin, C.J. 1986. A demotic lease from Philadelphia: P. BM 10560. *Journal of Egyptian Archaeology* 72: 159–73.

Menu, B. 1982. Le prêt en droit egyptien ancien (Nouvel Empire et Basse Époque). *CRIPEL* 1 (1973) 61–141. Reprinted in *Recherches sur l'histoire juridique, économique et sociale de l'ancienne Égypte*. Pp. 217–300. Versailles: Bernadette Menu.

——. 1988. Les actes de vente en Égypte ancienne, particulièrement sous les rois Kouchites et Saïtes. *Journal of Egyptian Archaeology* 74: 165–81.

——. 1998. Modalités et réglementation du prêt en Égypte à l'époque de la première domination Perse. In *Colloque international de l'ASPEP*. Paris, 1994. Reprinted in *Recherches sur l'histoire juridique, économique et sociale de l'ancienne Égypte*, vol. 2. Bibliothèque d'Études, vol. 122. Pp. 385–99. Cairo: IFAO.

Pestman, P.W. 1993. *The archive of the Theban Choachytes (Second Century B.C.). A survey of the demotic and Greek papyri contained in the archive*. Leuven: Peeters.

——. 1985. Registration of demotic contracts in Egypt. P. Par. 65; 2nd cent. B.C. In *Satura Roberto Feenstra*, ed. J.A. Ankum, J.E. Spruit, F.B.J. Wubbe. Pp. 17–25. Fribourg: University Press.

——. 1983. Some aspects of Egyptian law in Graeco-Roman Egypt. Title-deeds

and ὑπάλλαγμα. In *Egypt and the Hellenistic World*. Pp. 281–302. Studia Hellenistica, vol. 27. Leuven:
——. 1982. *Les Archives privées de Dionysios, fils de Kephalas*. Papyrologica Lugduno-Batava, vol. 22. Leiden: E.J. Brill.
——. 1978. L'impôt-ἐγκυκλιον à Pathyris et à Krokodilopolis (2ème–1er siècle av. J.-C.). In *Textes grecs, démotiques et bilingues*. Pp. 214–22. Papyrologica Lugduno-Batava, vol. 19. Leiden: E.J. Brill.
——. 1971. Loans bearing no interest? *Journal of Juristic Papyrology* 16/17: 7–29.
Pierce, R.H. 1972. Securities in the Demotic Papyri. In *Three Demotic Papyri in the Brooklyn Museum. A Contribution to the Study of Contracts and their Instruments in Ptolemaic Egypt*. Chapter 6, pp. 110–32. Symbolae Osloenses, Supplet. 24. Oslo: Universitetsforlaget.
Rupprecht, H.-A. 1997. Veräusserungsverbot und Gewährleistung in pfandrechtlichen Geschäften. In *Akten des 21. Internationalen Papyrologenkongresses Berlin, 13.–19.8.1995*. Vol. 2. Pp. 870–80. Leipzig: Teubner.
——. 1995. Zwangsvollstreckung und dingliche Sicherung in den Papyri der ptolemäischen und römischen Zeit. *Symposion*: 291–302.
——. 1995. Die dinglichen Sicherungsrechte nach der Praxis der Papyri. Eine Übersicht über den urkundlichen Befund. In *Collatio Iuris Romani. Études dédiées à Hans Ankum à l'occasion de son 65. Anniversaire*, ed. R. Feenstra et al. Vol. 2. Pp. 425–36. Amsterdam: J.C. Gieben.
——. 1994. *Kleine Einführung in die Papyruskunde*. Darmstadt: Wissenschaftliche Buchgesellschaft.
——. 1967. *Untersuchungen zum Darlehen im Recht der Graeco-Aegyptischen Papyri der Ptolermäerzeit*. Munich: C.H. Beck'sche Verlagsbuchhandlung.
Schnebel, M. 1933. Die Geschäfte des Γάιος ἰούλιος φίλιος. *Aegyptus* 13: 35–41.
Seidl, E. 1962. *Ptolemäische Rechtsgeschichte*. Ägyptologische Forschungen, vol. 22. Glückstadt: J.J. Augustin.
Sethe, K., and J. Partsch 1920. *Demotische Urkunden zum ägyptischen Bürgschaftsrechte vorzüglich der Ptolemäerzeit*. Abhandlungen der philologisch-historischen Klasse der Sächsischen Akademie der Wissenschaften 32. Leipzig: B.G. Teubner.
Taubenschlag, R. 1955. *The Law of Greco-Roman Egypt in the Light of the Papyri, 332 B.C.–640 A.D.* 2d. ed. Warsaw: Panstwowe wydawnictwo naukowe.
Théodoridès, A. 1971. The Concept of Law in Ancient Egypt. In *The legacy of Egypt*, ed. J.R. Harris. 2d. ed. Pp. 291–322. Oxford: Clarendon Press.
Vandorpe, K. 1998. Interest in Ptolemaic Loans of Seed-corn in the 'House of Hathor' (Pathyris). In *Egyptian Religion. The last thousand years. Studies dedicated to the memory of Jan Quaegebeur*, ed. W. Clarysse et al. Part II. Pp. 1459–68. Orientalia Lovaniensia Analecta, vol. 85. Leuven: Peeters.
Vleeming, S.P. 1991. *The Gooseherds of Hou (Pap. Hou). A Dossier Relating to Various Agricultural Affairs from Provincial Egypt of the Early Fifth Century B.C.* Studia Demotica vol. 3. Leuven: Peeters.
——. 1992. The Tithe of the Scribes (and) Representatives. In *Life in a Multi-cultural Society. Egypt from Cambyses to Constantine and Beyond*, ed. J.H. Johnson. Pp. 343–50. Studies in Ancient Oriental Civilization, vol. 51. Chicago: Oriental Institute.
——, and A.A. Den Brinker. 1993. *Check-List of Demotic Text Editions and Re-editions*. Leiden: Papyrologisch Instituut.
Zauzich, K.-T. 1994. Weitere Fragmente eines juristischen Handbuches in demotischer Schrift. In *Acta Demotica. Acts of the Fifth International Conference for Demotists. Pisa, 4th–8th September 1993. Egitto e Vicino Oriente* 17: 327–32.

CONCLUSIONS

Raymond Westbrook – Johns Hopkins University

I. Method

A large proportion of the legal documentation from the ancient Near East concerns debt. Notwithstanding the abundance of sources, the credit systems that lie behind them remain shrouded in obscurity. In part this is due to the incomplete nature of our sources, but it also reflects our ignorance of the economic and social structure of these societies, and of the practical working of their legal systems. Not only the broad issues of the economic and societal impact of debt, but even purely technical questions such as the interpretation of legal instruments and legal terminology associated with debt, stubbornly resist definitive answers. The contributions to this volume reflect these difficulties.

An initial problem, both for individual contributors and for comparison of their results, is the uneven quantity and range of sources available in each period. As Jasnow stresses, Egypt is particularly bereft in pertinent material before the Late Period. The bulk of the sources come from cuneiform records, but these are narrow in scope. They are mostly in the form of contractual documents, except for the Old Assyrian period, where the main source of information is the copious correspondence of Assyrian merchants trading in Anatolia. The Old Babylonian period has the widest variety of sources, if by no means the greatest quantity: contracts, letters, law codes and royal edicts. The neo-Babylonian sources, albeit more limited in type, are greater in quantity, and many come from identifiable archives. Reconstruction of the archives, as Oelsner demonstrates, may make up for the context that is lacking in the stereotyped formulae of individual documents. Ancient Israel is unique in having no documents of practice, the only source being the Hebrew Bible. Valuable information, however, may be gleaned from practically every genre in it, especially the narratives, proverbs and law codes. Overall, references to this topic in theoretical works such as the law codes are disappointingly few.

A second problem is the type of reality being presented by the sources. While all focus on the same single element of the credit system, security, the contributors differ in their emphasis. Most are concerned to establish the special terminology and mechanisms applied in their particular period. On that basis, it is possible to reconstruct the theoretical framework within which debt was regulated. Legal instruments, however, can create a world of their own, a self-contained intellectual structure, which does not betray the dynamic of their function in society. Some authors (in particular Steinkeller and Zaccagnini) have therefore gone further, seeking to analyze the effect of the legal mechanisms in practice. In doing so, they force us to reconsider how accurate a picture the theoretical framework gives of relations between creditors and debtors.

II. Typology

The principal cause of debt was loans, but indebtedness could arise from other circumstances, such as deferred payment for goods or services, penalties payable to the victims of delict and of course, taxes. Several contributors (e.g. Abraham, Oelsner and Radner) have noted the tendency in the later periods to recast obligations arising from other causes as debt-notes, thus making the remedies of creditors more widely available.

Two basic contractual instruments of security were employed in all periods, with varying degrees of importance: pledge and surety. Two further instruments are attested occasionally: joint liability and punitive interest.

Pledge in the legal records is confined to productive assets: land, persons (i.e. members of the debtor's household, whether slaves or family), and very occasionally animals. Scattered references make clear that non-productive assets could be pledged, but since such transactions were not deemed worthy of written record, we have no means of determining their legal nature or assessing their importance. The written instruments themselves tend to be extremely terse, often making it difficult to identify the exact type of pledge or its terms. Again, the scribes may not have seen fit to include some of the standard oral stipulations, or customary legal terms that applied automatically.

Pledge of productive assets was of two kinds: possessory and hypothecary. Possessory pledge was for the most part antichretic, i.e. the income from the pledge was taken by the creditor in lieu of interest, leaving the capital to be repaid in its entirety in order to redeem the pledge. Hypothecary pledge was left in the possession of the debtor until default. It is often difficult to determine from the terms of the document whether a pledge was intended to be possessory or hypothecary, but the latter appear to have been much rarer. They can sometimes be identified from indications such as a charge on all the assets of the debtor. Only the demotic sources appear to have dealt with the possibility of the debtor disposing of the charged assets in the meanwhile: Manning discusses a "trusteeship" device whereby interim possession is accorded to a neutral third party. Abraham points out that after default such a pledge could only be redeemed in special circumstances by payment of both the principal and accumulated interest.

A surety (guarantor) was a person who assumed liability instead of the debtor in case of default. The surety was not a co-debtor against whom the creditor could choose to proceed first, as in Roman law. Indeed, one form of suretyship was an obligation to make the debtor available to the creditor at the due date. Having satisfied the creditor's claim, the surety had a right of regress against the debtor. The identity of sureties is not usually given; sometimes they were relatives or business associates, but in many instances they appear to have been financiers themselves, who presumably took over the loan in return for stricter conditions against the debtor. As Veenhof points out for the Old Assyrian sources, a surety seems to have often been joined when problems arose at some point after the original grant of the loan.

The terminology of the Mesopotamian documents, including transactions between Old Assyrian merchants in Anatolia, sharply distinguishes between surety and pledge. Not so the sources from the periphery. As Skaist sets out in detail for Emar and Alalakh IV, and other contributors note for Nuzi and transactions between Old Assyrian merchants and native Anatolians, the Sumerian and Akkadian technical terms for surety are used indiscriminately for pledge as well. The reason for this looseness of expression is not clear. It could reflect the absence of separate terms in the substrate native languages—which suggests a concomitant lack of rigor in the local jurisprudence. Veenhof notes a similar confusion between primary liability of the debtor and the security provided by pledging persons or property in native Anatolian contracts, whereas in purely Assyrian contracts a clear distinction is maintained.

The two other contractual instruments of security are attested in various periods, but related to special circumstances. In the case of joint debtors it was the practice to insert a clause making each liable for the whole of the debt. One of the debtors might even be made surety for the others. Default interest or supplementary interest was imposed after the due date, mostly on short term loans. Evidently the creditor was more concerned about the willingness of the debtor to pay than about his ability.

One striking feature that emerged from the discussion at the colloquium is the existence of two parallel systems of credit, which we may term subsistence and commercial. The former is typified by agrarian loans to small farmers, either to provide capital for cultivation of their fields or subsistence during the inter-harvest period. The primary instruments of security were the debtor's land and the members of his household. Most of our sources on security are concerned with this type of credit, whether contracts exacting pledge or provisions restricting it. The Old Babylonian edict of Ammi-ṣaduqa expressly excludes commercial credit transactions from its cancellation of debts and restoration of debtors' property.

The commercial system is found mostly among merchants. It served to finance trade and was therefore more connected with contracts of sale. It is the foremost type of credit attested in the Old Assyrian sources, but in other periods is no more than a shadowy presence. Nonetheless, given the importance of trade and merchants in most periods, it must have had a commensurate role throughout. For merchants, Veenhof notes, the most important forms of security were their ongoing business and the support of their business associates. Given the at times huge sums involved, land was not considered adequate cover. Accordingly, pledge of land and persons played a less important role, more emphasis being laid on sureties and on special arrangements, such as penal interest or a floating charge on business assets or the right of the creditor to borrow from a third party on the debtor's behalf.

Nonetheless, the two systems were not separate from each other and overlapped to a considerable degree. On the one hand, a decree of the city of Assur discussed by Veenhof gave merchants as well as others the opportunity to redeem the family home lost to debt. On the other, Frymer-Kensky observes that the Bible allows economic forces to govern the system of credit, intervening only intermittently in order to level the playing field or to rescue the poor when they are on the edge of total deprivation.

III. Default

What happened if the debtor failed to pay his debt when it fell due? If a pledge had been taken, then it would naturally be forfeited to the creditor. In practice, that was by no means the end of the matter. Not surprisingly, the pledge contracts record the taking of the pledge, but seldom its subsequent fate. Where they do (mostly in Assyrian sources), two alternatives are offered: whenever the debtor (or someone claiming through him) pays what is due, he may recover the pledge (*Lösungspfand*), or the pledge is deemed to have been conveyed to the creditor (*Verfallspfand*). What, however, if the pledge were worth more or less than the debt? Did the creditor pocket the surplus as part of the spoils of default, or alternatively have to forego the shortfall? The ancient Near Eastern response to this question has significant implications for comparative legal history.

In his magisterial study, "The Pledge Idea," Wigmore (1896–7; 1897–8) offered a comparative history of pledge as a legal concept. The study covered ancient and traditional legal systems from all parts of the globe, including what was known at the time from the ancient Near East.

Wigmore's point of departure was medieval Germanic law, the primitive features of which he saw as prevailing at an early stage of all legal systems. In that system, language did not distinguish between loan, pledge and bet. The conceptual role of the pledge was that of a provisional payment, something given until such time as the debt would be met. If the pledgor later chose not to pay (i.e. redeem the pledge), the pledgee could not compel him to do so; he could look only to the object pledged for satisfaction. In other words, the notion had not yet developed that the obligation to repay a debt was independent of the pledge, and that the pledge was merely ancillary thereto. Under this primitive conception, until the due date the pledgee only had a defective title to the pledge, since the pledgor had not definitively abandoned it. On default, the pledge became the absolute property of the pledgee. He had neither the duty to restore the surplus if the pledge were worth more than the debt, nor the right to claim the balance of the loan if it were worth less. In the interim, profits on the pledge were not even considered, whether as interest or in reduction of the capital sum owed.

It was against this standard that Wigmore evaluated other systems in world history and assigned them to different stages in the development of the law. Ancient Near Eastern law was judged to be a little more advanced: "We know that the Chaldean civilization was a mercantile one, and that commerce was highly developed; and yet all this is consistent with a relatively primitive set of ideas."[1] Wigmore pointed in particular to simple terminology and lack of accounting for the difference in value between loan and pledge.

The Assyriological works on which Wigmore relied were based on the meager quantity of cuneiform legal documents then available—a trickle that has since swollen to a flood.[2] If his assessment is judged inaccurate in the light of present-day knowledge, it does not diminish the importance of Wigmore's scientific contribution. Moreover, Wigmore's view of historical development of the law, based upon the criterion of Germanic law, colored the thinking of the generation of scholars who founded the scientific study of cuneiform law. Koschaker, for example, saw Middle and neo-Assyrian pledge as still in the nature of a substitute payment (1928: 112–13). Wigmore's evaluation has therefore influenced the place of ancient Near Eastern jurisprudence in the history of ideas.

It is true that certain expressions give the impression that the pledge was considered a substitute for the obligation and that the creditor could not demand further compensation from the debtor. In the Middle Assyrian texts the pledge is said to be given "as fulfillment of" (*kī našlamti*) and in neo-Assyrian texts "instead of" (*kūm*) the debt. But as Abraham points out, already in the Middle Assyrian period such phrases are misleading. The debtor's primary obligation was to repay the principal, and his right of redemption depended upon payment of the principal and interest. Furthermore, the cumulation of two types of charge upon the property show that it could not have been in lieu of the debt for any particular one of them.

[1] Wigmore 1896–7: 412–13.

[2] Wigmore cited Revillout and the documents published by Meissner (OB) and Strassmeier (NB); he excuses his omission of Egypt on the grounds of the paucity of published pledge documents (412–15).

A further consideration is the valuation of the debt and the pledge. Westbrook calls attention to equivalency clauses in the Old Babylonian documents. In deliberately making the pledge amount to a substitute payment, these clauses paradoxically betray the fact that it was not automatically regarded as such.

The evidence from various periods therefore supports the conclusion that in the ancient Near East pledge was firmly conceived as an instrument of security ancillary to the loan. The creditor was entitled to satisfy his claim from the pledge, but might be obliged to hand over any surplus to the debtor. If creditors were under certain circumstances able to treat the pledge as a substitute payment, it was the result of conscious manipulation of the pledge idea.

The question of manipulation brings us to the views of Steinkeller and Zaccagnini, who argue for the Ur III period and for Nuzi respectively that the primary purpose of antichretic pledges was not security but investment. Their evidence is the fact that the annual yield of fields or labor far exceeded the return from normal interest rates. Thus the yield would soon have exceeded the capital value of the pledge. As these contracts could be open-ended or very long term (in the case of Nuzi *tidennūtu*-contracts often with a minimum term before redemption), they were *de facto* alienation of the land or person. This interpretation raises many questions that remain to be explored: what was the motivation of the creditors (why, for example, did they not purchase the property directly for the price of the loan?), how far this purpose reflected the true nature of antichretic pledge, and how prevalent it was in other periods.

If the creditor had failed to provide in advance for his own security, he had to fall back on what secondary measures of recourse the law provided. As far as we can tell these did not include the right to satisfy himself out of the debtor's property (or else pledge in advance would have been unnecessary). The most commonly attested measure appears to have been distraint, which in the Old Babylonian sources was confined to holding female members of the debtor's household captive on a temporary basis until he should pay the debt. Distraint of the debtor himself is not attested in this period, but Zaccagnini refers to a Nuzi document (AASOR XVI 73) in which a person was seized by his creditor (on the grounds that he was the surety of a defaulting debtor) and held in confinement for two days. As the creditor failed to prove his claim and was forced to pay his victim damages, it is hard to draw broad conclusions from this case.

We can be confident at least that the debtor's prison which was the shame of Victorian England and which Charles Dickens railed against in *Little Dorrit* was not a feature of ancient Near Eastern societies. Ironically, the situation of Dickens' Marshalsea Prison, where the debtor was confined but his family could come and go as they pleased, was reversed in the ancient Near East, where it was upon family members that imprisonment by way of distraint fell.

The same applies to physical measures against the debtor, such as beating and torture. Distrainees apparently could be beaten, but the law punished severely abuse of that power by the creditor if it resulted in death. Nonetheless, ancient Near Eastern law appears to have spared the debtor the treatment permissible in early Roman law according to a dramatic account of Livy given through the words of an escaped debtor:

> (He related that) . . . it (the debt) cumulated by interest first stripped him of the land of his father and grandfather and then of his other property; finally like putrefaction it reached his body; he was taken by the creditor not into slavery but into prison and torture (*Ab Urbe Condita* 2.23).

It is true that debt-slavery was a characteristic feature of ancient Near Eastern societies, but it was not so much a matter of confinement as of exploitation of labor. Furthermore, it does not appear to have been an automatic consequence of default. In the Bible, a widow complains that "the creditor is coming to take my two children as his slaves" (2 Kgs. 4:1). The legal basis for his right is not stated. The law codes and contracts, however, do not speak of a creditor taking a debtor involuntarily into slavery; the debtor is said to sell himself or his family into slavery by reason of the debt. Some contracts even go so far as to add that the persons in question are being sold of their own free will, even in cases where they could hardly have given informed consent.[3]

Were there conditions under which a creditor could enslave his debtor (or the debtor's family) for default, even without the debtor's consent? An international treaty from Ugarit provides:

---

[3] The clause is used in Arnaud Emar VI 205 with regard to two children who enter into slavery with their deceased father's creditor in circumstances almost identical to that in the biblical passage and in Arnaud Emar VI 217 of children sold by their parents, including a babe in arms.

> . . . And if silver of citizens of Ura is with citizens of Ugarit and they cannot repay it, the king of Ugarit shall give that man together with his wife and children into the hands of the merchant of Ura . . . (PRU IV 17.130:25–31).

Possibly an executive order or a court order could achieve what the creditor could not do on his own initiative. In Arnaud Emar VI 19 the plaintiff (actually the king's brother) records that having won a lawsuit concerning silver, he successfully petitioned the king to have the losing party handed over to him as a slave. These, however, may be very special circumstances. The rights of the creditor in the absence of contractual provisions remain obscure. Debtors certainly felt constrained to sell their land, their families and themselves rather than face the alternative, but what the pressure on them was, whether legal or economic, remains unknown.

What is known is that the treatment of debtors, especially the loss of their property and their freedom as a result of inability to pay their debts, was not altogether a matter of indifference to their rulers. Several of the contributors refer to official measures to relieve the burden of debt. In the Old Babylonian period redemption of property sold under pressure of debt was allowed, intermittent royal decrees annulled existing debts and released property sold or pledged pursuant thereto, and the Laws of Hammurabi ordered the release of debt slaves after three years' service. The same three possibilities are found in the Hebrew Bible, plus regular, cyclical annulment of debts and release of property. In Assur, an Old Assyrian decree allowed redemption of property and neo-Assyrian documents mention the imposition of debt-release decrees.

The more drastic of these measures, and certainly the combination of different measures, would be guaranteed to ruin all security for potential creditors. At the same time, Radner notes the presence of clauses in contracts purporting to override the effect of debt remission, a feature that has been noted elsewhere, for example in Old Babylonian Alalakh. If they could simply have been negated by a contractual clause, however, such measures would quickly have been abandoned as ineffective. Other contractual clauses, at Nuzi for example, acknowledge the power of the decree by claiming that the transaction in question falls outside its purview. This is not the place to canvass the question of the effectiveness of social justice measures in the ancient Near East, which has been the subject of debate for more than a century.[4] From the narrow perspective of the subject of this volume, it suffices to conclude that on the one hand intervention could have been neither so systematic nor comprehensive as ideologically driven sources like the law codes and royal inscriptions suggest, and on the other, contracts could not have imposed terms with such freedom as their terse documentation implies. In this perspective, the possibility of intervention to curb the worst excesses of creditors would have been a hidden factor influencing the formulation and execution of contracts, at least in some periods and under some regimes.

Nonetheless, hostility to the use of enslavement, at least of fellow citizens, as a means of securing debts eventually led to its disappearance and replacement with other instruments of security. The attitude is already evident by the mid-first millenium BCE in the injunction of Lev. 25:39–40 to treat a fellow Israelite who has been sold into debt slavery as if he were a hired hand. At around the same time Solon at Athens extended the scope of the debt release decree (*seisachtheia*) to abolish debt slavery henceforth for citizens altogether. In Rome, the *lex Poetelia* of 326 BCE abolished the last vestiges of debt slavery for citizens: the servitude of free persons to work off their debts and the sale of judgement debtors outside the jurisdiction. Security henceforth focused on property, with a partial substitute in the law of bankruptcy, which in Roman law and its successors not only led to a forcible auction of the debtor's total assets (*missio in bona*) but to *infamia*, a lowering of his citizenship status with loss of certain civil rights and sometimes even imprisonment. The latter, although generally abolished for private debts arising from loans, still lingers on for morally reprehensible debts such as alimony and taxes in many modern systems.

IV. Ancient and Modern

Tomlinson traces the development of many contemporary devices that were unknown to ancient Near Eastern law, such as bankruptcy, credit rating and bankers' commercial credits. It is true that rudimentary versions of some modern instruments did exist, such as the

---

[4] See the literature reviewed by North 1954: esp. 154–90.

floating lien, bearer bonds and possibly even garnishee orders (a court order to collect directly monies owed to one's debtor).[5] But the network of legal structures that underpins modern credit has no direct counterpart, even in the relatively sophisticated world of the ancient merchants. The dichotomy goes even deeper, into the conceptual universe of the ancient as against the modern legal systems. Modern systems tend to see the debtor as an individual, isolating him from his family and heirs, through devices such as the separation of marital property and the buffer of an estate administered by executors. The limited liability company may be seen as an extreme example of this tendency. By creating a legal personality to whose assets alone the creditor's security is confined, it effectively separates the debtor from his own person. By contrast, the ancient debtor was typically seen in the role of head of a household. Accordingly, as Radner notes, the household, including its subordinate members (i.e. wife and children) was in itself security, a part of the debtor's creditworthiness.[6]

Nevertheless, contemporary and ancient Near Eastern law stand comparison on a functional level. For example, information as to a borrowers' creditworthiness was no less vital then than now, and trading expeditions often needed more finance than an individual could sustain. Solutions were found within extended families, partnerships, and the association of merchants known in Akkadian as the *kārum*.[7] With the expansion of economic activity in recent centuries beyond those intimate spheres, valuable, if intangible, instruments of security were lost. Modern systems of information gathering, credit rating, bankers' references and bankers' credits are in effect a search for substitutes—attempts to reestablish the security furnished by familiarity and family relations in older systems.

By the same token, ancient debt-slavery and modern bankruptcy would appear to be totally alien institutions. To some extent, however, the possibility of discharge of a bankrupt that is built into modern

[5] Cf. a neo-Assyrian court record which appears to record a settlement based on the plaintiff satisfying his claim from the defendant's debtors: Jas: 1996, no. 48.

[6] Concerns that appear in the late first millennium to isolate the wife's dowry from her husband's creditors may be the first indication of a change from the collective to the individual approach. See Levine 1968: 283–85.

[7] The best known example is the Old Assyrian *kārum* which governed the affairs of the Assyrian trading colony at Kaneš. For a survey of its activities, see Garelli 1963: 171–204.

versions of bankruptcy has the same societal function as did the release of a debt slave after a period of service.[8] The purpose of the first modern Federal provision in the United States, in 1898, was described in the following terms:

> To do as nearly as possible to exact justice is the object of the law, and incidentally it tempers that justice with mercy and grants an honest bankrupt a discharge, an idea incorporated into the affairs of human life by Christianity, nurtured and developed by civilization; the same idea that prompts us to forgive our debtor and to throw the mantle of charity over his unfortunate past, and bid him again take up life's burden, freed from the shackles of debt.[9]

The same sentiments are already found in the mid-third millennium BCE, in the boast of King Entemena of Lagash that:

> . . . he caused the son to return to the mother, he caused the mother to return to the son, he established the release of interest-bearing loans.

They continue to find expression in the second millennium, in § 14 of King Lipit-Ishtar of Isin's law code:

> If a man has returned his slavery to his master and it is confirmed (that he has done so) twofold, that slave shall be released.

And they are still being voiced in the first millennium in the justification given by Deut. 15:18 for the release of a debt-slave after seven years:

> It shall not seem hard to you to release him, for he has served twice the hire of a hireling in serving you for six years . . .

The idea that annulling debt may be a form of security for the creditor is ironically demonstrated by the contemporary example of developing countries, which as sovereign states are impervious to legal measures to seize their territory or declare them bankrupt. Their financiers are experiencing some of the risks that ancient creditors had in financing agriculture in a world of limited resources and unpredictable harvests. Proposals to forgive the debt of such countries bear an echo of the debt-release decrees of ancient Near Eastern kings.

---

[8] Bankruptcy in English law did not originally make provision for discharge. It was introduced in the eighteenth century as a way to release the large number of debtors then languishing in prison. See Pakter 1988.

[9] Cited by Tabb 1999: 356.

In summary, creditors still look to the law to furnish them with a two-pronged security: the enforcement of pre-existing agreements, and if they fail or are lacking, the sort of recourse against the debtor and his assets that they would hope for by self-help. For all that the measures offered by modern law have radically changed, the prescient creditor today still has available the classic tools of security that were the mainstay of the ancient systems: pledge and surety. Then as now, they were formalized by word or document into obligations the parameters of which were well understood by all concerned. The very formality of a legal instrument brings certainty and predictability into the dealings of the parties but, as the contributions to this volume have shown, it can also be an instrument of oppression. Contemporary Civil and Common Law systems are the inheritors of these powerful instruments developed by ancient jurisprudence and still struggle to direct and contain their force.

Bibliography

Garelli, P. 1963. *Les Assyriens en Cappadoce*. Paris: Adrien Maisonneuve.

Jas, R. 1996. *Neo-Assyrian Judicial Procedures*. State Archives of Assyria 5. Helsinki: The Neo-Assyrian Text Corpus Project.

Koschaker, P. 1928. *Neue Keilschriftliche Rechtsurkunden aus der El-Amarna-Zeit*. Sächsische Akademie der Wissenschaften, philologisch-historische Klasse. Abhandlungen 5. Leipzig: Hirzel.

Levine, B. 1968. Mulugu/melug: The Origins of a Talmudic Legal Institution. *JAOS* 118: 271–85.

North, R. 1954. *Sociology of the Biblical Jubilee*. Analecta Biblica 4. Rome: Pontifical Biblical Institute.

Pakter, W. 1988. The Origins of Bankruptcy in Medieval Canon and Roman Law. *Proceedings of the Seventh International Congress of Medieval Canon Law*, ed. P. Linehan. Pp. 485–506. Vatican City: Bibliotheca Apostolica Vaticana.

Tabb, C. 1999. A Century of Regress or Progress? A Political History of Bankruptcy Legislation in 1898 and 1998. *Bankruptcy Developments Journal* 15: 343–81.

Westbrook, R. 1991. *Property and the Family in Biblical Law*. JSOTSuppl. 113. Sheffield: JSOT Press.

Wigmore, J. 1896–8. The Pledge Idea. *Harvard Law Review* 10: 321–50; 11: 18–39.

INDICES

I. Sources 343
Cuneiform Sources 343
Egyptian Sources 355
Biblical Sources 355
Classical Sources 356
English Legal Sources 356
French Legal Sources 356
United States Legal Sources 356

II. Terms 357
Sumerian Terms 357
Akkadian Terms 357
Demotic Terms 360
Coptic Terms 360
Hebrew and Ugaritic Terms 360
Greek Terms 360
Roman Legal Terms 360

I. SOURCES

Cuneiform Sources

A 1055 + 1070 269 n. 25, 271 n. 40
A 2427 271 n. 39
A 2527 280 n. 65
AASOR XVI 29 230–231
AASOR XVI 30 232
AASOR XVI 60 233
AASOR XVI 67 229
AASOR XVI 73 234–235, 333
AbB 1 89 86
AbB 1 93 84
AbB 1 101 79
AbB 1 137 85
AbB 2 113 81, 83
AbB 2 114 85
AbB 3 20 84
AbB 3 55 81 n. 41
AbB 3 67 87
AbB 5 228 85
AbB 5 234 85
AbB 6 41 84, 87
AbB 6 73 81
AbB 6 172 85
AbB 6 200 86
AbB 6 208 87
AbB 7 68 84, 85
AbB 7 75 79
AbB 7 125 85
AbB 8 81 65
AbB 9 27 81, 82
AbB 9 41 84
AbB 9 216 87
AbB 9 238 86
AbB 9 253 84
AbB 9 269 79
AbB 9 270 84, 85
AbB 10 1 84, 87
AbB 10 5 84
AbB 11 79 84
AbB 11 106 86
AbB 11 158 85, 87
AbB 13 131 84
ABL 387 286 n. 97
ABL 463 275 n. 54
ABL 702 286 n. 97
ABL 871 265 n. 4
ABL 1285 279 n. 63
ABL 1442 273 n. 44
Acta Sumerologica 10, p. 173 (Text A) 248
Acta Sumerologica 13, p. 335 (Text A) 238 n. 4, n. 10, 242, 246
Actes du 8e Congrès International no. 3 290
Adana 237E 137 n. 108
ADD 3 266 n. 5
ADD 5 267 n. 13
ADD 26 266 n. 5
ADD 58 271 n. 40
ADD 59 271 n. 40
ADD 60 271 n. 40
ADD 63 271 n. 40
ADD 64 271 n. 40
ADD 64' 269 n. 25
ADD 66 270 n. 30
ADD 67 271 n. 39
ADD 71 270 n. 31, 271 n. 40
ADD 72 269 n. 25, 271 n. 39
ADD 73 285 n. 84
ADD 74 285 n. 84
ADD 76 280 n. 66
ADD 77 282 n. 74, 283 n. 75
ADD 79 271 n. 39
ADD 85 282 n. 74
ADD 86 278 n. 61
ADD 101 274 n. 50
ADD 113 285 n. 85
ADD 134 268 n. 19
ADD 135 268 n. 19
ADD 152 281 n. 69
ADD 160 281 n. 70
ADD 161 281 n. 71
ADD 164 282 n. 72, n. 73
ADD 307 267 n. 9
ADD 629 285 n. 81, 285 n. 83

ADD 815+	286 n. 95
ADD 923	286 n. 95
ADD 926	286 n. 95
ADD 1154	271 n. 40
ADD 1165	268 n. 17
Ahmad 1996: no. 2	280 n. 67, 286 n. 91
Ahmad 1996: no. 3	280 n. 67
Ahmad 1996: no. 7	280 n. 67
Ahmad 1996: no. 11	280 n. 67
AKT 1 34	152 n. 145
AKT 1 44	128 n. 91, 134, 135, 139 n. 112, 140 n. 114, 143
AKT 1 45	136
AKT 2 18	126 n. 81
AKT 2 31	103 n. 21, 105, 124 n. 78
AKT 2 32	128
AKT 2 53	130
AKT 3 8	107
AKT 3 10	130 n. 98, 131, 151
AKT 3 14	151
AKT 3 27	100
AKT 3 28	100
AKT 3 59	105, 124
AKT 3 98	132, 146
AKT 3 104	133
ana ittišu 2 II 68–69	84 n. 48
ana ittišu 2 IV 21'–23', 27'–29'	64 n. 3, n. 5
ana ittišu 2 IV 30'–34	70 n. 15
ana ittišu 2 IV 35'–38', 49'–53'	65 n. 8
ana ittišu 3 II 41–45	81 n. 41
ana ittišu 3 II 51–53	79 n. 36
ana ittišu 3 II 54–55	80 n. 40
AnOr 6 19	99
AO 4506	275 n. 55
AO 19228	169 n. 29, 176 n. 69, 177 n. 72, 183, 184, 186, 187, 189 n. 120, n. 121, 201, 213, 214, 217, 221
AO 19229	162 n. 5, 169 n. 27, 201, 210 n. 9, 212, 219, 221
AO 20153	201, 216
AO 20154	193 n. 145
AO 20155	209, 214 n. 19
AO 20156	201, 215
AO 21380	169 n. 29, 171 n. 43, 175 n. 62, 176 n. 69, 180 n. 88, 201, 215, 217
ARM 8 31 + 72	64, 66, 67, 71 n. 18
ARM 8 52	63, 73
ARM 8 71	65 n. 7, n. 9, 70, 73–74, 75 n. 27, 81
ARN 105	64, 71
Arnaud 1987: 217–219	303
ARu 16	169 n. 28, n. 33, 201, 212, 218
ARu 53	169 n. 27, 192 n. 139, 213, 219
ASJ 10A	247 n. 18
ASJ 33	239–240
ASJ 35	238 n. 4, n. 10, 244–245, 247
ASJ 36	243
ASJ 37	243–244
Ass. A ii 27–iii 15 (Esarhaddon)	285 n. 83, 286 n. 98
AT 4	239 n. 12
AT 48	239 n. 12
AT 49	239 n. 12
AT 50	239 n. 12
AT 70	239 n. 12
AT 83	239 n. 12
AT 84	239 n. 12
AT 85	239 n. 12
ATHE 55	108 n. 39
ATHE 64	104 n. 27, 149 n. 139
ATHE 75	148 n. 139, 149 n. 139
AUCT 2 121	58
BE 3/1 1	50 n. 10
BE 3/1 19	57
BE 14 115	289
Bi 1	201, 214
Bi 2	169 n. 27, 174 n. 60, 176, 180 n. 88, n. 90, 201, 212, 219

Bi 3 169 n. 27, 174 n. 60, 176, 180 n. 88, n. 90, 202, 212, 219
Bi 4 169 n. 27, 174 n. 60, 176, 180 n. 88, n. 90, 202, 212, 219
Bi 4a 169 n. 27, 174 n. 60, 180 n. 88, n. 90, 202, 212, 219
Bi 5 168 n. 22, 169 n. 29, 189 n. 120, 189 n. 122, 202, 213, 217, 220, 221
Bi 7 164 n. 15, 210 n. 9
Bi 8 164 n. 15, 210 n. 9
Bi 9 187 n. 113, 209
Bi 10 165 n. 16, 171 n. 45
Bi 11 162 n. 5, 171 n. 42, 172, 210 n. 9
Bi 13 209
Bi 14 209
Bi 18 210
Bi 19 210
Bi 24 164 n. 11
Bi 25 165 n. 16
Bi 26 162 n. 5, 171 n. 42, 210 n. 9
BIN 4 4 98–99, 104 n. 26, 113 n. 51
BIN 4 112 132
BIN 4 218 106
BIN 6 27 105 n. 32, 121–122
BIN 6 35 104 n. 27, 113
BIN 6 68 130
BIN 6 90 132
BIN 6 109 106
BIN 6 123 106
BIN 6 178 155 n. 151
BIN 6 236 126, 135, 132, 137
BIN 6 238 113 n. 51, 114 n. 53
BIN 6 275 101
BIN 7 210 79, 80 n. 38
BM 74652 299
BM 103206 283 n. 77
BM 103390 = Fales 1983: 253 no. 13 277 n. 57
BRM 1 29 290
Camb. 306 299
CCT 1 11a 129 n. 95
CCT 1 13a 125
CCT 1 21d 95 n. 4
CCT 2 14 116
CCT 2 49a 104 n. 27
CCT 3 8b 104, 105 n. 31, 111
CCT 3 11 154
CCT 3 24 154
CCT 3 42 132
CCT 3 42b 132, 146
CCT 4 3b 155
CCT 4 29b 99, 132
CCT 4 35 132
CCT 5 2a 128
CCT 5 8a 105, 120, 122, 123, 145
CCT 5 17a 131 n. 100
CCT 5 24b 105 n. 30
CCT 6 34a 95 n. 4
CCT-MMA 1 84 106
CCT-MMA 1 84a 113 n. 52
CT 4 26a 65
CT 8 33a 83
CT 33 17 274 n. 49
CT 33 29 76
CT 44 83 289 n. 3
CT 48 108 83
CT 50 31 ii' 1–5 50 n. 8
CTN 2 10 285 n. 81
CTN 2 90 280 n. 64
CTN 2 91 280 n. 64
CTN 2 247 280 n. 65
CTN 2 248 285 n. 81
CTN 3 31 274 n. 52
CTN 3 59 286 n. 89
Dalley Edinburgh 5 238 n. 6, n. 11
Dalley Edinburgh 35 68, 71
Deller, Fales and Jakob-Rost 1995: no. 89 286 n. 94
Deller, Fales and Jakob-Rost 1995: no. 92 286 n. 93
Deller, Fales and Jakob-Rost 1995: no. 99 280 n. 67
Deller, Fales and Jakob-Rost 1995: no. 109 280 n. 67

Deller, Fales and Jakob-Rost 1995: no. 121 271 n. 39
Deller, Fales and Jakob-Rost 1995: no. 126 280 n. 67
Deller, Fales and Jakob-Rost 1995: no. 132 280 n. 67
DeZ 5662 = SH 86/8975 I 145 277 n. 58
Dialogue of Pessimism ll. 62–69 272
DSC 1: 46–47 210
Edict of Samsu-iluna 3' 76 n. 29
Edict of Ammi-ṣaduqa 7 87 n. 54
Edict of Ammi-ṣaduqa 20 74–75
Edict of Ammi-ṣaduqa 21 76
Edict X § H 76 n. 29
Edzard Tell ed-Der 21 65, 66
EL 2 127
EL 14 136
EL 15 126, 135, 150, 151
EL 20 130 n. 98
EL 21 148 n. 138
EL 24 129, 136
EL 55 151
EL 67 151
EL 75 121
EL 86 127, 136, 151
EL 87 152 n. 145, n. 146
EL 91 128, 136, 141, 149
EL 92 129, 136, 140, 142, 145
EL 94 149 n. 139
EL 180 130, 139
EL 184 104, 108
EL 185 152 n. 145
EL 186 107
EL 188 111, 131, 143
EL 190 125, 127 n. 90, 134
EL 215 121, 123, 144, 147
EL 217 129
EL 226 113 n. 51, 121, 133, 151
EL 227 104 n. 26, n. 27, 121, 134
EL 238 104, 106, 107, 110, 111 & n. 47, 112, 115, 117, 118, 119, 120
EL 252 129 n. 95, 130
EL 254 106, 107
EL 262 129
EL 273 95 n. 4
EL 292 128, 131, 132, 137 n. 109
EL 297 111 n. 49, 133 n. 104, 137, 140, 145
EL 306 109, 110, 112, 115, 116, 118
EL 320 + CCT 6 17a 132, 146
EL 321 113 n. 52
EL 325 105 n. 30
EL 325a 149
EL 326 106
EL 328 149, 150
EL 331–333 113
Emar VI 16 247
Emar VI 77 238 n. 5, n. 7, 240, 242, 247
Emar VI 86 244
Emar VI 87 238 n. 4, n. 7, 240
Emar VI 88 238 n. 4, n. 7, 240
Emar VI 119 238 n. 4, n. 7, 240–241
Emar VI 121 238 n. 5, 242–243
Emar VI 123 246
Emar VI 205 241, 334 n. 3
Emar VI 209 238 n. 4
Emar VI 217 334 n. 3
EN 9/1 181 229
EN 9/1 194 233–234
EN 9/1 265 232–233
EN 9/1 400 234
EN 9/2 152 230
EN 9/2 292 227 n. 9
EN 9/2 326 229 n. 12
EN 9/2 348 229 n. 12
EN 9/3 412 229 n. 12
EN 9/3 465 229 n. 12

Evetts Ev.-M. no. 13 300 n. 41
Fales and Jakob-Rost 1991: no. 1 276 n. 59
Fales and Jakob-Rost 1991: no. 28 267 n. 7
Fales and Jakob-Rost 1991: no. 31 267 n. 11
Fales and Jakob-Rost 1991: no. 33 280 n. 67
Fales and Jakob-Rost 1991: no. 34 280 n. 67
Fales and Jakob-Rost 1991: no. 46 269 n. 22
Fales and Jakob-Rost 1991: no. 53 280 n. 67
Fales and Jakob-Rost 1991: no. 90 276 n. 56
Falkenstein Gerichtsurkunden 195 122 n. 75
FAOS 16 932 59
FAOS 16 933 59
FAOS 16 1244 51
FAOS 16 1282 53
Fish Catalogue 60 51
FT 3 134
Gautier Dilbat 51 80 n. 38, 81 n. 42
Genouillac Kich D 39 85
Grant 1938 73
Grosse Prunkinschrift (Sargon II) 286 n. 96
H.K. 1005–5534 139 n. 113
Harris 1955: no. 3 65, 66, 67 & n. 10
Harris 1955: no. 4 70
Harris 1955: no. 5 66, 73
HSS V 66 228 n. 10
HSS IX 17 227
HSS IX 68 226
HSS XIII 171 228 n. 10
HSS XIII 259 229
HSS XIII 404 227
HSS XVI 238 227
Hunger 1970, no. 3 297
Hunger 1970, no. 14 298
Hunger 1970, no. 17 A 298
Hunger 1970, no. 17 B 298
Hunger 1970, no. 17 C 298
Hunger 1970, no. 17 D 297
Hunger 1970, no. 17 E 297
Hunger 1970, no. 17 F 298
Hunger 1970, no. 17 G 298
Hunger 1970, no. 17 H 297
Hunger 1970, no. 17 I 298
Hunger 1970, no. 17 K 297
Hunger 1970, no. 17 L 298
Hunger 1970, no. 17 M 297
Hunger 1970, no. 17 N 297
Hunger 1970, no. 17 O 297
Hunger 1970, no. 17 P 298
Hunger 1970, no. 18 298
Hunger 1970, no. 19 298, 300
Hunger 1970, no. 20 298, 300
Hunger 1970, no. 21 298
Hunger 1970, no. 22 298
Hunger 1970, no. 24 298
Hunger 1970, no. 27 298
Hunger 1970, no. 28 298
I 445 119 n. 66
I 475 99, 134, 145, 152 n. 45, 153
I 478 110, 118, 119
I 500 148
ICK 1 19 114
ICK 1 37 137
ICK 1 37b 132
ICK 1 61 129 n. 95
ICK 1 86 + 1 105 n. 29
ICK 1 86 + 2 110, 111, 113, 115, 116, 118
ICK 1 171 132
ICK 1 190 132
ICK 2 16 132
ICK 2 43 148 n. 138
ICK 2 95 152 n. 145
ICK 2 116 147
ICK 2 141 110 n. 41
ICK 2 147 152 n. 145, n. 146
ICK 2 262 149 n. 139
IM 63153 127 n. 83
ITT 2 6225 50–51 n. 10
ITT 4 7449 50 n. 8
ITT 5 6710 50 n. 8
Jacob-Rost 1968, nos. 1–4 293
Jacob-Rost 1968, no. 5 293
Jacob-Rost 1968, no. 6 293
Jacob-Rost 1968, nos. 7–12 293
Jacob-Rost 1968, nos. 8–12 294
Jacob-Rost 1970, no. 11 293
Jacob-Rost 1968, no. 15 294

Jacob-Rost 1968, no. 17 293, 300
Jacob-Rost 1968, no. 18 293, 300
Jacob-Rost 1968, no. 19 294 n. 17
Jacob-Rost 1968, no. 20 294 n. 17
Jacob-Rost 1968, no. 21 294 n. 17
Jas 1996: no. 16 283 n. 77
Jas 1996: no. 48 337 n. 5
JCS 14 10 no. 5 105
JCS 14, 17f. no. 12 148 n. 138
JEN 155 226 n. 5
JEN 263 226 n. 5
JEN 306 230
Ka 1096 140 n. 117
KAJ 7 192–193
KAJ 11 168, 169 n. 27, 170, 182 n. 96, 192 n. 139, 202, 212, 214 n. 18, 216 n. 28, 219, 221
KAJ 12 169 n. 29, 192 n. 139, 202, 213, 217
KAJ 13 130 n. 96, 169 n. 27, 183, 189 n. 121, 202, 213, 220, 221
KAJ 14 169 n. 27, 178 n. 74, 192 n. 139, 202, 213, 219
KAJ 16 168, 169 n. 30, 175, 179, 180 n. 86, n. 89, 181, 182 n. 98, 202, 212, 218, 219
KAJ 17 169 n. 27, 174 n. 60, 175, 189 n. 123, 202, 212, 213, 220, 221
KAJ 18 169 n. 27, 170 n. 37, 202, 212, 219, 221
KAJ 19 169 n. 27, 202, 212, 219, 221
KAJ 20 169 n. 27, 180 n. 86, 181, 190, 202, 213, 214, 220
KAJ 21 130 n. 96, 169 n. 27, 180 n. 86, 182 n. 98, 202, 212, 219, 221
KAJ 22 169 n. 27, 202, 212, 219, 221
KAJ 23 169 n. 27, 174 n. 60, 176 n. 66, 202, 212, 221
KAJ 25 169 n. 27, 170 n. 37, 203, 212, 219, 221
KAJ 26 169 n. 29, 175 n. 62, 186 n. 109, 192 n. 139, 203, 215, 216 n. 27, 218
KAJ 27 169 n. 27, 177, 178 n. 74, 184, 203, 213, 219
KAJ 28 169 n. 27, 170 n. 37, 175, 203, 212, 219, 221
KAJ 29 168, 169 n. 27, 170, 174 n. 60, 176, 180 n. 88, n. 89, 192 n. 139, 203, 212, 214 n. 18, 216 n. 28, 219
KAJ 30 169 n. 27, 189 n. 122, 203, 213, 220, 221
KAJ 31 169 n. 27, 175, 180 n. 90, 182, 203, 212, 219
KAJ 32 168, 169 n. 28, n. 33, 190, 203, 212, 218
KAJ 33 203, 215
KAJ 34 169 n. 28, n. 33, n. 34, 203, 212, 218
KAJ 35 169 n. 29, 177, 186, 186 n. 109, 203, 215, 218
KAJ 36 169 n. 27, 203, 212, 219, 221
KAJ 37 168, 169 n. 28, n. 33, n. 34, 190, 203, 212, 218
KAJ 38 169 n. 28, n. 33, 203, 212, 218

KAJ 39 168, 169 n. 28, n. 33, n. 34, 190, 203, 212, 218
KAJ 40 169 n. 28, n. 33, 203, 212, 218
KAJ 41 169 n. 28, n. 33, 175, 203, 212, 218
KAJ 42 169 n. 28, n. 33, 203, 212
KAJ 43 169 n. 28, n. 33, 203, 212, 218
KAJ 44 169 n. 28, n. 33, 204, 212, 218
KAJ 45 169 n. 28, n. 33, 204, 212, 218
KAJ 46 169 n. 28, n. 33, 175, 192, 204, 212, 218
KAJ 47 169 n. 28, n. 33, 204, 212, 218
KAJ 48 164 n. 11
KAJ 49 164 n. 11
KAJ 50 169 n. 28, 204, 212, 214 n. 19, 218
KAJ 51 164 n. 11
KAJ 52 187 n. 111, 204, 214
KAJ 53 169 n. 27, 175 n. 63, 192 n. 139, 204, 212, 219, 221
KAJ 54 164 n. 11
KAJ 56 164 n. 11
KAJ 58 169 n. 27, 174 n. 60, 178 n. 74, 180 n. 86, 182 n. 98, 204, 212, 219, 221
KAJ 59 204, 215
KAJ 60 169 n. 27, 175, 204, 212, 219, 221
KAJ 61 169 n. 27, 174 n. 60, 175, 178, 180 n. 88, 181, 192 n. 139, 204, 212, 219, 221
KAJ 62 204, 214
KAJ 63 169 n. 27, 190 n. 126, 192 n. 139, 204, 213, 219
KAJ 64 = 68 169 n. 29, 186 n. 109, 204, 215, 218
KAJ 65 168, 169 n. 30, 170 n. 38, 175, 179, 204, 212, 218, 219, 221
KAJ 66 169 n. 27, 174 n. 60, 175, 180 n. 87, 180 n. 88, 181, 184 n. 104, 190 n. 125, 205, 213, 219
KAJ 67 169 n. 27, 174 n. 60, 180 n. 88, n. 89, 205, 212, 219
KAJ 69 169 n. 28, n. 33, 205, 212, 218
KAJ 70 169 n. 27, 170 n. 37, 180 n. 86, 182 n. 98, 205, 212, 219, 221
KAJ 71 169 n. 28, n. 33, 205, 212, 218
KAJ 72 164 n. 11
KAJ 73 164 n. 11
KAJ 74 164 n. 10, 208, 216
KAJ 75 164 n. 11
KAJ 76 164 n. 11
KAJ 77 189, 205, 214
KAJ 78 205, 215
KAJ 79 192 n. 139, 210
KAJ 80 165 n. 18
KAJ 81 205, 214
KAJ 82 162 n. 5, 164 n. 10, 208, 216
KAJ 83 188 n. 117, 211, 215
KAJ 85 169 n. 28, 205, 212, 218
KAJ 86 205, 215
KAJ 87 169 n. 28, 205, 212, 218
KAJ 88 205, 215, 216 n. 29
KAJ 89 164 n. 11
KAJ 90 164 n. 11
KAJ 91 164 n. 10, n. 11, 191 n. 133, 192 n. 135, 208, 216 n. 30
KAJ 92 210 n. 9, 162 n. 5, 172
KAJ 93 164 n. 11
KAJ 94 164 n. 11
KAJ 95 164 n. 11, 165 n. 16, 208, 216
KAJ 96 169 n. 27, 205, 212, 219, 221
KAJ 97 205, 216
KAJ 98 164 n. 11

KAJ 99 165 n. 16
KAJ 157 184 n. 102, 210
KAJ 159 209
KAJ 162 162 n. 5, 174 n. 60, 184 n. 102, 210, 220
KAJ 165 174 n. 60, 210, 220
KAJ 166 210
KAJ 167 192–193, 194
KAJ 168 175 n. 63, 193–194, 210 n. 10
KAJ 170 162 n. 5, 175 n. 63, 185, 210
KAJ 171 172
KAJ 268 162 n. 5, 210
KAJ 310 162 n. 5, 210
KAJ 315 162 n. 5, 165 n. 16
KAJ 318 165 n. 16
KAJ 319 164 n. 15, 165 n. 16
KAV 45 268 n. 19
KAV 197: 25–37 267 n. 9
KAV 211 162 n. 5, 184 n. 102, 185, 210, 220

Kennedy-Garelli 1960: no. 1 104 n. 27
Kennedy-Garelli 1960: no. 2 149
Kennedy-Garelli 1960: no. 5 123
Kienast 1976: no. 3 135
Kienast 1984: no. 6 147
Kienast 1984: no. 10 128, 138 n. 111
Kienast 1984: no. 26 138 n. 111
Kienast 1984: no. 27 138 n. 111
Kienast 1984: no. 28 114 n. 55
Kienast 1984: no. 32 138 n. 111, 140
Kienast 1984: no. 33 98 n. 10
Kienast Kisurra 1 70
Kienast Kisurra 4 65, 70
Kienast Kisurra 5 66
Kienast Kisurra 6 66, 67
Kienast Kisurra 8 66, 67
Kienast Kisurra 9 66
Kienast Kisurra 92 77
Kienast Kisurra 193 66, 67
Kienast Kisurra 203 67 n. 10, 77
KKS 3 106 n. 34
KKS 5 106
KKS 8 108 n. 39
KKS 13 108 n. 39
KKS 15 128 n. 91, 134, 135

Kleine Prunkinschrift (Sargon II) 286 n. 96
kt a/k 300 110, 112
kt a/k 447a 127
kt a/k 477 143
kt a/k 1044 140
kt a/k 1411 149
kt b/k 121 144, 147
kt c/k 680 150
kt c/k 1340 127
kt d/k 43 129
kt f/k 71 151
kt f/k 82 143
kt f/k 94 151 n. 144
kt f/k 171 131
kt k/k 16 128
kt k/k 114 154
kt m/k 104 142
kt m/k 118 136
kt m/k 126 105
kt n/k 71 142
kt n/k 75 147
kt n/k 101 117
kt n/k 519 154, 155
kt n/k 1139 107 n. 35
kt n/k 1528 130 n. 96
kt n/k 1716 134
kt n/k 1830 137
kt v/k 28 143, 147
kt v/k 156 106, 121
kt v/k 157 140
kt v/k 160 148 n. 138
kt v/k 161 153
kt v/k 171 136, 140
kt 84/k 169 147
kt 86/k 202 128 n. 91, 134
kt 87/k 96 136
kt 87/k 104 136, 138
kt 87/k 293 113 n. 51, 114 n. 53
kt 88/k 1050 143
kt 89/k 119 132
kt 89/k 231 124
kt 89/k 282 130 n. 98, 131
kt 89/k 307 108 n. 39

kt 89/k 312	134, 135, 140	LH 114	86, 154
kt 89/k 313	130	LH 116	84
kt 89/k 341	150	LH 117	75
kt 89/k 352	110, 112, 113, 118	LH 119	73
		LH 122ff.	131
kt 89/k 371	143	LH 151	90 n. 58
kt 89/k 419	110, 111, 113, 116, 118	LH 152	90 n. 58
		LL 14	76 n. 28, 338
kt 91/k 1	134	MAD 4 36	50 n. 8
kt 91/k 107	128	MAH 20613	274 n. 51
kt 91/k 107 + TPK 1 100	145	MAL C+G 7	71 n. 16
		Manana 29	64, 69
kt 91/k 125	113 n. 51	Manana 35	66, 71 n. 18
kt 91/k 127	106, 121, 124, 125	Manana 47	67
		Manana 63	66, 67, 71 n. 17
kt 91/k 135	114 n. 53	MDP 23 250	68
kt 91/k 173	122	Meissner BAP 61	79, 80 n. 38
kt 91/k 179	132	Moldenke II 2	291
kt 91/k 200	103, 106, 121	MVN 3 336	51
kt 91/k 228	137 n. 109, 139	MVN 8 168	58
		NATN 17	56
kt 91/k 426	129 n. 93	NATN 163	50 n. 6
kt 92/k 173	135	NATN 305	56
kt 92/k 178	135	NATN 307	57, 67 n. 11
kt 92/k 179	132	NATN 346	50 n. 6
kt 92/k 206	132 n. 102	NATN 472	50 n. 6
kt 92/k 212	132	NATN 539	50 n. 6
kt 92/k 228	135	NATN 748	58
kt 92/k 1038	134	NATN 836	57
KTH 13	133	NBC 8618	76 n. 29
KTH 15	106, 113 n. 52	Nbk. 138	300
KTK 68	132	Nbn. 375	300
KTK 94	149	Nbn. 619	300
KTK 95	131, 139 n. 112, 141	ND 2078	267 n. 11
		ND 2089	267 n. 12
KTS 29b	154	ND 2316	280 n. 65
KTS 47c	132	ND 3444	266 n. 5
KTS 2 9	135, 137, 142–143	ND 5480	267 n. 7
		NRVN 1 104	50 n. 6
KTS 13 28	132	NRVN 1 192	58
KUG 48	149 n. 139	NRVN 1 197	50 n. 6
Langdon 1928: 322	301 n. 44	NRVN 1 239	57
Larsen-Moller 1991: 227	129 n. 94	O 3684	106, 110, 111, 112, 113, 115, 118
Larsen-Moller 1991: 230 no. 3	128 n. 91, 134		
		OECT 9 2	301 n. 45, 303
LB 1218	147	OECT 9 3	289 n. 3
LE 22	86	OIP 27 12	130
LE 39	72, 73	OIP 27 35	155
LH 49	68	OIP 27 59	128–129
LH 50	68 n. 13	OIP 79: 89 no. 5	164 n. 13
LH 52	69	PBS 8/2 207	80
LH 66	68 n. 13	PBS 8/2 245	80–81
LH 113	85	PBS 13 39	67 n. 10, 71 n. 18

POAT 12 150
PRU IV 17.130 335
PSBA 33, no. 29 68 n. 12
RA 8, 70 77
RA 8, 197 no. 21 50 n. 6
RA 60, 123 106
Radner 1997a: 390 270 n. 28
Radner 1999: no. 35 273 n. 47
RE 10 244
RE 58 238 n. 5, n. 10, 244–245
RE 90 246
Scheil 1925: 147 274 n. 51
Schwelleninschrift Typ V (Sargon II) 286 n. 96
SÉ 104 267 n. 11
SHLF viii 3–10 67 n. 10
SLHF viii 11–15 70 n. 15
Strassmaier 1888: 129ff. no. 13 289 n. 3, 303
S.U. 51/44 = Finkelstein 1957: 139 278 n. 62
TBR 5 242 n. 16
TBR 25 244
TBR 26 245
TBR 27 238 n. 5, n. 7, 240
TBR 28 245
TBR 29 245
TBR 34 238 n. 5, n. 9, 245
TBR 36 245–246
TBR 39 247
TBR 40 247
TBR 53 238 n. 5, n. 10, 246
TBR 74 246, 247 n. 20
TBR 82 243
TBR 84 245
TC 1 25 154, 155
TC 1 43 154, 155 n. 152
TC 1 103 109
TC 2 46 154, 155
TC 2 61 132
TC 3 28 110 n. 41, 117, 118 n. 62
TC 3 29 149 n. 139
TC 3 51 130
TC 3 60 103, 154, 155
TC 3 63 128
TC 3 67 105, 122
TC 3 69 133
TC 3 110 114
TC 3 218 130 n. 98, 151
TC 3 221 137
TC 3 222 128 n. 91, 134
TC 3 232 99, 134, 128 n. 91
TC 3 233 134
TC 3 237 131, 150
TC 3 238 131
TC 3 240 137
TC 3 240 + TC 2 66 132, 135, 139
TC 3 252 146, 147
TC 3 255 138 n. 111
TC 3 266 131 n. 100
TCL 1 2 84, 90
TCL 9 10 229–230
TCL 9 59 165 n. 16
TCL 9 68 275 n. 55
TCL 17 74 85
TH III 908c 274 n. 51
TH III 1160 274 n. 52
TIM 3 149 51, 53
TIM 11 14 280 n. 65
TIM 11 17 271 n. 36
TIM 11 18 284 n. 79
TPK 1 21 126, 137
TPK 1 21a 132
TPK 1 26 144 n. 127
TPK 1 46 144–145, 147
TPK 1 85 98 n. 9
TPK 1 88 136, 137, 139
TPK 1 91 153
TPK 1 100 128, 141
TPK 1 106 127
TPK 1 108 149 n. 139
TPK 1 138 151
TPK 1 156 102
TPK 1 156a 140, 143
TPK 1 157 105 n. 29, 114
TPK 1 160 132
TPK 1 166 104 n. 27, 124
TPK 1 169 152 n. 145, 153
TPK 1 170 122
TPK 1 171 105 n. 29, 110, 112–113, 115
TPK 1 192 155 n. 151
TPK 1 194 127, 140
TR 100 209
TR 101 162 n. 5, 209
TR 102 209

TR 104 169 n. 29, 175 n. 62, 206, 215, 216, 217
TR 110 163 n. 7, 206, 208, 215
TR 112 170, 206, 214 n. 18, 215, 216
TR 115 210
TR 129 164 n. 11
TR 2015 209
TR 2021 + 2051 206, 216
TR 2028 164 n. 11
TR 2039 162 n. 5, 209
TR 2045 164 n. 11
TR 2052 169 n. 27, 174 n. 60, 180 n. 88, n. 90, 206, 212, 219
TR 2057 209
TR 2058 209
TR 2061 210
TR 2062 + TR 2905 209
TR 2065 209
TR 2069 + TR 2908 209
TR 2903 164 n. 11
TR 2907 206, 215 n. 23
TR 2913 163 n. 7, 206, 208, 215
TR 3001 174 n. 60, 184 n. 103, 210, 220
TR 3002 174 n. 60, 184 n. 103, 210, 220
TR 3007 169 n. 27, 179 n. 84, 206, 212, 219, 221
TR 3011 209
TR 3012 210
TR 3013 206, 215
TR 3014 206, 214
TR 3015 206, 214
TR 3016 187 n. 113, 209
TR 3021 169 n. 27, n. 32, 170 n. 39, 175, 206, 212, 219, 221
TR 3022 169 n. 29, 170 n. 36, 175 n. 62, 176 n. 69, 180 n. 88, 187, 189, 206, 214, 217
TR 3036 206, 214
TTC 14 149
TuM 2/3 104 299, 303
TuM 2/3 38 300
TuM 2/3 41 290
TuM 2/3 42 290 n. 7
TuM 5 48 50 n. 8
TuM 5 216 50 n. 8
TuM n.F. 1/2 32 57
TuM n.F. 1/2 246 60
TuM n.F. 1/2 247 60
TuM n.F. 1/2 248 61
TuM n.F. 1/2 249 58
TuM n.F. 1/2 250 59
TuM n.F. 1/2 253 59
TuM n.F. 1/2 254 60
UCP 9/I 2 299
UET 3 11 50 n. 6
UET 4 56 296
UET 4 61 294, 295
UET 4 62 295
UET 4 63 295
UET 4 68 295
UET 4 69 295
UET 4 70 295
UET 4 71 295
UET 4 72 294, 296
UET 4 73 295, 296
UET 4 74 295, 296
UET 4 75 295
UET 4 76 295, 303
UET 4 77 296
UET 4 78 296
UET 4 79 296
UET 4 80 296
UET 4 81 295
UET 4 82 295
UET 4 83 295
UET 4 84 299
UET 4 87 296
UET 4 88 296
UET 4 89 296
UET 4 112 296
UET 4 113 296 n. 25
UET 4 114 296 n. 25
UET 4 146–148 294 n. 18
UET 4 174 296
UET 4 182 296
UET 4 183 294 n. 19
UET 4 186 294 n. 19
UET 4 195 296 n. 25
UET 4 196 296 n. 25
UET 4 197 296
UET 4 198 294, 296, 303
UET 4 202 296 n. 25
UET 4 203 296

UET 5 9 85, 86
UET 5 300 71 n. 18
UET 5 323 64, 71 n. 18
UET 5 425 80 n. 37
Urad-Šerua 5 164 n. 11
Urad-Šerua 33 171 n. 42, 210 n. 9
Urad-Šerua 49 172 n. 52
Urad-Šerua 56 172 n. 49
Urad-Šerua 60 162 n. 5, 210
Urad-Šerua 65 172 n. 46
Urad-Šerua 69 171 n. 44
Urad-Šerua 76 162 n. 5, 210
VAS 1 96 268 n. 21
VAS 1 97 266 n. 6
VAS 1 101 274 n. 51
VAS 4 5 299
VAS 8 26 79
VAS 13 73 78
VAS 13 96 63, 65, 71 n. 18, 73 & n. 22
VAS 15 2 289 n. 3
VAS 19 8 209
VAS 19 19 169 n. 28, 175 n. 61, 207, 212, 218
VAS 19 20 169 n. 29, 189 n. 120, 207, 213, 217, 221
VAS 19 23 162 n. 5, 165 n. 16
VAS 19 36 169 n. 29, 190 n. 125, 207, 213, 217
VAS 19 38 210
VAS 19 47 164 n. 10, 172, 191, 192 n. 135, 208, 214 n. 18, 216 n. 30
VAS 19 51 162 n. 5, 209
VAS 19 67 165 n. 16
VAS 26 1 130 n. 97, 132
VAS 26 37 117, 118 n. 62
VAS 26 60 132, 133
VAS 26 112 105 n. 30
VAT 5604 274 n. 51
VAT 5605 266 n. 6
VAT 5606 268 n. 21, 283 n. 76
VAT 8232 280 n. 67
VAT 8270 280 n. 67
VAT 8274 280 n. 67
VAT 8280 280 n. 67
VAT 8643 268 n. 17
VAT 8656 273 n. 47
VAT 8893 271 n. 39
VAT 9137 280 n. 67
VAT 9323 268 n. 19
VAT 9326 267 n. 9
VAT 9695 269 n. 25, 286 n. 94
VAT 9703 276 n. 56
VAT 9758 278 n. 60
VAT 9778 280 n. 67
VAT 9838 280 n. 67
VAT 9868 286 n. 93
VAT 10491 285 n. 86
VAT 14451 278 n. 59
VAT 17888 162 n. 5, 164 n. 12
VAT 17889 162 n. 5, 164 n. 12
VAT 19495 280 n. 67
VAT 19500 270 n. 28, n. 31
VAT 19511 280 n. 67
VAT 20341 267 n. 11
VAT 20350 267 n. 8
VAT 20351 280 n. 67
VAT 20374 284 n. 80
VAT 20396 269
VAT 20398 269 n. 22
VAT 20688 280 n. 67
VAT 20782 268 n. 17
VAT 21000 280 n. 67
VDI 80/70 217
VDI 80: 71 168, 169 n. 30, n. 31, 175 n. 61, n. 62, 178, 179, 180 n. 87, 182, 183, 185–186, 190 n. 125, 206, 213, 218, 221
von Weiher Uruk 5 308 289 n. 3
von Weiher Uruk 5 309 289 n. 3
von Weiher Uruk 5 311 289 n. 3
Waterman 37 78
Wiseman Alalakh 18 65 n. 6
Wiseman Alalakh 22 80 n. 37
Wiseman Alalakh 82 127 n. 84
Wiseman Alalakh 83 127 n. 84
Wiseman Alalakh 84 127 n. 84
YBC 12860 162 n. 5, 206, 215, 216
YBC 12861 162 n. 5, 210
YOS 4 5 51

YOS 4 7	50 n. 6
YOS 4 21	51
YOS 4 55	50 n. 6
YOS 5 114	80 n. 37
YOS 8 35	77
YOS 8 78	71 n. 18, 73 & n. 22
YOS 13 42	83
YOS 13 273	80
YOS 13 312	83 n. 45
YOS 13 315	83 n. 45
YOS 13 327	83 n. 45
YOS 14 35	70
YOS 14 85	73
YOS 14 158	79–80, 81, 82
ZA 53, 87 no. 24	56

Egyptian Sources

Admonitions	37
Amenemope 16/1	42
Any	38, 42
Cairo 43371	37
Coffin Texts	35
Eloquent Peasant	35
Harkhuf	40
Hekanakht	37
Hermopolis Legal Code	35, 319
Installation of the Vizier	35
O. Cairo 25553	38
O. Cairo 25572	38
O. Chicago 12073	36, 310
P. dem. Adler 10	315
P. dem. Adler 15	321
P. dem. Adler 20	321
O. Gardiner 204	38
P. Berlin 3048	39, 43
P. Berlin 3106	317
P. Berlin 3108	317, 318
P. Berlin 3110	322, 323
P. Berlin 3139	317
P. BM 10425	320
P. BM Glannville 10525	310
P. Brookl. Pierce 1	322
P. Hauswaldt 18	319
P. Hibeh I, 34	323
P. Kahun 13	37
P. Lansing	36, 41
P. Loeb 48 + 49A	316
P. Louvre E 3228b	40
P. Mattha	319
P. Mayer A	311
P. Philad. 15	319
P. Philad. 16744	315
Ptahhotep	35
Statue Inscription of Djedkhonsefankh	39
Tale of the Eloquent Peasant	37
Tale of Wenamun	37

Biblical Sources

Gen. 38	253–254
Gen. 44	256
Exod. 22: 21–27	259
Exod. 22: 24	251
Exod. 22: 25	254, 258
Lev. 25: 8–12	260–261
Lev. 25: 17	259
Lev. 25: 35–37	252
Lev. 25: 39–40	336
Deut. 15: 6	251
Deut. 15: 7–8	251
Deut. 15: 9	258, 259–260
Deut 15: 11	251
Deut. 15: 12–18	259
Deut. 15: 18	338
Deut. 24: 6	254
Deut. 24:12	254
Deut. 24: 18	41
Deut. 24: 20	255
Judg. 11: 3	257
1 Sam. 22: 2	257
2 Kgs. 4: 1	334
2 Kgs. 4: 1–7	257
2 Kgs. 6: 1–7	257–258
Isa. 50: 1	257
Jer. 15: 10	252
Jer. 32: 6–15	258–259
Jer. 34: 13–16	260
Ezek. 18: 7	255
Ezek. 18: 12	255
Ezek. 18: 16	252
Ezek. 33: 15	255

Amos 2:8	255	Prov. 14:21	251
Amos 5:11	252, 256	Prov. 17:18	256
Ps. 109:11–12	257	Prov. 20:16	256
Ps. 119:121–122	254	Prov. 22:26–27	256, 257
Job 22:6	255	Prov. 27:13	256
Job 24:3	255	Ruth 4	259
Job 24:9	257	Neh. 5:1–5	257
Prov. 3:27–30	251	Neh. 5:6–13	260
Prov. 6:1–3	256	Neh. 10:32	260
Prov. 11:5	256		

Classical Sources

Diod. Sic. I, 79	312, 322	Livy, Ab Urbe Condita 2.23	334
P. Col. Zenon II 83	312		

English Legal Sources

Statute of Acton Burnett (1283)	7	Statute of Westminster II (1285)	8–9
Statute of Merchants (1285)	7–8	34 and 35 Henry VIII, ch. 4 (1542)	11 n. 22
		Twyne's Case (1601)	16

French Legal Sources

Code Civil (1804) Art. 2076	16	Code de Commerce (1807)	12–13
Code Civil (1804) Art. 2078	15 n. 33	Loi relative au redressement et liquidation des enterprises (1985)	13 n. 31, 21

United States Legal Sources

Bankruptcy Act (1898)	13, 24 n. 65	*Sturges v. Crowninshield*, 4 Wheat. 122 (U.S. 1819)	25 n. 68
Uniform Commercial Code	19–20, 25, 28, 30	*United States v. Reynolds*, 235 U.S. 233 (1914)	31
Uniform Trust Receipts Act	18		

II. TERMS

Sumerian Terms

en-šu(meš) 238, 240–241, 247, 267
kú 69
kù(-ta-gub-ba-)šè . . . gub 56 no. 2, 64
lú-dam-gàr 282 n. 74
lú^{meš}-ú-lu^{lu} 247
lú-silim-ma ù lú-gi-na 83–84
MA.U 226
máš a-šag$_4$-ga 53, 54, 57 no. 5, 58 nos. 12, 13, 59 nos. 14, 15, 16, 17; 61 no. 21
máš(-bi-.šè) 56–61, 64
šu(meš)^{ti} 238, 242, 243, 245
šu ba-(an)-ti 56 no. 3, 57 nos. 5, 6, 8; 58 nos. 9, 10, 11, 12, 13; 59 nos. 15, 16; 60 nos. 17, 18, 19; 97, 239
šu-du$_8$/dù-a 50, 80, 127 n. 84, 239
šu-du$_8$/dù-a-ni in-gub 50 n. 7, n. 10
šu-du$_8$/dù-a-ni šu ba-an-ti 79–80
šuku 54, 57 no. 4, 58 nos. 12, 13; 59 nos. 14, 15, 16, 17; 60 nos. 18, 19, 20; 61 no. 21
ú-gu . . . dé 66
ugu . . . in-tuku 97
ur$_5$-ra 64, 227

Akkadian Terms

abākum G 111
amēlūtu 111 n. 48, 244, 247–248
(an)durāru(m) 75, 284–286
apālum G 107–108, 112, 123
balāṭum G 97
be'ūlātum 102, 134 n. f
dagālum G 129, 136 n. h, 141, 142, 149, 270 n. 32
ebuṭṭum 95
edannu 184, 216 n. 28
eli . . . išûm G 97
erābum G 126–128
erābum D 127 n. 88, n. 89
erēšu Gt 177, 180 n. 86
erēšu Gtn 189 n. 124, 217, 219, 220
erubbātum 99, 122, 126–128, 133–135, 138, 139, 140, 142–143, 153
esip tabal 68–69, 79
ezābum G 95
gimillum 97
ḫibiltu 266 n. 6, 268 n. 21
ḫubullu(m)/ḫabullu 64, 95, 225, 226, 227, 229, 234–235, 267 n. 8, n. 9, 273, 277 n. 57, 278 n. 59, n. 60, n. 61, n. 62, 280 n. 64, 282

n. 74, 286 n. 95, 295 n. 22, 297 n. 29
ḫubuttūtu 293, 295
iṣṣer . . . (išûm) 98, 104, 122, 131, 150
iṣurtum 95 n. 4, 132, 146 n. 133
iḫiltum 65, 75 n. 27
imittu 289 n. 3, 291
ina muḫḫe/i 163, 164, 187 n. 113, 190 n. 128, 193 n. 146, 208 n. 4, 209, 210, 290, 294, 295 n. 20, 310 n. 44
ina pān(i) 164, 265, 290, 293, 295, 296
izuzzum/izēzum G 65, 106–107, 129, 145 n. 131
izuzzum/izēzum Š 64, 106–107, 112, 119, 295
ka'unum D 108
kammusu D 270
karāmu 226 n. 6
kārum 94, 95 n. 4, 111, 112, 113, 118, 132, 143, 337 n. 7
katā'um G/D 103, 108, 154–155, 168 n. 24
kattû 161, 167, 168–170, 173, 175, 181, 186, 201–208, 212, 218
kī našlamte 168, 178–179, 185, 217, 219
kīma/kīmū 138, 144, 178–179, 185, 217, 219
kīmū ṣibtāte 168, 177 n. 72, 186, 189
kullum/ka'ulum D/Dt 101–102, 110 n. 41, 112, 127, 129–130, 136 n. a, n. f, n. g, 144 n. 127, 168, 177, 187, 189, 218, 219, 220, 232, 245
ukâl (lien) 168–170, 174–184, 186, 187, 189, 201–208, 213, 217
kūm 178 n. 79, 268 n. 21, 271, 278 n. 59, n. 62, 280 n. 66, 281 n. 69, n. 70, 282 n. 72, 283 n. 75, 283 n. 77
kutu'ātum 154
lapātum Gt/N 105–106, 121, 122 n. 74
leqû(m)/laqā'um G 97, 98 n. 9, 140, 145 n. 131, 180, 184, 185, 186, 187, 190 n. 128, 190 n. 128, 193, 218, 240, 241, 246, 278 n. 61
māḫiṣ pūti 225–227, 231–235, 296
mallu'um D 153
maškanu(m) 128, 237, 291, 293, 310 n. 44
maškanūtu 270, 291
mazzazānu(m) 64, 72–73, 75, 107 n. 37, 128, 237
mazzazānūtu(m) 64, 65
mušallimānu 172
naṭālum Gt 70
nadā'um G 95, 99
nadānum Š 164 n. 15, 187
nadānum/tadānum G 111, 112, 115–120, 163, 164, 165, 187, 231, 241 n. 15, 243, 278 n. 61
naruqqum 95, 149, 150
nasāqu G 177–178, 186, 218, 219
nepûm G 84, 87, 154
nipûtum 84–88
nisḫu 273
nupārum 85, 154
palāḫu 244, 246, 268 n. 21, 280 n. 66, 281, 282 n. 74, 283 n. 75, 283 n. 77

paṭāru(m) G 140, 180, 220, 280, 282 n. 74, 283 n. 75, 283 n. 77, 284 n. 79, 284 n. 80
pāḫat . . . naši 171, 172
paqādum G 112, 118
puḫu
  ana puḫe leqû 164 n. 10
  ina puḫi našû 265–266
pūt . . . maḫāṣu 234
pūt . . . našû 291, 294, 298, 300
qaqqadu(m) 80, 130 n. 98, 148–149, 185, 290
qātam šakānum ina 128–129
qātātu(m) 79, 81, 104–106, 114, 238–246, 268
  bēl(ū) qātāti(m) 105, 122, 125, 171, 267
  ša qātātim 80 n. 37, 104–106, 109, 110 n. 41, 111, 112, 115–120, 122 n. 74
qāti nasḫat 80
qerbu
  ša qerbi 300
qiāpum G 95
qīptum 95, 111, 124
rakis (rakāsum G) 130–131, 148–152, 168 n. 25, 169, 172, 173, 212
rašû 291, 292, 294, 295, 297, 298, 310 n. 44
rubbû 271, 282 n. 74
ṣabātu(m) G 75 n. 27, 76, 102, 103, 128, 131, 136 n. 1, 137 n. 109, 140 n. 116, 144 n. 127, 168, 177, 187, 217, 219, 220, 233, 241 n. 15, 242, 246, 248
ṣibittum 85, 154
ṣibtum 95, 131 n. 99, 190 n. 128, 214 n. 19, 216 n. 28, 217, 219, 220
šakānu(m) G 177, 219, 220, 240, 244, 270
šalmum (u) kīnum 83–84, 130 n. 98, 148–152, 173
šapartu(m) 65 n. 8, 99, 126, 127, 129, 131, 132, 133, 135–137, 138, 139, 146, 151, 161, 162, 167, 169, 174–184, 201–208, 219, 220, 229, 237, 269
še'āum G 123
šiprūtum 65, 66
ṭuppa ṣabātu 188
ṭuppa(m) ḫepû 165, 173, 187
ṭuppu ṣabittu 188, 209
ta'urum D 111
tamkāru(m) 95, 99, 121, 133, 134 n. h, 135, 136 n. c, 138, 272
tarā'um G 135, 136 n. m, 140, 141 n. 120
tidennu/tidennūtu 224, 225, 228–234, 333
u'iltu 164 n. 9, 290, 291
uppu laqi 184, 186, 187, 218
uriḫul 229, 232, 233
waṣûm G 66, 99 n. 12, 139 n. 112
waṣûm/uṣû Š 130, 271, 280, 281 n. 71, 282 n. 73, n. 74, 283 n. 75
wašābu/ušābu G/Š 177, 180 n. 86, 219, 220, 271 n. 36
wuššurum/waššurum D 75, 104 n. 28, 112, 125, 130, 140
zaku 175 n. 61, n. 62, 176, 184, 192, 201–202, 206, 208, 217, 284 n. 79
zakû D 284 n. 79

Demotic Terms

ꜣkr 317 n. 43
ỉwꜣ 311
ỉwy.t 43, 311
ꜥrbṯ 35, 321
ꜥkr 317 n. 43
ms 310
ḥw 312
sẖ n wy 35 n. 6, 316
sẖ n rꜥ-wḫꜣ 309
sẖ n-ḏbꜣ ḥḏ 35 n. 6, 316, 318, 321
šꜥr 319
šꜥ.t n hn 321
šwty 41
šp dr.t 42, 310
ṯꜣb.t 37
ḏꜣḏꜣ r ms.t 310

Coptic Terms

ⲙⲏⲥⲉ 310
ϣⲡ̄-ⲧⲱⲣⲉ 310 n. 16

Hebrew and Ugaritic Terms

ʿerabôn 127 n. 83, 253–254
ʿarubbā 127 n. 83
ʿrbn (Ug.) 127 n. 83
ʿaboṭ 251, 253, 255
nôšeh 251, 252, 257
ḥabol/ḥabolah 253, 255
ʿrb 254
ḥbl 255
ḥob 255
yšb 255
nqh 255
ge'ulah 258
ṣeʿaqah 258
dror 260–261

Greek Terms

arrabon 127 n. 83
enkuklion 321
horoi 320
hypallagma 319, 322
seisachtheia 336

Roman Legal Terms

fideiussio 225, 226
fideiussor 115
fiducia 54 n. 17
hypotheca 225
infamia 336
missio in bona 336
pignus 54 n. 17, 225
vindex 115